PENGUIN BOOKS
THE WRITERLY LIFE

R.K. Narayan was born in Madras in 1906 and educated there and at Maharajah's College in Mysore. His first novel *Swami and Friends* (1935) was set in the enchanting fictional territory of Malgudi. Narayan's other novels are *The Bachelor of Arts* (1937), *The Dark Room* (1938), *The English Teacher* (1945), *Mr Sampath* (1949), *The Financial Expert* (1952), *Waiting for the Mahatma* (1955), the Sahitya Akademi award-winning *The Guide* (1958), *The Man-eater of Malgudi* (1962), *The Vendor of Sweets* (1967), *The Painter of Signs* (1976), *A Tiger for Malgudi* (1983), *Talkative Man* (1986) and *The World of Nagaraj* (1990).

Besides six collections of short stories (*A Horse and Two Goats, An Astrologer's Day and Other Stories, Lawley Road, Malgudi Days, Grandmother's Tale* and *Under a Banyan Tree*), Narayan published two travel books (*My Dateless Diary* and *The Emerald Route*), five collections of essays (*Next Sunday, Reluctant Guru, A Writer's Nightmare, A Story-teller's World* and *Salt and Sawdust*), translations of Indian epics and myths (*The Ramayana, The Mahabharata* and *Gods, Demons, and Others*, published together as *The Indian Epics Retold*), and a memoir, *My Days. A Town Called Malgudi, The World of Malgudi, The Magic of Malgudi* and *Memories of Malgudi*, collections of his fiction, and *Malgudi Landscapes*, a selection of his best writings, are available from Penguin Books. *Malgudi Schooldays*, a volume of Narayan's children's writing, is available in Puffin.

In 1980 R.K. Narayan was awarded the A.C. Benson medal by the Royal Society of Literature and was made an Honorary Member of the American Academy and Institute of Arts and Letters. In 1989 he was made a member of the Rajya Sabha. In 2000 the Government of India conferred on him the Padma Vibhushan.

R.K. Narayan died in May 2001.

S. Krishnan taught English literature at Madras Christian College and at Annamalai University. He spent many years with the United States Information Agency in their educational and cultural programmes. He is now a weekly columnist for the *Hindu*, the consulting editor with the *Indian Review of Books* and senior editor of *Shruti*, a music and dance magazine. Krishnan has edited several volumes of R.K. Narayan's writings for Penguin Books. He lives in Chennai.

By R.K. Narayan in Penguin Books India

The Emerald Route

The Indian Epics Retold

Indian Thought: A Miscellany

The Magic of Malgudi

Malgudi Landscapes

Malgudi Schooldays

Memories of Malgudi

My Dateless Diary

The Ramayana

Salt and Sawdust

A Story-teller's World

A Town Called Malgudi

The World of Malgudi

A Writer's Nightmare

The Writerly Life: Selected Non-fiction

THE WRITERLY LIFE

Selected Non-Fiction

R.K. NARAYAN

Edited by S. Krishnan

PENGUIN BOOKS

Penguin Books India (P) Ltd., 11 Community Centre, Panchsheel Park,
New Delhi 110 017, India
Penguin Books Ltd., 80 Strand, London WC2R 0RL, UK
Penguin Putnam Inc., 375 Hudson Street, New York, NY 10014, USA
Penguin Books Australia Ltd., 250 Camberwell Road, Camberwell,
Victoria 3124, Australia
Penguin Books Canada Ltd., 10 Alcorn Avenue, Suite 300, Toronto,
Ontario, M4V 3B2, Canada
Penguin Books (NZ) Ltd., Cnr Rosedale and Airborne Roads, Albany,
Auckland, New Zealand

First published in Viking by Penguin Books India 2001
Published in Penguin Books 2002

The essays in this volume were previously published in *A Writer's Nightmare*, Penguin Books
India 1988; *A Story-teller's World*, Penguin Books India 1989; and *Salt and Sawdust*, Penguin
Books India 1993. *My Dateless Diary* was first published by Indian Thought Publications 1964.

10 9 8 7 6 5 4 3 2 1

For sale in the Indian Subcontinent and Singapore only

Typeset in Sabon by Mantra Virtual Services, New Delhi
Printed at Chaman Offset Printers, New Delhi

CONTENTS

Later Essays

The World of the Writer

PUBLISHER'S NOTE

R.K. Narayan's writerly life spanned seven long and illustrious decades, from the 1930s to the 1990s. Almost throughout his career, he wrote non-fiction pieces, and his essays written at various times indicate his growth as well as concerns as a writer. Starting with pieces written as a weekly contribution to the *Hindu* in the late 1930s (after his first three novels had been published to critical but not popular acclaim), Narayan's interest in the short essay form led him to comment, over the next few decades, on just about every aspect of the world around him that held his interest. It was the short subjective essay that was Narayan's forte, since it was the perfect platform for building on his gift for keen observation and anecdotal narrative.

His essays have been divided into four sections for the present collection. The first group of short essays was written over the earlier stages of Narayan's non-fiction career, during the late 1930s, 1940s and 1950s. The second section comprises short essays written in the 1950s, 1960s and 1970s, while the pieces included in the section titled 'Later Essays' were written during the 1970s, 1980s and early 1990s. All of Narayan's essays on the subject of writing, written between the 1950s and 1980s, have been brought together under the rubric 'The World of the Writer'.

Many of Narayan's earlier essays are not dated, and for reasons of consistency dates of composition have not been provided for any of the essays in this volume. However, the essays included in each section fall into the rough chronological categories described above, and delineate Narayan's progression as a non-fiction writer.

The essays selected for this volume were previously published in three collections of essays, *A Writer's Nightmare* (1988), *A Story-teller's World* (1989) and *Salt and Sawdust* (1993). This volume also includes *My Dateless Diary*, Narayan's travelogue about America, derived from his jottings during his first visit to the United States in 1956, and first published in 1964. *My Dateless Diary* is in fact a collection of short subjective essays, which is why it has been included in this selection of non-fiction, while *My Days*, Narayan's very personal memoir, has not. With the exception of *My Days* and a few short pieces, *The Writerly Life* represents the majority of R.K. Narayan's non-fiction that has been published in book form.

FOREWORD

This introductory note is taken from R.K. Narayan's 1988 collection of essays, A Writer's Nightmare.

In my BA class (we had a three-year course then) fifty years ago, we had a professor of English who perhaps could not stand the stare of 200 pairs of eyes from the gallery and so decreed, the moment he approached the dais, 'Head down, pencils busy', and started dictating notes right away, even before reaching his chair. He taught us *Essays and Prose Selections* and dictated practically the same notes every year, which began with the sentence 'Definitions of the Essay are numerous and positively bewildering . . . ' The poor man suffered this bewilderment throughout his career.

When I began to write for a living later, I realized that definitions of the essay were neither numerous (as our teacher claimed) nor bewildering. I realized there were only two kinds of essays—the personal and the impersonal or, in other words, the subjective and the objective.

First, let me talk about the objective essay. One may go through the impersonal essay for information, knowledge and illumination, perhaps, but not for enjoyment which is after all one of the purposes of literature. Unfortunately, I was compelled to read certain authors in the category of heavy essayists. My father was a fervent admirer of Carlyle, Macaulay, Froude and so on. He read Carlyle and company far into the night and felt I should also be reading them for my edification. I obeyed. To speak the truth, I found them unreadable but went through the pages as a matter of self-mortification and to show I was a dutiful son. I particularly recollect the hardship I experienced while plodding through 'The Times of Erasmus & Luther' by Henry Froude in his volume *Short Studies on Great Subjects*. Carlyle terrified me. So did Macaulay. I could only marvel at my father's capacity for enjoying tough writing unrelieved by any light moment. So much for the heavy essay. I felt my college professor was justified in using the phrase 'bewildering'. He probably felt the same way that I did. I have always been drawn to the personal essay in which you could see something of the author himself apart from the theme—a man like Charles Lamb, or more recently, E.V. Lucas or Robert Lynd (to mention some names at random) are good examples of discursive essayists. The personal essay was enjoyable because it had the writer's likes, dislikes, and his observations, always with a special flavour of humour, sympathy, aversion, style, charm, even oddity.

Unfortunately, this type of essay is not in vogue today. You see it sometimes here and there but generally it is almost extinct. Yes, we have feature writers in magazines and newspapers, astute political analysts, profound scholarly and historical writers in academic journals, earth-shaking editorials in newspapers, but not the discursive essayist. This is because the discursive essay can come not out of scholarship or research but only out of one's personality and style. The scope for such a composition is unlimited—the mood may be sombre, hilarious or satirical and the theme may range from what the author notices from his window, to what he sees in his waste-paper basket, to a world cataclysm.

I cannot claim that I fulfil all the grand conditions I have enumerated. I have written the following essays because I had to. I had to write to meet a deadline every Thursday in order to fill half a column for the Sunday issue of the *Hindu*. I had rashly undertaken this task not (to be honest) for artistic reasons, but to earn a regular income. Three of my novels had already been published but they had brought me recognition rather than income. I had approached the editor of the *Hindu* for help, and he had immediately accepted my proposal for a weekly piece. I had not the ghost of an idea what I was going to do. As he had left me to do anything I wanted within my column I started writing, trusting to luck; somehow I managed to fill the column for nearly twenty years without a break.

In conclusion I should say that the essays reproduced in the following pages should enable the reader to get a better sense of my idea of the 'discursive essay' than any theorizing I could do about it.

Short Essays I

These essays were written by Narayan during the late 1930s, the 1940s and early 1950s for his weekly column in the Hindu. They are all set in the South India of Narayan's early years and showcase his ability to charmingly etch the characteristics of the world around him in a few words.

NEXT SUNDAY

SUNDAY IS THE day most looked forward to by everyone. It is the one day which suddenly evaporates before you know where you are. Everyone knows the Saturday-evening feeling, with all the pleasures of expectancy, and the Sunday-evening feeling already tainted by thoughts of Monday. What happens to the day? It is the day on which so many items are thrust—promises made to children for an outing, promise of a little shopping, calling on someone, and so on and so forth, all promises, promises. There is no way out except by stretching the twenty-four hours to do the work of forty-eight. Before one notices it the forenoon is gone.

In the morning one decides to stay a little longer in bed and one does it till one is worried out of bed by the noises which start earlier than usual, because it is a Sunday. A radio enthusiast in the next house who has been waiting for this day to tune in an hour earlier, a motor car with its engine going to pieces, children's shouts of joy because they have no school today; all this goes on while the Sunday devotee is planning to spend an hour longer in bed. The man gets up in a slightly frustrated mood and that is not a very good way to start the day. It knocks all charm out of existence at the very start itself. When one has got up in this mood it is no use hoping for a good life again. It is better to accept it for what it is: that the Sunday is nearly gone. Next, one begins to notice things. On other days one has no time for all these scrutinies and examinations. I know a person who is a very gentle being on all working days but completely turns a somersault on a Sunday. He becomes ferocious and difficult to deal with. He sees that everything at home is going wrong. He is a hobbyist, one who likes to repair things with his own hands. This man draws up a heavy schedule of work for Sundays. Hanging a picture, fixing a leaky tap, choking off the squeak in the radio, or oiling the watch or bicycle, are all jobs for a Sunday. All through the week he keeps making a mental note of what he proposes to do on the Sunday. If he could have his way he would have to work far into midnight and a part of the Monday morning also. But he never gets through this arduous programme. No doubt he opens up a radio or a watch the first thing in the day, and squats down like a great god in his workshop. Francis Thompson said of Shelley, 'The universe was his box of joys.' We are reminded of this picture when we see this man sitting amidst his toys; but with this difference: Shelley was pictured as being lost in the delight of creation, while this man is unable to do anything because he finds so many articles missing. A nail which he cherished, a piece of string or wire which he reserved for future use, a precious nut or bolt, and something or the other is always missing, and it enrages him. He has a number of children and his losses are in direct ratio to their numbers. This is not a thing that this irate man can take casually. The children have been helping themselves to various articles all through the week. A blade for pencil mending, a wire for tying up something, something else for something else, and a nut and bolt because they look nice. This man's anger knows no bounds. He calls them, lines them up and starts an investigation. The investigation may lead to useful results or it may not. It is in the laps of the gods. One child, impressed by his father's manner, may give up his loot and another may out of a desire to earn a certificate, or they may do nothing of the kind but remain unyielding of their treasures. The man sitting with his box of toys is clearly frustrated. His suspicion is roused and he now proceeds to take stock of all his losses. He hurriedly gets up and opens his cupboards, and presently the household keeps ringing with, 'Where is this?' or 'What has happened to that?' in varying degrees of petulance. But like Jesting Pilate's, his questions are destined to perish without an answer. People would answer if they could. Others know no more where that hammer is gone, which no one has ever seen, than he does. He realizes that he lives in a most unhelpful world. He shoots his question apparently in the general air, but actually aims it at his wife who is busy in an inner part of the house, and at the children who are gleefully watching their father's tantrums and are only waiting for a chance to run away. One child of seven years, an intuitive escapist, with apparent innocence suggests that probably such and such a thing is in such and such a place, and should he go and look for it? The irate man falls prey to this guile. No David more easily vanquished a Goliath. Before the man knows what has happened the young fellow is gone, and once the line-up is broken it is broken for ever. The man gets absorbed in something else, probably a book or magazine on his table, and forgets all about it for a while, till he sees the same children unconcernedly playing in the next house. He calls them back by a lusty shout through the window. They all troop back, and the man opens the offensive by asking about their books and schoolwork, clearly a sadistic design. This leads to an examination of their educational progress and propensities. He discovers that his children have not been developing on the right lines at all; he had not noticed till now how badly they were growing up—an oblique reference which at once brings down a hot denial from an inner part of the house. He bullies the children for a while and grows tired of it very soon. Now he discovers that half the Sunday is irrevocably lost. There are only a few more hours of sunshine left. He is now reminded of all his promises for this day after he had his midday meal and has acquired a pleasant mood. He promises to fulfil his obligations after a short nap. When he gets up after his rest he realizes that he simply cannot take his family out today. He simply will not spend the balance of this much-battered Sunday at bus-stops. He recollects how sometime ago he had to spend two hours at a bus stand with all his children howling with hunger, and all of them had to trek back home late at night. He shudders at the memory and suddenly cries, 'Please, let us stay at home. I will take you all out next Sunday.'

THE CROWD

ANY CROWD INTERESTS me: I always feel that it is a thing that deserves precedence over any other engagement. I always tell myself that an engagement can wait, but not the crowd. It may disperse by the time I return that way again. And so I make it a point to drift directly towards any gathering that I may see on a roadside—often incurring the displeasure of my companions. But I am convinced that a good crowd is worth any sacrifice in the world. Seldom have I been disappointed: it always turns out to be something startling and instructive: a scorpion-gatherer on the pavement with his commodities; an inventor of toys who sells for eight annas a couple of dolls which execute an uncanny dance at the ends of invisible strings; a quite unexpected array of books and journals; or a medicine-seller who tries to establish his worth by performing breathtaking conjuring tricks with cowrie shells and Chinese Rings; or, I'm ashamed to confess—even a quarrel between two persons.

In a crowd a man can attain great calm—he can forget himself for a few hours. There are different types of crowds and you have to choose the kind most suited to your temperament. There is a kind of pleasure in frequenting the radio stand at the Marina; you get a somewhat different pleasure out of, say, passing through the Flower Bazaar Road at about six in the evening; or you may buy a platform ticket and take your seat on a bench at the Central Station platform till the last train departs: I know a person who spends his holiday evening thus and draws the finest enjoyment out of this occupation; or you may pass slowly along with your eyes open from Parry's

Corner to Moore Market. During such a journey you have a chance to watch humanity as in a peep-show: in a dazzling variety and shape of colours, forms, voices, appeals and activities.

A slight abnormality comes over people in a crowd. They cease to be their usual selves. The shell which insulates an individual ordinarily is broken in a crowd: someone's affairs, whether he is holding up a medicine, or singing, or quarrelling with another, become everybody's concern. A quarrel is a private affair till a crowd forms, when it becomes state property and those who form the crowd set aside for the moment all their own occupations and thoughts and get absorbed in the central object, and try to view the problem before them with a judicious mind.

In a crowd how eager everyone is to spread a piece of information! You have only to ask: 'What is it all about?' and a dozen persons will be found thrusting themselves forward to give the information, or again you may pitch your question to a man who hasn't known what has been going on but he will helpfully direct you to another who may be properly informed. There are many persons of this type in a crowd—people who are there just for its own sake, not bothering to know what it is all about. We have often known instances where one man keeps looking down a parapet on the roadside, and another comes up to find out what he is looking at, and another and another; and all of them stand there intently looking down the parapet. The question: 'What are you watching?' will receive the reply: 'I don't know, they were looking down and so I stopped . . .'

Our ancestors fully realized the value of a crowd. A temple festival, lasting over a week, is a unique opportunity for an entire mass of people to gather in a place. The fragrance of flowers, the cries of sweet-vendors, the colourful paper toys exhibited for sale; and above all the music of the piper reaching out to the largest mass of people with the simplest means possible, are all subtle ties, which bind hundreds of people together in a common experience.

The misanthrope who declares that he hates a crowd does not realize what he is missing in life. For human beings the greatest source of strength lies in each other's presence.

OUR DRESS

IN ALMOST ALL parts of the world we hear the common complaint that men dress in a monotonously uniform manner, but ours is one of the few countries to have risen above this limitation. One has only to pause for a moment at Round Tana or Broadway to realize what a wealth of pattern and colour this freedom has produced. Here is a man wearing a long-sleeved shirt, a vest-coat and a *dhoti* tied Bengali style; there goes another, as a contrast, wearing a natty *banian,* a green towel over his shoulder, and a *dhoti* in the straightforward Madras manner; at the bus-stand is someone in a three-piece suit, soft hat and complete with cane. If the observer's luck is good he may even detect a couple of flowing Rajput turbans of the colour of the evening sky. Or someone crowned with an inch-broad, coffee-coloured felt cap of other days. Where has this cap gone now? I think it was the first article to face annihilation when nationalism surged up in our hearts and the *khaddar* cap made its appearance. However, many people may still remember the early days when one went into a cap-shop, and keenly examined the lining of each cap for the imprint of 'X & Co., London'. What a prized possession it used to be (in spite of its faint resemblance to the lid of a milk can). The man who wore this cap, along with a stiff collar, tie and vest-coat, was surely something of a fop in those days.

Now and then we hear talk of standardizing dress in India as if such a thing could be achieved by an edict. Considering all things our present system is perhaps the most sensible, leaving each man to put himself into any dress he chooses according to his taste and convenience. The busy office executive has no use for loose flowing garments. One belonging to the musical profession would sooner cut himself in two than get into a pair of trousers. The journalist or writer feels that a *khaddar*-shirt, with a shining fountain-pen-clip peeping from below the third front button, is quite adequate for his needs. There are others who advance the claims of shirt and *angavastram* as the most graceful combination devised. You may be sure you will find an equal number to decry the upper cloth as a useless impediment (particularly if you have to struggle for space in a bus every day). There are inspired people ready to swear that they were the first to arrive at the combination of *dhoti* and shirt, with just a simple coat over it: they also believe that all mankind will ultimately adopt this dress.

The suit, like the English language, holds a very undefined position in our country. One can never be sure how far 'Quit India' should apply to it. Its champions claim for it manifold virtues—varying from the purely aesthetic to the purely utilitarian: it improves a man's appearance (if he has potentialities that way); it helps a man deliver (somehow) convincing sales talk to his prospective customers; and above all it entitles a man to be treated as a gentleman by fellow-beings. Those opposed to this system of dressing have quite a catalogue of its defects to offer, the chief one, which cannot be gainsaid, being that in wearing a suit a man acquires far too many things to look after: the time spent every morning polishing the shoes, pressing a tie, and covering the holes in the sock, and in getting in and out of all these, precludes any other engagement for mind or body.

Of course each man is free not only to dress as he pleases but also to press his own point of view unreservedly. Fortunately ours is a very tolerant country in such matters. There is also another virtue we possess. We are generally free from the tyranny of having to dress for the hour or for the occasion. Here and there, no doubt, we come across persons who rigorously classify their dress items and would sooner appear with soot over their faces than in a set of clothes supposedly of another hour. These are, however, a select group living in a rarefied atmosphere, the sort of people who would ask when invited to dinner, 'Indian style or?'—a very strange type of question, which has been possible only in this country. In this connection I cannot resist quoting a recent author: 'The Englishman who religiously sits down to his solitary dinner in a dress coat in the sweltering heat of equatorial Africa at least obeys an obscure impulse to safeguard his self-respect. The Indian who imitates this ritual from a muddled feeling that it is somehow necessary to his own self-respect is merely a figure of fun.'

NOISE

THIS AGE WILL probably be known as the noisiest in human history. We create a lot of noise not only to show that we are in a happy, festive mood, to canvass votes, to advertise a commodity or a point of view, but also for its own sake. Noise is the greatest bane of modern life. Every moment of our existence we are being distracted by it, necessary noise, unnecessary noise, purposeful noise, and the purposeless, enough to fray our nerves and madden us. If the average Indian's life is only twenty-six, we have only ourselves to blame for it. The noise in and around us is wearing us out at a terrific pace.

Someone noted recently that present-day babies are peculiarly loud throated. They look elegant and sweet, no doubt, but the moment they open their mouths they let out a shattering volume of sound. Schoolteachers do their best from the beginning by ordering every few seconds in the class-room, 'Silence, silence.' But it does not appear to have any effect on children. They remain the noisiest creatures on earth. I think there will be an all-round benefit if a period of absolute silence is introduced in every class timetable with a prize at the end of the year for the softest spoken in the school.

Hawking in the streets has, of late, assumed dangerous proportions. It seems impossible to concentrate on any study or writing at home, particularly if one's window looks over a street. Even if one retires to the back of the house one may not be saved since the hawker seems to set the pitch of his voice on the basis that you should be searched out and pierced through and through even if you are hiding in the innermost recess of the house. At the moment I am writing this I see and hear two plantain-sellers coming on each other's heels, almost trying to bark each other out of existence. I fear that the Grow More Food campaign has brought in only more plantains since I notice two more hawkers coming in with the same commodity. Now for a variation, I suppose, a seeker of old paper and empty bottles is expressing his wish in a rich, space-filling baritone, a knife-grinder is employing an anguished cry like one caught in a trap, and many others follow in succession, all that we understand about them being that they are shouting something; it may be anything from gingelly-oil-cake to lotus flowers, brinjals or bangles. We are surrounded by a moving, vociferous market all the time.

I have a dread of living next to a man owning a motorcycle. When a motorcyclist starts out, the agitation he creates lasts half-an-hour, even after the machine itself has gone out of sight. On Sundays this enthusiast tests and touches up his engine, whereupon the whole locality is converted into a sort of gold factory. I say gold factory because, in my experience, it is the most deafening place on earth when the ore is pulverized before being treated with cyanide. This was all I could catch of the whole process when I visited a gold-mine some years ago. My guide was explaining everything to me in great detail, but I could only see his lips move, there was such a clatter all around. It has been the same experience for me in any factory. I have often been taken around many types of factories, but as my guides gesticulate and move their lips I give up all attempts at knowing how cotton or silk is converted into yarn and fabric. The noise of machinery is always at a higher *sruthi* than the voice of the guide, a fact which is generally overlooked by those who take people around factories. While all the explanation is going on, my mind keeps feasting on visions of a zone of silence.

I abandoned a very comfortable house once because of a neighbour who switched on his radio every morning at five, long before even the gates were unlocked in any radio station. The result of such an early switching-on was that the radio (the neighbour's) kept up a sort of humming, a most harassing accompaniment, unbroken like the humming of a thousand bees. I fear that this simile may mislead my readers by its poetic association, but far from it; this humming was like the skewering of one's brain by many instruments of torture, something like a pneumatic drill operating at one's temples. Why my neighbour should have queued up so early in the day in order to receive a radio programme was a thing I could never understand. Its only effect was to make me get up early since I did not like to lie in bed wallowing in uncharitable neighbourly thoughts first thing in the day. Moreover I was not without hope since a friend who knows all about radios told me that my neighbour's habit of switching on the radio when the transmitter was still cold was the surest way of destroying the valves, if not the radio itself . . . But nothing occurred along those happy lines, and I had to move on.

I sometimes feel that God, who constructed the human body with so much forethought and solicitude, seems to have become weary when he came to the ears, and left them as the most vulnerable portion of a human being. The result is that we spend all our hours hankering after something that we cannot attain, namely Silence.

COFFEE

I NEVER TIRE of writing about coffee. It seems to me an inexhaustible, monumental theme. I sometimes feel that it is a subject which may well occupy the space of a whole saga, if we may define a saga as a worthy theme expanded to a worthy length. I am planning a noble work running to two hundred thousand words, a mighty work, not the fiction with which my name is generally associated but an accurate and factual piece of work as solid as the table on which I am resting my hands now. The work will be called *A Study of Coffee*. The first part will describe the life and philosophy of Bababuden, a Muslim saint who brought coffee to India. He came from Mocha, bringing with him a handful of seeds, and settled himself on the slopes of a mountain range in Kadur district, Mysore State. This range was later named after him, and anyone can see his tomb even today if he will undertake a short trip from Chickmagalur. The origin of coffee, thus, is saintly. It was not an empire-builder or a buccaneer who brought coffee to India, but a saint, one who knew what was good for humanity.

After this historical prelude I will go on to examine how far this vision of the saint has been fulfilled. This will take us into the intricacies of making coffee, a definition of good coffee, its colour, texture, and taste. Incidentally we may have to deal with the question of milk and milk supply, sugar production, etc. We shall have to study the different techniques of coffee-making, pause to consider what should be the right temperature of the water boiled for decoction, the actual fuel used for boiling the water, the hardness and quality of water, etc. There are persons with highly cultivated tastes who can at once declare whether the coffee they are consuming has had its water boiled over faggots, charcoal, or an electric heater, and whether the water has been taken from a river or a well. All factors that affect the ultimate quality of coffee will have to be examined, and then there should be a dispassionate assessment of the relative value of decoctions filtered through white drill, flannel, and metal percolators. What should be the precise meeting point of flavour and strength, aroma and taste, are questions that involve the higher aspects of the coffee habit. A few observations will be necessary on the question of coffee temperature. This section will be called Thermodynamics of Coffee. In this section we shall strive to decide the right temperature at which coffee may be sipped. It must be understood that the temperature has to vary according to the occasion; the hot cup you may demand at home may not be suitable when you have to gulp down a mouthful and run back to your seat in a train whose engine has just whistled and just started moving; and then the social classification of humanity—at one end of the scale those who sip coffee so hot that the tumbler cannot be held except by wrapping a towel round it, and at the other end those who demand iced coffee, which must be characterized as a spoilation of both good ice and coffee. I shall also attach a map of the country showing spots where 24-carat coffee is provided.

So far I have confidence that my outlook as well as writing will be pleasant, but when I come to write on the economic aspect of coffee, I fear I shall lose my equanimity. I fear my tone may become bitter. I shall demand to be told why coffee should be made so expensive as to make an ordinary consumer despair every time he goes to buy some. Is it the aim of the Coffee Board to make every coffee-drinking citizen a bankrupt? I shall ask how far we need an elaborate and costly propaganda machinery for a commodity which is too well-known. Why run elaborate coffee bars in order to demonstrate how to make and taste good coffee when the humblest amongst us can do it with a spoonful of powder if the mechanism of supply does not stand in our way? The fallacy of this organization will be fully explored and exploded in my book. Over-organization has a tendency to make simple things complicated. Don't we know that the betel leaf of which we can buy half-a-dozen for a copper can become rare as uranium if it is handed over to a Betel Leaf Propaganda and Marketing Board under the authority of some ministry? Such organizations have a habit of being preoccupied with the question of how to earn foreign currency rather than how to make our people happy.

There are one or two unforgettable remarks thrown in by persons in high places which seem to explain the present position of coffee supply. They say, in a heavily jocular manner or seriously (we cannot judge from news-reports), that people ought to drink less coffee. If they mean it they should wind up the propaganda machinery, and then issue an ordinance forbidding the drinking of coffee. As law abiding men we shall make a supreme effort to obey this order: we shall pray to Saint Bababuden to give us the necessary resoluteness to overcome the mad desire that seizes us first thing in the day, and then give up coffee for ever.

THE WINGED ANTS

THE SWARM COMES in the evening. We don't notice it at first, but as soon as the lights are on, there comes along the first member—a pale little body poised on flimsy transparent wings. It circles round the light. One would think that it had a purpose or limit, but its circumambulations grow beyond count. Before you say, 'Here is another!' there are five more, and very soon, imperceptibly, as many as thousands have gathered round the light—quite a cloud of them, like the photograph of bombers poised over a doomed city. They go on circling round and round the light at a giddy pace, hitting us in the face, dropping into our food, and becoming a general nuisance. They gyrate till their wings drop off and then trail along the edge of the floor behind one another helplessly, 'eyeless in Gaza'. When the flight nuisance is at its height, as any householder knows, a basin of water placed under the light draws away most of the circumambulating crowd to a watery grave. Their attempt to reach the light within the bulb has itself been an illusory pursuit, their attraction to the reflection in the basin of water has proved a disaster! Here is sufficient stuff to keep a philosopher thought-stricken!

For all the flutter it creates, the ant's whole existence lasts only an hour or so. God knows why they come out at all. Any evening, particularly if there has been a downpour of rain, we may anticipate the coming of the swarm. If we watch the crows and sparrows in the garden, we should see them engaged in a lively activity: they have found their ideal dinner, also a limitless one, coming their way, emerging from the ant-holes in the ground, and they catch them in flight. Not many of the winged creatures have a chance of coming out further until the birds retreat for the night. And then they come out full-fledged towards every source of light and flutter their brief life out.

Millions arrive, fly about, and get destroyed in various ways. What is Nature's purpose in devising this extravagance?

An entomologist has given me the answer. Millions come out and perish so that an elect may survive. Out of the multitude the queen is protected and led back to their subterranean home, where she is fed and pampered and encouraged to breed. Once this aim is achieved, it does not matter how many are trampled under human feet or swept away with a broom.

Why has Nature made the white ant so prolific and important? Some day, I hope people will give sufficient thought to the subject. I feel there must be some purpose in having in our midst a creature who will destroy anything. Consider the termite and its activity. First and foremost, it builds laboriously a home—perhaps not for itself but for the deadliest enemy of man: the snake. Tunnelled, sheltered, full of passages—an architecturally ideal home for the snake. Should we view the white ant as the sworn enemy of man, one that provides a concealed home for the viper and then proceeds to nibble away everything that a human being values? The importance that Nature attaches to the breeding and welfare of the white ant ought to give us food for thought. Man should once for all get rid of the presumption that the universe is created for his convenience.

Imagine for a moment a world without the white ant. The possessiveness inherent in man will crowd the world beyond all reckoning. There will be no standing room owing to the accumulated junk everywhere; old newspapers, government records, classics in ancient editions, and old furniture. Once I removed to the garage a basketful of classical works whose pages had become verminous. A month later when I opened the garage door and peeped in I found not only the classics gone but also the basket in which they had been heaped. I felt depressed at first, but the impartial annihilation that the white ant had effected struck me as something cosmic.

In my profession I accumulate too much paper; review-cuttings, typescripts, galley proofs, correspondence which makes no sense now, manuscripts in various stages, mementoes of various kinds, all things that should have been dumped into a disintegrator ages ago but weren't because of a vague irrational thought that they may have value or utility some day. Observing myself with honesty, I realized that I had not touched any of it a second time in twenty years, while they went on choking all the available space in every room, shelf, desk, and drawer. Twenty years is an adequate period for testing the usefulness of anything. Now when I wish to clear up I put everything into a basket, leave it in the garage, and forget about it. And in less than a week I won't even remember what I have lost. There is something to be admired in such a consummate corroder: it saves the world from becoming clogged.

BEHIND ONE ANOTHER

WHEN OUR COUNTRY was less civilized, persons who had gone abroad to acquire a Barristerhood or an Oxford degree, generally came back with a lot of contempt for our own people. It was a sign of refinement to display a distaste for what may be called the Indian Way of Life. They generally spoke of two things—noticed by them in London—with admiration. One was the unvarying good cheer of the London 'bobby' (the 'native' took time to grasp what it meant), and the other was the Londoner's habit of queueing up. 'Queueing up? What is that?' asked the innocent stay-at-home. The gentleman cleared his throat and explained at length what it meant, contrasting it with the habits of our own people.

It used to be quite a normal feature of our existence to struggle for a ticket, for any sort of ticket, whether for a journey or for an entertainment. I remember how years ago when cinema was a new art and they were trying to show the first Indian film at a Madras theatre, we could not approach the ticket window for days and weeks. At last we took a wrestler along with us, a hefty man, who took a few paces back and charged into the crowd with a shout; he carried on his neck, tightly gripping it with his knees like a jockey, another medium-sized man, who pushed in the cash and took the tickets the moment they reached the window, while Samson's own arms were engaged in warding off the tide of humanity threatening to engulf him. He brought us our tickets but most of his clothes were gone and there were scratches all over him. Neither that man nor anyone else felt that there was anything unusual in it: the man who flourished his ticket wore the look of a winner. Our social conscience had not developed too much and we never thought that there was anything wrong in it—till the young barrister expressed his horror at it, comparing it with what they would have done in London under similar circumstances. From the way he spoke we felt ashamed of our country. All our heritage of philosophy, learning, art, the Taj Mahal, religious teachings, *Bhagavad Gita,* temple towers, etc., seemed to mean nothing culturally; the absence of the queueing system branded us as barbarians.

Today there is enough of it in the world to gladden the heart of the most perfervid queue-champion. When the history of civilization pertaining to this period comes to be written, the queue-behaviour of the men of this age is certain to find a mention. The future historian will in all probability say, 'There are ample signs that people everywhere stood behind one another for hours and hours and the file stretched away for miles. Why they did it we will never understand, particularly as there seemed to have been plenty of space all around where they could have spread out. They seemed to have learnt the style from ants. The one behind took exactly the same number of steps as the one ahead, and if he stopped the other stopped. Why they did it we can never understand as we have no means of judging the inner stresses of those times. All that we are able to gather is that if a man's longevity was twenty-seven years, he spent a total of twenty years standing in various queues, at bus-stands, railway stations, ration depots, cloth-shops, cinema houses, and every kind of public place. Considering the time spent this way it is surprising how they managed to find the time to carry on their normal domestic or economic activities.'

When I project thus into the mind of a future historian I am doing a piece of wishful dreaming. I hope in the future queues will be unknown. It must be admitted that the queue is a necessity, but a cruel necessity. It is a sign of an abnormal, confused, and congested existence. Except for the young barrister of those days, no one likes a queue for its own sake. There is something comical in standing so close to another, watching the back of his ears for hours, with another person doing the same thing behind you. Even the most hardened person never likes to be seen standing in a queue. It is always recommended for others. Even your best friend looks away when he waits for his pair of *dhotis* at the controlled rate. It is no doubt a sign of self-discipline and social conscience to stand sandwiched between unknown persons, but secretly everyone tries to avoid it. Everyone hopes that he will be able to find someone else to do the standing for him. I read the other day of a Delhi refugee making a living as a stand-in at a bus-stop for *babus* in a hurry. Who knows how this will develop? It may become a specialized job, depending upon one's 'standing' endurance. Perhaps the understudy may employ sub-agents, organizing and controlling the whole business from his office table far away. It may perhaps become a new guild or the government may find it necessary to class it as an essential service. The possibilities seem infinite. With all that I hope the queue system will interest only antiquarians in the near future.

RESTAURANTS

SOMEONE RECENTLY COMPLAINED that the serving boy in a hotel dipped all his five fingers into a tumbler while fetching drinking water; this brought out the indignant repudiation from the manager, 'How could he have had all the five fingers in? It must have been only four. Otherwise he could not have carried the tumbler.' This seems to me typical of the utter divergence in outlook between two sections of the present-day population: those who visit hotels and those who run them. Probably in order to improve the situation a questionnaire was sent out sometime ago, intended to catch all aspects of the problem. I believe when the investigators attempted to elicit facts all that they got were complaints from the servers regarding work and wages, complaints from hotel-goers regarding quality, quantity, cost and everything. I think the committee gathered a voluminous quantity of paper, properly filled up. It is probably too early even to say what they will do with it.

Most people are miles away from their homes at tiffin time. This is a characteristic of urban life. Students, office-goers, businessmen, have no choice in the matter. It would be unthinkable for a man from Adyar working in First Line Beach to return home for his afternoon coffee; nor can he wait till the closing of his office. At office awaiting the tiffin-break is one of the pleasantest states of existence. When one returns to one's desk an hour later chewing a *beeda* one has definitely acquired a pleasanter outlook. Now, I would like to examine what has happened to the man between his leaving his office table and returning to it an hour later. No doubt when he returns our friend is chewing betel leaves and looking the picture of satisfaction, but he has been through a trial.

He goes to his favourite hotel as fast as his feet can take him, but he cannot enter it. He has to wait, then push his way through a file of others moving in, and finally stand in a corner scanning the hall for a vacant seat. It is most awkward standing there, he has a feeling of waiting for a dole. His trained eye catches someone at a table sipping the last few ounces of coffee in his cup, and our friend knows that the other will presently get up. He cleverly slips through the crowd and approaches the about-to-be vacated chair cautiously: he does not like to appear too inquisitive about the other man's movements lest it should look ungracious but hovers about the back of the chair with a look of unconcern while the man is enjoying the last drop. If the man at the table knows that his seat is wanted he will try to brave it for a while but will ultimately vacate it, unable to bear the silent, implacable pressure exerted by the one waiting behind him. If our friend is lucky—that is, if someone else more nimble-footed does not descend on the seat like a bolt from the blue—he can feel certain that he has won his seat. I don't think any election candidate could reflect with greater gratification on his triumph.

When our friend gets his hard-won seat, what happens? He looks at the time. Half-an-hour wasted in manoeuvres alone. The sands of time are running low, he will have to be back soon at his office. He desperately tries to draw the attention of the man serving at his table as he catches glimpses of him here and there. At this point one is reminded of the epitaph for a restaurant waiter, 'God finally caught his eye.' Finally, when the server comes, his demeanour may be affable or sour according to his constitution; but it is patent that he is extremely harassed and fatigued. If he should run amok he would knock down all plates and cups and tiffins and tiffin-eaters as the greatest irritants in life . . . But he asks formally, 'What do you want, sir?' And then the counter-question, 'What have you?' It is a routine question that a hundred others have already asked although the whole menu—Sweets, Savoury, and Today's Special—is chalked up on the board. The server mechanically repeats the catalogue of edibles at lightning speed, takes his order, and goes out of sight.

As our friend awaits the arrival of his food he notices that his table is littered with used cups and plates and remnants left by other people, and as he eyes them distastefully, a tremendous cry rings out, 'Table clean!', and a man arrives with a bucket overflowing with unwashed crockery and vessels, reaches over the shoulder of our friend, leaving him in acute suspense for the safety of his clothes, and clears the table: he then rubs the table-surface with a very damp blue cloth, which our friend would rather avoid looking at. There are a few other things which he attempts to ignore while he is in the process of appeasing his hunger. He tries not to look at the wash-basin right across his table which sprays around a vast quantity of water as person after person comes up to wash his hands, some of them none-too-gently. The general noise in this hall is something that frays his nerves—the radio (somehow our restaurants seem to have stations to tune in to at all the twenty-four hours), the deafening clatter of vessels dumped out for cleaning, somebody shouting orders to the kitchen, shouting across of the bill amount, customers greeting each other . . . through all this babble our friend can hardly make himself heard. He ignores the crack in the china cup which bears his coffee, and the notches and grease on the spoon given to him. He thinks these are minor terrors which ought to be borne patiently. When he carries his bill to the payment counter and the man there sticks it on a miniature harpoon on his table while sweeping the cash in, our friend is happy that he is out of all this trouble. Perhaps that's why he wears such a merry look coming out of a restaurant.

THE CAT

AMONG ANIMALS, I admire the cat for its poise and equanimity. Except when some important issue is to be argued out with an intruder from another territory, and that mostly at midnight seated on a wall, at all other times it is very silent and composed, soft in movement and unobtrusive, taking good care to avoid being noticed. Among human beings it may have a favourite whom it will greet by arching the back and mewing in an undertone, sometimes going to the lengths of brushing against his leg too. That is all. Never more demonstrative than that.

Recently at the Madras Music Academy, during the festival, I sat with a thousand others and tried to listen to the music, but it was not always easy, since there is a habit among our people of moving about and carrying on conversation during a concert, not exactly in whispers but a little above the *sruti* of the singer struggling to establish his voice in that vast hall.

In contrast to the human behaviour, a cat sat on the platform, perfectly still, facing the singer. I noticed him only on the evening of D.K. Jayaraman's performance, but learnt later that he would be present on the platform every evening, especially at the prime hour between 5 and 7.30. He sat so still that one could mistake him for a decorative piece. Sometimes he sat with his head half-turned towards the auditorium, quietly watching the public in their seats, but looking at no one in particular, very much in the style of a VIP chairman. At some point he would tuck in his limbs and tail and shut his eyes in total relaxation, displaying a model behaviour in a music hall.

He was not generally noticed because of his unobtrusive manners as well as his perfect camouflage: he merged perfectly in his surrounding of sombre carpets and saree patterns of the assembly on the platform. Nature had endowed him with a coat of grey and black, with a dash of yellow, and polka dots here and there, making it rather difficult to specify his complexion in a single phrase. He merged into his background while he was there, but suddenly at some point he would not be there, so smoothly making his exit that you might wonder if you had suffered a hallucination all along. During subsequent studies, I discovered the exact point at which he would vanish. During *thani avarthanam* of mridangam, especially if the percussion maestro belonged to the hard-hitting class and generated enormous decibels out of his instrument. At such times the cat hastily picked himself up and raced down the wooden steps of the platform. (He never committed the indignity of jumping away while in the hall, but, though in a hurry to leave, carried himself with poise proper to the occasion.) He avoided the place during Bharat Natyam performances, feeling perhaps that so much of stamping of feet and convulsive movements are not conducive to a peaceful evening for a cat. He avoided the morning sessions too when there would be much excited talk and debate. At such times, I have noticed him curled up under a chair in the Special Reserved Class, away from the platform.

Others who have noticed the cat speculate that he might be a savant or maestro of the last century preferring this guise so that he might arrive and depart without fuss or embarrassment to the management. (Incidentally you may remember how God Indra assumed the form of a cat, in order to try and slip away when the husband of the woman in his arms arrived home suddenly.) There is also a view that the Academy cat might be an ancient musician who never made it to Sangeeta Kalanidhi though he aspired and manoeuvred for it all his life.

But for me such notions are far-fetched. I see no harm in taking a cat for a cat. Why not? As good a creation of God as anything else.

Man in his arrogance concludes it is impossible for a cat to enjoy music. He cannot tolerate the idea of music appealing to a cat unless he anthropomorphizes the creature. To me this is just a cat with an ear for music and respect for the institution. However when he folds up, shuts his eyes and remains immobile, even during a dull patch in the concert, he may not express disapproval, out of good manners, but might just switch off his mind and turn his thoughts to the mice scuttling under the wooden platform, or he may brood over his affairs in the alley: for, though he is seen in the Academy, it is not his home. I have noticed him at midnight going up the corridor of the deluxe block of the Woodlands Hotel nearby, and I learnt from the watchman that this cat belongs to the hotel but enjoys a wide jurisdiction. I think he creates the same illusion in the hotel next door, in the next two bungalows, as well as at the Music Academy, of belonging to each place. T.S. Eliot, who shows profound understanding of cats, mentions in his *Book of Cats* a particular cat who was a conjuror and could create an illusion of being at several places at the same time.

CAUSERIE

MY LITTLE NIECE, Shanta, went on repeating the ditty:

Nicely want, nicely want;
Shame, shame, poppy shame;
All the girls know your name.

I noticed her uttering these lines whenever she found us lost in some little predicament such as having a pencil point broken while signing, or losing in a game, or getting snubbed unexpectedly. I tried to analyse its meaning. Evidently it was her way (as well as that of her companions) of gloating over another's moment of awkward plight.

From this general understanding, I tried to make out a particular meaning. What was 'nicely want'? A phrase which looked so agreeable could not possibly have any unpleasant meaning. But after much questioning I found out that it was a literal translation of a vernacular idiom—*nanna venum*—said by one who watched, unsympathetically of course, someone else in trouble; example, a younger brother watching the ears of his bullying elder brother being twisted by the arithmetic teacher; the idiom indicates a state of mild vindictiveness and the satisfaction arising therefrom. No one who has no sense of our own idiom could ever understand the statement. It is one hundred per cent *swadeshi* like the towers of our temple or our rasam.

What was 'poppy shame'? I asked, for enlightenment, and the little girl at first said that she did not know, but later explained that it was 'like the poppy flower'. How many of us have seen poppy flowers? Is it poppy of the drug or of the flower garden? Does it signify oblivion to everything except the state of shame such as '. . . of hemlock drunk and half a minute ago had Letheward sunk'? Or if it is the harmless flower-bed poppy, it perhaps means a little embarrassment, delicate and finely-patterned like the poppy flower; just enough to make one blush to the tint of a poppy in the garden and no more? What really intrigued me was 'All the girls know your name'. I thought no boy would mind that, whatever may be the reaction of girls to the prospect; but the little girl disillusioned my mind by spelling it out. She said it was 'no' your name, not 'know'. Ah, could it mean that word was used as a verb without an auxiliary? 'All the girls "no" your name' might be a picturesque way of saying that all the girls will cry 'no' in one voice the moment your name is mentioned. Does it mean they won't accept any date in the modern sense or is it a relic of the old *swayamwara* days when a girl could say yes or no unmistakably? I am still thinking of this verse. Anyway it holds a pretty dreadful prospect for one fallen from grace.

*

I read of a country in which there were so many holidays that the dates of the calendar were generally printed in red, the working dates being indicated by a small sprinkling of black letters. I think we are fast approaching this stage. On one side, there is talk of the Five Year Plan and its urgency; on the other side our readiness to pull down the shutter any minute. Religious occasions, the birth or death of eminent men (in some instances the date of someone's birth is celebrated without prejudice to the observance of his date of death later), Saints' Days, National Celebrations (two sets again), and several New Year's Days. I do not wish to be a killjoy but I do want to be able to receive my mail in time and to ask for my cash at the bank for the maximum number of days possible in a year. A very urgent communication which I had been expecting arrived on the

14th of August, but I was not at home when the registered packet arrived; the 15th of August was a holiday; on the 16th the postman could not get at me again; he had left the post office when I went there in search of him; he had left our area when I went back to look for him. In this hide-and-seek another day was lost; the 17th was a holiday again; on the 18th our usual postman had a headache and a substitute was sent who delayed so long in finding each address that the letter missed me again. There was no use in my going to the post office because it was a Saturday and the shutters were down at 1 p.m. The 19th was a Sunday. I succeeded in taking charge of my urgent letter on the 20th (after a delay of nearly a week) by presenting myself at the post office at 6 a.m. long before anyone should leave the building. I leave the subject there without further comment.

*

A recent essay I wrote on the cosmic nature of the white ant's activity has brought me much support. I have been receiving lists of articles consumed by the white ant. Going over the lists I am more than ever convinced that there is a design and plan in the activities of the white ant. A friend who was addicted to playing on the 'leg harmonium' went away on a holiday after pushing his instrument into a corner and covering it with a blanket. After his holiday when he wanted to resume his musical exercise, he found the white keys left suspended in mid-air as from a ghost musical-box; the bellows as well as the box portion of the harmonium were gone. This no doubt distressed the harmonium player himself but brought immeasurable relief and joy to his neighbours.

A devoted husband cherished the heavy crayon drawings and the garish watercolours done by his wife, and compelled his friends to appreciate them whenever they made the mistake of visiting him. The wife was a prolific artist, the husband's devotion knew no limit, the friends suffered acutely and began to drop off. It threatened to create tension between the gentleman and his good friends. Luckily for the friends, white ants got into the almirah in which the art treasures were kept. Presently, it was discovered that all the crayon work as well as watercolours had been impartially devoured. The lady lost heart and took a vow never to touch a paint-box again. The friends resumed their visits.

*

The brightest piece of news for the week has been the placing of the English language on 'Open General Licence' again. Till now we had worked ourselves into a position where the language took on the aspect of a contraband article. To change the metaphor, the English language was almost like an outlaw who could not be actually outlawed. We saw him here, we saw him there, we saw him everywhere, but no one could do anything about it. You fulminated against him, you denounced him unreservedly, and you put a price on his head, but still he moved about unconcerned, with an air that things would be all right in the end. In our dislike of Imperialism we made the mistake of identifying the language with the Imperialist. One might as well forswear all military uniform because our English rulers wore them. But the language itself has an independent colonizing habit: it goes 'native', and becomes so rooted in the soil that it cannot be uprooted. Let us thank providence that this fact has now been recognized and that we may speak and write this language without feeling all the time that we are engaged in an un-national activity.

ALLERGY

THERE ARE TWO aspects of medicine, the concrete and the abstract. The concrete used to be seen in cases such as malaria, cold, etc., unmistakable troubles for which well-known remedies were provided out of bottles. The sufferer drained off the medicine with awry face, demanded a pinch of sugar to counteract the bitterness on the tongue, repeated the procedure, and then forgot all about it. This was the good old medical system as practised in any normal L.F. Dispensary (it took me long years to understand that L.F. stood for Local Fund). The doctor wrote a great deal on the leaves of a brown register. Although the ink used was faint and dilute, the entries afforded a rough-and-ready cross-sectional view of public health. After every 'name' and 'age' there was a column for 'disease'. This column was invariably filled with malaria, influenza and indigestion, in a regular pattern, with an occasional 'general debility' thrown in, whenever something turned up which seemed to be beyond this classification. The good old doctor wrote with one hand while feeling the pulse of his patient with the other. The compounder in the adjacent room issued readymade mixtures out of gigantic bottles and placed his stamp on the prescription with an air of dismissing sickness for ever. I have lost touch with this institution, but I believe that it is not so popular now as it used to be. Nowadays people do not like things to remain so elementary and simple.

The days of glancing at the tongue and dashing off 'mist' this or 'mist' that, are past. Bitter medicines with a pinch of sugar are unacceptable to the modern mind. This is an age of scientific terminology. A thing has no value unless it is clothed in respectable, scientific expression. Everybody has recognized the hypnotic value of scientific or scientific-sounding phrases. Manufacturers of various beautifying commodities nowadays are trying to attract clientele by claiming that their products contain this element or that principle or some fabulous vitamin. Medical science is also progressing on these lines. Doctors' clinics have been resounding with new terms for over a decade now. Vitamins became very popular at one time. An elaborate vitamin-consciousness developed in people, driving them to maintain a perpetual hunt for vitamins in all their diet. It was followed by calcium deficiency. Even now the cry is all calcium deficiency, but one suspects that it has fallen into a routine and the fervour is lost. And then came a time when no doctor would look at a patient unless he had all his teeth pulled out first. The trend of medicine seems to have been all along from the seen to the unseen. Medical science is becoming more and more metaphysical.

I am saying this with the thought in my mind that we are hearing the word 'allergy' too much nowadays. Calcium and vitamin seem to have yielded the place of honour to allergy. In a week I heard four different doctors mention allergy under four different conditions. A person who was suffering from rashes was said to be in a state of allergy. A person who was racked with cough was also said to be undergoing allergy. Another who was feeling fidgety was also allergic. And another nearly unconscious with high fever was pronounced to be in a state of allergy. This is a very generous and compendious word meaning anything. It is applied to every kind of symptom from sprained toes to raving mania. When a doctor says of some symptom, 'Oh, it's just allergy,' he seems to say in effect, 'Don't bother me with this any more. I don't know how you have got it, and I can't tell you how you can be rid of it. Grin and bear it until it leaves you. God knows when . . .' It satisfies the doctor that he has looked over the case as best as he could, and the patient that he has had the benefit of expert advice. When a doctor says that it is just allergy he also implies that you must cure yourself of it after discovering the cause that led to it. It takes a person on through a process of self-analysis and self-discovery. Allergy has converted the doctor's room into a confessional. While you are writhing with pain or irritation you will hear the doctor say, 'Just throw your mind back and see where you have erred. Just recollect all the things you have eaten, all the clothes you have worn and all the thoughts that have passed in your mind—pick out the thing that has caused this and avoid it; that's all, and you will be well again.' There is a great deal of comfort in this process. It is good to think that a hammering toothache is thoroughly unreal, and is a fancied state caused by that horse-hair stuffing in the sofa you sat upon, or the attack of asthma which twists you up is an illusory condition which you could have easily avoided if you had not bothered about those unpaid bills. If this process is followed, I am sure it will be possible to say someday, pointing at a passing funeral, 'That man is not dead, but is only allergic to life.'

HORSES AND OTHERS

I HAD A most illuminating conversation with the driver of a tonga a few days ago. All along the way from the market he kept explaining why we should have more and more horses in our midst. His talk made me yearn for a horse and carriage. Its economics were alluring. You could own a turn-out for an outlay of five hundred rupees. What vehicle could you hope to acquire for this value? You could maintain a horse on two rupees a day and engage a driver for less than thirty rupees a month. You did not have to visit a workshop every morning as most motor owners do. Perhaps you might have to go to a vet or look for medicinal leaves if the horse caught a cold or slight fever, but one ought not to grudge this little attention to an animal which took one about, generally without any trouble, thirty miles a day. The horse created a salubrious atmosphere all around, it made the surroundings auspicious enough for Goddess Lakshmi to come and reside in.

His talk gave me a glimpse of a world with which we are fast losing touch—the world of the horse, its trappings, the perfume of leather upholstery, the shining brass lamps with little green crystals stuck at their sides, the fragrance of steaming gram and, above all, the coachman with his coat buttoned up to his neck and his turban, and his hand lightly resting on the whip handle. My mind went back to the days when my uncle had a carriage in Madras. I don't know what they called it: phaeton, dogcart, victoria, governess (or governor's) cart. It was a yellow carriage with windows, and bench-like seats inside. You could sit comfortably facing other passengers and also look out of the window. The driver's seat was screened off with a panel. He sat high up, and you had to put your head out and tell him where to go and when to stop. It was a beautiful experience. You had to warn him a couple of hours ahead what your programme for the day would be since he had much to do before getting the horse and carriage ready for the road. He had to groom the horse ('malish', as we heard him call the process), strap on to it various leather bits, give it gram and water, and tuck a small quantity of green grass under his footrest for the way, which engendered a perpetual smell of green grass about this vehicle.

The double-bullock cart with its arched springs and mat-covered roof is another thing that comes to my mind. It may be the trick of reminiscence that endows it with so much charm now. One of the most enchanting memories of this kind of locomotion was an all-night journey I had to undertake years ago when I returned home for the summer vacation, the train putting me down thirty miles from my town. The bullock carts moved in a caravan, winding along a dark, tree-shaded highway. Robbers were known to attack such caravans about ten miles from the railway station at midnight. This menace was warded off by a simple expedient. One of the cart-men walked ahead carrying a lantern and a staff and throwing bloodcurdling challenges to the night air. 'Hey! Keep away, prowlers, if you don't want to have your skulls pulped . . . Who goes there?' and so forth, the other drivers also sitting up and urging their bullocks on with the loudest swear-words. This was kept up till we passed a jutting rock beyond the twelfth milestone; the moment we crossed this spot the challenger went back to his cart, curled himself in his seat and fell asleep, the entire caravan following this example. By some strange law or understanding the robbers never seemed to step an inch beyond the jutting rock. It always seemed to me that the robbers were wasting a fine opportunity to attack with all the cart-men fast asleep and the only wakeful person being myself as I tried to sleep on a pile of straw expecting any moment to be killed. But nothing happened and we reached our destination sometime the next day, the jingling of ox bells persisting in a re-echo for nearly a week after the journey.

Death due to movement, in various forms, is an inescapable condition of living today. We move about and carry on our work, dodging an oncoming wheel all the time. 'Caution', 'Speed Limit', 'School Zone', 'Halt and Proceed' are all there, but is there anyone who takes these instructions seriously? The pedestrian is the only person likely to notice these signs, with every chance of being knocked down while pausing to study the directions meant for the motorist. In a world where the pedestrian seems to be of so little account—he is blinded by motor lights, deafened by screeching horns and chased about by reckless speed fiends—it is soothing to think of a horse and carriage or a bullock cart.

THE VANDAL

THE REAL OLD-TIME vandal came in as an invader, if not a conqueror. The moment he marched in he picked up a hammer and knocked out the noses of all the sculptured figures in his new domain, and he, alas, spent considerable time breaking their arms and legs. He carried out his task as matter of routine. After this, if he saw any building of architectural value standing he lost no time in demolishing it.

This was a conscious and deliberate vandal who did what he did because he had the strength and the chance to do it. He probably told himself, 'Well, there is too much art plaguing the world anyway—let me do my bit to mitigate it.' There is no way of remedying this man's handiwork. We have to accept it as a historical process, but the work of the not-so-historical vandal is the one that should cause us concern now. I visited an ancient temple recently, famed for the minute sculptural work on its pillars, walls and ceiling. Painstaking work by ancient craftsmen was in evidence everywhere, but even more painstaking were the efforts of those who had attempted to effect improvements later.

These should be called the real vandals. They seem to have been telling themselves, 'It was all very well for the old sculptors to have attempted so much, but they don't seem to have paid much attention to brightening up their surroundings.' And forthwith they sanctioned out of the temple funds the purchase of large quantities of aluminium paint, cement, lime and mortar, and plastered every cornice, wall, and pillar with lime or cement. Figures that could not be so easily dealt with were given two special coatings of aluminium paint, with the comment, 'Now there is something to be proud of. The figures look as if made of silver.' Actually the figures now look as if they had been shaped out of old aluminium vessels. I noticed cigarette foils also employed for effecting improvements. A huge quantity of it was used for covering the inlay work on an inner door. I could not help asking the temple authority for an explanation of his activities. He said, 'You know this is a famous temple, and our Minister visits it often. I shouldn't like to give him the impression that we are neglecting it in any way.'

The vandal in authority is the person to be most dreaded today. He is capable of making a hash of the architectural pattern of an entire town. He can never set eyes on a building without wanting to do something or other with it. His words carry weight with the executives following him, with notebooks in hand, when he is out on inspection. When he points at a building and suggests improvements, those behind dare not contradict him. The building may be a concrete, streamlined modern structure, but he may order a huge lotus bud to be carved on its top, or he may demand that floral designs be carved on its pillars, or that the entire building be given a dome and Mogul turrets; or an ancient French villa-type building may suffer the addition of an utterly modernistic cantilever.

Vandalism may be direct and obvious, as in the instances above, or it may also be hidden or implied. I cannot stand the sight of unfading crepe flowers in vases. Putting crepe flowers in vases is an act of vandalism according to me. Shiny plastic curtains over doors and windows give me an uneasy feeling; also the sight of indiscriminate assemblage of ferns and potted plants in verandas, or monstrous creepers trained to cover an entire building. This is an entirely personal view. I am sure that the man who has gathered those flowerpots or hung those curtains views them as achievements and may not care to be labelled a vandal in his own home. I respect his sentiment. I shall never let him see my own catalogue listing what, according, to me, are vandalisms. Each individual is free to draw up his own list.

There cannot be what may be termed a standard list of vandalisms which may be of use to those about to undertake the task of furnishing their homes and surroundings, however much we might standardize the pattern of society. Those that love calendar pictures will not rest till they cover the walls of their homes with all the calendars issued on the new year by all the business concerns in the country; a lover of group photos will cover every inch of space in his home with portraits of all the friends and relations that ever came his way; the organizer who is determined to sell space in the music hall will ever hang placards announcing the virtues of asafoetida or soap on every pillar there, and the man who is bent upon painting his home deep blue and illuminating it with an abundance of green tube light must have his way. When confronted with such acts we gently avert our looks and mumble indistinctly rather than shout our views from housetops. It is in the interest of harmonious human relations. It would be unseemly otherwise. But the line must be drawn somewhere. When the vandal emerges from the privacy of his home or immediate surroundings and attempts at improving nature or art on a large, public scale, then it is time for us to start an uninhibited 'down with—' campaign against him.

THE NON-MUSICAL MAN

THE MAN CANNOT understand why so much fuss should be made about music. He can never make out how people could sit in their chairs for hours in a hall gazing on a musician and shaking their heads. In his view the whole thing is a piece of hypocrisy practised by a group of persons who wish to look different.

In a sort of superior way the musical enthusiast feels a pity for this man. Says he to himself, 'Ah, this poor fellow is deaf to music. What a lot he misses in life!' And he goes to him with the idea of improving his outlook. He tells the one deaf to music, 'You must come and hear so-and-so's music on Sunday,' peremptorily, with the air of a physician forcing a draught of quinine.

The other looks scared. The prospect is frightening. He tries to withdraw, but he is compelled to spend the Sunday evening at the music hall. The most unacceptable thing there for him is the mournful silence that he is expected to maintain. He cannot discuss weather or politics with his neighbour. He has to speak in whispers, if at all, and generally conduct himself as if he were in a Presence. His democratic nature does not permit him to tolerate such restrictions. He sits silently fretting in his seat. He feels bored. He tries to count the electric bulbs in the hall. He studies the faces around him. He spots a friend across intervening heads, far off, and feels like shouting, 'Hallo, long time since we met!' but he swallows the greeting. He studies a watch on someone's wrist four chairs off. He reads an advertisement board stuck on a pillar, forward and backward, spelling it out letter by letter. He feels bored with all this activity very soon. He sits back in a mood of profound resignation. He looks at the dais.

The programme is attaining its zenith: the singer and his accompanists are negotiating their way through a tortuous *Pallavi*. Our friend notices that the drummer is beating the skin off his palm, the violinist is jabbing the air with his elbow while attempting to saw off the violin in the middle, and the vocalist is uttering a thousand syllables without pausing for breath. A triangular skirmish seems to be developing among the three on the dais. Evidently someone seems to have emerged a victor presently, for the audience which was watching the fray in rapt attention suddenly breaks into thunderous applause. There is a stir in the crowd and a general air of relaxation as the instruments are being tuned and touched up after the terrific battering they suffered a while ago.

Our friend hopes that this is the end of all trouble, but he notices, to his dismay, that it is only a pause. The audience shows no sign of leaving. The musician clears his throat and starts once more, and involves himself in all kinds of complicated, convulsive noise-making. Our friend, who had a brief moment of joy thinking that it was all over, resigns himself to it again, reflecting philosophically, 'Everything in this world must end sometime, even music.' A most consoling thought.

When the performance ends he leaves the hall with an iron resolution never to go near music again. If he remains an unknown, insignificant man he may exercise his fundamental right of keeping away from music; but if he becomes a man of consequence he will have to bow to other people's will. He will be invited to attend an eminent artiste's performance. He will be received at the gate by the organizers of the show. He will be conducted to an honoured seat while an audience of a thousand watch his movement with wonder and respect. The programme will not start until he is well settled in his seat.

Why they want him to attend this musical function is a question that can never be precisely answered. It may be for a variety of reasons. His presence may lend weight to the occasion; he may be in a position to cast favours, such as ground for a building, or funds; there may be a dozen reasons why they want him there, all except that he likes music or knows anything of it. He has to sit through the music fully conscious of his own suffering. He knows that he is imprisoned in his own status. He is not a whit changed inside. His bafflement at the goings-on on the dais is still the same. He still wants to break out into chatter or call up a distant friend. He still feels the same impulse to rise and dash out of the hall at supersonic speed (to quote a young nephew of mine addicted to comics and science fiction), but he simply cannot do such a thing. He cannot afford to hurt anyone. If he gets up, it is feared, the musician may lose his inspiration, it may dishearten the organizers, or throw the audience into confusion.

Usage makes him a hardened music listener in due course. He can sit through a four-hour performance without turning a hair. Gradually, he wreaks a subconscious vengeance on those who have dragged him into it, by beginning to talk about music in public and in private. He can explain what is good and what is not good in music. He classifies music as classical, heavy, light, bantam, folk, meaningful or meaningless, compares their respective values, and prescribes what is good for whom. This may safely be taken as the point of danger for music as a whole.

ON HUMOUR

'IF YOU LOVE humour don't talk or write about it,' said an eminent guru to his disciple. Commendable advice. For, nothing evaporates so swiftly as humour the moment it is examined or explained. Nothing kills it so successfully as analysis and study. I am happy, and feel repeatedly happy at the thought, that humour is not made a subject of study in our universities, which has spared us from the predicament of having Ph.Ds of humour in our midst. I often speculate what question a 'theory paper' on humour might have contained if it had been a university examination subject: explain with diagrams the anatomy of laughter; distinguish between chuckling and grinning; trace the relation between gravity and humour; explain the origin of smiles; write short notes on buffoonery, sally, clowning, quip and innuendo. The 'practical paper' might probably have asked the candidate to apply his theory and make an attempt to move at least one of his examiners to emit a loud guffaw.

Humour is still not a public speaker's theme. Had it been one, eminent men presiding over the celebrations of the national humour week might be found exhorting their audience, 'Be humorous. We must all strive to wear out grimness wherever we may meet it. Remember grimness is our national enemy number one. Humour lightens the burden of existence, and so let all the good citizens of our country exercise their sense of humour (without detriment to their avocations) during their weekly holidays and all other recognized government holidays.' As our good fortune will have it, no government on earth has bothered to create a ministry of humour, although some have come perilously near it with their zeal for cultural activity. Humour fortunately still remains an individual business. Otherwise we should be having experts, bluebooks and statements of annual turnover of jokes emanating from various secretariats.

I have a secret conviction that the Posts and Telegraph, more than any other government department, possesses a sly sense of humour, and arranges its affairs in such a manner as to enjoy a quiet chuckle now and then in its contacts with the public. Otherwise how could we explain some of the most bewildering things we see them perform now and then? A bridegroom receives a greeting telegram on his wedding day with just the message, 'Number Eight'. I have found this mysterious message creating quite a lot of speculation and bewilderment in an otherwise peaceful household just setting down to a restful afternoon after the wedding festivities. 'Number Eight' assumes all the sinister quality of a message in code passing between deadly conspirators until one goes to the nearest post-office and finds out that it is just the code number of a greeting which calls upon heaven to shower its choicest blessings on the happy couple.

Further, one may notice the presence of small metal discs on the footpaths of any city, stuck at regular intervals. Each disc rears itself up like an angry cobra, a foot above ground: the inscription on the disc explains itself as a 'CTD cable', placed there by the telegraph or telephone department. Only a dull, humourless mind would protest against it. If you watch closely you will find dozens of feet coming on proudly and then suddenly stumping on one or the other of the discs: some go limping forward, some step away in surprise, some execute a tango in sheer pain. When the traffic police compel pedestrians to walk on the footpath—ah, that is the time when the CTD discs fulfil their mission without a doubt. This piece of humour is no doubt of the class of circus clowning, but nonetheless it is some kind of humour and let us give the credit where it is due.

Humour is such an individual matter that it would be difficult to generalize about it. I feel distressed whenever I find serious, solemn persons enquiring, 'Have we a sense of humour?' The question will have to be answered by each according to his capacity. But there is also this danger: one might think oneself humorous, but others may not perceive it. There is none so tragic as the man who has delusions in this respect. There is nothing on earth more miserable than the man of anecdotes and constant jokes studiously learnt and cultivated. I know of a public speaker whose most cherished possession is a bulky book containing quotable anecdotes and jokes. He picks up a couple of them at a time, carefully rehearses himself before a mirror and brings them out in the evening. His audience anticipates all his humour and enjoys it unreservedly, although knowing fully that it is all derived from a vast storehouse of quotations. When the lecturer pauses to say, 'I am reminded of an anecdote . . .' the audience laugh in advance. It only proves that the public loves to laugh and that it possesses a better sense of humour than its humorous speaker.

Our cartoonists, humorous writers and columnists are now fully alive, deriving their inspiration from the absurdities and contradictions seen in public life: in the pomposities of self-important men, the elaborate pageantry surrounding the arrival and departure of a VIP, the ridiculous fuss bureaucrats make everywhere, and above all the plight of the modern unknown warrior, who is the middle class common man, and who is unable to bear all the improvements and benefits that his would-be champions attempt to heap on his head. It would be impossible to survive these if we did not possess a sense of humour: that itself is a proof that we have an abundance of it.

THE SCOUT

I REMEMBER I was very proud of being a scout. I spent several sleepless nights revelling in visions of myself in a scout uniform: Khaki shorts and shirt, green turban (those were still days of turban), colourful shoulder-straps and the mighty staff in hand. There was really no need for me to spend my time in mere dream but for the fact that my scout teacher seemed to have told my people that they could take their own time to provide me with a uniform. I don't know why he said it, but probably he felt that my novitiation was incomplete; he must have had a better measure of my stage and worthiness than I. I thought no end of my accomplishments, although now looking back, any competence I exhibited must have been only in regard to the holding of the staff, and in giving the scout salute. But this was obviously not enough. If I had been asked: 'What is the fourth law of scouting?' I am sure I should have felt flabbergasted. Or, 'What are the three promises?' I was sure to bungle because the easiest thing that came to my head was, 'On my honour I promise to do my best for God, Crown and Country.' But we belonged to an association which had decided to drop the *crown* in their promise, deftly substituting something else, perhaps *truth*, in its place; but I always stumbled on to crown, under the strong influence of a friend from another troop, which followed the orthodox line. In addition to my own handicaps another important reason why I could not have the uniform was that my people at home believed that good khaki could not be easily obtained except by using someone's influence. Their line of thought was: 'I know someone who knows someone who alone can get the best khaki at the cheapest price.' This meant agonizing trips for me, up and down, and waiting on the arrivals, departures and moods of a contact man who, beside this business of finding me the best khaki on the easiest of terms, had plenty of other things to do for himself, and so could not view or remember his promises with the singlemindedness I expected of him. But all this meant only delay and not actual frustration.

Eventually the khaki pieces arrived, to be followed by countless journeys on my part to the tailor, who was probably unused to the business of stitching shorts and the scout shirt, with so many pockets and straps and flaps; finally he did produce something approximating our design. It turned out to be a little prolonged here and a little curtailed there, but by judicious tucking-in, slicing-off and re-stitching, he gave me something that might have seemed a little ill-made to impartial eyes, but enough to fill my heart with pride and satisfaction when I viewed myself in a mirror; khaki turban and streamers at the shoulder. The picture that the mirror gave me was so imposing and self-inspiring that I had no doubt I was one of the pillars of the nation. I would give anything to feel that again now with such genuineness and intensity. I had a feeling that I had ceased to be just a boy hanging around the fringes of the world of elders, but someone of consequence. I belonged to a very vital group. We stood at attention, turned right and left, saluted each other and uttered patrol calls. When we marched in the streets in a file we had a feeling that we were the objects of envious watching by the whole town. We had certain esoteric, secret training and abilities; by glancing at the marks on the ground we could say where a companion had gone or where a buried treasure could be located. We knew what to do if someone was drowning, how to light a fire in a storm with a single matchstick (I never passed this test), how to tie a reef knot, the mysterious purposes of sheep shank or clove hitch, how to bandage a cracked skull. All this knowledge filled us with the pride of accomplishment and performance. And how anxious we were to place our knowledge and training at anybody's disposal, always waiting to be asked to regulate crowds, help people out or watch over something. It was incumbent upon a scout to record at least one good turn a day in his diary. It was not at all as easy as it might sound. I can recollect the desperation some days when the world seemed to be so perfectly organized that one looking about to perform a good turn hardly got a chance. It was harrowing to feel that perhaps the page would have to be left blank for the day. Driven to desperation, one did all sorts of things. If one could somehow salvage my good-turn diary of years ago one would find therein such profound entries as 'Chased away a big dog when it came to bite a small dog,' or 'Saw the old lady in the fourth house suffering from stomach ache, ran to the opposite shop and fetched a bottle of soda water,' and 'Guided a stranger to the toddy shop'.

Of course there were badges and decorations for special achievements, but they were not the chief source of inspiration for the performance of shining deeds. The important thing was finding an occasion for performing a good deed; all else was secondary.

GARDENING WITHOUT TEARS

A LITTLE GARDENING goes a long way, and I view with apprehension the recent outburst of horticulturism that is evident everywhere. What one needs is not a mere garden, but a garden which leaves one in peace. If someone will draw a blueprint for gardening without tears I shall be the first to support it. The gardening enthusiast is the most anxiety-ridden person on earth. He is constantly racked with the feeling that he has to contend against evil forces all his life. He visualizes himself as a victim of all the malicious forces in the universe which are ever ready to frustrate his dream, coming to him in the shape of straying chickens from the neighbourhood looking for seeds, seedlings or sprouts; or a laughing child dancing on a patch of soil cultivated with blood, sweat and tears; or just a dignified visitor whose dignity would be injured if told not to let his finger play mischief with the foliage on the way. Every fervent garden-maker becomes a cranky neurasthenic full to the brim with complexes. There is something in gardening which affects what may be called the norms of human temperament.

There are at least two gardens within every compound—the seen and the unseen. What a visitor sees in the first round is only a small portion of what the proud gardener actually has in view. The lover of plants lives in a sort of fourth dimensional plane. Many things that you as visitor will not notice are already there: that plot of turned up earth is just a forest of roses, the small twig sticking out a green shoot a tenth of an inch long is not actually a stick but *plumeria, poinciana* or *spathodia*, rare and noble trees which have transformed the landscape. Their very names possess magic and poetry. There is much to commend in the use of botanical names, which apart from other things act as passwords among the community of plant-lovers, shutting out the Philistine who cannot distinguish between cacti and cannae: and which also keep alive in our midst Latin, probably the only language which has not spread widely enough in our country to create a problem.

There are at least as many types of gardens as there are temperaments. Our tradition is to start a piece of gardening, whatever may be the size of the area, with a coconut seedling on an auspicious day, and follow it up with other things. The coconut is for posterity, hibiscus and jasmine for the gods in the *puja* room, vegetable for the kitchen, and lastly come those that afford merely visual pleasure. It is in contrast to the quick gardening that, for example, a foreign visitor taking a house for a few months would plan: pansies, asters, phlox and zinnia, and this and that, which come up within a few weeks, brightly wave their multi-coloured stalks, and as swiftly wither away without a trace. I once observed an American who took a house for a few months; he hustled the earth with phosphate, sulphate and compost, and grew lettuce for salad, maize (corn on the cob) for snack, and cut flowers for table decoration, and gave an impression of creating a garden overnight, but it was a strictly utility garden that would not outlast the lease. I observed that there was no semblance of a garden left a week after he vacated the house.

A plant, no doubt, can be a man's best friend: silent, unobtrusive and (more or less) responsive. The great thing about plants is that they don't move or make noise, the two great evils that beset us in this world of ours. We are all the time so much battered by noise and movement that it ought to prove a tonic for us to watch things that don't move or talk. But we must first examine ourselves and ask, 'Are we worthy of this great company?' Unless one makes sure of it, one is likely to suffer (and also cause suffering) by contact with plants. Who is the happy gardener? It is he that hath the hope and resignation of a gambler, the nerves of a circus acrobat, the unfading wonderment of a growing child, the detachment of a seer and, above all, the forbearance of the eldest of the *Pandavas*.

THE GREAT BASKET

IN A NEW ORDER of things I hope the wastepaper basket will receive the recognition and status that it deserves. It is not just a receptacle that you keep under your table for flinging unwanted papers in. Unwantedness, in any case, is a relative term. The urgent paper of today becomes the unwanted one of tomorrow. If a new symbol is needed to indicate Time it should be neither the hour-glass with falling sand nor the hands of a clock, but a wide-girthed wastepaper basket into which all papers vanish and attain a final equality. This tax notice, that cinema folder, that reminder of an old bill, even letters from friends or foes whose contents have been read and digested, and invitation cards so laboriously prepared and printed, where do they end?

I have discovered a most practical way of dealing with unnecessary correspondence. I suffer from the privilege of receiving letters from strangers, most of whom desire to tell me how to write or what to write about. I go through them with reverential care, but I am never able to acknowledge them. It is not because I am not able to appreciate the brilliance of the advice or the spirit in which it is given, but, having to write for a living, it is impossible to engage oneself in the same activity at the end of day's labour. If a writer does not always display the courtesy of acknowledging a letter it must be put down to nothing worse than the psychological difficulties of his profession. And so what happens? I read the letter, send up a silent thanks to the writer and then gently toss it under the table. I know where it will fall. By long practice I know exactly how far a gentle fling will carry a piece of paper. I don't have to look a second time. It is rarely that I overshoot or undershoot and find the letter or paper lying under the table. When that happens it means that the missile must be an abnormal one, of an unusual density or volume, such as a questionnaire form or a catalogue. It may seem unjust that this should happen to the most carefully composed forms and lists, but no one who is reasonable can ever object to this disposal. What else can one do with them? It is with reluctance and regret that I consign such papers to the basket, constantly asking myself what else I could do about them. If I keep them in sight on my table, they will go on bothering my conscience. I don't wish to go through existence with a gnawing conscience all the time. By putting that letter out of sight I remove one possible strain on my conscience. I make the wastepaper basket my conscience-keeper. I never crumple a letter while slipping it into the basket. I leave it whole with all its postmark intact on its envelope. I never have my basket cleared except once in a while. This helps me take a second look at my correspondence when occasion calls for it. I remember quite a few occasions when I have pulled out a letter from the basket and written a reply on second thoughts.

Apart from other considerations there is the question of space. You may have the largest study and the most capacious table but yet, day by day, there is bound to be gradual and steady encroachment on all the available space, and a time may come when (to quote Shaw in a favourite saying that also appears elsewhere), 'The dead may crowd the living out of this earth.' The word dead must not be resented by anyone. Keep any letter for a week and it becomes dead, and then the only thing to do with it is to put it out of sight and no one is the worse for it. When examined after a week what seemed pressing and inescapable seems just cold and inconsequential. Only government offices enjoy the unique privilege of keeping in ponderous files what had better be entombed in the great basket. Their fear is that all sorts of papers may be necessary for some reference at some future date. My view is that this world would be a better place to live in if there were fewer references available on any question. No question is valued on its own present worth but in relation to a deadweight of its past.

I feel that a little more liberal use of the W.P.B. will also solve all accommodation problems in this world—everywhere there is a cry for more accommodation—not for human beings alone but for papers and files. It is just here that the W.P.B. can help humanity.

The basket is an equally good place for sudden and voluminous literary effusion. There is a cold impersonality about its reception of literary matter which always appeals to me. I have sometimes found it necessary to consign to it several thousand words of a new novel representing weeks of hard work, and I have felt the better for it. When one can bring oneself to the point of doing it, one feels light and free and able to resume an obliterated chapter with a better perspective.

Apart from its association with much paper, the great basket is an article worth possessing for its own sake. It is the shapeliest article ever made by human fingers. It has symmetry, poise, accessibility and balance, and it certainly deserves a better place than the dark regions under a desk.

OF TRAINS AND TRAVELLERS

I HAVE A weakness for odd trains, some shuttle or passenger which will crawl through the countryside and stop long enough at unknown stations to enable one to gain an idea of the life and habits there. I like to reach my destination by a series of such hops rather than by a masterful, purposeful mail rushing along to its terminus without pausing to look this way or that. The disadvantage of travelling by such a strict train is that one glides past most places at dead of night. For instance, Salem or Jalarpet are stations which I have crossed hundreds of times these many years, but without any idea of what they look like. In order to remedy this deficiency in general knowledge, I have taken to travelling by unspectacular day trains. Not the least part of the delight of such a journey being that you find the human element within the compartment as attractive as the landscape without. During a night journey, preoccupation with the problem of sleep distorts the human personality.

The bearded *sadhu* who occupies a corner with scorn on his face for all worldly goods including railway tickets; the meek paterfamilias taking his wife and numerous children somewhere, always consumed with anxiety lest they should be crowded out of their seats; the businessman and his friend lounging back and continuously shouting over the din their prowess in market operations; the bully stretching himself out on a complete seat in full luxury, daring anyone to approach him; the glutton who can never allow a single edible pass outside the window without stopping and buying one, every time haggling over price and quality and showing no inclination to produce his cash till the train actually begins to move, compelling every vendor to trot beside the train; the season-ticket student showing off his familiarity with the railway by perching himself precariously on the footboard or at the doorway; these are familiar characters one meets in any journey.

There is one other type of person who grips everybody's attention the moment he enters a train. He is the loquacious man. He can never leave anyone alone. His air of assurance and friendliness wins him a new listener, if not a friend, every moment. It may be said that this man attempts to guide the life and thought of everyone in the compartment. There a child may cry. Our friend will not persuade the child to remain quiet but also explain to the mother how children should be brought up, what should be done if they suffer from stomach ache, how to treat a cold, how to tackle bad temper or mischief. If need be he can move everybody and clear a space for the young mother to spread out a piece of cloth and put her child to sleep. He once cleared a lot of space for elders by persuading all the children to sit in a row on an upper berth. One might take him to be a child specialist until one sees him turn his attention to the next subject. He may happen to notice the glutton eat his orange when he will yell out, 'How much did you pay for the orange?' and follow it up with a discourse on the ups and downs of the orange trade, the method of its cultivation and the geography of the country where it is grown. If he happens to see the actual transaction, this or any other, you may rest assured he will throw his weight on the side of the buyer and force the vendor to bring down his price. If he overhears some others in a corner talking among themselves of political matters, he will step in and put an end to their conversation, compelling them to listen to his own talk. He is one who knows all that goes on behind the scenes at New Delhi. He can explain why this policy is being pursued or why the other one is dropped. He knows who is at the back of everything. He may even claim to be the one who originated the Janata Express, Shatabdi Concession, or the Hindusthan Coach, through his mysterious agencies in the proper quarters. When he mentions the Parliament he assumes the look of one who bears it like a burden on his back. He knows all the persons that pull the strings that move the puppets in the Parliament and in the Cabinet. His hints about his own participation in various political activities, builds up a background to whatever he says and gives them a touch of credibility. He can mention most of the personages at Delhi by their pet names; it may take time for an ordinary man to spot them out under his terms. Not for him the words Prime Minister but just Jawahar; for most of the others in the government he employs mystifying initials and abbreviations.

This man gives one the impression that he travels for no other purpose than to gain first-hand impressions of how people are faring. He demands very little from others except a hearing which he will get anyway. He hardly keeps a seat for himself, always surrendering it to anyone who may look for more space. I have always wanted to ask whether he possesses a ticket or not, but could never muster enough courage to put the question to him.

UMBRELLA DEVOTEE

I READ WITH great pleasure the recent news that the prices of umbrellas (why not 'umbrellae' for plural in order to add to the dignity of the subject?) have fallen. I am one of those, I believe it is a somewhat select group, who believe that every adult should have a minimum of three umbrellas: one for personal use, one for lending and one for reserve in case all the umbrellas suddenly vanish from the face of this earth through some freak action such as an atomic blast. Deep within, the umbrella devotee is prey to all kinds of phobias. And not all the phobias are unfounded, if we remember how well-founded is his impression that all are frantically attempting to get at his umbrella all the time. He cannot leave it resting in a corner and be sure that he can find it there when he wants it again. Everyone thinks that he can pick up any umbrella that he sees. The man who would hesitate to pick up my ring never hesitates to snatch away my old umbrella hanging in its stand. It is this utter disregard for ownership in umbrellas that is responsible for all the confusion and irritation that we notice in the umbrella business today. I heard a friend confess recently, 'I have five umbrellas and five hundred enemies.' He explained, 'I make enemies this way: I have five umbrellas because I like to have five, that is all. I have as much right to have five umbrellas as I have to have five fingers. Anyone who questions why I should possess five umbrellas sounds impertinent to my ears and gets the appropriate reply. And then when they ask me to lend them my umbrella I invariably refuse to do so; that makes people call me selfish and I retort appropriately.

People are sometimes persistent and will plead and cajole till I give them my umbrella. Of course it is given with stern warnings and stipulations regarding time and place of its return, but I am yet to come across a single creature who remembers this injunction; ninety out of a hundred will not remember their obligations. In the end I have to undertake a trip to retrieve my umbrella, and then I do not hesitate to tell a person what I think of him. Moreover, it is a well-established fact that ninety-nine out of a hundred do not know how to hold an umbrella: when I find a tear in the cloth or a loosened rib or handle, I tell the borrower plainly that he ought to be sent to jail for it. People do not appreciate forthright comments. I am sorry to say that most persons do not know how to handle an umbrella; some have the distressing habit of twirling its handle while walking, or holding it too high or too low, right over their skulls as if it were a cap; all this will ruin an umbrella.

'There is a technique in using an umbrella as in all things. There should be neither stiffness nor too much flexibility at the wrist of an arm that holds an umbrella; it must be adjusted properly to the pressure of the wind. Wind is an insidious enemy whose effect is most wearing; the ribs may be made of iron but it is as a broomstick to the wind. What must protect an umbrella is an understanding wrist. How can everyone understand this subject, when most people never think of an umbrella except when it rains? I wish they would include a course in umbrella-holding in all educational institutions. Just fifteen minutes a day for two or three days in the week and it would produce wonderful results. It must be based on the same footing as compulsory military training. Another reason why all these unpleasant things exist about umbrellas is that there are far too many persons in each of our households and too few umbrellas. In a normal joint-family household there are at least ten persons in a house, but how many umbrellas are there to be found? Just one, where it ought to be really thirty on the basis that everyone should have at least three umbrellas. What happens is this; one umbrella probably belongs to an enthusiast, but everyone has his eye on it whenever he wants protection from sun or rain. It is either sunny or rainy, one or the other, and the umbrella is in danger of getting into circulation. Fortunately nobody asks for your umbrella when there is the moon. I believe it is due to that wonderful proverb which says that only an upstart will hold an umbrella over his head at midnight. We need more and more of such proverbs. I believe one way in which people may be induced to own their umbrellas is to include the question in every form that is to be filled out. Form-filling for one purpose or another is a necessity for ration, passport, education, employment or anything, in which a lot of questions are asked regarding age, ancestry, etc. of every person, and among all that host of irrelevant questions why not add one more, 'Do you possess an umbrella? If so, how long have you had it? How do you manage to keep yours?' This may not always bring forth truthful answers but it will at any rate put people into a proper frame of mind. Nowadays umbrella lovers are viewed as cranks, which is most unfortunate. People openly brag, 'Oh, I cannot think of carrying an umbrella in the streets; oh, no, I would never be seen with one.' This is a very unhealthy attitude. They go even a step further and say, 'I have lost nearly twenty umbrellas this year.' Somehow this is said in a tone of pride. Why should it be made a matter of boastful talk rather than one to be ashamed of? If this braggart has lost twenty umbrellas, you may rest assured that the losses are someone else's and not his. Existence will not be perfect until it becomes as impossible for a person to carry another man's umbrella as carrying another man's driving licence. 'I do not accept the statement that the slump in the umbrella trade is due to the successive failure of monsoons. No true umbrella devotee will ever be put off by such fickle causes as weather. A man loves his umbrella for its own sake. He would hug his umbrella, whether it is a London-imported variety rolled to look like a stick or whether it is the heavy-canopied flabby one with a cane handle, not because it is hot or rainy but because he has true affection at heart for it.'

THE SYCOPHANT

SYCOPHANCY IS ONE of the oldest professions in the world. Old King Cole was a merry old soul because he could afford to be so. He would have felt choked by his surroundings but for the sycophant who stood by and helped him attain peace of mind. The sycophant may well be called the provider of peace of mind for those in authority. He acts as a shock absorber—even this word is a little ahead of the sense: it would be nearer the mark to say that he acts as a shock repeller. The sycophant is ever watchful and manages to keep his chief from feeling unduly bothered by conscience or common sense. The sycophant's genius lies in showing a feeling that is not his own but his master's. He cannot afford to assume any colour of his own. His survival depends upon his capacity to take on the hue that his master is likely to assume at any given moment. Hamlet points to the sky and asks Polonius: 'Do you see yonder cloud that's almost in shape of a camel?'

Polonius: 'By the mass, and it's like a camel, indeed.'

Hamlet: 'Methinks it is like a weasel.'

Polonius: 'It is backed like a weasel.'

Hamlet: 'Or like a whale?'

Polonius: 'Very like a whale.'

I quote this because it seems to me a masterpiece of sycophancy, although Polonius had perhaps other aims, such as wanting to humour a madman, in making himself so agreeable.

The essence of a sycophant's success lies in his capacity to remain agreeable under all conditions. He may not be a lover of children, least of all his master's favourite, the seven-year-old devil. He may feel like spanking him and putting him in his place whenever he sees him, but his first sentence, his opening line for the day, always is: 'How is the little charmer, sir?' He has to show a keen interest in the boy's games, books, hobbies and friends; and cherish for timely use one or two quotations from the young man's speeches which displays his wit and wisdom. There is a certain amount of self-abnegation involved in it. The sycophant is one who sacrifices much and bears much, and it is no small strain to remain agreeable under all conditions. After all, when we come to consider it, what is his personal gain in all this? It is not much. All that he seeks is that he be allowed to bask forever in the sunshine of his master's presence. This gives him a reflected glory and an authority which seem to him the most important acquisition in life; the material and other advantages that may arise therefrom are mere by-products. He practises sycophancy for its own sake, for the pleasure it gives, for the sense of well-being that it spreads all around. This man I would place at the summit of the category. One who practises this fine art for the sake of obvious gains can take only second place in this hierarchy. It has all the difference that we observe between one who is a devotee of art for art's sake and the utilitarian who uses art for propaganda. When we see a man employing sycophancy for some cheap purpose we are seized with the same sense of bathos as overwhelms us while seeing a film, perfectly made in every way, but out to show only the virtues of the caterpillar wheel or of chemical fertilizers.

When the history of mankind comes to be written more fully, I expect a great deal will be included about the sycophant and his influence on human affairs. How many rulers of men, how many despots, lived in worlds of their own, unperturbed by contrary views and outlooks? In the *Fall of Berlin* there is a historic instance, which may be of questionable accuracy, but the portrayal itself seems significant. Hitler is told that the fall of Moscow is imminent, a matter of a few minutes. He keeps looking at the time and frets and fumes. A military adviser suggests that Moscow may, probably, never be taken since, in the course of its history, many an invader has had to turn back from its gates. This man is dismissed instantly and a courtier who blindly assures Hitler that the German troops are at the moment marching in the streets of Moscow is promoted very high. We may question the propriety of this presentation but it is a perfect example of the sycophant's role in human affairs.

The American colloquial expression for it is more direct: 'yes-man'. It seems to me that this expression may not exactly mean sycophancy but something more. 'Yes-man' appears to be a democratic word. Sycophant was quite adequate for one-man rule, when the ruler did not have to worry about public opinion, but nowadays the ruler has to get through his business with the backing of his yes-man, which alone can give it a democratic touch.

The yes-man's role is not necessarily confined to politics. Of late he has made his appearance in the scientific world also. When a scientist becomes a yes-man he will assert that the earth is square or flat or crooked, just as it suits his master's mind. Galileo's trouble was that he could not show this accommodating spirit and hence suffered persecution all his life. Now in some places the scientist obviously avoids the folly of Galileo, and is ready to assert that man and not nature should decide how much time wheat or some other corn ought to take to grow and ripen, if his master shows any signs of annoyance at the time-table followed by nature.

I have tried to trace the origin of the word 'sycophant'. The dictionary says: 'perh. orig. "one who informed against persons exporting figs," from *sukon* "fig", see *Syconium*', which injunction I could not lightly ignore. I looked up *Syconium* to know that it was Greek for fig or a near-fig-like fruit. I have found it very illuminating on the whole. I realized that we have after all been bandying about a word without being aware of its association with the fig business, its export restrictions and possible controls, the men who profited by flouting the law, and the greater profit that other men derived by watching (and informing against) the men who profited by flouting the law, and these last were known as sycophants. This is all only an incidental discovery. My original purpose in turning the pages of a dictionary was to know if sycophant had a feminine form. I am sure it will be a heartening piece of news for many to know that there is no 'sycophantess' just as there is no such thing as yes-woman.

THE MAHA

A JUDICIOUS ADMIXTURE of Sanskrit and English, I find, produces sometimes a marvellously handy idiom. It may not have the approval of pundits of either language, but I think it is effective. For instance, how fluently speaks one whose sentences fuse into Tamil and English alternately: the tongue naturally selects the easy way. This is not to say that the mongrel breed is the best in a language, but sometimes it is the most effective. English, at any rate, has been so pliant and absorbent that it has become the most resilient language in the world.

I wish to add to this language a new phrase, maha superiority. *Maha*, the Sanskrit word, seems capable of going in harmoniously with any word in any language; and it is just the word that can add a degree to superior. We want now a word which is above the ordinary superlative; it is achieved by coining 'maha superiority'.

What is maha superiority? It is a state beyond the ordinary standard of snobbery. The ordinary snob pales before this man. The common snob may like to show off his wealth or wit, but his horizon is apparently bounded by another class which can show off more wealth or brighter wit. This is the secret sorrow of every snob. He is ever conscious, through all his preening and measured swagger, of a higher snob, to reach whose place is the secret hankering in his heart all the time. He has a sense of superiority to a certain class of persons around him but he has not that absolute sense of superiority which is the privilege of one who comes under the 'maha' class. The maha superior man has no secret misgivings about his eminence. He feels that the world is at his feet. His uniqueness, he feels, can rouse the envy of gods.

You can generally spot him by his cigarette holder which is the only one of its kind in the world, by his pocket screw pencil of which only a dozen are known to exist in the world. He may not play cricket or any game in the world, but he has a cricket bat given to him by Bradman himself with his autograph. His familiarity with all the names which are only newspaper names for the rest of mankind is breath-taking. Don't be surprised if you hear him say, 'Once, when I put my hands into the Aga Khan's pocket at Nice, do you know how many diamonds I could pick up in a handful?' Or he will talk of the various personal comments made by Clem, Winston or others. 'When I ran into them accidentally at Prague last time . . .' or 'Franco is not really a bad sort. He once told me . . .' or 'At that time I was in a hurry to catch the plane but neither Chiang Kai-shek nor Madame Chiang would let me go without supper, and their chief of air force phoned the airport to delay the plane for three hours.' He is a walking autograph book. He refers to most celebrities by their first names so that most times you may not recognize the person to whom he is referring. If he says Ingrid or Cecil or Harry, he is quite clear in his head whom he means, though his listeners may take time to sort out the famous star, the famous producer, the President of America. America? You will never catch this gentleman using the word. He will always refer to it as the States. 'When I was in the States . . .' You, a simpleton, are likely to think that unless you say USA or America in an obvious heavy style, you will not be understood (remembering your political-science definition that a state is one which has an area, population and government, and that there are thousands of states in the world), but this man has no such doubt. He has a mind free from any kind of misgiving or doubt. His conviction is that what is clear to him ought to be clear to the rest of mankind. What he does not notice is not worth noticing. His talk has always an international background. He is a product of too much travel. He is the sort to say, 'My second son is in Manchester, training in textiles . . . My daughter is in Cambridge; I put her there directly after she passed her high school; I had to rush up to see about her admission personally although I was busy in Rio de Janiero at that time. After all we must take the trouble to settle our children's lives . . . I have always been keen on my children getting a cosmopolitan outlook. Our standards must become international in all matters.'

The air-travel bag has now taken the place of the Kaiser-i-Hind medal or the old decorations of Dewan Bahadur. The maha superior man's contempt for the slow-witted land—or sea—travellers is unbounded. He is ever trying to impress on them the casual ease with which he performs his journey. 'Do you know I never carry anything? I go on with just a *dhoti* and a *banian* . . .' You are astounded. You thought in your innocence that one had to put on a tie or a long coat or things like that. It is all for lesser folk; here is the man who has a feeling of ownership with the airlines. 'You mean to say you can go with a *dhoti*?' you ask innocently. 'Why not? It is our national dress; I always like to attend even formal dinners . . . For instance, when I was in Paris last year . . . where many ambassadors were present, I sat down to dinner in shirt and *dhoti*. People stared at me, that is all; let them,' he concludes. He likes to have people stare at him; in fact, he thrives on it. If others value elaborate dressing up he at once advocates simplicity. He is bound to strike out an independent line for himself. 'Don't imagine we can go up before others like clowns. We have to observe certain proprieties, remember.' He advocates an international outlook till a lot of others also joined his way of thinking, when he might suddenly say, 'All this talk of internationalism is all very well, but we must first think of own homes . . . I have seen these folk at conferences; each is interested in his own affairs. I tell you they are no good. We must set our house in order before we think of anything else.'

HEADACHE

OF ALL THE blessings conferred on mankind by a benign providence, the most useful is the headache. But for it there would be many great embarrassments in life. Factual explanations are not always either palatable or feasible. In such circumstances a headache acts as a sort of password. I remember at school, the very first letter-writing lesson I was taught was: 'Respected sir, as I am suffering from headache, I request you to grant me leave . . .' I always wondered what made our headache an excuse, even in a specimen letter. I think it was very much in everybody's thoughts, useful alike to the pupils, and their master. For us a headache was a boon. We used to have drill after school hours (which I still think is an unfair and undesirable practice). We disliked this hour. On the drill ground almost all appeared to be afflicted with 'Splitting headache, sir', and our drill instructor put an end to it by decreeing one day, 'Those suffering from headache will hold up their arms.' It raised our hopes, but he added, 'Since I wish to detain them for some special exercises that will cure their headache.' Not one lifted his arm, at which the instructor declared, 'Now all of you take off your coats and get through the usual drill. I am glad to find that the class is going to exercise in full strength today.'

Headache gives the sufferer a touch of importance. All other aches sound crude and physiological, and sensitive people would not mention them. No other ailment can be so openly mentioned with impunity. You could mention headache in the most elegant social gathering and no one would be shocked by it. The only expression which is superior to headache is 'indisposition'. Whenever I see that word I wonder what it exactly means. It is one of those curious words (like 'inanity' which has no 'anity'), which do not necessarily mean the opposite without the 'in'. You cannot say, 'Owing to disposition I am not taking the medicine,' whereas you can say, 'Owing to indisposition I called in the doctor.' What exactly is this indisposition? I have never been able to understand it, except that it sounds very well in press notes or health bulletins or in messages from eminent men to gatherings to which they have been invited. 'Indisposition' cannot generally be said by the person directly afflicted. It does not sound very well for anyone to write directly, 'Owing to indisposition, I will not be attending your meeting.' It sounds unconvincing. It sounds better in the third person. It implies that the gentleman is an eminent one, has a secretary or a deputy who can speak for him. 'Mr So-and-so regrets his inability to attend the meeting today owing to indisposition.' People will understand and accept the statement and will not question, 'What is that indisposition? Is he down with flu or malaria or cold or rheumatism? I know a doctor who can cure it . . .' On the contrary, they just accept it at its face value and pass on to the next item. Indisposition could be used only at a particular level, not by all and sundry. A schoolboy who says, 'As I'm indisposed, I want to be let off,' will have his ear twisted for his precociousness.

I think I should shock mankind if I suddenly said, 'There is no such thing as headache or indisposition. It is all just an excuse, an elegant falsehood, for have I not seen dozens of headache cases walking or driving about gaily, to be seen everywhere except where they ought to be at the particular hour!' The world is not yet ripe for such outspokenness. A man cannot say, 'I am not attending the meeting today since I don't feel like it.' A clerk who writes to his master, 'I am not attending office today because I am not inclined to look at any paper today,' will lose his job, whereas he is quite at liberty to say that he is down with headache.

A headache is essential for maintaining human relationships in working order. We cannot do without it either at home or in public. In any normal household one can see a variety of headaches, curtaining off a variety of uncomfortable situations. The mother-in-law, who forswears her food on the plea of a splitting head, is clearly not on the best of terms, at least for that day, with the daughter-in-law or her son; the son, who pleads headache, may want to keep away not only his friends and officers but would like his wife not to press him too much to fulfil his promise to take her out; the little man who pleads headache has definitely skipped his homework, and would like the tutor to be sent away. As I have already said, it will not do at all to be bluntly truthful on all occasions. The sign of cultured existence is not to pry too deeply, but accept certain words at their face value, as expressed by the speaker.

Headache has become such a confirmed habit that a huge trade has developed in providing a cure for it. Some people feel lost unless they carry a tube of some headache remedy in their pockets all the time, and opticians give glasses guaranteed to relieve headache. These are instances to show that mankind easily begins to believe in its myths.

THE CRITICAL FACULTY

THE CRITICAL FACULTY is the most potent one in the human make-up. Its pervasiveness and force have not properly been recognized because, like breathing, it is so much a part and parcel of human activity. The difference between a simpleton and an intelligent man, according to the man who is convinced that he is of the latter category, is that the former wholeheartedly accepts all things that he sees and hears while the latter never admits anything except after a most searching scrutiny. He imagines his intelligence to be a sieve of closely woven mesh through which nothing but the finest can pass.

The critical sense is essential for keeping social transactions in a warm state. Otherwise life would become very dull and goody-goody. The critical faculty is responsible for a lot of give and take in life. It increases our awareness of our surroundings; it sounds dignified no doubt, but it seems also to mean that we can watch someone else's back better than our own! We never know our own defects till they are pointed out to us, and even then we need not accept them. We always question the *bona fides* of the man who tells us unpleasant facts. On the surface it is all very well to say, 'I want an honest criticism; that will help me, not blind compliments.' I wish people would mean it. In my experience I have met only one person who took my views literally and tore up the story that he had brought to me for an opinion. He could very well have turned round and said, 'The stories you write are certainly no better. I see no reason why I should accept your judgement,' but he tore up his manuscript into minute bits and scattered them out of the window, and turned his attention to other things immediately, and later became a distinguished anthropologist. His book on the subject, a respectable demy-size volume priced at thirty shillings, is about to be published by a famous press. I sometimes flatter myself with the thought that perhaps it was my critical sense that helped the young man turn his energies to a vocation that suited him best. However, it is an isolated insance and not likely to occur again. No one ever accepts criticism so cheerfully. Neither the man who utters it nor the one who invites it really means it. Any artistic effort has a lot of ego behind it and can never admit criticism. The only two categories that a writer or a musician recognizes are those that admire and those that do not have the wits to understand. It takes several years of hardening experience for a writer to become really indifferent to what others say about his work, but at the beginning of his career every writer watches for reviews of his book with a palpitating heart. If the review is all praise, then the author feels that the reviewer is a clever fellow full of subtle understanding, but if it is adverse he cries, 'These fellows lack elementary intelligence and discrimination! I don't know why some papers give the reviewing work to their office boys.'

I have discovered that a lot of interest that people show in each other's affairs comes just out of a desire to exercise their critical faculties and to measure how far below one's own the other's achievement is. It is particularly applicable to those in the same profession. It is only an engineer who can properly deprecate another engineer's handiwork. I have noticed that anyone who has recently built a house shows an undue zeal in inspecting every new house that he can possibly reach. It gives him a lot of pleasure to be able to say, 'Oh lord! How that contractor has cheated the poor man! What a lot of space they have wasted, and what hideous pillars on the veranda! I wish he had seen my house before starting on his own!'

The democratic machinery is kept going through the exercise of the critical faculty. If someone should ask, 'How should an Opposition function?' the best answer would be, 'In the manner of a traditional mother-in-law who watches the performance of household work by a daughter-in-law and follows her about with her comments.'

BEAUTY AND THE BEAST

IT HAS BECOME a fashion to choose the beauty queen of the year in each place, but her majesty's reign is strictly limited in tenure and jurisdiction. For instance, the beauty queen of 1951 may be forgotten an hour after the 31st of December, I suppose. Or the beauty queen of, say, California, may hardly receive recognition in Calcutta. Presently we may have a beauty queen selected for each month, who will not be looked at when her hour has passed. A surprising philosophical admission seems to be implied in this scheme—the utter evanescence of all appearance. It seems a rash, impractical activity all the same. Even for the briefest duration, how could anyone fix 'the most beautiful'? 'The young one is a golden pet for even the cow,' says the Tamil proverb. What a parent sees, others definitely don't. It is not merely confined to appearance, but also to accomplishments and quality. 'My little fellow, you know, is very smart; oh, that fellow is terribly mischievous.' This may be said of an infant which still lies flat on its back, kicks its legs and emits gurgling sounds. The fond parents are able to interpret so much in that sound and movement and look, although to a rank outsider it may mean nothing. A parent is openly boastful when his offspring is only a few months old, and he keeps it up till the child is five or six years old. Thereafter he adopts a little reticence, and gradually gives up openly boasting of his son's unique qualities. The parents may be reticent, but you may be sure they have not, inwardly, moved a jot from the standpoint they assumed when they declared to a polite-minded rank outsider, 'See him, don't you think he is too clever and understanding for his age? And I'm sure he is the most lovely.' And the rank outsider peeped into the crib with the appropriate show of agreement, although having his own views in the matter.

But a rank outsider has no place in the assessment of beauty of either personality or person. That is why any elaborate beauty contest, with judges, fills me with wonderment. How can beauty be judged by means of tape and weighing machine? Perception of beauty seems to be an entirely personal matter, peculiar to each individual and even to each country. This is the reason why we remain unmoved when we see in our newspapers photographs of beauty queens of other lands. What is beautiful in one country or in one part of the country may be viewed differently in another. Among certain aborigines piercing the upper lip and riveting on it several layers of metal discs is considered indispensable for any lady of social standing. In our part of the country nose-ornaments are very popular, and not so in the north; green eyes and red hair are probably considered masterly touches of nature in the West, while we think they handicap a girl's future.

It's not only in a perfectly measuring figure, but also in features that real beauty is to be perceived; and this perception may turn out to be a highly individual view. For this reason a photo-finish for deciding beauty is not feasible. The eye of the camera, though perfect in judging neck-to-neck of horses, is no better judge than the human eye, where human beauty is concerned, for the simple reason that its data, once again, will have to be verified and accepted only by us. The camera cannot be an absolute instrument of perception. Sometimes people look better than their photographs and sometimes photographs are better than the originals. It is for this reason that any astute would-be bridegroom refuses to be led away by photographs when he has to make up his mind, but insists upon holding over his decision till he has a chance to view the girl, which becomes really a turning point in any young man's life. It is all, as anybody knows, elaborately staged and arranged. The girl is decked and dressed in her best. She is induced by her parents and sisters to come forward and show herself properly. The young man has to watch the curtain or the doorway through which she has to come with the greatest anxiety and curiosity, and yet not seem to watch for the sake of propriety. The girl may come up and take a seat opposite, but it does not help the young man. He is afraid to stare and judge. He is for the moment a beauty judge, but handicapped by proprieties which will not let him stare and assess. All his impressions will have to be finalized by darting looks and side glances, while keeping up a general flow of conversation with a lot of uninteresting people around. When the interview is over, the man is tortured with the feeling that he wasted precious moments which ought to have been spent in proper scrutiny. 'I didn't notice whether her nose was slightly arched or straight.' He wishes he could have another look before saying yes or no. But few get such a chance. And even if a man says yes with a lot of secret misgivings, he never displays any regret later in life. He has no doubt that he has made the right choice. It is this that led a cynic to define beauty as something we derive when we have got used to the beast. There must be some degree of truth in this statement. Otherwise no one except a handful of universally acclaimed paragons can ever have a chance of marrying and settling in life.

It'd be interesting if somebody sponsored a world ugliness contest. If ugliness, too, could have a commercial value. I'm sure it would find its sponsors: a sweater-making company which can declare, 'We will make you look like the devil,' a draper or outfitter who can say, 'We will make you look like a tub,' a railway or a bus service claiming, 'A two-hour journey on our lines will transform you into an ogre,' a film producer looking for ghoulish players or a hat-manufacturing company intent upon making people look like fools. In due course many may sigh for that bulbous nose or the tapering forehead which gave the winner of the contest his holiday in Europe, his photograph in the papers and the film contract at the end of it all.

MEMORY

IT IS SAID OF Faraday that he was so absent-minded that he was constantly writing on slips of papers reminders of what he should be doing next. His pockets were stuffed with hundreds of these slips; there they rested untouched, for there was no way of reminding him of the existence of the slips. Men of genius are particularly absent-minded. They have reason for it; their minds are engaged in noble pursuits. It is understandable. But why should we ordinary mortals also be afflicted with it? Faces of persons: 'Your face is familiar,' is the elegant formula which covers an unpardonable lapse. A face seen every day behind a counter in a bank or a post office becomes unrecognizable in the street. 'He is a pleasant and helpful person, but where have I seen him before?' you wonder secretly. It would be a pity if this caused any bitterness, for no one is to be blamed for it. We are all at the mercy of an erratic faculty: memory. It proves particularly treacherous where proper names are concerned. You go about feeling confident that all the names you need are properly labelled and stocked in your mind, and that you can call up any at will. The occasion arises. In the middle of a dignified and fluent sentence you realize that you cannot get at a particular name. Your ideas scatter, and you become incoherent while you frenziedly pursue the name that recedes like a chimera. Others look on and smile half-sceptically as you tear your hair and wail, 'It was on my lips a moment ago.' You are now in an awkward situation, as if you had been tripped from behind. Later, when there is no occasion for it, the name will intrude upon your attention and will not leave till you repeat it irrelevantly.

There are numerous suggestions as to how memory can be developed. I have found none of these tips practicable. Most of them are based on what may be called associative thinking. It works in the following manner: I am unable to remember fourteen. All that I have to do now is to remember thirteen on one side and fifteen on the other. Or, taking another instance, if I cannot recollect where I left my bunch of keys, all that I must do is to sit back and mentally go over every place I visited in the last three or four hours. This exercise will leave an ordinary man so exhausted at the end that he will have little interest in his lost possession, and by itself it seems such a feat of memory that those who are capable of it are not likely to misplace things.

The child under four is acknowledged on all counts to be an ideal being—a creature who has an almost unearthly delight in living. He is able to attain this grand state because he is unaware of the existence of the thing called memory. He has no clear-cut notions of past and future. Many of his plans and aspirations are placed in a tomorrow. He hardly remembers anything that has happened in the last hour. If he only remembers the admonitions given him by his elders, the physical ills he has suffered and the frustration of his little life, he would cease to be a child. However, he is not left in this happy condition very long. Presently the home tutor comes along with his multiplication table and rules of grammar; henceforth he must study and remember. From this moment existence becomes an endless hide-and-seek between him and memory till old age overtakes him. By the time he reaches seventy-five his mind has turned itself into a vast jumble of memories which makes the immediate life around entirely unacceptable to him.

It is for this reason, I suppose, that poets have always cried for the mercy of oblivion. For, in our present stage of evolution, we have not yet understood the precise use of this power. It is like having a storage battery on hand for no special purpose. The result is that we constantly suffer from too much of it or too little of it, and have no clear notion as to whether we are the masters of this faculty or its servants.

A WRITER'S NIGHTMARE

A FEW NIGHTS ago I had a nightmare. I had become a citizen of a strange country called Xanadu. The government all of a sudden announced the appointment of an officer called the Controller of Stories. All the writers in the country sent up a memorandum to their representative in Parliament, and he asked at the next session of the house: 'May we know why there is a new department called the Controller of Stories?'

From the government benches came the answer: 'Through an error in our government printing section five tons of forms intended for the controller of *stores* were printed controller of *stories,* an unwanted "i" having crept into the text. Consequently the government was obliged to find a use for all this printed stuff.'

'What sort of use?' asked the member.

'Since the stationery was inadvertently ready a department of stories was started.'

'Was a new incumbent entertained for the post of Controller of Stories and, if so, will the Honourable Minister quote the public services commission circular in this regard; what is the cost of this post and where are you going to get the money for it and under what head is it going to be charged and who will be the deciding authority and will you place on the table a copy of the auditor-general's remark in this regard?' went on the Parliament member, trying to get the Minister into an entanglement of linked-up questions. The Minister was familiar with such tactics and curtly replied, 'The answer to A is in the negative, B the government is watching the situation, C the question does not arise, D see B, E it will not be in public interest to answer the question at present . . .' He spoke so fast without a pause, that the questioner got derailed and lost track of his own questions. Undaunted, he asked again, 'Will the Honourable Minister explain if this is in keeping with the government's recent economy drive?'

'The answer is in the affirmative.'

'Will he kindly explain himself?'

'Yes. In the first place we have managed to utilize a vast quantity of printed paper. Anyone who is familiar with the world shortage in paper will appreciate this move, and in the second place there is no extra expenditure involved in starting this department since the Controller of Stores will be *ex officio* Controller of Stories and will generally conduct the affairs of this department, for after all stories are also stores in a manner of speaking.'

'May we know the why and how and what-about-what and wherefore of this department?'

'I am glad to have an opportunity to speak on this issue. The government is becoming increasingly aware of the importance of stories in our national life. Since this is a welfare state the government is obliged to keep a watch over all the activities that affect our citizens. It has come to our notice recently that sufficient attention is not being paid by the authors in this country to the subject of story. The government has observed that next to rice and water, stories are the most-demanded stuff in daily life . . . Every moment someone or other is always asking for a story. It may be a child asking his teacher or a novel-reader his author or a magazine-buyer his editor or a film producer who has spent lakhs and lakhs and has every equipment ready except a story, and of course all our radio stations and theatres, too, demand stories. The demand is far in excess of supply, and may I add even where a story is seen it turns out to be deplorably bad stuff? The government has made up its mind that they will not tolerate bad stories any more.'

At this point the question-master interrupted with, 'May we know what is meant by bad stories? Will the Honourable Minister quote instances?'

'No. I cannot mention any specific bad stories at this juncture, since that would lead to the suspicion that invidious distinctions are being made, but I would like to point out that bad stories are stories that are not good, and our honourable friend must be satisfied with it for the moment.'

'May we know how this department is to function?' asked the member.

'Presently, the Controller of Stories will undertake the formation of a body called the Central Story Bureau which will immediately go into the business of formation of a Chief Story Officer for each state.'

'May we know what it will have to do with the story writers in the country?'

'Every story writer must fill up Form A, obtain a local treasury certificate for ten rupees, and forward both to the Central Story Bureau (general branch), and he will receive an endorsement entitling him to call himself a registered story writer. Thereafter, whenever he has an inspiration for a story, long or short, he will have to send a synopsis of it in quadruplicate to the C.S. Bureau (technical branch), and obtain its approval before proceeding to expand the work further.'

'Why should it be in quadruplicate?'

'For facilitating procedure. The Central Story Bureau (technical branch) will consist of four directorates, one each for plot, character, atmosphere and climax, and each section will examine the proposed story in respect of its own jurisdiction and may suggest emendations and improvements in respect of the story before issuing a final authorization certificate to the author, which must be prominently displayed in his study. Any author who attempts to write a story without proper authorization will be fined five hundred rupees and imprisoned for a period not exceeding eighteen months . . . The government has every desire to avoid these extreme measures, its sole aim being improvement of national culture, and we have every hope that all this will bring about a revolution in story writing within the next ten years. Incidentally I wish to inform the House

that we are presently inaugurating a national story week which will
see the birth of a write-better-stories movement all over the country
. . .' He concluded, 'All this is in the nature of an effort on the part of
the government for improving the standard of story writing in this
country. We shall watch the results, and let me say,' here he raised
his voice, 'let me warn all bad story writers that I shall not hesitate to
smash their ink bottles. We don't want bad stories in this country in
any form. We shall watch the situation and see how it develops, and
if writers fail to show any improvement, which we shall be in a
position to judge from the quarterly reports submitted by the
regional story officer, I have no hesitation in saying that we, on this
side of the house, will take to story writing ourselves . . .'

And, at this stage, I woke up.

My Dateless Diary

An American Journey

Narayan wrote this travelogue—in the form of daily entries in his journal—during his first visit to the United States in 1956. Drawing on the style of the short essay which he had already perfected, My Dateless Diary *presents a composite (if fragmented) view of what was for Narayan a new world.*

NEW YORK DAYS

Over a Cup of Coffee

Yesterday, at the self-service cafeteria, I made the mistake of waiting for someone to ask what I wanted. Today I know better. You enter the cafeteria, pull out a 'check' (on which prices are punched) from a machine, pick up a tray and spoons, and study the various dishes displayed on the long counter under a glass cover, trying to judge what's what and how far a vegetarian could venture—whether that attractive yellow stuff might not be some prohibited food such as lobster; the men here evidently do not like anyone to stare so long at their display; one of them asks in a surly manner, 'What do you want?' (instead of the ever-polite 'Can I help you?') They are black-haired, hatchet-faced men, possessing a Latin temper perhaps; not the blond, soft-spoken *Mayflower* descendants. How differently you got through a restaurant-session in Mysore. You took your seat, asked for the morning paper and a glass of water—just to mark time before deciding whether you should have *Masala Dosai* again or *Idli,* or as you generally felt inclined (but resisted), both; but indecision could never be an end in itself, and you devised a further postponement of issues, by asking, when the reading of the paper was over, 'What have you?' A routine question. The waiter would give a quick recital of the day's menu—nothing new or startling, but you enjoyed hearing it all over again. Coming from a civilization used to this pace of life, I felt unequal to the speed of a Broadway cafeteria. If you hesitated with the tray in hand, you blocked the passage of others and made them silently fret. I fumbled and obstructed only for a day. Today I was as good as my neighbour. I picked up my breakfast and assembled it with deftness, and had on the whole acquired so much smartness that when I approached coffee and was asked, 'Black or white?', 'Neither,' I said haughtily. The server looked up rather puzzled. 'What do you mean?' he asked. 'I want it neither black nor white, but brown, which ought to be the colour of honest coffee—that's how we make it in south India where devotees of perfection in coffee assemble from all over the world.' He must have thought me crazy, but such leisurely talk is deliberate, like the extra-clutches on the track of a train rolling downhill. I wanted to apply a deliberate counteraction to Broadway's innate rush, just to study the effect. It could prove disastrous, as I learnt later about an Indian anthropologist who went to an Automat and nearly paralysed all business while he beamed at everyone with, 'Well, my man, how are you?' or 'Where do you come from?' or 'How many children have you?' and so forth. He attempted to make genial conversation with all and sundry, got in everybody's way, fumbled with his purse, asking elaborately: 'Can you give me change please?' at the wrong place, while all the time five-cent coins were rolling out, as from the mint, at the right place. He felt so discouraged at the end of it that he slipped away losing all hope of mastering the art of ordering food in New York; he subsisted for a week on hot chestnuts sold at the street corner.

Today I wanted to discourse on the philosophy of brown coffee, but there were other breakfasters, holding their trays, standing behind me inexorably, to secure their coffee and race for a table space. They were too well-mannered to push, but I knew they were fretting inside, each must have had a dozen things to do after breakfast, and how dare I block their business? Still I was in a communicative mood; I smiled at those behind me and said, 'Sorry.' I told the coffee server, 'When you have more time, come to me, I'll tell you all about brown coffee.' I bore away my tray and sat at a secluded table and began to work my way through cornflakes and milk, marmalade and toast, which were to be my main diet for the next ten months. A man in a sports-jacket came over and asked, 'Do you mind?' 'Not at all,' I said. He set his tray on the table and said, 'I overheard your remark about coffee. You know of any special trick in making it?' God-given opportunity for me to start off a lecture on coffee, its place in south India (in the North they favour tea), its place in our social life, how the darkest condemnation of a family would be the warning uttered at their back, 'Their coffee is awful', how at wedding parties it was the responsibility of the bride's father to produce the best coffee and keep it flowing all day for five hundred at a time; how decoction drawn at the right density, on the addition of fresh warm milk turned from black to sepia, from which ultimately emerged a brown akin to the foaming edge of a river in flood, how the whole thing depended upon one's feeling for quality and eye for colour; and then the ding of sugar, just enough to mitigate the bitterness but without producing sweetness. Coffee-making is a task of precision at every stage. I could not help mentioning my mother who has maintained our house-reputation for coffee undimmed for half a century. She selects the right quality of seeds, almost subjecting every bean to a severe scrutiny, roasts them slowly over a charcoal fire, and knows by the texture and fragrance of the golden smoke emanating from the chinks in the roaster whether the seeds within have turned the right shade and then grinds them into perfect grains; everything has to be right in this business. A daughter-in-law who comes into the family will have to go through several weeks of initiation before she may dare to make the family coffee. 'Three spoons for six persons. Place the powder at the bottom of a stainless steel vessel and pour boiling water over it and then strain it slowly through a piece of cloth.' She is a fanatic and insists on straining coffee only through thin cloth; no power on earth can ever make her change over to a percolator or the more common brass coffee-filter. She considers all such contraptions inimical to her coffee ideals. She gleefully boasted once, 'I have made over a hundred persons throw away their coffee-filters and use a cloth for straining. I shall persuade many more before long. Ultimately coffee-filters should cease to have a market . . .' Such a fanatic, I wondered what her reaction would be to the preposterous question, 'White or black?' She would be infuriated at the very terminology. 'White' coffee actually means, according to her, milk with dash of coffee which is administered only to sick persons; black coffee should never be drunk! 'Cream' itself she would object to as it can never help good coffee. Only pure milk, untampered and taken straight from the cow, can be a true coffee component.

Ageless in New York

After breakfast I emerged into Broadway. My life in New York had not yet fallen into a routine. I felt free to do what I liked. l could have gone to see my good friend Gilpatric, but he was in hospital. It was a pity, since my whole visit had been planned by him and he was to do so many things for me. He could not be seen for another week. That left me somewhat uncharted.

I walked up and down, and decided that I might as well spend the week trying to learn something of New York.

I passed down 50th Street, and sat on one of the benches at Rockefeller Plaza in order to study my diary of engagements. Through a corner of my eye I also watched the goings-on around. The Dolphin Fountains and gardens look much more attractive in the 'View-Master' slides. The View-Master has accustomed us to a richer-than-life outlook. People were skating on ice. Young figures clad in coloured jerseys were executing beautiful ballet-like movements. Middle-aged persons skimmed along precariously, held in position by uniformed attendants. Why were aged persons attempting the feat with that air of daringness? Perhaps they enjoyed the sensation of movement without the lifting of feet, or perhaps the spirit of youth bubbled irrepressibly within old frames. The aim might be to ignore age and defy time. With so many facilities in civilization one simply could not afford to grow old. I remember one evening a big-hatted cheerful man at the lobby of my hotel, who after dining well stood at the staircase and joked aloud, pointing at all the women coming out of the restaurant. 'Age has no chance in New York,' he announced. 'Look at these women, they are trying to look young with all those hats, earrings, paint and girdles—but how long can you cheat age? Not for ever. Even in New York people will have to look their years sooner or later.' He was in a rollicking mood, and all the women walking past him giggled. He found the women's headgear, in particular, funny. It might sound ungracious to comment on women, but I found myself in agreement with this man's views. Hat designers have persuaded American women to carry on their heads fantastic oddments in felt, fluff, and what not. Some wore hats which had the aesthetic finish of the lid of a marmalade can, some of the women's hats produced the same visual impression as Christy's felt cap of ancient times. I wonder if any one remembers or knows about Christy's caps. At the turn of the century, Christy's caps were considered, in south India at any rate, the acme of men's fashion. Men shaved the front portion of their heads, grew a tuft at the back and tied it into a knot. The shaved portion of the head was covered with a Christy's cap, which was just half an inch or an inch high, while the tuft stuck out of the rim of the cap at the back. The ensemble was complete with a couple of gem studs on the ear lobes. With the advancing standards of civilized appearance this scheme was given up, and after losing sight of it for years in India, I noticed it now in New York—cap like Christy's, sparkling studs on the ears, tuft at the back; and even the skirts and jackets had a resemblance to the *dhoti* that South Indians wear. I was taken aback to see the abandoned masculine fashion of India adopted by the women of New York as the latest. Another fashion that I noticed was a flat piece resembling a castor-leaf, placed on the head of a stylish woman. Peasant women, working under a tropical sun, sometimes cover the tops of their heads with a castor-leaf, which is supposed to keep the brain cool even under the hottest sun. There is every reason for the village women of India to try castor-leaf under a hot sun, but what excuse could the women of New York have to imitate the fashion (with felt, velvet or whatever it might be) in the middle of the night in Broadway? This was puzzling to me as, to be frank, it lends a touch of irresponsible clownishness to the appearance of women, and seems particularly unsuited to some of the portlier types one notices here and there. Our discussion on fashion was over. The big-hatted man gave me his card and said,

'Any time you visit Texas, you must visit us. Drop me a card and my station wagon will pick you up at the rail-station. I enjoy receiving guests, I've a house with 12 guest rooms. You will find the women in our state different; they are not like the women here.'

Guided Men

Most of these men and women were obviously visitors to New York. New York is perhaps the most visitor-filled city in the world; unlike Paris or Rome, where the visitors are from other countries, New York is full of Americans themselves, from other states. Later, in every small town or state I found the local resident proudly recollecting his visit to New York last year or five years ago. 'Oh, I can't stand the pace of life there,' he would invariably conclude. But while doing New York, he likes to do it thoroughly. They are all over the place; they form the bulk of the shopping crowd in Fifth Avenue, they follow the guide at the Rockefeller Centre, looking up faithfully at the murals above when his finger points down. They fill the Empire State Building, they cram every inch of available space in Manhattan cruise boats, swarm over the Statue of Liberty, and above all they are the people, if my guess is right, who skate on the ice at Rockefeller Plaza; they are definitely out to enjoy life, every inch of them proclaiming this purpose.

India Behind Glass

Passing down 49th Street, I suddenly come upon a show window, in which Indian bric-a-brac are displayed. Being Sunday the door is shut, but it is studded with mysterious lettering, reading something like G-V-N-T F I-DIA TOU-ST OFF-E. By guessing one might comprehend it as 'The Government of India Tourist Office'—someone has probably been banging on the door to make so many of the letters drop off. At the window the display is almost bare—but for a heavy Tirupathi wooden doll. Beside it stands an ivory figure, which might be anything—a god or a paper-weight. It is tucked far away at the back. The only other Indian article on display here is a brocade and a gaudy picture of a Mogul garden. It leaves me wondering as I have wondered at every tourist office, how this is going to help whom. As though in answer to my query, a passerby stops to look at the articles in the window. His hat and correct Sunday dress proclaim him to be a weekend visitor to New York. He glues his face to the glass sheet in attempting to study the article inside. I am curious to know what attracts him:

'Can I help you?'

'What's that white stuff? What do you call it?' he asks.

'That's ivory—'

'What does the figure represent?'

'An Indian god, you know, one of the hundreds of gods in India.'

'I'd like to have it. Know where I can order such things?'

Immediately I write down for him a few addresses in Mysore, and explain, 'Mysore is in the south-western part of India. In its vast jungles elephants flourish, and the figure you see here is carved out of the tusk of an elephant, by craftsmen who have done nothing else for generations.' It sounds so romantic that I am myself impressed by it.

No doubt the American is moved by my description. He confesses: 'My wife likes them. She is fond of such things.' He produces his card. He is from Milwaukee; and his card announces him to be the Director of the American Association of Bowling.

'What is bowling?' I ask innocently. He explains, 'It's one of the finest American Institutions. It helps people get a little entertainment, and at the same time just that extra cash everyone needs, you know. More than anything, it has kept down juvenile delinquency, which is a pressing problem in our country.'

'Why don't you visit my country some day and organize bowling there; we are desperately in need of a lot of diversion as well as extra cash. Juvenile delinquency, though not a very big problem yet, may be nipped in the bud, you know . . . Incidentally your wife may buy any quantity of those ivory figures in the bazaars . . .'

He is impressed with my sales talk and has promised to plan a visit to India.

Gandhi Land

Consulting my pocket book, I walked down East 68th Street, looking for a doctor from India, whose address had been given to me at London. People give us addresses for a variety of reasons. Sometimes it's purely mercenary—some will want us to carry pickles and spices from India to their kith and kin abroad. Apart from the utilitarian motive, quite a number of persons offer the addresses of persons known to them, I am sure, in order to be helpful to a man going into strange lands: 'If you see so and so, he'll give you the maximum assistance.' I didn't have the heart to confess that my friend Gil's help was quite adequate for me officially, personally, and in every conceivable way. I had accepted all the introductions unthinkingly. Now I suddenly asked myself, 'Why should I see this doctor?' There was no logical answer to it. I didn't come ten thousand miles to see an unknown Indian doctor. I dropped the idea of seeing him, but going down to its very end, I acquired a working knowledge of 68th Street.

Saw a subway opening at the end of the street, and went down. Held out a coin through the window, as I saw others do, and received what I took to be two coins but what were actually a dime and a token. I asked where it'd take me. The man at the window asked:

'Where do you want to go?'

'Anywhere.'

'Uptown or downtown?'

I was not sufficiently educated yet to know what up- or downtown meant. So I said, I just want to look around. He looked sickened by my vagueness and aimlessness, and refused to comment further. I slipped in the token as others did, turned the stile and jumped into a train. Whether it was down or up—I had no idea. Everybody was getting out of the train all the way. I was the only passenger when the train reached its terminus. I got out, and wandered through a park full of mighty trees with leaves changing colour—one of the finest sights of New York in this season. Fine sunshine. Youngsters in bright sweaters were playing a game.

Walked down a road admiring a row of new villas, and went back to my starting point. Felt hungry and slipped into a shop and asked for food, explaining that I was a vegetarian. I uttered the word 'vegetarian' with the greatest caution, since it stirred people in unexpected ways; and dismayed them as if I had said I was a man-eater. So I generally softened the blow by asking, 'Can you give me lunch, please?'

'Yes.'

'But, you know, I don't eat meat.'

'Oh, that doesn't bother me, I can give you fish.'

'No fish, please.'

'I can give you, perhaps, an omelette?'

'No eggs please, I don't eat fish, fowl, or meat.' Before he or she looked completely shattered, I added in a sort of constructive way, 'Maybe you could fix me a meal with toast, cheese, fruit, yogurt, rice, carrot and tomato?'

'Oh, yes,' and they proceeded to give me my food, without any more difficulty. Someone might occasionally ask, 'Why are you a vegetarian?'

'I don't know. Have never been anything else.'

'Are you a vegetarian by conviction or religion?'

'I am a born vegetarian. I cannot eat anything except rice, greens, and dairy products.'

'Extraordinary! Wonder that you are alive.'

I ordered my lunch. The lady bustled about. She was kindly, interested, and sympathetic, and said, 'I'll fix it, don't worry,' and gave me bread and coffee, and apple pudding. When they learnt that I was a writer from India, they gathered around me. They held me as a show-piece, presenting me to their customers coming in for cigarettes and ice cream. The woman's husband, an old man, came forward and said, 'I like Gandhi, but Nehru is not like Gandhi, am I right?'

'No, you are wrong,' I said.

'Nehru is friendly to the Communists, isn't he?'

'No, if you read the Indian papers you would understand his views better.'

'Oh, I don't know. Anyway, Gandhi was great. I've tried to read everything about him.'

Another young man who worked in an automobile firm in Manhattan and came here every weekend to visit his grandmother at a nursing home, joined us and added, 'Gandhi was a sturdy man. What a strong man he was!'

'But he weighed only ninety pounds,' I added.

The talk was all about Gandhi and his life. They listened to my description of the Mahatma with interest, and gasped with surprise at my description of the mighty congregations at his prayer meetings. They were very happy and proud that I should have come all the way from Manhattan to Bronx, just to see the place—which seemed to them an impossible feat—as city-dwellers live and die rigidly within their own orbits. They were more impressed with my visiting Bronx than my coming all the way from India. Children were dropping in for ice cream and milk shakes, pausing to listen to my talk. When I rose to leave, the old man came forward to shake my hand, really proud to have seen a man from 'Gandhiland'.

On my way back, got in and out of all the wrong buses. Got out of a bus which terminated at University Avenue. No bus seemed to go in my direction. North, South, East and West looked confusing near University Avenue. Finally, went down the steps of a subway, to ask for directions at the ticket-window. Found a communicative American at the ticket-window.

'Downtown, get off at 50th Street, change to a local to 59th Street and walk a block.' He peered at me through the small window and asked, 'From India?'

'Yes.'

'What do you think of Nehru?' he asked straightaway. Second time someone was asking about Nehru.

'Fine man,' I said.

'Is he good?' he asked.

'In every way,' I said, although I was talking so confidently about one whom I had never met. He merely said, 'Just wanted to know, that's all.'

Portugueseness

At the hotel I phoned for the service of an electrician, something having gone wrong with my reading lamp. A heavy man in a blue overall knocked on my door. He examined the light, pulled out its wires, and looked worried as he said, 'Someone has badly done this.' He looked like a detective sitting over a corpse. I hoped that he didn't imply that I had tampered with it. 'I will fix it,' he said, with a touch of menace in his voice. 'But it must be righted here first,' he said, obscurely tapping his head. I expressed agreement with all his views because he smelt faintly of alcohol. He added, 'Don't talk to me if you don't want to; I must not be seen talking to you; they may fire me.'

'That's all right—You can talk to me,' I said.

'Sure, you won't tell them?'

'No, I promise,' I said.

'It's good to talk to you,' he said. 'I know Polish, Portuguese, Spanish and English—two and two, four languages,' he said, holding up four fingers.

'But I hope your Polish etc. are better than your English,' I said truthfully.

'Yes, yes, sure,' he said, 'I know Spanish well,' and added, 'You know Spanish?'

'No . . .'

'Portuguese?'

'No . . .'

'But you are Portuguese, aren't you?'

'No . . .'

'You look like Portuguese. You are very much a Portuguese,' he repeated obstinately.

I wanted to look into a mirror and verify. He seemed relieved to know that I was not a Portuguese, and said with disgust, 'I have travelled. But in South America they speak no Spanish, only Portuguese: they call it Spanish. But it's no Spanish, but Portuguese.'

'What a pity!' I said, although it was all the same to me.

'Sure you don't know Portuguese?' he asked and after I

reaffirmed my non-Portugueseness, he asked, 'Where do you belong?'

'India.'

He repeated, 'India! Never heard of it.' He remained in thought for a while and said, 'Say it again?. . . Where is it? Funny! Sounds familiar,' he said.

'Mention a place there, may be I've been there in my ship—but—' he tapped his head woefully, 'Mention a place.'

I said, 'Madras . . .'

'No, never heard of it, mention another.'

'Delhi.'

'No, first time I hear the name.'

'Calcutta,' I said.

'No such place,' he replied shaking his head.

'Bombay.'

'Ah, Bombay! Sounds like a place I know. Is it India? Is it a port? I am sure I must have been there, but you know I was the sort that never went ashore. My business was in the engine room and there I stayed. I went round the world for thirty years but never went ashore anywhere, until I gave up service and landed in New York.' Before leaving he tore off the lamp from its holder and took it with him, promising, 'You'll see a new lamp on your bed when you come home tonight.' He made a request before passing out of the door, 'If you meet them down there,' indicating a vast horde of managers and employers, 'tell them your engineer is a good guy, that'll help me.'

Missing Letters Dropped

After all, found the India Tourist Office open and walked in. A couple of young men in the office downstairs got quite a thrill out of meeting me and instantly proposed that I should address the Indian Students Association at New York. Warded off the proposal gently since I loathe all lectures and hope to survive the American visit without adding my voice to the babble around. The boss of this establishment proved to be a happy, friendly soul, who immediately set up a phone call to the Indian Consul and tried to involve me in a forthcoming party there in honour of the Indonesian Tax Commission or some such highly eclectic body. Out of consideration for his kind-hearted effort, I simulated a provincial enthusiasm for the party, but in a strictly non-committal way. Seeing him at close quarters I found it impossible to be critical of his Tourist Office. Even the missing letters on the door did not seem to matter: I never mentioned it, leaving the rectification of such errors to the gods.

Publishers

Being published by a University Press is a distinction no doubt, but a disadvantage commercially speaking. Booksellers, who are an inevitable link between an author and his public, will not stock a university publication. You may print on the cover of your book, as boldly as you will, that it is a work of fiction, guaranteed not to enlighten, bore, or instruct, quoting all the reviews, but still the bookseller will have his misgivings when he sees a university imprint. He has a fear that under the jacket of fiction someone is attempting to sell him a heavily loaded PhD thesis.

For nearly twenty years I managed without an American publisher, and year after year my English agent reported that the time was not ripe yet. I accepted it as an inevitable state of affairs until around 1953, the late Lyle Blair became Director of Michigan State University Press, and the first thing he did was to wire us an offer to publish all my books. He was a man, though we had never met, of tremendous personal enthusiasm for my writing; he used to publish my books in England, and in Europe. He was the first publisher to bring out an English book in Europe after the war, and that was my *English Teacher* printed in Vienna in the Guild Edition. I've always felt that if Lyle Blair were at the head of a Law Publishing firm, he'd still find an excuse to reprint one of my novels in their series. He published five of my books within a period of eighteen months. The reviews were always favourable, but unfortunately as he himself confessed in his note to *Swami and Friends*, the sales were poor; but he was still prepared to go on with the publications, unmindful of the results. When I arrived in New York, the late

Harvey Breit, my good friend, (then) of the *New York Times,* made it his mission to find me a New York publisher purely for commercial reasons; he also took the responsibility of smoothening out the human side of it with Lyle Blair, who was then away in Australia.

Harvey Breit telephoned me a list of publishers to see. He had made appointments for me, morning and afternoon, so that I should meet a new publisher every two hours. After breakfast one morning, I started out and beginning with Viking at 625 Madison Avenue, I worked my way up and down strictly on a schedule. After seeing all of them I was to decide who was to publish me. There was a touch of unreal ease about it. I had really no notion what I should say to them since I had no manuscript to offer. I went through it because it was going to be fun knowing the publishers of New York. I did not think anyone would seriously bother about me. All my life I was used only to publishers who could not be moved, and who were wary and on the defensive when they met a writer. But here were men who did not believe in being cautious or diplomatic and who plainly stated within ten minutes of our meeting that they would like to be my publishers. It's good for an author to feel wanted. It became harder to choose as I saw more and more of them. I was impressed with all the men I met. Myer, editor of Scribners, who seemed so full of refinement and high values. Harold Strauss of Knopf, whose wonderful conversation held me spellbound. James Laughlin himself of New Directions, an old friend since an evening long ago when he had walked into my Mysore home (as I was struggling to produce my Sunday article for a paper), after flying from Bombay to Coimbatore and motoring a hundred miles from Ooty. Saxe Commins of Random House, who admitted total ignorance of anything I wrote but still wanted to try me, and whose talk of Einstein and Gandhi fascinated me. Or Storer Lunt, genial, warm and extraordinarily human, with whom I had an unforgettable dinner at a restaurant and then a drive around New York one night. He spoke of New York with love and excitement and in the three-hour drive with him, I saw the subtle beauty of this city, especially at night when its buildings are lit and its waters scintillate, and the skyscraping windows are aglow. Simon Bessie of Harpers, one of the liveliest minds, who quoted from my novel *Waiting for the Mahatma*. How could I make a choice, when all of them were so good and friendly? I despaired of being able to choose, and requested Harvey Breit to cancel a few other names he had had on his list.

Reminiscential Dog-lover

To the East River side just to investigate this part of New York. Automobiles were speeding off south and north as if in a delirium. I got into the wrong track and then into a curving tunnel prohibited to pedestrians. I had no idea of the prohibition; but I noticed passing motorists throwing curious glances at me. Later, emerging from the tunnel, I read the sign outside, *'Pedestrians prohibited'*. While in the tunnel I had to stand for nearly an hour pressing myself close to the wall, with automobiles speeding past within half a foot of me, and a gust of wind hitting me in the face each time a car passed. I feared that if an extra-fat model came along, it'd plaster me to the wall. Or at least, I feared, I might never leave the spot again, until I dropped down through fatigue and they picked me up and carried my famished self—a martyr to no nobler cause than pedestrianism.

It was a relief to come into the open, under the open skies again. I climbed a pedestrian's overbridge in order to take in uninterrupted the beauty of the river, barges and boats cruising along, the evening sky, and the mighty bridge spanning the river. From my eminence, I could watch with detachment the traffic flow by: long cars, longer cars and still longer cars in multicolour. In any other country's traffic, there'd be a mixture of long cars and not-so-long cars and (in our own country) bullock carts and stray cattle thrown in, but here in New York, there was a continuous parade of elongated vehicles—going in three layers or four—on the bridge, below the bridge, on the road, over the road—up and down. As I stood watching, an old man came up the steps of the pedestrian bridge leading two dogs—a venerable man, with a handsome face and God-given wrinkles and blue eyes. One of his dogs was an Alsatian and the other was a very short, puny, indistinct variety. We were the only two on the bridge. Standing in this eminence, we could afford to take a lenient view of the excited traffic below. 'Won't bite?' I asked as an opening. 'Oh no, just playful you know. Wants to play, but if I unchain him, I will have to pay a fine of twenty-five dollars. Can't afford it.'

'You love dogs?' I asked.

Such questions, however banal, have the effect of bringing humanity closer. 'Oh, dogs mean everything to me,' he said. 'I had a Great Dane once, so high,' I said, recollecting Sheba, black and white, so beautiful and gentle and big that she was often mistaken for a heifer. He came closer and told me about dogs, their pedigrees, the best years of their lives and so on. 'Six is the best year of a dog's life, but at ten he is like me; he likes to curl up and sleep all the time. What's the use? He's then a dog only in appearance. Until he is two he is no good as a dog either. I had another one—' More about dogs and then he asked me about myself and India. 'Is it a fact that you have a population over 400 million? Oh God, what a number, and most of them die of starvation?' In his view was a limited granary and a stampede by a mass of humanity for it. He wanted to know what we did for food. 'You have pigs, cattle and poultry—yes? Then what's the trouble? How is the winter there?'

'In most parts of the country—the sharpest winter day is like what we have in New York now,' I said. He was astonished, and started off on his weather experience. He told me about himself: a Swede who had come with his father as a boy of fifteen, fifty years ago. Served as a valet in the household of a famous chain-store magnate and travelled widely in all the states. 'When he died his daughter inherited the business and married an Italian count, who didn't even know English—and let me tell you a secret: he already had two children and a wife, but married again for money . . . Money is everything still. Money speaks. Do you think people elect? . . . It's money which decides to have someone there and someone not there . . . that's all . . . I'm voting for whosoever will prevent atom bombs exploding in the seas and poisoning the fish I eat . . . Anyway why should there be atom bombs? . . . See, all these buildings destroyed and wounded children mean nothing to a man bombing from the air—so I was told by a man who had been a pilot in the war. He took an abstract view of destruction and death while releasing his bombs. War is unnecessary, there should be no war. You are an Indian, I am from Sweden; are we not getting along now? We are all one; no need to fight even if we are all different . . . Come to Sweden some time. Oh, when I think of Stockholm . . . I want to go back and die there, but my wife loves her sister, who lives in Long Island, and won't part from her. We've no children, but these dogs I love. Going down the riverside? Oh no, you can't at this hour. Listen to my advice; there are bums and dope-fiends who will assault and rob you. Don't go down; if you live in Broadway you should turn back and come along with me, and take the bus. I've lived in this area for fifty years. For thirty years I lived over there in a house on Second Avenue. In those days, you didn't have skyscrapers . . . Only a few old houses and open spaces and buses were parked right here where you see this huge building, twenty stories high with its elevator and all. It's all wonderfully changed now . . . All these places belonged to Rockefeller once, and he gave them away. After the 1914 war I saw respectable persons queuing for bread and white-collared men sleeping on newspapers in the subway. Bad times: factories closed and all kinds of things happened . . . And then a war came up and things picked up. But war is bad . . . When you go to Sweden, don't miss Stockholm, that's my place. I like to talk to people. It's so good to have someone to talk to. Nowadays nobody finds the time to stand and talk. Thank you very much indeed and God bless you . . . Get into this bus. Goodbye. It'll take you to your hotel.'

Mrs X

Awakened by the telephone, emerge from the mists of sleep and stretch out my hand for the receiver, but it's at the foot of my bed. I hide my head under the blanket again in the hope that the telephone will cease, but it is insistent. I'm not destined to sleep. Like Macbeth I shall sleep no more.

'May I know who is speaking?'

'I am Mrs —. I want to ask you . . .'

'Who did you say?'

'You remember we met the other night at J's home where you had come to dinner.' I did not think I should pursue this research anymore. Not in a clear condition of mind. I could perhaps sort it out later.

'Yes, yes, what can I do for you?'

'You see, the psychic portions in your 'Grateful to Life and Death' *(The English Teacher)* interested me. I want to ask a few questions.'

'Go ahead.'

'Is it all fact? I am eager to know whether it's all fact or fiction.'

I could not catch much of her speech on the phone. She had borrowed J's copy of *The English Teacher* and read it. 'I want to meet you. Could you come for dinner on Tuesday?'

'Yes,' I said, to end the conversation, as it was becoming too metaphysical and obscure.

Later I tried to recollect who she might be. It had been a short-notice dinner at J's a few evenings before. I had called on him at his office earlier in the evening and he could give his wife only an hour's notice for preparing a suitable dinner for me. He had also invited a few others to join us after dinner. It had been an enjoyable party, but for the harrowing thought that perhaps my hosts, out of consideration for me, were starving themselves on rice and greens, adopting for the moment my own diet. The others at the party were: the editor of a home magazine, a young man working in Burma on a Ford Foundation assignment, the editor of a highbrow review, and a lady who came with him and whom I (mis-)took to be his wife. This was the lady telephoning me now. This lady, I recollected, had been firing off all through the evening a number of questions on idol worship, symbolism and Gandhi, and it was difficult for me to answer them because I could not be sure whether she was trying the Socratic method or whether she genuinely sought answers to her questions; her husband's (as I took him to be at the time) English I could not follow. He was a Russian, and spoke a sort of Russian-English, in a sort of through-the-pipe-drawl; he had a rough, authoritative style of speech in a low, growling pitch, and was too positive-minded and intimidating.

Luckily I didn't have to hear this trial too long. At about ten o'clock Santha, her husband Faubion Bowers, and Donald Keene (head of the Japanese section at Columbia), entered, sat down on the carpet since all the chairs were occupied, and commanded all the rest to cease talking so that the conversation might be all about *The English Teacher*, which they had just read.

The telephone woke me up again this morning.

Mrs X again. 'I'd like to see you sometime today. What time are you free?'

'We are meeting at your home tomorrow, aren't we?' I said.

'Yes, but I want to see you today at your place . . . What time are you free?'

'Two o'clock,' I said without a thought, unable to turn the leaves of my little engagement diary with one hand, while the other held the telephone.

'What's your time?' I asked. Thus do I exploit all those who call me in the morning, since I do not possess a watch.

'Nine-thirty,' she said and I decided not to go back to bed. I made myself a cup of instant coffee with hot water from the bathroom tap. It was eleven o'clock when I emerged from my room. Felt extremely reluctant to visit the cafeteria and so skipped breakfast, not feeling well enough to bear the smell of carrot in that place. Walked down to E 65 to call on Mrs Gilpatric, intending to take only five minutes of her time in order to enquire about her husband's health, but I stayed on. We had so much to talk about, she knew Mysore and its people, and we had common subjects for a whole day's talk, and so I didn't notice the time passing. When I started back for my hotel, I glanced at the clock on a wayside shop, 1.30 p.m. At 2 p.m. Mrs X would be at my hotel. This was going to leave me no time for lunch. While hurrying along to meet Mrs X, at a crossroad, encountered the lady whose name I never caught at Harvey's party the other evening, but who sat beside me and chatted for a whole hour. Before leaving she had said, 'I should not monopolize you. Will you call me sometime to say when you will be

free?' I'd like to take you round to visit some of our book-shops.'
Now she met me at the corner of Madison Avenue, and said, 'Hello,
I expect your telephone call tomorrow morning, remember,' and
passed on with a friendly smile. I was on the point of confessing that
unless I knew her name I could not call her on the phone; but I could
not bring myself up to it. I had let her assume too long that I knew
her. She had even shouted her telephone number to me over the din
of the party that evening, but I had forgotten it.

Mrs X was waiting for me at the hotel lounge. I was fifteen
minutes late. She carried a huge bunch of red flowers in her hand.
She followed me to my room, and bustled about to find a place for
the flowers.

'Have you a vase?' she asked.

'I'll call for one; meanwhile, let me keep them in the sink.' I took
charge of the flowers, all the time wanting to burst out:

Oh Lady, I crave for lunch
Not blooms in a bunch.

'How much time have you for me?' she asked. I looked through
my pocket diary.

'Half an hour perhaps,' I said. 'I have an engagement at the NBC
at three.'

She said, 'After hearing Faubion speak about it, I borrowed J's
copy of *Grateful to Life and Death* and read it. It has made me feel
that we have a common experience. I too lost someone dear to me.
He was my friend, an obstetrician who helped me deliver my baby
about a year ago. I loved him. There was profound understanding
between us; he meant everything to me. Ten days after my baby was
born he died in a motor accident. I was convalescing in our Long
Island home—it is a large house but we do not live there—only in a
rented flat in New York—for the sake of my husband's business and
my daughter's school. By the way, if you need a quiet place for
writing, please go up and stay there whenever you like and as long as
you like.'

'You were telling me about your doctor,' I said, bringing her back to the main subject.

'Yes, during that period of convalescing I was rather sensitive, I suppose. My friend said goodbye to me, gave me some routine instructions, and started out on a long drive one day. I felt all along that I might probably never see him again. Within an hour of our parting I learnt that his car had skidded. I was rather sensitive and felt his spirit hovering near me. I felt that he was reproaching me for not stopping him from going out that day when I knew all along that he would never return. I might probably have saved him with a word. Why did I not say it? I am anxious to communicate with his spirit. Do you think it will be possible? I feel psychically sensitive. I don't want to do anything,' she said, 'that may seem odd and eccentric to the American eye. I feel inclined to fast once a fortnight and I feel psychically sensitive. I go to my church and meditate regularly . . . Still I feel there must be a technique. Please tell me what I should do to develop myself fully. I live comfortably. I love my husband. I love my children. They are all very good to me. I write, I paint, I do various things, still I feel there is something else that I should do. I want your help. Your book tells me that you know about these things.'

I didn't know what to say. At no time did I think that my book, however close it might be to my own life and outlook, would ever involve me in a practical problem. I wanted to think over it. I didn't like to say anything light or irresponsible. She seemed earnest and greatly troubled in mind, and at the same time high-strung; any severe concentration or psychic effort, I felt, might upset her. I told her, 'I will try and answer your question when we meet on Tuesday.'

'Many thanks. Dinner will be at six-thirty. Could you come at five-thirty? My husband and children will be home at six, and I shall want half an hour's talk with you before we settle down to dinner.'

'Yes, I will try.'

'I don't want others to take me to be eccentric you know,' she said. She added, 'The other day at J's house you saw a millionaire's flat. You should also see how an ordinary, common American family lives. We are not rich. We work hard to make both ends meet. You should see us. That's why I am inviting you to our house . . .

Well, another thing. My friend's name was . . .' She wrote it down
for me on a piece of paper. 'If you manage to contact his spirit, tell
me what he says. Tell me if he has any message for me . . . See those
flowers, he was fond of red. That's why I have got them here. I am
sure if you keep those flowers with you, you will be able to tell me
something.'

Super-Guide

Finished my lunch at four-thirty which is nearer the American dinner
time, and hurried along to the National Broadcasting Corporation
studios at the Rockefeller Centre. An efficient guide took us along:
he was witty, smart, familiar, factual, as he took us through room
after room, and showed us with a good deal of explanation a few
persons miming beyond a sheet-glass; and he pointed out elementary
things such as boom, camera, monitor, etc. He behaved like a
cheerful elementary schoolteacher taking his children through a
museum. We were an assorted crowd: men, women and children had
converged here from the forty-eight states, all of course, like me, on
their first visit. The guide's smartness, kindliness, elaborate speech
and ready wit got on my nerves because it was so well-practised; his
smooth speech, I suddenly realized, took the place of actual exhibits;
after walking along endless corridors and up and down flights of
steps, one realized that one had finally seen only charts and dummies
and heard the guide's lectures on the technicalities of television. He
reminded me of the chief character in my new novel—a tourist guide
who conjured history and archaeology out of thin air. I suddenly
recollected the amusing sight of visitors streaming along the gardens
of Gemini Studio in Madras, behind a Public Relations Officer. 'This
is the cutting room, that is the laboratory,' he would say indicating
the exteriors of various sections, never showing them anything
really, while the crowd followed patiently, hoping till the last second
to get a peep at a star or a scene being shot. I couldn't stand it any
more. Suddenly I slipped away from the crowd and strode down the
corridors, saying 'Excuse me' to people standing in the way, and
everyone here thinking everyone else an executive in a hurry, made

way. I merged with a crowd at the elevator, who had completed their travails and were being seen off by their guide.

Two Tickets or None

I owed my visit to the National Broadcasting Corporation to that energetic soul Miss Roser of Anta (American National Theatre and Academy). I had met her at her Broadway office in her little cubicle beyond the receptionist, surrounded by masks and costumes. She was an extremely active person. Theatre organization was the very breath of her life. She took immediate charge of anyone who wanted to see the stage or understand its working in America. The first thing she did on our meeting was to make me write down my name phonetically and rehearse her in pronouncing it. She was interested in India and had a fantastically remote, unguessable link with it. She confessed that she had done the part of Shakuntala when Kalidasa's play was staged, I don't remember where, years and years before, and she confessed that it was one of her proudest memories. Within half an hour of meeting me, she picked up her telephone and fixed a number of appointments for me to watch rehearsals and plays, meet theatrical men and so forth. She promised also to give me a series of introductions so that I might contact theatre men in every corner of the country. She proved too fast for me, giving me no time to think and reply; Wednesday afternoon Anta Theatre, Thursday 7.30 Carnegie Hall 'Johnny Johnson', Friday television studios and so on and on. She would suddenly pick up the telephone and say, 'Hello, this is Roser of Anta speaking. You have been so good to us at other times that I am tempted to trouble you again now. You see the problem is I have now sitting here right before me a distinguished gentleman from India who has come on a Rockefeller to study the theatre movement in this country. He wants to see a rehearsal . . . I would appreciate your help—all right I'll hold on, tell me your time and date . . . Yes, certainly he is a distinguished visitor from India, interested in the theatre, of course.' She would cover the mouthpiece with her palm at this stage and plead, 'Really, do you realize I know nothing about you? Please sympathize with me and give me a note about yourself so that I may tell these folk the truth about you.' She would then resume her telephone conversation and tell me finally:

'Go to such and such theatre, and mention your name at the box office and they will have two tickets for you.'

'Two? Why two tickets?'

'It is always so. Two tickets or none, is an inflexible principle in this country.'

Rain and Reason

The last day of October looks like the last day of the world with its unceasing rain since the morning. I get drenched before reaching the Rockefeller Building four blocks off. Adding to the rain, a taxi splashes up all the road water over me, drenching me up to my ears. Mr July (of the Foundation) must be aghast at the picture I present, and suggests that I return to my room and change. Of course, I see no point in changing, since I have to be moving about and will surely get drenched again. My tour programme is finalized. I shall leave New York in a couple of days.

Next I have to go to the Viking Press. Viking is entering a practical phase in tackling me. A telegram came to my hotel last evening inviting me to lunch.

I could easily walk there from Rockefeller Centre, but it is wet outside, and I feel I shall be wise in taking a cab. And so I stand on Fifth Avenue watching taxis dash past. After half an hour's gesticulation I am able to stop one. When I reach Viking the meter shows 35 cents. Give the driver fifty cents. He remarks, 'Big nickel! I can build a house with it, I suppose!' I don't know why he says this or what he means. The sight of coins provokes taxi drivers in strange, unexpected ways.

Hour of Decision

Keith Jennison introduces me to Harold Guinzburg, the president of the firm, who at once refers to Graham Greene for whom he has admiration as an author and affection as a person, and concludes,

'Graham is our author, and you will be in good company. I am sure you will be happy with us.' I am hesitant, having misgivings about my ability to face a commitment. There is no rational basis for this hesitation since it is a first-rate firm and their approach to me is also first-rate. But I think I like to postpone a decision, because it is so much easier. We adjourn to a nearby restaurant for lunch, dashing across in the rain and hopping from awning to awning. 'Somehow, I will always, from now on,' wrote Keith Jennison to me later, 'associate the rainiest days in New York with you. The afternoon we officially became your publishers was wet enough to have made me feel like a fish *ever* since,' which was appropriate since the novel I was planning but despaired of writing had much to do with rain. At the restaurant I made no announcement regarding my preferences but quietly ordered a vegetable plate (during my subsequent visits to this restaurant the waiter fetched a vegetable plate at the sight of me). The luncheon party consisted of Keith and a couple of others from the office. We sat at the table talking and eating till three in the afternoon and on going back to his office Keith seated me in a chair opposite him, and said point-blank, 'Have you made up your mind about a publisher?'

'No,' I said, undecided as ever.

'You started with us, and after one round of visiting the publishers, you are back, the cycle is complete now. We'd like to publish your books. We shall be glad to sign a contract with you and give you an advance on your next book. Have you any reason why you should not immediately say yes?'

'How are you sure of my next novel?'

This was not a mere point of argument but a real fear. I am never sure of my book at any stage. I dread any commitment ahead. 'We'll take the risk, that is all,' said Jennison. 'We do have faith in you as a writer from our knowledge of your books, and we hope what you write will be OK, but if something goes wrong we won't hold you responsible, it is a part of the risk of a publisher's business.'

I said, 'I may not like to take any money in advance before I write my book.'

'As you wish. But you are going about travelling, all that may be expensive, and if you need funds at any time, just let us know . . .'

Very gentle and roundabout reference to money.

I am impressed with their delicacy. Money should always be a roundabout, hinted-at subject between friends, only then is it possible to maintain the dignity of human relations. Finally Jennison bursts out, 'After all this is your agent's business, let him speak to us about it.' I ask for another day to remain undecided and leave.

Charred Halloween

Mrs X stands at her doorway watching the street. She is delighted to see me although I'm half an hour late for the engagement. I am happy to see her 'average American home'. They live on the ground floor, the furnishing is almost Indian in its simplicity. I see no one around yet. She shows me to a seat and immediately asks, 'What have you to tell me? Did those flowers give you any message?'

I have to explain to her that occult experience cannot be ordered, and then she asks, 'What about my problem? Have you a solution for me?'

'Don't attempt any concentration, meditation, or any such activity for at least six months. Just allow your mind to be restful, that is all I have to say. In due course if you are destined to have a new experience it will come to you. You cannot seek it by force.' I am sorry to sound so heavy and pontifical, but this is the only way in which I can caution her against straining her mind. As she opens her mouth to ask something more, a sudden charred smell fills the air. 'Oh, dear, I have let those Halloween seeds get charred!' It is Halloween time and pumpkin seeds were being roasted for the children, according to the custom on this day. The lady put them in the oven and came down to the street to look for me and forgot about them. Now the pumpkin seeds have turned into carbon and fill the kitchen and the house with acrid smoke. Her daughter comes running into the kitchen, sees the charred seeds, and looks sad. 'You have done this, Mummy!' The girl is nearly in tears. Mrs X apologizes to her. It brings in her husband also from another room. I realize what a blunder I had almost committed. I had all along treated her as the wife of that grumpy intellectual editor, just because they happened to arrive together at J's house the other evening. Here the real husband is different. However, it has been a purely subjective blunder and hurt no one. We sit down to dinner. It is a nice happy family centring round a chubby baby with four teeth. The husband is in business. Over dinner he asks, as everyone does here, about Gandhi, Nehru, and India in general, and about my writing. The dinner is fine but I am as ever bothered by the thought that perhaps my hosts were starving themselves for the sake of courtesy, on a meal of avocado, carrot and apple. I am delighted to note that Mrs X gives no sign in her husband's presence of her psychic and philosophical trials. Her husband is good enough to drive me back to my hotel at night. I like him, he is a level-headed, hardworking businessman, with a modicum of information on all matters. There is no reason to doubt his devotion to her or her devotion to him. Yet the wife has secret pressures on her mind. I only hope she will not harass him with her artistic, psychic, and other angularities, all of which he may find particularly baffling.

Pride and Prejudice

Americans like to know how far they are being liked by others. They have a trembling anxiety lest they should be thought of badly. We Indians are more hardened, having been appreciated, understood, misunderstood, represented, misrepresented, rated, and overrated from time immemorial both in factual account and in fiction; we take it as a matter of routine to be roused to indignation when we find India attacked and create quite a scene, but it is never more than a passing indignation, nor do we honour our detractors by saying that we are pained by such and such comments. We stop bothering about an unjust, cantankerous book, the moment its sales go up as a consequence of public protest; it is different with Americans, who seem to feel genuinely pained by ill-informed criticism. I came across quite a number of Americans who personally loved Graham Greene's writing, but could not bring themselves to reading *The Quiet American* for fear that it might upset them. Americans do not mind others enjoying themselves moderately at their expense, poking fun at their speech, habits, prosperity and gadgets, as most English writers have done since the time of Dickens. Americans have always displayed great hospitality to a writer or lecturer who is humorous at their expense; but they hate to be hated, although in order to put you at ease, your perfect host will indulge in a mild disparagement of American habits, gadgets, or the TV.

Within the country itself there are small prides and prejudices which one must fully appreciate if one is to understand the country and its people. The test of a visitor's understanding is his sharing of local prejudices.

There is a marked difference of view between North and South and between East and West as anywhere else in the world. To a Southerner the rest of the United States is an immature, undeveloped country, a sort of geographical appendage; the New Englander is proud of his heritage of sober English qualities and the beauty of his landscape; the West Coast is an extremely proud country, their weather, their mountains, roses, grapes and tomatoes are ever a source of continuous pride and they like to hear someone say, 'Oh, I can't stand the pace of New York or its weather. What a relief to be here!' There is no great harm done in letting people cherish their prejudices and even sharing them yourself as long as you don't air your views in a family gathering where, as it often happens, New England and California or Mid-West and Oklahoma may be united in matrimony, when polite conversation on prejudices will have to be carried on with circumspection.

*

It's raining hard, and so reach Mrs Dorothy Norman's house at 70th Street in a damp state for tea. It's an impressive house in the heart of Manhattan, filled with pictures, images, manuscripts and books—right from the street door all the way along the staircase to the hall upstairs. Looks like an art gallery. Dorothy Norman had made tea and tit-bits, and we sit overlooking her garden beyond the french window, and talk of a hundred things: philosophy, Gandhi, religion, Gita, the universality of human types, and ancient Indian handicrafts. She has been in India and knows her India. She says that she likes South India more than the North, a very pleasing thing to hear, as pleasing as it would be for a North Indian to be told that Madras is detestable in every way.

(Gil said yesterday that he preferred Mysore to Bangalore—excellent sentiment, sir, the finest test of a visitor's understanding, as we have already seen, is his participation in local prejudice.) We discuss at length the effect of architecture and sculpture on the temper of pupils, and their social life as seen in old South Indian temples—with their colonnades, corridors and halls and skyscraping towers. She asks me to say what characteristics, according to my understanding, mark off an average American from an Indian. I cannot help confessing, 'I definitely feel man to man, an average American is totally materialistic in the best sense of the term, work, wages, good wife, and good life—are all his main interests; while an Indian will be bothering about the next life also, in addition to all this.'

*

At the Indian restaurant, a new American waiter in attendance at dinner. I feel rather apologetic about ordering *a la carte* rice and yogurt, and explain, 'You know, we in India live on rice and yogurt!' He replies, the gentle considerate soul, 'Why not, sir? Excellent thing. I myself try and take a lot of rice and yogurt whenever I can.' So that puts a stamp of absolute correctitude on the whole issue.

Limp Biscuits

I must have been observing fantastic timings today. When I woke up and made myself coffee, I did not ask for the time on the telephone (as I generally do); but sat down and wrote letters, and then asked for the time. Came the answer, 'Twenty past three, sir.'

'Thank you,' I said, trying not to sound shocked.

I had been under the impression that it was noon. It was getting beyond a joke, my timeless existence in the heart of New York! I decided to buy a watch at once (not pursued, really). I had missed both breakfast and lunch. I hurried out for a snack at four o'clock and then to fulfil a tea meeting at 5 p.m. Still another day come and nearly gone and I have had no time again for anything—seeing Gil or saying 'How do you do?' to Harvey or buying a shirt, all of which I had proposed to do. This lack of time was getting to be a nightmare and I decided to do something about it as soon as I could find the time for it. The tea proved the most wasteful engagement one could ever accept. I had to search for the house at a back of beyond downtown area. Had to change buses twice, once legitimately and once through a blunder, and then had to explore the alleys for number 240A. Added to it was a persistent drizzle. Finally found the household perched on a staircase landing, with the lady of the house very loud and casual. Perhaps when they invite you to tea they expect you to drink Martini; when I was offered and declined liquor, they provided me a tea that tasted like rainwater flowing down the roof tile; and to go with it was a biscuit that had the look of Salvador Dali's 'Limp Watch'. My host, I realized, welcomed visitors because he wanted an audience for his incessant chatter at high speed! I suddenly realized that it was a mad evening, with an engagement that I ought to have waived with grace and dignity. Moral: don't readily accept any and every engagement hereafter. While you are extremely selective and inflexible with regard to public engagements, someone has only to suggest 'Come to our house,' and you are there the next moment. Move with caution and use your judgement, if you do not want to waste your lifetime hunting up streets where monologous hosts with their loud-voiced wives reside! A valuable day in New York totally destroyed. Suddenly got up in the midst of the other's peroration and said thanks for a lovely evening and goodbye.

Key Obsession

Dinner at the Indian Consulate. The Consul General, a friendly soul without any of the feather and war paint that officials generally love to wear. Other guests for the dinner are an ex-Maharaja from India, whom everyone deliberately 'highnesses' much to his delight. Royalty in exile is generally very exacting. His Highness was a jovial man, with whom I came to backslapping terms before the dinner ended; a morose Muslim officer from the Central Revenue Board, Delhi, who had never heard of me; a Jewish doctor, before whom everyone was afraid to mention Egypt, but whom everyone asked about 'Tranquillity Pills', in order to cover up the Egyptian question which we had been discussing before he arrived. The dinner was a triumph, establishing once and for all the supremacy and the tranquilizing qualities of South Indian food—*rasam, sambhar, masala dosai,* pickles and so forth. I'm more than ever convinced that the South Indian diet marks the peak in the evolution of culinary art and that the South Indian, however well he may be received, will never feel really at home anywhere in the world unless he can have his spices too within reach. My regard for His Highness went up when I found him uttering little cries of joy at the sight of *sambhar* and *dosai.* I knew then that the man could do no wrong. It was a commentary on the march of democracy in India that when I mentioned a discount house, where radio sets and refrigerators could be purchased at a reduced price, His Highness became alert and wanted me to note down the address for him. I did it cheerfully, and also gave a copy of it to our Muslim officer, who brightened up ever so slightly on receiving it and asked what sort of a writer I was and which newspaper I represented (I had to explain to him gently the distinction between a novel and a newspaper). The good turn I did in providing the address of a discount house so much endeared me to His Highness that he put his arm around my shoulder and cracked a few jokes. He apologized to me in the car when he lit his cigar. All of us compared weights and he envied me for being only 140! He was 196 or thereabouts, but was dieting all the time, which only had the effect of making his suits lose shape ('I have discarded a dozen suits within the last six months!') without any decrease in weight. We went to the United Nations where a debate was in progress in the General Assembly. Mr Menon put us in the VIP's gallery, where with the aid of the earphone and push-buttons on your chair you could hear a speech in five languages. It was an impressive setting with a big crowd, colourful furnishing and lights, and a general air of festivity. For a while I diverted myself by listening to a speech in five different languages by pushing the button for a new tongue halfway through each sentence, but still I grew bored with it. His Highness was showing me a gold gadget in his vest pocket, which looked like a small pen-knife but was actually a miniature pair of spectacles, with which you could study only a menu card or a list of wines (not at all necessary for one who was reducing). He felt very pleased when I mistook the gadget for a knife, and explained how he always carried it in his vest-pocket with his latch-key. The word 'key' made me look for my own room key. It made me anxious when I did not find it in my pocket, and I feared that the stern men at the reception desk of my hotel might refuse to produce a duplicate and leave me to freeze in the open. This thought working at the back of my mind produced an anxiety neurosis in me and completely spoilt for me the United Nations session. I got up abruptly, took leave of His Highness, and rushed back to my hotel, where they gave me a duplicate key without fuss. But when I went up I found that I had not shut the door at all when leaving my room in the morning.

THROUGH THE MID-WEST

What Caste, Traveller?

On the train to Detroit. Very comfortable bedroom suite. Slept soundly. At 5.30 a.m., the steward knocked on my door. Shaved, dressed, and ready at 6 a.m. Detroit at seven o'clock. I had learnt the art of dealing with porters. I carried two of my bags and left the porter to carry only the other two—so only fifty cents to pay. The porter dumped my bags at a place and told me to await the arrival of the 'transfer' man. 'Plenty of time, don't worry.' I wondered what was meant by 'transfer'. But one gets used to new phrases and awaits with interest the dawn of their meaning. A new man turned up as promised: 'Lansing, have you got the transfer?' He examined all the papers in my possession, tore off a bit and said, 'OK, plenty of time. Hang on to your half of the ticket.'

'Grand Rapids? Get in all passengers for Rapids,' a conductor was shouting and gesticulating on a platform. I said, 'I'm going to East Lansing. Is this the train?' 'Get in, get in,' he cried impatiently. When I hesitated, he said, 'The train leaves in five minutes, get in.'

I showed him my ticket. He brushed it aside and cried, 'First get in, don't waste time, of course this is your train.' He was excitable like a schoolboy on his first excursion. I hesitated outside for a moment to enquire about my luggage, but he cried, 'If you don't get in—' gritting his teeth, gesticulating wildly like an air-raid warden ordering the population into the shelter. I could no longer resist this man's unreasonable, irrational, imperiousness. I went in and took a seat. No sign of my luggage. It was a crowded compartment. I asked a passing official, flourishing my ticket, 'Are you sure my seat is here?'

'Ask him,' he pointed at the impatient conductor outside. I was getting worried about my luggage, which a porter had already carried ahead, noting as usual the number of my seat. It was no good hesitating any longer. If my trunks were to be left behind in Detroit, that was just where I was also going to stay. No sense in reaching Lansing to borrow a shirt off the first person I saw. I noticed the hasty conductor already crying 'All aboard', and preparing to lift the step. I made a quick decision and jumped out, and said, 'My luggage has not come.' He looked at me despairingly as if I were a Peeping Tom, and said, 'The train is about to move—' I lost my temper and cried, 'Can't you see that I must have my baggage, what do you mean by hustling me like this? A porter took it from me, where is he?'

Now he showed a better appreciation of my state, 'Let me see your ticket.' When he saw my ticket, his manner changed.

'Oh, your seat is three carriages—further up there; you have a parlour seat reservation, sir.'

'Indeed!' I said, and added, 'And you had no patience to show me my carriage.' He was contrite. A parlour seat belongs to the high-caste traveller; and he had subjected me to the indignity of showing me a coach-seat! I had every right to put on the look of a proud soul, deeply hurt. I moved to my parlour car. My suitcases were there; the attendant said, 'Watch your step, sir,' and 'That is your seat, sir,' 'Let me take your coat.' And, 'Breakfast will be served in a quarter of an hour, sir.' All of which are marks of respectful attention to which a parlour-car passenger is entitled as a birthright, as opposed to the coach-class one who is generally left alone. The caste system works rigorously in this field. I sat in a swivel chair at the window, through which you could watch the landscape gravely.

Steely Thoughts

At the breakfast table a man sitting opposite smiled and said, 'How do you do?'

'Good, thanks.'

'From India?'

'Yes.' I smiled back affably.

'I am—' he interrupted his breakfast to produce from his pocket a card. It was inscribed: 'Mr So-and-so, Steel Corporation, Detroit.'

'I am honoured to meet you, sir,' I said, sufficiently impressed. There was a young man by his side.

'This is my boy who is on vacation. He goes to school in Chicago. He is Tom.'

I bowed to him too. The man asked, 'Is this your first visit to this country? How do you like it?' These were routine questions, which I could answer in my sleep. And through the window he pointed out:

'Those are our factories, you know.'

'Wonderful, must be . . .' I had no idea how one progressed conversationally with a steel-magnate. To say, 'Must be exciting to produce steel,' or 'You must be making a tremendous lot of money' might sound silly. So I kept quiet. I looked at Tom appreciatively as he took out a cigarette and lit it. The proud father said, 'We are going to Rapids for a day.' Rapids! It conjured up visions of waterfalls cascading over smooth rocks and little glades, the play of sunlight on water producing a hundred rainbows—but it was Frank Thomson of Michigan Press, who knocked this vision out of my head by explaining that Rapids was nothing more than another town with its underground car park and market street, not known for anything in particular.

'I am going to East Lansing,' I said.

'Are you connected with the University?' he asked.

'No, just visiting.' He now buttonholed me and asked:

'Are you connected with the steel purchasing mission from India?'

'Why?' I asked warily.

'We'd like to sell steel to India, I hear river projects are under way.'

I could now understand his interest in me. I had shone in borrowed feathers. It was a pity that I should soon be disillusioning him, but I couldn't keep up a steel-talk and was bound to be discovered soon.

So I replied, 'No, I'm not connected with the steel mission.'

I wondered what part of my personality had a steel purchasing touch about it. Then he swung to the other extreme and asked, 'Are you studying in East Lansing?'

'Oh, no, I'm a writer, I mean an author.' It was now his turn to be dumbfounded.

'Must be wonderful to be an author,' or 'Must be making a lot of money' were probably statements he could not make without feeling silly. So he said, looking at his watch, 'Excuse me, we'll have to be getting back.' He smiled, and was off, followed by Tom, puffing away. It made me brood for the rest of my journey how he had come drawn to me like a piece of iron to a magnet, and was repelled the moment he realized I was only an author. For the rest of the journey he hid himself behind his newspaper.

East Lansing

One never expected a mere Lansing to exist in reality—one always thought there could be only East Lansing. At ten-thirty, Lansing—a small station. Two men were looking for me. Frank Thomson of the Michigan State University Press, and his Indian friend. From that moment Frank devoted his entire time to me. He drove me in his car to the Kellogg Centre (unforgettable breakfast name)—a magnificent hotel, run by students undergoing a hotel management course. A very attractive campus—reminded one of Cubbon Park in Ooty.

Pantheon, Parthenon, and Push-Button Ballot

Attended Professor Edward Blackman's lecture on Roman architecture. Forty boys in the class—sat in the last seat of a classroom, after years. The professor spoke on Roman viaducts and Ionic columns and pantheon and parthenon, coliseum and so forth. The presence of slaves in ancient Rome made life easy and created a large class of Romans without any occupation. It became necessary to build huge structures and give them continuous free entertainment and enough accommodation to keep the whole population engaged. Some days there were as many as five hundred fights and contests—between men and men, men and animals, and animals and animals—fantastic and bloody spectacles. The Romans used an enormous quantity of water, '300 gallons per head, that is they consumed each day more water than all the citizens of East Lansing use in a year.' Statistics makes sense only when they are applied to known analogies. I felt impressed. The Romans soon exhausted all the water supply for baths and fountains, and had to devise means of bringing water from distant sources and so built their viaducts.

This was the day of the big election. Impossible to think that one would lecture on a subject like this and anyone would listen to it, while a national election was in progress. No one seemed to care about it. No holiday. In our country it'd be unthinkable to have schools and offices working on a day like this. Election day ought to be a day of complete, total, abandonment to political excitement.

In my fevered imagination I had expected election day to be full of noise, crowd and movement, with all normal work suspended; and above all, loudspeakers rending the air.

Evening, a little more activity was noticeable. People were queuing up before the fire station; pushed my way through the queue with Frank's help and went in. The polling officials, most of them women, were good enough to explain the working of the mechanical ballot—whereby a push-button records your vote for a party, a member, or a mixture of parties from the President, Supreme Court Judges, down to the Inspector of Drains and Municipal Supervisors. Considering the complete overhaul an election involves, surprising that people are not more excited. People went into a curtained booth and recorded their votes. They were silent and businesslike. We passed on to another centre, a grammar school where ordinary ballot-paper voting was in progress. Being a grammar school, children were playing in the corridor and moving around with a greater sense of ownership. (At the Fire Station too, a child had insisted upon being enclosed with her mother in the booth while the officials tried to explain to her how it could not be done.) There were fantastic scrawls and figures on the walls. A child held a large collie by his collar at the door. Four children were watching a garden snake kept in a glass. Women smirked and giggled and commented on political matters. Here again the officials were good enough to explain to me the procedure in voting and the identification of voters was foolproof.

Kindly Host But—

I must make a mistake in every place and today the mistake was to get tied up with one of my countrymen whom I shall call Joshi. He was a horticulturist, who having married an American, and not knowing where his sympathies lay, stopped and debated politics at every corner with all and sundry, to whom in all fairness to myself, I should have said 'No'. I found the horticultural things he took me round to see very limited and uninteresting. I was not interested in watching tropical plants such as banana or coconut raised in glass houses maintained at 70°; while out of my window at home I see nothing but these. We get more horticultural delight in Lal Bagh, Bangalore, or any Mysore nursery. But I had to pass through several glass houses politely admiring very common, ordinary plants. Like a museum, an official flower garden is a bore. I was tired of the whole thing, but resigned myself to it. I could also sympathize with him—he possessed so much spontaneous friendliness, although he was messy in arranging things. He tried to tie me to a lunch with his office colleagues at eleven, when he knew full well that I had had my breakfast only half an hour before. It was painful to say 'no' when his friends wanted me to join them. Joshi also had to put off his own lunch for my sake. Later he took me to the university cafeteria, but forgot that I ate no meat. On the whole confused. I wish I had not put him to the strain of entertainment.

After lunch I was back in my room for an hour. Frank came back to my room and took me to a fat, cheerful, television expert, in an office downstairs, where I found Professor Blackman waiting. He was to appear in a television programme along with me. Frank was also in the programme. They both looked very nervous and scared, the television expert kept repeating, 'Television is nothing. Just be natural, don't think of it as something terrible. Forget the boys with their cameras—only just don't do what you were doing now; were you aware that you had your finger across your lips while you spoke just now? It is a thing you simply must not do in a television programme . . . and raise your voice slightly please—not much—but . . .' All of which made Frank so panicky that when he lit his cigarettes in a chain his hands shook, and he confided to me, 'I've never been in this sort of thing before, you know, and I am terrified.'

Financial Expert

After television, a visit to Professor Useem's evening class. I was interested to know that my novel *The Financial Expert* had just been studied analytically in that class. I went there dreading how I was going to come through it, not remembering much of my own book. It gave me an odd feeling to reflect that a book written in joy and hopefulness in that lonely splendour of my home in Yadavagiri should now be turning up to plague me thus. The class was ready—questions came on to me from various angles: a hand was raised, and a question fired at me:

'Is this typical?' 'Is that social tension common?' 'Is that so and so?' 'Do brothers quarrel in India?'

'Of course brothers would quarrel anywhere in the world,' I said and delivered a long discourse on joint-family living in India. About fifty answers, always reminding the audience in conclusion that *The Financial Expert* was a work of fiction, not a treatise or a document, and the story was about an individual and was not portraying a type. 'There are 380 million people in our country, and as many types if you please,' I said, this being the only way in which I could explain my point of view.

Ten p.m., applause and close. At the end of the session, one of my audience, an elderly person, came up and produced out of his wallet a small group photograph, consisting of about twelve persons—a father, mother, eight sons and two sisters. He explained, 'This is our family, my parents, and brothers. That's me. Till recently we all lived together. It's just to prove to you that some of us also live a joint-family life. As long as my parents lived, we were not allowed to leave the old home and live separately. And, that was the happiest period of my life.'

Govind

I have to refer to an Indian friend by a pseudonym because I am making a note about his private life. What happens to an Indian who gets culturally mixed up, was a question that I often put to myself whenever I saw my countrymen abroad. Here, in a nutshell, this friend provided an answer. I shall call him Govind. He was from an orthodox family in Bombay. He had come to the United States about seven years ago for higher studies. Before he left India, he had been a fervent nationalist, engaged himself in political activities, performed *satyagraha*, was jailed by the British government, came under the spell of one of the political leaders of Bombay—an austere associate of Mahatma Gandhi. This leader is known for his spartan outlook, a stern practitioner of Gandhian principles of simple living, dedication, non-killing (for food), and temperance; a man of absolute personal purity in life, and an uncompromising fighter for the principle he feels to be right. Govind came fully under his influence and became his political and personal attaché. When he went to the United States for higher studies, Govind was being catapulted into the land of comfort, gadgets and beef steak. He went to school and did well in his studies. He kept in touch with his master, who often wrote him detailed letters of what was happening in free India, although he was a busy politician. He had real affection for Govind, and promised him that he would personally help him to get suitably settled when he returned to India after his studies. After three years, the young man fell in love with an American (or European, I don't remember) girl, and wrote to his master of his intention to marry her. The master wrote a circumspect letter in reply, saying that if Govind felt sure that he was not being carried away by a momentary attraction, he might go ahead. With this blessing, the young man married. This was the starting point of complications. His own father, a very orthodox Hindu gentleman, could not view his son's marriage to a European girl with equanimity. He ostracized him from the ancient family. The boy took it calmly, secured a lecturer's post in the university, and settled down with his wife. He had a car, a home, a wife, but still he clung to his orthodox habits and did not eat meat. This created certain domestic complexities and after three years of trial he gave up his orthodoxy, and took to American food. This change of diet seems to have had an unexpected effect on him. For he soon wrote to his master of his conversion. He almost said that he had groped in the dark all along, sticking to the precepts of his orthodox family, and after all light had now dawned. He was now eating meat and was beginning to like it. 'Am actually eating not just ordinary meat, but beef, the best in the world, and it has not done me any harm, it has not destroyed me physically or morally. On the contrary I have never felt better in my life. My point in writing to you about this is this. India will never become a modern nation, unless we Indians get over our blind superstitious prejudice against eating beef. What a shame that we should be begging the world to supply us food? I feel so small when I read in the papers that India is begging for American wheat. We Indians here bow our heads in shame when we read such a piece of news. Instead of it why should we not retain our national self-respect? Beef-eating will solve fifty per cent of our food problems. We allow old cows to stray in public places and remain an economic burden on us; how sensible it would be to slaughter them for food. It will solve our food problem through own effort, and we won't have to be taking around the begging bowl . . . And now this is my point. You must set an example to the nation yourself. You are the first man in our state. If you set an example, others will surely follow you. I would advise you to adopt forthwith beef-eating as a national duty.' This boy had completely lost touch with the realities of an Indian background. Probably, suggesting the eating of beef may not sound abnormal in most parts of the world, but in India where the cow is a sacred object, beef cannot be eaten, no rationalization is ever possible on this subject.

The venerable recipient of this advice felt so outraged by the letter, that he wrote a brief reply through his secretary to say that he would prefer not to hear from the young convert again. This episode had its sequel, as it made it impossible for Govind to look to his master for support if ever he should return to India.

Govind could stay on in America, but as his wife explained he was gradually becoming homesick. For about six years he had not thought of his home, his father having cut him off completely. But suddenly his father relented and started sending mementoes every now and then: sweets for Diwali, a silk scarf, a brightly-patterned, hand-woven counterpane, and so on. Mrs Govind explained that every time a parcel arrived, Govind would go out of his mind completely. He would parade the gift, and give himself over to sentimental outbursts: 'After all one's parents', 'No place like home', and such things. Govind began to feel that if he wanted to return, his father would certainly receive him and his wife in their ancient home. How this could be practically worked out in an orthodox joint-family, where several others also lived together under the same roof, was a real problem and not a mere matter of detail as our friend had thought. He concluded, 'Well, one of us will always have to be homesick, I suppose, either myself or my wife.' His wife said, 'Don't bother in the least about my homesickness, if you feel sure you want to return home and know what you want to do there.'

'Ah, that is the problem,' he said. 'What am I going to do in India? My master will not help me in the least, and I can't get a foothold anywhere without his help . . . I made a mistake in writing him that letter. But you see it is only common sense which I wrote, what is wrong in it?' Add to this the fact that they were expecting a baby soon. I will leave him at that, with his 'buts' and 'howevers' as unresolved problems.

Self-immolation

The junior member of the staff wanted to 'buy me a cup of coffee' at the coffee house across the road—a cosy place, but smoke-ridden.

Talked to them—heaven knows what about. One of the professors of the English department came down, joined us and suggested that I should address the Literature students assembled in his class. Walked back to the college. Answered questions about Kipling, Forster, and about myself. On the spot, evolved a theory that I started a book on being provoked by an odd and eccentric character. All questions were based on this assumption, and I got plunged more and more into the morass of this hypothesis. Such literary theories are easily enunciated but difficult to maintain unless you hold the monopoly of speech; the moment one begins to be examined on this issue one is sure to lose ground. I could not maintain my hypothesis too long, finding that my own books would not support the theory. And so when a student asked, 'What about your *English Teacher,* in what way would you call him eccentric or odd?' I was flabbergasted. The boys in their generosity turned to question me on *A Passage to India* and on Kipling—safe subjects from my point of view.

Last day at East Lansing, packed up in order to 'check-out' at 3 p.m. Met the famous American artist Rattner and his wife at the cafeteria for a few minutes and got involved in a discussion about the need for prayer and meditation in daily life (particularly for Americans). Saw some of his pictures and felt baffled by his style but felt too polite to say so; he looks so venerable.

*

At noon, over lunch, faced an interview by a press reporter. He had had an appointment to meet me at breakfast, but actually turned up during lunch at the restaurant table, explaining that he had been called away by a sudden scoop about a triple murder. I wanted to know all about it, but he would not say anything more. He treated it casually—I'm afraid with a deliberately put up professional air of boredom and casualness. He looked fatigued and bored—from three corpses to a live Indian author was all in his day's range of work, undoubtedly. I could not get over the feeling that he was not a real reporter (just as I could not help the feeling that the Kellogg Centre with its perfect service was a make-believe place), but a type out of the pages of a whodunit—the sort of reporter who beats both the detective and sergeant at their game of investigation. Over the soup he asked, 'What solution would you offer for the American civilization? What can save it?'

'What is wrong?'

'We have everything in the world, yet are unhappy. We as a nation are terribly bored; and so seek continuous forgetfulness in excitement, gadgets and so forth. Our suicide rate is increasing, our divorce rate doubling. What do you think it's due to? What solution would you suggest?'

'Meditation and withdrawal—for about fifteen minutes a day,' I said, echoing the talk with Rattner in the morning. 'In every Indian home we have a place called the *puja* room or God's room, where the members of a family could generally withdraw and pray. Most Indians pray and meditate for at least a few minutes every day, and it may be one of the reasons why, with all our poverty and struggle, we still survive, and are able to take a calm view of existence. I cannot say that we have an appreciable suicide rate in our country; practically no divorce.'

'Do you attribute it to the presence of the special room in every Indian home? What do you call it?'

'*Puja, puja* in Sanskrit means worship.'

'Will you please spell it for me?'

He fishes out of his pocket a crumpled piece of paper of almost the size of a bus ticket, from amidst his handkerchief, cigarette-packet etc., smooths it out, jots down in a corner the word 'Puja', and stuffs it away back into the folds of his kerchief and matches. He then goes on to enquire about the literary trends in modern India, and of course I have to mention our epics, and so he has to retrieve the bus ticket again and again to note down names. If ever anyone has an occasion to take a look at that bit of paper he will find on it 'Ramayana', 'Mahabharata', 'Tagore', 'Gandhi', 'Sathyagraha', 'Nehru', 'Tamil', 'Telugu', 'Sanskrit', etc. I don't know if he had the patience or the space to write down all the names I kept mentioning as I found him attempting to make a note, jotting a vowel or a consonant, and abandoning it immediately. I speculated about how he would weave all this jumble into a copy. Perhaps on the other side of the bus ticket was the sketch of the triple murder. Would both get a page-wide splash in whatever paper he was representing? Is it possible: *The Three-in-One Homicide* juxtaposed with *Indian Author Recommends Quarter-Hour Meditation for Would-be Suicides* or *Puja Room Abolishes Divorce in India*. I had all along thought that he was there as my guest, but he suddenly called for his check, paid for his portion of the lunch, and was off, and I had no chance of asking what he proposed to do with all that jumble of names on his bus ticket.

On to Madison

The train from Chicago to Madison is not a very serious train. It reminds one of the Nizam's State Railways of old days. I held a first-class ticket but no one would let me into a 'parlour car' because all the seats had been reserved for a 'Football' crowd.

'Are you going to the ball game?' the guard kept asking. 'No,' I said.

'Then, you must go up, we can't take you here.'

I had to walk the entire length of the enormous train and then they put me into a crowded 'coach' which is, as I have already said, parallel to our third class. No one cared to understand what I said as I kept repeating that I held a first-class ticket.

The train strolled along at its own pace—an unpunctuality which no one would have dared to attempt in our country (at least in olden times). It stopped and switched off the engine at various stations, a big noisy football crowd streamed in all along the way and choked up all the space, crying, 'Scandalous arrangements!' Football was too much in the air. Everyone asked of everyone else something about North-Western and Wisconsin. This was a bad day for normal travellers—the Saturday afternoon train. I was again and again asked by ticket-checking officials whether I was going to the match. 'No, no, no.'

'Then you will have to move up to the other coach, this is stopping at the football ground.'

I am a heretic in this land of football worshippers. In other days they might have burned me at the stake. With all this diversion the train arrived at Madison late beyond belief, and when I was hoping to leave the train once for all, it stopped within sight of the station, a furlong away, and spent another half an hour detaching the coaches occupied by the football patrons.

Henry Hart, whom I had known intimately at Mysore, and his little daughter Nancy, are there to receive me. When I finally manage to find my way out of the carriage. This is another penalty that a 'coach' traveller has to pay—he'll have to wait till everyone ahead has cleared out of the carriage. Talk of class distinctions! Remember I had a first-class ticket all the time in my pocket! I'm entitled to a refund, I think, but no one will explain to me the procedure for claiming it.

Adam Street

Henry and Virginia give me a room in their lovely home in Adam Street. It was Nancy's room till a moment ago; for her toys peep at me from their various corners of concealment. I feel completely at home. Henry, Virginia, Benny and Nancy, and their huge shaggy dog Tippy (mixed collie and Airedale), form a happy household; with another Virginia, a bright girl in a green dress who appears at the dining table and vanishes unobtrusively into her own room upstairs. She is a student who has room and board here in return for helping Virginia with household and baby-sitting a couple of days in the week when Virginia goes out of town to teach. Within a couple of hours of my arrival, I am involved in parties. Cocktails somewhere, and then on to a dinner at a French professor's house, where through Virginia's gentle hints I am provided with a plate of rice and vegetables. A young man who has just won a seat in a local election and his wife, a well-read tiny French girl, seem to be the guests of honour today, and the talk is all about the elections at Milwaukee and the machinations of the opposite camp. The young man never speaks a word for hours, until someone starts him on the subject of elections, and then he reels off all the stories of individuals, groups, unions, uptown or downtown associations, which attempted to wreck his chance. He doesn't seem to have got over the surprise of getting through the election successfully. He speaks in a sort of monotonous iambic meter, moving no part of his face except his jaws, his wife collaborating in the narrative in a sort of undertone running commentary. I feel completely lost. The French host's friendliness and cheerfulness are stimulating, but alas, he speaks so little. He just smiles and serves food and drinks, while the budding Milwaukee politician and his wife do all the talking—the rest are just so many pairs of ears for them. Before leaving I say to the Milwaukee monologist, 'Hope you will end up in Washington someday,' at which his face relaxes. Rather a handsome gesture on my part since neither he nor his talkative wife ever bother to ask who I am, or how I have come to find myself in their midst.

A Bright Sunday

Sunday morning. The day is bright when I wake up at nine o'clock. Find the family ready for breakfast. A sunny and promising day. It stimulates people to make plans and announce them.

Henry says, 'I am going to get into old clothes and fix Benny's cart.' This is a dog cart, a two-wheeled trap to which the hefty Tippy is yoked and driven about by Nancy or Benny, flourishing a whip. A nice contraption which may be seen in front of Henry's house at Adam Street any time of the day or night. But Henry is a perfectionist who likes to work on the sled again and again. He has a complete workshop at the basement, and his idea of relaxation is to fix things at his workshop. He disappears after this announcement. I say, catching the mood of the hour, 'I will go for a walk,' the only way in which I can enjoy a bright day.

Virginia says, 'There is a park nearby with a zoo, let's all go there with the children.' The children receive the proposal with a whoop of joy. I go upstairs to dress. Benny, Nancy and Tippy go after Henry. I come down an hour later, dressed and ready to go out. Virginia is washing dishes.

'We will go after this,' she says to me.

Henry comes in unobtrusively and lends a hand in washing. Over the splash of the faucet Virginia suddenly asks, 'Where is Benny?'

'I managed to fix his carriage, now it nicely fits on Tippy. They are there—playing.'

'Have you left Benny alone with the dog?'

'Nancy is also there.' Silence.

Over the sound of flowing water Virginia says quietly, 'They should not be left alone by themselves, Henry.'

'Why not?'

'Oh, I don't know, they may run away. Why have you left them there?'

'I came to help you wash.'

'No, I don't like it Henry.'

'I will go back to them presently.'

'Leave me to do the washing. Please go.'

'I insist upon helping you,' says Henry jocularly. The humour is lost on her.

Virginia says in deadly seriousness, 'I don't think you should leave them alone, Henry.'

'Nancy is with them,' says Henry.

I notice the same set of arguments coming up in a second cycle while the faucet splashes, their talk is being carried on in the gentlest undertone but gradually gathers emphasis. I feel that my presence embarrasses them and that they might perhaps have it out a little more decisively if I left them free. I quietly withdraw from the scene and go back to my room and settle down to do a little writing. I write my diary notes of four days, having been in arrears, and I am occupied thus for an hour. When I finish writing I strain my ears to hear their voices and to guess what stage of the debate they may be in now. There is dead silence below. I conclude that peace must have again settled on the household and that Henry must have gone back to guard the children. I put away my papers and go downstairs. Virginia is cleaning up the gas stove with a sort of grim determination. I wonder if she will be free now to come out into a bright day with me. She hears my footsteps. As I pause at the door she says quietly, 'Benny is lost.' She adds, 'I knew something would happen. Henry has gone to search for him.'

'What about Nancy? Wasn't she with him?'

'I don't know,' she says without lifting her head. She is probably in tears. Benny had been seated in the sled carriage with Tippy yoked to it at the time Henry had come in, offering to do dish-washing. Nancy, who was supposed to be with them, was hailed by a friend and moved away absentmindedly, leaving Benny alone. By the time they were all back to look for him, Virginia's premonition had been fulfilled. Virginia looks so unhappy that I cannot help asking, 'Why are you so worried?'

'He is so small, anything may happen to him, with so many cars about . . .'

I suddenly feel that I ought to join in the search for Benny. I go out.

At the end of the street I see Henry leading Tippy, who is of course strapped to his carriage, but without Benny in his seat. 'I caught Tippy running down Randal. Benny and Nancy must have gone off together somewhere,' says Henry, the optimist he is.

'So it is OK, they should both be back soon.'

But this is a false lull. Presently Nancy comes running down the road from another direction.

'Where is Benny?'

'I didn't see him,' she says innocently baring her gums. 'They were here,' she says assertively indicating the spot where she last saw them. She catches hold of Tippy by his shaggy ears and shouts, 'Tippy, where is Benny? Where is Benny?'

Tippy merely sweeps his huge fan-like tail, pants, and puts his tongue out. Henry bends close to Tippy and says, 'Tippy my man, look, you have really tipped Benny over somewhere. Where is he?' Tippy shakes his entire gawky frame, rolls his eyes, and lets out a bark in joy at being addressed, and tries to stand on his legs and jump although hindered by the harness and reins of the sled; giving almost a demonstration of what he could do with a rider sitting in the carriage. All of us stand looking helplessly at the animal wishing that he could speak.

Nancy says, 'I will go and look for him.'

'No Nancy, go back home, I don't want to search for you next.'

But Nancy begs, 'Daddy, I won't get lost. Let me look for Benny please.' It is evident that she enjoys the thrill of this search, and will not miss it for anything. She runs down the road again out of sight. Henry now looks serious. He goes up the steps and peeps in at the kitchen door just to report to Virginia, 'Not found yet,' and goes out again, on his bicycle this time. Virginia sits unmoved in the kitchen chair and murmurs, 'Something terrible must have happened to him. He is so small. He can't even speak. I don't know. . . Probably he has been kidnapped. That sort of thing is common here. I don't know if I shall ever see him again.' I say inanely, 'He couldn't have gone far.' 'What is he wearing?' I ask.

'A brown jumper and green cap. I must telephone the police.'

'Oh, no, don't,' I say, somehow not liking the idea of the police being involved in it.

'He has probably been kidnapped, such things are common here.'

I go out in search of Benny. Though Madison is not a very big town, when it comes to searching for someone its streets look endless and complicated. I walk up and down and across the streets and go back and forth, looking for a brown jumper and green cap. To me every child looks like Benny. Benny is chubby, round-headed, and pink, about a foot and a half high; that is all the impression I have of him, nothing more detailed. Being a sunny Sunday, scores of Benny-like children are moving around and most of them seem to wear green caps. I stare so much at every child I pass that they start running at the sight of me. I block the passage of one or two to say 'Hello!' and ask, 'Where are you going?'

'I am going home.'

'Where do you live?'

My questions have the effect of making them run back to their houses. So I watch every child get back to his house, rather a complicated process of eliminating non-Bennys. I believe I am scaring all the children off the streets this morning, as I go about with that fixed examining look. I notice here and there at a crossroad

Henry pedalling his cycle slowly with his eyes on the passing children. About an hour later, I notice a van slowly perambulating with policemen peeping out of it, obviously looking for a green cap. The children of the town must be having a puzzling morning with everyone staring at them so purposefully.

I give up the search after about two hours. I go to a milk bar for a drink and start homeward to report failure. Virginia has laid the table for lunch and is waiting for me. Benny is back. I find him engrossed in his lunch, perched on his high chair. He must be ravenously hungry after his outing and cannot wait for the others. Virginia is her usual cheerful self again.

'Did the police pick him up?' I ask.

'No. They had come to say that they could not find him and wanted to alert the neighbourhood. When they went back to their car, they found Benny examining it; and then they picked him up and brought him in; actually, you know, no one found Benny. He found himself.'

'Where did you go, Benny?' I ask.

He pauses with the soup wet around his mouth, smacking his lips.

'There,' he says, pointing from his seat of eminence, indicating a faraway beyond.

'Where?' I cannot help asking out of curiosity.

He merely replies, 'Walk,' and with that monosyllable returns to his lunch, dismissing the affair once and for all from his thoughts, having successfully neutralized all our elaborate plans for a bright Sunday morning.

Speech Correction

In the evening visit the University Union to hear Katherine Anne Porter read her short stories. Very unimpressive show. Her masterpiece 'At the Circus' which is so good to read sounds feeble and pointless at her reading. Moral: an author should never give a reading of his or her own masterpiece, nor should he try to explain it.

It always produces an effect of bathos. The hall is full. To think that people have bought tickets for this. Extraordinary habits. In our own country, the way to assure an empty hall would be to announce a price for seats at the lecture. On the contrary, speakers being so much more eager than their audience, they may have to tempt them with gifts in order to fill the seats. But this is a land where anyone would gladly give a dollar or two for sitting through an hour's lecture.

Rest of the evening at the Union cafe—smoke-filled, beer flowing. Students were dispersed here and there; some were writing their assignments. This was the only student organization where beer was served because as someone explained there was a large body of Germans here, and also because the Milwaukee breweries were nearby and had something to do with the universities. Noisy music. We sat chatting at the top of our voices sipping our drinks.

Conversational atmosphere rather spoilt by one of the ladies, Mrs R—, who caught me telling Virginia, 'Gil suddenly developed pneumonia,' and would not let me proceed, her amusement at the way I said *develop* was so great. 'All Indians say *develop, committee;* instead of De-Vellop, and Committee—does *pneumonia* develop?' she said, which I found very irritating. I merely replied, 'So much of an accent seems to me a waste of good breath; we've always been taught to speak without accent. Do you imagine your way of accenting is the most desirable, which the whole world should copy? In any case, why don't you let me finish my sentence so that you may catch the sense of what I am trying to say?' I could not speak more rudely since she was cheerful and nice otherwise, and had left her car at our disposal the whole day. She was not to be curbed so easily. The whole evening she kept repeating, 'So pneumonia developed! H'm!' and enjoyed the joke afresh each time although the rest of the company could not share her humour and wanted to talk of other things. Before bidding goodnight she again concluded, 'What did you say, "pneumonia developed", is it?' and giggled.

I had a premonition that this preoccupation with pneumonia would do her no good. My premonition was confirmed when I received an unsigned postcard two days later with the message:

The pity would be
If by accident or design
Your present accent ever stopped
Accept an admirer's wishes
That you continue to say
Your friend's pneumonia *developed.*

On the day I left Madison, I telephoned this lady intending to say good-bye; but I could not reach her as she was indisposed and could not be disturbed. A month later Virginia wrote to me, while giving me local news, 'Mrs R— was down with severe double pneumonia. I am happy to say that she is out of danger, but still the doctor says she will have to be very careful for some months.' I could only wish that she would not invite a relapse by recollecting me and attempting a fresh set of verse on pneumonia.

Space and Time

The problem of parking is one that lends a touch of irony to the whole development of modern transport. Every third person has a car, which means every third man needs a space of twenty-two by five, wherever he goes. Everywhere one turns one notices the warnings: 'Parking between . . .', 'Reserved for . . .', 'Absolutely no parking', 'No parking at any time', places where one must jump out of a moving car in order to reach one's destination. The problem is to get to a place in a car and get off at the right spot, otherwise you might as well walk from the starting point itself. There are parking facilities for only twelve minutes' duration or for ten hours. You slip the appropriate coin into the meter and return in time to take out the car, otherwise the inexorable dial betrays you to the police and brings you a ticket tucked behind the windscreen wiper—a long envelope at the sight of which the driver knows that he will have to part with several dollars on the following day. It means you will have to be watching your watch, which incidentally seems to support the sale of watches. Parking in certain places is permitted for higher officials and a junior who demands it will not get it: there is a local tale of an indignant junior, who resigned his job, stood for elections, became a senator and parked his car at the best place in the same compound within a year. There are radar beams which betray the speed and cameras which photograph the number plate of the offending motor car; there are young men who hold up placards to say 'Radar-check beware' in order to confound the police trap.

Live Lobster

At 12 p.m., Henry took me along to meet Miss—, someone or the other, name has gone out of my mind, Chairman of the English department, who was all excited about a conference she was attending at Washington. Lunched with her and three others of the English department. As usual with the English department anywhere, they were cautious and on the defensive. They may not have heard of me or read my books, quite understandably, but they were in suspense lest I should shoot questions at them. I for one do not in the least mind if others don't read me. They are not bound to. I don't read the books they write. So it is all right with me. But what I do object to is their defensiveness in my presence. They seem to be all the time in suspense, lest I should put questions to them on my work. 'Compare my *Financial Expert* with *Swami and Friends*,' 'What is the English title of *Grateful to Life and Death?*' 'When was *Mahatma* published?' and so on. I am a very considerate author, never referring to my work unless I am forced to. At this lunch, my neutral attitude proved encouraging, because in a short while conversation began to flow. My hosts ventured to ask, 'How many languages are there in India?'

'Fourteen.'

'So many. Are books being written in all of them?' 'What are the literary trends most noticeable?' 'After Independence, has Indian writing shown any notable change?' etc. etc.

And then they came near to the most dangerous question, 'Are your books translated?'

'Into what?'

'English?'

'I write in English.' This brought the conversation on to the edge of the precipice. Fortunately we had got through the dessert by then and everybody looked at his watch, and planned his retreat, saying, 'I've a class,' 'Oh, I have a meeting,' or 'I'm flying for a conference in Washington. I must catch the plane . . .' English studies work on the basis that a dead author is a good author. He is passive and still while you explain and analyse him in the classroom; having a living author on hand may be like having a live lobster on your plate.

Wrightism

One of Henry's friends, who is interested in architecture, brings his car in order to take me through the town and show me Frank Lloyd Wright's designs and Sullivan's before him—fantastic houses with horizontal lines at all costs. Frank Lloyd Wright's deliberate *negligé* (leaving portions of a building rugged, without plaster or dressing) seems to us rather affected, but one must see them through the eyes of Americans who are probably sick of machine-finish everywhere, and who may have a fascination for the half-finished look. To me such an ultra-modern building appears like the house of a man, in our country, who has run out of cash and cannot induce his contractor to plaster the walls. Americans cherish antiquities—in many of the homes, the most cherished object is a piece of mat or a brass vase or a verdigris-covered image from India, while in an Indian home the proudest possession would be a chromium-finished cigarette-lighter or a cuckoo-clock from Switzerland; one half of the world always yearns for something that the other half possesses but does not care for. In New York, in some of the more fashionable restaurants, an extra attraction is provided by the announcement, 'Charcoal broiled steak', and behind the glass, the roasting is done in public view, with firewood burning in brick kilns with real smoke going up, similar to the open-air kitchens built in preparation for a large-scale marriage feast in any household in an Indian village.

*

Returned home and went out for a walk; Nancy insisted upon keeping me company (riding) in her dog-cart. This proved a too complicated companionship. She was in her sled drawn by Tippy with me on the road, the dog sometimes racing up, sometimes at a standstill or sometimes prancing like a pony. So persuaded her to go back home and leave me alone. After a walk returned in time for an Indian dinner, of rice and curry devised by Virginia; a number of professors and their wives were invited. After dinner shut the doors and built a fire with all the guests sitting around—really cheerful and cosy, the temperature outside being very low. The fire was built as usual with the Sunday issue of the *New York Times* (which Henry maintains is excellent, adequate fuel). The children were sent to bed early. If they were around, lighting a fire became an elaborate ritual—the children being ever ready to feed the fire with varied literary fare. Henry had only to announce, 'Let us build a fire,' and Nancy and Benny would gather all the magazines, books, letters and manuscripts they could lay hands on and dump them in the fireplace. While Henry always thought this an excellent disposal of much of his correspondence and unwanted library stock, Virginia sometimes complained that some of her letters were thus destroyed even before she got a chance to see them. The climax was reached one day when Benny tore sheets out of a brand-new copy of *Oxford World Atlas* for feeding the fire. He was punished for it (as at times when he hit Nancy) by being carried to his bed; his protests on such occasions took the form of blood-curdling cries and shouts from behind the door, and then he'd kick against the door (to which Tippy would respond by barking merrily and scratching the door with his claws from this side), until sleep overcame him, the rest of the family going about their business unmindful of the uproar.

*

When Nancy peeped in at my door, I asked, from my bed, what the time was. She promptly said 'Eight' and withdrew her head. Continued to sleep, for half an hour more, believing her; but found that it was nearly eleven when I got up and had my first coffee.

Skipped breakfast and went up to pack. Packed and ready to leave at three.

No Time for Goodbye

The train is at 5 p.m. At four-thirty we are all out in the street looking for a wireless-summoned taxi. I cannot say goodbye to Nancy as she is away somewhere else, playing or watching television. Benny is coming with us to the railway station. He is excited at the prospect of seeing a train, asking a hundred questions, employing over and over again the limited vocabulary at his disposal and trying to squeeze the maximum sense into them. At the station the official behind the window says, after taking a look at my ticket, 'No parlour seat in the five o'clock train, only coach class.'

'But you sold us a first-class ticket yesterday!'

'Oh, that was a mistake. You can travel coach and claim a refund later.'

I feel that for the next few months I shall have no time for anything but writing claims for refund of tickets sold by mistake. When the train steams in, Henry, like a good host, will not let me touch a bag but carries all the five pieces himself, into a coach, hauling them up, and moving them to a corner.

And now a train official comes up to look at my ticket and exclaims, 'You have a first-class ticket, you must go further up.'

'But they said there is no first class on this train!'

'Who? The office staff there, they wouldn't know.' No one seems to know of any matter precisely. I refuse to move again, preferring to continue where I have found myself. But they won't hear of it. Never heard of a coach class seat being occupied by a parlour car traveller (although this was exactly what had happened to me while coming to Madison on that day of the football match). So once again we are on the move. Only a few seconds left. The ticket has once again to be taken to the office for revised payments and checking and so on, Henry runs to the other end of the platform for endorsing a reservation. I pick up my baggage and get a porter to move my baggage to my legitimate seat in the parlour compartment, where a set of grim, determined patricians are elegantly leaning back in their swivel chairs reading their papers, pausing ever so slightly to watch the last minute arrival into this exclusive paradise. Virginia and Benny are waiting to have a few words before I leave. It is so difficult to squeeze in a word in all this confusion and last minute make-shift. Benny does not care, his gaze being riveted on the engine, of which he has now a near-view. I hardly have the time to thank Virginia for all her kindness, the train is about to leave, Henry comes running with the new reservation tickets. There is just enough time to snatch the ticket from his hand and jump into my compartment before the steps are removed. All through the journey I am racked with the thought that I ought to have managed to spend a little more time talking to Virginia and Henry instead of letting my luggage monopolize my attention.

CHICAGO

In Professors' Midst

Between Singer, Redfield, and Shils, eminent professors whose knowledge of India was profound and who had each spent at least a year in different parts of India, my stay in Chicago was most rewarding. Between them they unobtrusively took care of my food, shelter, and movements.

On the morning of my arrival while talking to Redfield in his room, Milton Singer came in to say that Chamu was arriving from New York next day. Let no one be puzzled about the identity of Chamu. He is Dr M.N. Srinivas, an eminent Indian sociologist of Oxford, Baroda, Bombay, Manchester and Delhi, who was a great friend and neighbour of mine in Mysore. Years ago when I wrote my first novel *Swami and Friends,* and found none to read it, a very young college fellow came forward to go through the manuscript; he read and certified it as readable, which was very encouraging. That was Chamu. He was then a college student; now he is a senior, respected professor—many academic activities and distinctions having come his way. His research and studies constantly took him out of view, if not to another corner of the world at least to another part of the country. However I always had an annual glimpse of him, when he came down for a couple of weeks each year to see his mother and brothers in Mysore. Our literary contact, started years ago with *Swami,* continued. He always goaded me on to write my next and not to waste my time; whenever I saw him I discussed with him the subject I had in mind for a new novel, and through his reaction I always got an objective view of anything I might plan to write. So he continued, through the years, to be not only the first reader of my first book, but also a critic and adviser on many unwritten ones.

Now I was happy to know that I should be seeing him next day, not only because I longed to speak Tamil to someone, but also because I hoped he would be able to give me a small quantity of betel-nut to which I am addicted. I had exhausted my own stock of it weeks ago; above all I wanted to speak to him about my new book and the problems connected with it.

I stayed at the Quandrangle Club, a residential club for Faculty members and their guests. I had a comfortable room upstairs and everything was fine. After breakfast Professor Shils called on me and took me along to the college. In the afternoon Milton Singer suggested that I might attend a class (or was it a seminar, I can never say, the only difference between the two being that in a seminar the students light their cigarettes during the lecture but in a class probably they don't. Here I found in Cohn's classroom everyone smoking). Milton Singer and I sat at one end of a horseshoe table.

The lecture is on the Indian joint family. Joint family is almost a rage in academic circles in this country. Wherever I go questions are fired at me on joint family, their real wonder being how so many different persons could live, work, and budget-balance, under the same roof. The point I have always stressed about the joint family is that this system of living affords protection to the oldest and the youngest in a family. A family in which several brothers live together with their wives and children produces an extreme sense of security in the children, who move with all the members of the family freely, and when their parents go out there is no problem of engaging a baby-sitter; the children do not feel lonely, as they generally spend their time with their cousins, uncles or grandparents. As a matter of fact, in a big household children hardly ever cling to their parents. They get a balanced training as they are always watched by someone or the other and if they are spoilt by their parents, they certainly get disciplined by uncles or others and *vice versa*. Anyway, children grow up very well in a corporate household, without neurosis, angularities, or over-sensitiveness. For old people their original domestic life has an appearance of continuance, the old parents never lose touch with the affairs of the family, giving plenty of advice and guidance, sometimes offering even a different point of view, all of which gives them a feeling of having something to do.

Cohn has drawn an elaborate chart of a joint family with a lot of sociological jargon thrown in; he has also drawn a chart of the interior of a large village home to show how members are dispersed in a large household. It is interesting to watch all this, and the variety of questions asked by the boys on this complicated arrangement. It is very interesting to view myself as a specimen of this system. At the end of his lecture I am asked questions on my book *The Bachelor of Arts*, which has been just studied in the class as an example of Indian life. The boys fire questions at me and once again I am at a disadvantage, having read and written so much else after *The Bachelor of Arts*. As usual they ask, 'Is that scene on page such and such typical of an Indian family household?' 'Could Chandran's life be considered an example of joint-family living?' and so on.

The Chair

Yesterday Lyle Blair's long-distance call from East Lansing woke me to say that he was coming to see me today. Early this morning a phone-call again from him to say that he will not come, as the plane flights have been cancelled owing to bad weather. Dark, dismal day with a cold wind blowing. After breakfast ventured out for a walk. Saw a barber's shop on the way and walked in, with slight misgivings as I remembered the following story told by Balaraman of New York. An Indian artist on a travel assignment from India happened to be in Chicago and went to a barber's shop for a haircut. The barber refused to admit him owing to his colour. The man was so demoralized by it that he returned to New York and shut himself in his room, not having the confidence to show himself outside again. Balaraman had to visit him each day and persuade him to venture out as he feared that the artist was going to starve and die in his room—ultimately the man had to cancel all his plans for a study-tour and return home. But this Chicago barber welcomed me. 'Salon' same as ours, only the pictures hanging on the wall were less garish. The barber wore a snow-white apron and blue trousers, and ran an electric-clipper over one's scalp. He turned the chair away from the mirror while cutting the hair—sensible arrangement as it saved the contemplation for a prolonged period of one's head in a composite frame with the barber's. When he felt that you were entitled to have a glimpse of yourself in the mirror, he flicked the seat around asking: 'Is it all right?' Before you might study yourself too well, he turned it away again. After a few slight touches with scissors he held up a hand mirror for a second, too close to your eyes, and you saw yourself blurred.

'Awful weather, isn't it?' I said to make conversation.

He shook his head, 'The temperature is going down if anything, too cold—it ought not to be so at this time of the year, surely.'

'I had my last haircut in Bombay,' I said to impress him.

'That was a long way back for a haircut, sir,' he said. He was interested to know that I would be going to California.

'You are going to a fine place, let me tell you,' he said. As usual in all strata of society, California spells magic. Meanwhile the other barber who had been listening to the radio, said, 'Fifty thousand persons to have Thanksgiving dinner—with turkey and everything. Who pays for it? The taxpayer,' he said with a profound, disturbing civic conscience. He explained to me how and why these things happened, and what and who were at the back of all that show. After the haircut was over, a little flick off here and there, and a run of the comb on the hair (no lotion and dressing as in our country, unless perhaps you asked for it). When I got up, my barber went to the cash machine and said without facing me, 'That'd be two dollars twenty, today, sir . . . because,' he felt a little apologetic, 'it's Thanksgiving tomorrow.' Everything was now hitched to Thanksgiving. Ahead, back, and on the day itself, Thanksgiving Day seemed to loom large. The charges as printed on the wall were only 1.75. He had raised it by 25 cents and added another twenty to it. I paid up with a look of

casual ease and cheerfulness, without any betrayal of shock, feeling
that my barber in India would not earn it from me for a whole year's
attention to my head.

Visited the museum, and started back for my room. The barber
waved to me from his seat when I passed his shop again. Evidently
the extra forty-five cents had cemented a friendship between us.

*

Night: dinner with Shils. I am moved by his solicitous hospitality. He
prepares my dinner with his own hands; he lays the table, serves,
changes plates, and is constantly moving in and out. He is a complete
host. I protest against the extraordinary trouble he is taking but he
brushes aside my protest. 'I enjoy doing this for you,' he says.

After dinner adjourn to his study where books cover the walls
and rise to the ceiling. He is a man of varied studies, knowledge and
incisive observations—it is engrossing to hear him talk:
personalities, politics, and books.

As we sit there lost in conversation, we hear the thud of a falling
object in the next room, followed by a scream. Find that his child has
rolled off his bed in sleep and fallen down. I feel unhappy. Perhaps I
am indirectly responsible for this mishap: normally perhaps Shils
and his wife would have retired with the child and prevented its fall.
Shils looks anxious, still makes an effort not to leave a guest alone. I
take my leave, being the only thing I could do to help him. He is good
enough to say: 'Don't go, he'll be all right,' though his face is full of
anxiety. While giving me my coat, he notices that it is light. He
fetches his own heavy coat and wraps it around my shoulders,
remarking, 'Should you catch a cold, of all places, in Chicago?' and
sees me off. Later I was relieved to learn that the child continued his
sleep unmindful of the fall and woke up quite normally in the
morning.

*

Thanksgiving Day. Awakened by the telephone call from the

manager's desk.

'Breakfast being served, sir, and will close in a few minutes. If you are coming down I can tell them to wait for ten minutes.'

'Thanks, time please? . . .'

'Nine-twenty . . .'

'I'll come down in a second.' I jump out of my bed, hurriedly wash and dress up, and go down to breakfast. Thanksgiving drives everyone away, and depletes the town of all its useful men and women.

Chandran of US

I know that all the restaurants close today at seven. But still attempt to go out to try my luck, protected with ear-muffs (which always make me feel silly) and Shil's greatcoat, dreading the cold outside. But the young man at the desk comes to my rescue. He opens the store and brings me a tray of food in my room, although he confesses that he is not sure if he has the authority to open the store. However, it saves me from starvation or the alternative of searching for an open restaurant and getting frozen in the process.

After dinner go down for a chat with the young man. His name is Montague something. He feels Montague rather Shakespearean and unlucky in romance. His girl is in California. They love each other but still have not decided whether they should marry. He is preparing for a diploma in 'Fine Arts' but also works part-time at the hotel desk. Hopes ultimately to make enough money to take a trip to California. He has not decided what he should do for a career—he alternates between various proposals and possibilities; he is the American version of Chandran of my *Bachelor of Arts*. He is thrilled to hear that I shall be visiting at Palo Alto—where his sweetheart is studying.

'I don't know, I don't know, what we are waiting for,' he says. He adds, 'After I marry, I shall also become a vegetarian like you, because I think it'll save us a lot of money. You look OK without eating meat. Why should I also not try? In any case, after I'm married, I may not afford to pay for meat. Another thing—I once saw a chicken killed in our kitchen and never got over the shock. I have no right to eat something which I can't see killed.'

On Thanksgiving seventy (or 700) million turkeys are consumed in the state—on this day the general paralysis of public life is thorough—no letters delivered at all! No shop, no bank, nothing doing, 'no, nothing' (to quote a Los Angeles downtown hotel clerk). This is a 'legal' holiday, which means it is a complete one. Friday, that's tomorrow, is going to be a holiday without much legal mention, I'm sure, because it's wedged in between Saturday and today.

At the Zoo

S—, who teaches in the University, with his brother and all the members of the family, called at my hotel at 10 a.m. in order to take me to the zoo. It was a very considerate act on his part, considering the fact that the car was full of the members of his family who had come for Thanksgiving. He took me to the zoo, stopping at the Chicago Bank for my sake, where I sent off a remittance home. We drove through the snow: glorious white everywhere. Driving was difficult. At the zoo it was impossible for me to move about—the temperature was probably 20° all through and the cold was intense; my toes were numb inside the shoes, my nose felt like a wood-chip, losing its sensitivity. Everyone expected with a lot of thrill tonight's temperature to go down to 5°! The zoo was very much like other zoos, with miserable animals in heated chambers—the monkeys, elephants and tigers seemed resigned like those under a life sentence. I was impressed with the gorillas I saw. S— had a habit like zoo visitors all the world over, of making animal noises on his side of the cage, and disturbing the dignity of all those reposeful animals. At the conservatory their wonderment at the sight of mostly yellow chrysanthemums surprised me. Lunched with them at a restaurant across the road on spaghetti and tomato. Very soon I got tired of the zoo, and felt convinced that I had messed up another day. On the way back Mrs S— insisted upon being driven through a certain road and in front of some houses, where she had spent her childhood. She became very sentimental in this district and narrated anecdotes of how she used to go up such and such a distance which seemed so big then. At the zoo also she had been excitedly pointing at various objects, a Viking ship (1000 AD) which she used to admire as a child, a water fountain where she used to stand on a slab of stone to reach the spout. 'Oh, how high up it seemed to be then!' All of which was appreciated and approved with screaming giggles by S—'s sister. I fear that gentle S— found all this reminiscing a little tedious and embarrassing. Reminiscing might not always be a suitable occupation, it should be something personal, like one's bank balance. It may not thrill everyone to see a house where one was born or bred, unless the person happened to be a Shakespeare or Keats. There were other fallacies too in this attitude: Mrs S— was not really removed far enough to reminisce and feel sentimental either in time or space. She was recollecting something that happened less than five and not seventy years ago. And the place was only a couple of miles from where she now lived: someone even asked why she didn't think of coming up here all these days to indulge in reminiscences, instead of waiting for our company. I realized soon that I was no longer fit for company, and when S— suggested that I might go with them and see slides projected in his house, after tea, I politely explained I'd like to go back to my room and write.

Overload

When I reached Chamu's room in the hotel, his wife, Rukka, cried through the bathroom door, 'So you have come! Don't go away. I must talk to you.' I liked the mystery and menace of her tone. The moment she was ready to meet me she said with considerable warmth, 'Did you want to work off a grudge against us by mentioning our name to Mr— of Mysore before leaving? A nice situation you created for us after you left!' I understood what she meant. On the eve of my leaving Mysore, with a dozen things to do by way of getting my papers and baggage in order, a man locally employed in a scientific institution clamoured to meet me although I repeatedly sent word that I was too busy. He said he wanted only a few minutes with me, that he would very much like to say goodbye to his favourite author. No author is so hardened that he cannot be won by such an approach, and so I found for him a quarter of an hour on the day of my departure. I settled him in my study, offered him a cup of coffee as usual, and he told me for exactly the space of five minutes how much he admired my Sunday *Hindu* articles (which anyone may talk about even without reading them); and then mentioned his real business with me. He had his daughter and son-in-law studying in a university in New York State; he wanted me to carry a hamper of condiments, chilli powder and spices for them. He assured me that the whole thing could not weigh more than a pound, but I excused myself all the same, being an air passenger, explaining that if I had space for another pound I should probably take a woollen sweater or some such thing. He looked as if I had refused to carry some life-saving drug to one in dire need. And so I said (this is where Chamu comes into the story), 'If it is so urgent why don't you try and send it through Dr M.N. Srinivas, who is coming to the States by boat?'

The man brightened up immediately and said, 'Oh, I know that family so well. His brother was my classmate. His aunt was—was good to us when we were in Kolar, his cousin has married my nephew,' and so on and so forth. He found so many approaches to Srinivas that I felt at the rate of a pound per bond of kinship, he could ask Srinivas to carry a whole shipload of sweets and spices. The next part of the story is best presented through Chamu.

'That man got at me through my brother with whom he renewed his acquaintance. He had been a cricket player once upon a time and you know how my brother melts at the sight of an old cricketer. I told him to send his package along next day. Next day, when I returned home at night, I found the passage of our home choking with a wooden chest, the sort of thing the thirteen pirates sat on, a burlap sack, apparently filled with coconut, a smaller trunk containing sweets, judging from the swarm of ants, a basket containing possibly brinjals and cucumbers, and three more nondescript bundles. I had come home at midnight from a farewell dinner, and the sight of this luggage upset me. I summoned the man next morning and lectured him and said that unless he reduced the bulk of his gift to his son-in-law by seventy per cent, I would leave it behind. He again started off on how his cousin was married to our nephew, how devoted he was to my cricket-loving brother, how he had watched my Oxford career with pride and satisfaction, but I was adamant. He had to take them away. Later in the day they were ready in the passage again, for me. All that he had done was to substitute a steel trunk for the old pirate's chest, the other articles remained unchanged. It was too late to do anything about it now. You may imagine our plight as we lugged all this around, the trouble we had at Bangalore, Bombay, Southampton, London, Manchester, every port, custom, and railway station, porter's tips, vigilance, counting and recounting, in addition to the problem of our own baggage. This trip was completely ruined for us thanks to your introduction, and by the time we arrived at the New York port our patience was at an end; just when we were hoping to be rid of the whole thing we found that the man's son-in-law had not arrived to collect his baggage as promised. The port was in the throes of a dock strike. I had to spend eight hours trying to get help to move the goods to my hotel. Finally I had to dump them in the hotel corridor because they were too unwieldy and large for any normal check room. I wrote to his son-in-law, telegraphed, and finally called him on the telephone, because I was leaving New York but still no one turned up. I waited as long as I could and finally left the goods in the hotel corridor and came away. I don't know or care what happened to them . . . I have only to thank you for all these travails.

Opiated Cocoon

Picked up by Milton at eleven—lunch with sociologists at Faculty Club. After lunch visit Chicago Museum of Art in the company of some friends, where there is the added attraction of a Sullivan architectural exhibition, mainly photographs of various Chicago and New York buildings.

Sullivan's specialities, such as an arch, a railing, a bracket, a grill, a floral design or filigree on an elevator door, are highlighted. These are viewed as exciting flights of architectural imagination and of daring originality, but do not leave me speechless with wonder, probably because of the odious but inevitable comparison with similar specimens in India in stone and metal which one sees in the ancient temples, and which make these look just casual. But I suppose it is not right that I should see them in a mood of comparison; my aim should be an 'absolute' viewing, rather to know what it means to those for whom it's meant. One notices in this country a continual effort to 'build up' tradition in architecture as in other matters—although the tradition may stretch only to fifty years rather than five hundred, and this exhibition is of value from this angle. The conception and execution of skyscrapers are a daring adventure (here again remember the immense towers of South Indian temples), and Sullivan's work shows sober development in contrast to the eccentric and outrageous efforts of Frank Lloyd Wright. (Possibly Frank Lloyd Wright wants to outdo everyone and himself with his recent promise of a one-mile high skyscraper in Chicago). Quotations from Sullivan expressing his views and aspirations show a lot of feeling for his work, but sometimes sound naïve. My own comments on all this may be out of place, since I know nothing about architecture, and dare to pronounce them here only because this is my own personal diary.

The whole museum is too big. Extensive collection of paintings, which require a day-a-room technique of inspection. I could see only a portion of the great collection, for want of time and also because I was already afflicted with 'museum knees'. But was thrilled by the large landscapes by Innes, which are captivating. The modernist collection at the end of the section was exasperating, except one piece entitled 'Rock', which with its glowing colours and exaggerated expressions conveyed some dynamic point of view. Particularly baffling were a splash of pigments on a very large canvas, entitled 'The Grated Rainbow', which considering the criss-cross of strands might also have been called, with equal logic, 'The nightmare of an opiated cocoon'. But logic is out of place in this particular gallery, as my friend who brought me here, explained.

'We must not view these with any preconceived set of notions, expectations or habitual attitude of mind.' There was a 'wire sculpture' entitled 'Street Car', which might logically be also named, 'Balloon Hangers', and another very elaborate, tall one called 'Family Tree', which started with something like a lobster at the base, and ended with an assemblage of television aerials; it seemed to symbolize (this wretched orthodox habit of mind!) the development of amusement from crab-catching to television, or it might have also meant with equal reason skeletons in the cupboard or the need for more hat-stands and coat-hangers in a growing family.

*

At the Quadrangle, Milton Singer comes down to collect us and our baggage at noon. Then a drive to Redfield's home thirty miles away, through heavy snow-covered roads, and flurry-curtained air. See a great deal of Chicago on the way. Heavy flurry drifting down like winged ants after a rain and covering the road. Very cold and dim.

Redfield's ancient cottage set in a remote site full of trees, now bare and snow-covered—is at the point of the river where the Red Indians crossed into this part of the country in their westward passage, and the grave of a chief is said to be in the compound, left untouched, although once inadvertently dug up in the days of Redfield's father and covered over again. Mr and Mrs Redfield civilized and warm. Their household breathes the utmost charm. Nothing seems to be out of tune here—the mellow Redfields, the timber-beamed cottage, the antique furniture, the reminiscential touches of India in the shape of little bronze pieces on the mantle. Through the window frames the snow-covered woods have an unreal postcard picturesqueness. A couple of robins perch outside the window in the bird-shelter, which we can view closely through the glass pane from our side. Abundant conversation, abundant lunch, extreme care being taken not to outrage the vegetarians in the slightest manner—an admirable experience although I am constantly harassed by the thought that we might perhaps get snow-bound, seeing how thick it was falling. We bid farewell to the

Redfields at four-thirty. Singer drives us back to Chicago, difficult driving on snow-covered, slippery roads.

At six take leave of Singer and his wife at Chicago Union Station. Before parting, Singer slips over my shoulder a camera case. It looks imposing in its leather case. 'Though it looks stylish like a Leica or Rolliflex, it's only a box camera. Try to take pictures with it. If you graduate from the box you may go up to costlier ones,' he says. I don't like to be burdened with such contraptions, but he won't hear of it. He insists on proselytizing me to photography.

WESTWARD BOUND

On the (rail)road to San Francisco, with Chamu and his wife in another compartment, four doors off. Life in train for the next forty hours. Food in the train, bath in the train, and neighbourly visits to and from Chamu, with many occasions to narrate my new story, and discuss it with him. It is so comfortable that I enjoy having an illusion of being a permanent dweller here, and so arrange my little possessions around on that basis. Find a comradeship with all and sundry—including the very fat, crew-cut teenager, always tottering with drink. He is a nuisance, as he pushes the door of every compartment in the corridor and peeps in, much to the consternation of Mrs Chamu.

Our life is punctuated by movements to and from the dining car at various intervals—pushing and pulling the heavy doors all along the vestibule. Our biceps are greatly strained. Chamu and I have divided the labour, each doing it one-way. We march along, as everyone in the lounge stares at Rukka's colourful sari with open-mouthed wonder. We notice, however, a red-haired girl and two others being exceptions, who never look up, maintaining a concentrated gaze on their beerglass, all day. The steward is proud of being able to give us rice and buttermilk, and watches over us, as Rukka produces from her hand-bag South Indian condiments and spice-powder to help us through our meals. We form such a close community (although lasting only forty hours) that even the drunken teenager begins to say, 'Good morning,' 'How do you do?'

and 'Excuse me,' every time we pass.

I plan to do some writing, but the hours pass unnoticed. I cannot take my eyes off the window where grand mountain scenery passes. I think we are passing through an elevation of six thousand feet, farms and towns at night, the beacons on hill-tops look mysterious; wayside towns with their streets, shop-windows, and above all the used-car lots, brilliantly lit all night although the population is fast asleep, and the lights of passing lorries and automobiles on the highway. At some small hour of the night we pass Reno—the haven of divorcees. I fancy I see the sign 'Court' on a building. I cannot help craning my neck to watch if any couple is getting down the steps and parting on the road in silence and tears. But it is an hour at which I suppose, even the turbulence in a divorcee's bosom is lulled into sleep.

Berkeley

Tuesday. Arrive Berkeley. We decide to get down here rather than go up to San Francisco. We climb down by means of a step-ladder. Professor David Mandelbaum and his wife are there to receive Chamu and wife and take us to a hotel. I have a feeling of being an intruder, the real expected guest being Chamu. I have got down here because Chamu is here, otherwise I should have gone to San Francisco and then on to Palo Alto which was really my original destination. But I never get there.

I think Chamu is the luckiest house-hunter in the world. Over lunch at Mandelbaum's he was suggested a house at Albany, a suburb of Berkeley. After lunch David went upstairs to his study and Ruth drove us to Albany—1050, Peralta Avenue (the name attracted us). This was practically to be my second home in Berkeley for the next two months. Rukka saw the house, liked it, Chamu endorsed her view even without looking at the house, on hearsay, and there they were ready to move in as soon as the lady of the house who had recently lost her husband and was going to live with her daughter in New York was able to move her things out. I never saw anyone make such a quick decision about a house. Chamu is a philosopher and a logician, a man who can specify what he wants. I sometimes envy him his clearheadedness and luck. What a contrast to my own management of my affairs. Having decided to stay away at Berkeley, I was next involved in hunting for a flat or apartment for myself. With Ed Harper's help I am engaged for the next couple of days in house-hunting, which Berkelians assure me is an exciting, unrewarding occupation. I find an apartment which is available for sixty dollars a month, which figure appeals to me instead of the seven dollars a day for a hotel room. But this apartment is too big, empty, and unfurnished, and I shall probably be obliged to spend all my time like a newly-wed equipping the pantry and bedroom and the front room. I shall have to be thinking all night about sheets and pots and pans, not to speak of grocery, which in any case I shall have to bother about. The heating primitive: you'll have to open a gawky apparatus and apply a match, and when it goes off apply it again and so forth. I never knew that a bare house could look so terrifying and discouraging—all due to its vast emptiness. To add to the emptiness, someone, a weird-looking woman, at the basement, a woman with seven or seventeen (as they seem) children, all in one room, a creaky staircase going up and up, full of thuds. The only reason that such a huge apartment is coming to me for sixty dollars is that the county council has marked it for demolition. Very wise of them. There is a beautiful elm tree in front of the house, which is a point in its favour. There is a spring settee in a landing on which Harper and I settle down to consider the matter. It's a crucial point; if I'm keen on an apartment, this is my opportunity. I shall not regret later that I didn't take it when it came. On the contrary we run over mentally all the things that one would have to do to make it habitable. Out of it a story develops. A helpless man like Dr A— (an Indian anthropologist) arrives at Berkeley on some important research assignment. He inherits this apartment, and starves for a day or two before he can make a cup of coffee for himself, and a friend like Ed Harper helps him and fills the house with labour-saving gadgets. Dr A— spends his time learning the technique of house running with American gadgets and in tidying up the place. At the end of a month he finds he has not read a line nor written one—no time. He has all along been trying unsuccessfully to learn how to operate a can-opener, how to turn off the gas, and how to dish-wash. He is helpless, incompetent and unpractical—until a girl arrives on the scene who is writing a thesis on his work and wants his help to finish her thesis. She starts running his household for him and complications arise.

'How old is she?'

'Twenty-six.'

'How about looks?'

'Charming.'

'Blonde or . . .?'

'Of course, blonde.'

After this refreshing dream we go out, and Harper drives me to another house—seventy-five dollars a month; which I reject for the opposite set of reasons. It's too full of gadgets and articles and equipment, which I shall be responsible for, the owner going away for a time. If I take this house, I fear, I shall become a caretaker, a sort of my man Annamalai (who guards my Yadavagiri home for thirty-five rupees a month), with the difference that I should have to pay rent in addition to watching the house.

We come to the conclusion that it's no good deciding on a house in a hurry, and walk back to where Ed has parked his car. In all this preoccupation with fact and fiction, he seems to have forgotten the parking restriction, and when we reach the car, a long envelope is stuck at the windscreen—he has a police check, which means probably five dollars fine. 'I generally pay ten dollars a month in fines,' he confesses.

Today I create an unprecedented confusion for myself by checking out of my hotel at 2 p.m. I had all my baggage taken down to the lobby, and within half an hour came back to the hotel to ask for my room again. It happened thus. After deciding against the ramshackle house, with Ed Harper's concurrence, I had decided to move to an apartment on Haste (sixty dollars a month). But at the last moment Rukka mentioned that David Mandelbaum did not quite approve of my taking a room there. When she said this, there flashed to my mind all kinds of defects in the apartment, which I had already noticed through a corner of my eye—its carpets were frayed, its towels were not fresh and were brought in by the hotel proprietrix herself, who also registered at the desk; there were cracks in the wall of my room, the place was full of old people moping in the lounge, the elevator was rattling and grill-ridden, and above all, the address was Haste and Telegraph, which sounded impossible, as I feared I might have nightmares of 'Haste makes waste' or people might address my letters 'Post and Telegraph'. And so I went back to tell them I would not take the room and came back to my hotel, much to the astonishment of my hotel manager.

Evening dinner at an Indian restaurant in San Francisco, our host being Ed Harper. Its elaborate and self-consciously planned Indian atmosphere, dim light, long coats, bogus Indian tunes out of gramophones hidden in the arras, more bogus bric-a-brac are deliberate, but I suppose, commercially successful. Chappati and Indian curry are genuine and are not bogus. A waitress clad in a sari, an usher in a long coat buttoned to the neck, create an Indian atmosphere, which seems to appeal to San Franciscans as I find all tables booked, and women dressed in caps and gowns, which outdo Fifth Avenue style, sit with an air of facing an impending adventure, while reading the menu card, and utter little cries of 'delicious, delicious', when they sample a curry. The story of Dr A— goes forward in this setting. He decides to find a suitable bridegroom for the blonde—taking a fatherly interest in her (after taking time to realize that he is too much her senior and has a wife and children at home). Being a busybody and match-maker in his own country, he has affection for John, a scholarly bachelor, and makes it his business in life to 'arrange' a marriage between the two; he casts their horoscopes, compares to see if the stars match; all in correct Indian style; and this imports into United States the first 'arranged' marriage! A promising theme, which I must take up immediately after *The Guide* is written. After dinner one half of the party returns to Berkeley, while I stay back with John and others to see a little more of San Francisco. John takes us to a Bohemian place, where brandy served with coffee is a speciality. There are suggestive pictures everywhere on the walls, lewd sayings in glittering letters—framed gaudily; deliberate joviality, and girls who affect to be intoxicated and throw themselves on all and sundry.

*

John is a linguistic scholar, teaching Hindi in Berkeley, who sought me out a couple of days before at my hotel, offered to drive me around and show me the places of interest. He had spent some years in India and explained:

'When I was in Mysore, Mr— was so hospitable that I like to do anything I can for anyone from Mysore.' He is a gentle, sensitive, civilized and cheerful being. He drove me to San Francisco, over the Golden Gate Bridge at sunset, initiated me into the mysteries of photography with my box camera; and helped me to de-sensitize my first spool of negatives. With my camera he first took a picture of me standing below the Golden Gate Bridge, forgot to turn the film, then handed me the camera and allowed me to take a picture of him under the Golden Gate Bridge on the same film; when it was later developed I saw on the negative two Golden Gate Bridges with a double-headed, four-armed monster standing under it—my first photographic effort. He gave me a supper of pizza at an Italian restaurant, took me to visit Biligiri, who gave me scented betel-nut to chew and suddenly proposed that we go to Oakland to see the haunts of Jack London.

The inn where Jack London wrote and drank himself to death is still there. It is a shack made out of an old boat, the entire floor sloping as in a ship's bar, and the state of cleanliness and furnishing remaining unchanged since the days of Jack London. The waiter is a genuine admirer of Jack London's writing. Beer is served in the bottle, and the man explains, 'It's anyway hygienic.' People drink straight out of the bottle as they do in a roadside soda-shop in Madras, tilting back their heads. Faded photographs of Jack London at various stages clutter the wall, and the waiter throws a torch-light on them while he lectures on Jack London's life and philosophy. He (the waiter) also mentions Raja Yoga, Gnana Yoga and the Bhagavad Gita. He confesses to being a book-lover, spending all his spare cash and time in reading. He is interested in Indian philosophy because Jack London was interested in it too. He quotes and explains the basis of various Jack London stories. I suggest that he become the narrator in a Hollywood picture on the life of Jack London, but he says that his boss secretly nurtures such an ambition himself and so his own chances are poor. When he learns that I'm an author, he abandons the other guests to another waiter and sits up with us. He notes down the names of my books and he sees us off at the door with a simple goodbye; although his routine statement to every outgoing couple would be, 'See you in the spring,' and after they say, 'Thanks,' he would add, 'if you get through the mattress.' Full of double, treble, and shocking meanings, but no one minds it. And he generally utters this lewd quip mechanically, without any zest, as if it were an awful duty cast upon him by his boss.

An Encounter

I loafed around San Francisco till 7 p.m. and returned to the Key Station, in order to catch a streetcar for Albany, where I was to dine with Chamu at 8.30.

I paid 45 cents and took a ticket. I asked at the barrier, 'Where do I get the car for Albany?'

'Albany?' said a man standing there. He pulled out a time-table from his pocket, and said, 'There is one leaving in five minutes. Go, go . . . go straight *down* those steps.' He hustled me so much that I didn't have the time even to say 'Thanks'. I was in a hurry. I went down and saw ahead, on the road, two coaches with passengers, ready to start. As I hurried on, wondering which of them I should take, two men standing at the foot of the stairs called me to stop, and asked, 'Where are you going?'

'Albany. If that is the bus . . .'

'Where is your ticket?' I held up my ticket. One of them snatched it, crumpled it into a pellet, and put it into his pocket. These men evidently liked to keep me at the San Francisco station. They were well-dressed, and looked like the presidents of a railroad or a college; one of them looked quite distinguished in his rimless glasses. I demanded an explanation for their arbitrary handling of my ticket, but they strolled away and disappeared into the shadows around a corner of this grim building. Not a soul in sight. It was past eight. I dashed back to the ticket office and asked for another ticket of the woman (I purposely avoid the indiscriminate American usage 'girl') at the window. She said, 'You took one now!'

'Yes, but I need another one for a souvenir,' I said. She said, 'You don't get the next bus until nine o'five.'

'Is it a bus or a coach or a train or a streetcar? What is the vehicle one rides in for Albany?' I asked.

'Why?'

'Each time I hear it differently.'

'I don't know, ask there,' she said out of habit and went back to her work.

I went round the station asking for directions. No one was precise. It was surprising how little anyone here cared to know the whereabouts of Albany, only half an hour's ride away. They behaved as if they were being consulted over some hazardous expedition beyond uncharted seas; while the fact remained as any citizen of Berkeley or Albany will confirm, 'F' trains and 'E' trains shuttling between Berkeley and San Francisco wailed and hooted all night, keeping people awake.

The station was getting more and more deserted and I didn't want to miss a possible bus or streetcar that might start from some unsuspected corner of it. So I went round looking for a conveyance. At a particularly deserted corner, I was stopped by the two men who had misappropriated my first ticket. They blocked my way. I tucked away my new ticket securely into an inner pocket. I was not going to give it up again. One of them grabbed the collar of my jacket and said, 'Let us talk.' The other moved off a few yards, craning his neck and keeping a general look-out. The nearer man said, 'Don't start trouble, but listen.' He thrust his fist to my eyes and said, 'I could crack your jaw, and knock you down. You know what I mean?' Certainly, the meaning was crystal clear. I knew at a glance that he could easily achieve his object. It frightened me. In a moment flashed across my mind a versatile, comprehensive news-headline,

'Remnants of Indian novelist found near Key Station. Consulate officials concerned—'. I realized these were men of action.

'What do you want?' I asked simply.

The one on sentry duty muttered something in the local dialect. The collar-gripper took his hand to his hip pocket. I thought he was going to pull out a pistol, but he drew out a gold watch with a gorgeous gold band. He flourished it before me and said, 'How do you like it?'

'Don't hold it so close to my eyes. I can't see what it is. Take it back.' Yes, it was a nice, tiny watch. He read my thoughts and said, 'I'm not a bum, but a respectable member of the merchant marines. I'm on a holiday and have been gambling. I want money. Take this.'

It was of course an extraordinary method of promoting watch sales, but I had to pretend that I saw nothing odd in it. He said in a kind of through-the-teeth hiss, 'I don't like trouble, that's all. See what I mean?' His hand still held the collar of my jacket, and the watch was sunk within his enormous fist. It was very frightening. The lub-dub of my heart could be heard over other city noises. I'm not exactly a cowardly sort, but I am a realist. When I encountered a fist of that size I could calculate its striking force to the nearest poundal. I have always weighed 140 pounds, whatever I did, whether I starved or overate or vegetated or travelled hectically. My weight never varied. I felt, in my fevered state, that the man before me must weigh as much between his fist and shoulder. No police in sight. The entire force seemed to have been drawn away to meet a graver emergency elsewhere. I looked casual, as if it were a part of my day's routine, as if someone were always turning up doing this sort of thing to me every two hours. I tried to assume the look of a seasoned receiver of ladies' watches. The whole scene filled me with such a feeling of ludicrous staginess that I suddenly burst out laughing. The man looked puzzled and annoyed.

'You think it funny?' he asked.

'S-u-r-e,' I said in the most approved drawn-out manner, dreading that my tactics might misfire. He gave my jacket a tug. I said curtly, 'I hate to have my jacket pulled. I hate anyone hanging on to my jacket. It shows an infantile mind and mother-fixation.'

'You are a professor, aren't you?' he said sneeringly.

I asked, 'Whose is that watch?'

'My own. I would not be selling it otherwise.'

The other man turned round to say, 'Of course it is of course his. Should you ask?'

'I don't believe it,' I said. 'Maybe you are a guy with a slender-enough wrist to wear that strap. Let me see how you manage to put it on! Seems to me it's a lady's watch.' At this he repeated his threat about my jaw. I had by now got used to hearing it; and almost said that if he broke one jaw, another was sure to grow in its place. I still marvel that he didn't hit me. I took off my spectacles as a defence preparation. I didn't want splinters in my eyes. He ran his hand over the entire surface of my person, trying to locate my purse. Ignoring his action I repeated emphatically, 'It's a lady's watch.'

'It is Pat's,' said his friend.

'Who is Pat?'

'His wife,' he said.

'What does she do now to know the time?' I asked.

'I got her another one,' he said. 'That's why I want to sell it.'

'Does she know about it?' I asked.

'Sure. Peggy will do anything to help me.'

'Peggy?' I asked. 'Who is she and how does she get on with Pat?'

'What are you talking about?' he growled. We had now arrived at a level of conversational ease which must have looked like the meeting of three old school-ties around the corner. The only unsavoury element in it, if one peered closely enough, was that he still had his fingers firmly on my collar. He assumed a menacing tone suddenly, and asked, 'So you don't appreciate our help?'

'Thanks a lot, I don't. You are really mixed up. Your wife, if you have one, must be either Pat or Peggy, not both, unless you are a bigamist who lets two wives manage with a single watch, or am I going to hear about Sally and Jane too? Are you a bigamist or a polygamist? Are such things allowed in this country?'

'Oh, stop that, you talk too much; that's what's wrong with you. Jack made a slip, that's all,' the man said with a touch of sadness.

'What's your time now?' I asked. 'I've a dinner engagement at

Albany—' He looked at his own watch. He applied it to his ear and cried, 'The damned thing has stopped.'

'No wonder,' I said. 'All that clenching and flourishing of fist would reduce any watch to pieces,' I said. 'Why don't you look at the cute one in your pocket, Peggy's, is it?' He pulled out the little watch, peered at its face and said, 'Can't see anything in this blasted place.'

'Why don't we all adjourn to a better-lit place?' I suggested.

'And have a drink, eh?' he said.

After Jack had had his laugh at the joke, the other one said, 'Professor, you are a good guy; learn to use an opportunity. You don't appreciate our help. Do you know what this watch actually costs?'

'Do you?' I asked.

He paused to think up a reply. His friend, Jack, turned round to say, 'It cost him one hundred forty dollars,' without taking his eyes off the corner.

'What's your offer?'

'Not even the twenty cents that I am left with now,' I said. 'I would not accept it even as a gift. You know why?'

'Why, Doctor?'

'I've no faith in watches. I never wear one; I've never had a watch in my life. Only recently, for the first time in my life, I bought a two-dollar alarm clock, because every morning I slept till twelve noon, and was in constant danger of missing trains and planes. So now I have a clock, which I strictly look at only once in a day; just to know whether I should get out of bed or continue to sleep.'

'How do you keep your appointments?' he asked.

'I never keep them. I should have been eating a dinner now at Albany. But where am I? What am I doing?'

'Now you know we want to help you.'

'I'll never buy a watch even if I miss all the dinners in the world,' I said emphatically.

'Perhaps you should take this to your girlfriend,' he said.

'No such luck. Never had one in my life,' I said. 'Even if I had one, I'd never inflict a watch on her. It's a misleading instrument. What's a watch-time? Nothing. You don't even know how to look at

Sally's or Pat's watch in your pocket. Your watch has stopped; I'm sure Jack's watch is showing some wild time of its own. It's a different hour now at New York; something else in Chicago; morning time in the other hemisphere, Greenwich Time, Summer Time, and God knows what else. What's the use of having an instrument which is always wrong by some other clock?' He looked overwhelmed by this onslaught. His fingers slackened on the collar of my jacket, and I took the opportunity to draw myself up proudly, turn, and briskly walk away, with my heart palpitating lest they should grab me back. I walked off fast.

I don't think I overcame them by my superior wit and escaped. I cannot claim any heroism on that score. I think they let me go because they must have felt that they had caught a bankrupt and a bore. Or it may be Jack espied the police somewhere and they let me go. Although I missed my dinner that night, I was glad to be back at my hotel with my bones intact; and as long as I stayed in Berkeley, I took care not to visit the San Francisco Key Station again.

Sunday Excursion

Half the Sunday spent in finding my way to Chamu's house at Peralta Avenue in Albany. In this process came across a number of places with picturesque names, such as Euclid, Scenic, Cedar, Spruce, Sonoma, Pomona, Carmel. Felt tired. Finally managed to reach Albany. Mrs Chamu was good enough to keep rice and curry and curd for me. Evening, John came down to take me for the Diwali celebrations at the International House. I resisted going there at first—afraid of the air of fraternity. But yielded for want of a better occupation. A number of dances—sketchy and extremely amateurish. The usual ingredients of Indian cultural fare were there: wick lights, vague, slow, plaintive and drawn-out music, women clad in saris going round each other, gently swaying their arms, interspersed with definitely crude stuff such as Hindi film-hits played on the harmonica by two youths (which seemed to appeal to the audience more than anything else), phoney folk-songs in languages nobody knows, and all the distance from the home country could not excuse the performance, considering the big, eager crowd that had turned up. Speech by the Indian Consul. The air was so heavily, deliberately Indian that I felt oppressed and persuaded John to come out. An American standing in the corridor, wearing a South Indian dhoti, jibba and khaddar cap (style of any waiter in a restaurant in South India)—and pointedly refused to shake hands, when I stretched my hand, but performed a namaste, perhaps showing off his familiarity with India, where some foundation must have taken him to learn this trick. I don't know whether it's hypocrisy or ignorance that makes them do such things. Where is the point in mimicking a piece of Oriental courtesy when you perpetrate occidental bad manners by ignoring a proffered hand? We went to the campus bookstore for browsing—always a most desirable proposition.

*

At the bookstore John met a friend—a Dr Schurman, an expert in Chinese, Japanese and Arabic, who proposed that we adjourn for a drink somewhere. He drove downtown in search of 'Lemon and Cat' or some such well-known 'quiet' pub. It was as usual dim-lit, 'atmosphere-ridden', but so full that we had to get out again and search for another place; finally he drove us to his flat, where he could provide us fruit juice and beer. I was impressed with this man's knowledge of Eastern languages. For light reading he read Chinese literature in the original, and Greek and Hebrew when he wanted to bite into harder stuff. Being a woeful failure at learning languages, not knowing any except Tamil and English, I was definitely impressed and wanted to proclaim that he should be the grand moderator at the Tower of Babel. We dispersed at midnight.

Picked up by John at noon, and then on to Chamu's for a South Indian lunch. Chamu, the saviour! After lunch, John drives us over the Berkeley Hills, Tilden National Park, Grizzly Peak, and Redwood forests, till sunset—all through wonderful mountain scenery.

I was getting obsessed with the thought that I was not putting my camera to good use. So brought it out today and exposed a few rolls—delicately framing each picture around huge elms and redwoods, with Chamu, wife and John in each spot. I took so much time to compose each picture that the others became impatient. I begged them to stand still. But unfortunately I forgot to readjust the shutter from where John had set it for time exposure under the Golden Gate Bridge the other evening, and so no one turned up in recognizable shape when the films were later developed; thus lost a chance of immortalizing the magnificence of the scenery and company that we enjoyed that afternoon.

End of a Quest

Another day of house-hunting, having firmly decided to stay in Berkeley rather than at Palo Alto in order to write my novel. Scrutinizing of advertisements in *Berkeley Gazetteer,* following up hearsay accounts of apartments available; thanks to Ed Harper's help, visit the University housing centre, and tell one Mrs Keyhoc (I could not concentrate on business as my inner being clamoured to know if 'Keyhole' was being misspelt) that I almost belonged to the university faculties, before she could take an interest in the proceedings, and then she telephoned a number of places and gave me a list, very reminiscent of Roser of Anta in efficiency and thoroughness; she gave me the impression of running everyone down to earth. 'Here is a man who wants a room for writing, with kitchen facilities, private bath, prepared to pay etc, etc,' she poured forth into a telephone. Finally we march out with a list in our hands. My preference is for Albany, because of Chamu's proximity. In Albany we do go to a house owned by an old Japanese lady, who knows absolutely no English and who is feeding several noisy, scraggy dogs; the apartment upstairs is good, but without bed or blankets, to be provided by myself. Sixty dollars a month. I am delighted with the prospect and, as usual, almost promise her on an impulse that I'd take the flat and come and occupy it next day. Edward Harper drops me at Chamu's and goes away. After dinner Chamu's wife phones the news to Ruth Mandelbaum and they all come to the conclusion that it would be madness to pay sixty dollars for a bare apartment without bed or utensils, and they remind me that the apartment I declined the other day had everything for sixty and yet I wouldn't take it! And then the fundamental question: whether it is worth living in far-off Albany for Chamu's sake or in Berkeley with all the amenities around. I feel hopelessly lost. I already have a feeling that I am going to let the dog-loving Japanese lady alone. We sit discussing several prospects, but come to one conclusion—that I should quit my hotel as it takes away seven dollars a day, while I spend most of the day in the streets looking for food and shelter. I return to my seven-dollar hotel in a taxi, my mind full of problems. Get off at the bookstore. While browsing around the campus bookstore, I suddenly look up and notice Hotel Carlton staring me in the face, never having noticed its presence before. Walk in and find Kaplan, the manager, extremely courteous and full of helpful suggestions—he's willing to give me a room where I may use a hot-plate for cooking my food, daily room service, separate bed and study, ideal in every way, the perfect hotel for me. And it costs seventy-five dollars a month.

Check out of the seven-dollar-a-day hotel at two and check in at Carlton at five minutes past two next afternoon. That very night acquire an electric hot-plate, a saucepan, and rice, and vegetables, and venture to cook a dinner for myself. Profound relief that I don't have to face again the cafeteria carrot and tomato fare!

For the first time a settled place where I don't have to keep my possessions in a state of semi-packedness. I am able to plan my work better. I am enchanted with the place, everything is nearby: two cinemas, three or four groceries, and any number of other shops. I can walk down and buy whatever I may need and peep at the Campanille clock to see the time; its chime is enchanting.

Palo Alto

Mrs K— is good enough to drive me to Palo Alto, thirty miles away. Nice in every way, but for the restless presence of Joe, her five-year-old son who talks too much and often blames his mother for monopolizing all the talk and so they come to an agreement: Joe to shut up till such and such a place is reached, and his mother to shut up till they are in such and such a place. Joe to do the talking when we arrive on the bridge. You know how interminable San Francisco bridges can be, and Joe exercises his right of chatter and refuses to recognize that the bridge is past. A duel goes on between the mother and the son, and it is the mother who appeals for a truce each time; the result is that our conversation gets to be extremely jerky and incoherent, full of interruptions; add to it the strain of driving at sixty miles an hour, keeping an eye on the lane, watching the route. Children should recognize that elders generally have the right of way in conversation, and a little firmness in handling them will go a long way in avoiding conversational chaos. The lady confesses that she is no good for the strain of such a long drive, but had ventured out today because of a hope that she might talk to me on the way. But unfortunately this cannot be realized. Between the strain of watching out while driving, and keeping Joe satisfied, she has no chance of saying anything worthwhile, and when we arrive at Palo Alto she turns me over to Robert North and goes away for over an hour, out of a delicacy of feeling that she may perhaps seem intrusive while I confer with North.

I had mistakenly thought that Robert North would be upset over my choice of Berkeley instead of the original plan to stay at Palo Alto and that I might have to be apologetic, but he seemed relieved that I had settled at Berkeley. He announced, 'This is a place where you can't get a house or a hotel room.'

I feared he might want to hold me at Palo Alto at least for the evening, but he merely said, 'We must have lunch together, some afternoon. I'll find out about the time from one or two others and call you—' I could understand Mr North's preoccupied condition. In his study you couldn't flick a finger without knocking down a pile of books and papers. He was surrounded by a mountainous quantity of reference for writing (if my impression is right) a study of the political developments in the East. He looked overwhelmed by the amount of material he would have to wade through.

I could not say I cared very much for Palo Alto either. To me it was like selecting Srirangapatna for a prolonged vacation; and so when Mrs K— returned to drive me back to Berkeley, I was ready for her.

In all this, nearly a hundred miles drive up and down, one saw automobiles moving in a string at night, like an endless torch-light parade, up and down the Bay bridge, along several lanes, but there was not a single pedestrian to be seen anywhere, nor a dog, nor a cow, nor a tree. This gave it all a touch of grim, machine-ageness (one of H.G. Wells's nightmare visions). The pedestrian has been successfully liquidated on the freeway, which may be defined as the most mechanized patch on earth.

'Phoneme'

I find Biligiri most fascinating. A brilliant student of linguistics, always dreaming of his girl in Mysore. One who looks both rugged and sensitive at the same time. He gave us all a dinner at the Mexican restaurant, run by a Goanese who has married a Mexican woman—truly a marriage of culinary experts. The food was very Indian and very enjoyable. Only after the dinner my hosts could think of nothing more stirring than a lecture on phonetics by a visiting expert. I went along with them and took my seat in the hall.

As I listened I was appalled at the dryness of the subject of phonetics. The professor read a paper, suppressing a yawn all the time in the mumbling rapid manner of a nervous secretary reading an annual report. I didn't follow a word of what he said; I caught 'phoneme' or 'phoney' constantly. The audience sat through in dead stillness; in a state of morose resignation. The only sentence that came near to making any sense at all was some quip about making a synchronic approach to diachronic studies; which stirred the audience to a brief fit of polite laughter. I felt that I had wasted an evening in sitting through this baffling function: everyone pretended that the lecture had been too simple and elementary and not at all what they expected of such an eminent expert. Even if the men had really understood this lecture, what about their wives, who rallied round in good number and sat through as if it were an after-dinner entertainment?

Visit Biligiri. He has paid five dollars and bought a fancy notebook, gilt-edged and bound in real cowhide, with ivory pages. He takes it out of its case and shows me the poems he has written on its pages—an offering to his sweetheart. He reads me one of the poems in Kannada. It is entitled 'Neenu' ('you' in Kannada), and says 'In the thorny thicket that is my heart, appeared a rose that is "you" . . .' etc.

After dinner picked up by John to join a party on the hill at Ed Harper's. The view from the hill is beautiful: several times magnified view of Mysore from Chamundi at night. I find the party itself unbearable. Bunches of anthropologists, all talking simultaneously and no one listening in particular, drinking and filling the air with smoke.

At a cocktail party, men and women arrive who don't care for each other or for the function, hold glasses which they would rather throw away, sip drinks with an air of doing so under compulsion, say things which are inane, utter remarks which no one hears. Everyone shouts at the top of his voice, and contributes his mite to the general din; no one should stand apart and look out of the window. He must munch monkey-nuts, wash them down, and contribute to the babble, smoke, and confusion.

I looked about and saw Chamu engaged in an earnest conversation with a young professor, in the quiet seclusion of the fireplace. I approached them with a feeling of relief at finding someone to talk to; but they stood with their backs to the assembly and were engrossed in their own talk. I overheard Chamu say, 'Tell me, do the Australian aborigines correlate copulation with population?' I asked Chamu later why he should bother about the question. He said, 'Oh, anything to keep his mind engaged. Otherwise, he would have bothered me to explain the caste system in India.'

Nothing much to record, the same routine. I have got into the routine of writing—about one thousand five hundred to two thousand words a day anyhow. I have the whole picture ready in my mind, except some details here and there, and the only question is to put it in type. Some days, when I feel I have been wasting my time, I save my conscience by telling Kaplan at the desk, 'I am going to be very busy for the next few weeks trying to get on with my book.' A restatement of purpose is very helpful under these circumstances. Graham Greene liked the story when I narrated it to him in London. While I was hesitating whether to leave my hero alive or dead at the end of the story, Graham was definite that he should die. So I have on my hands the life of a man condemned to death before he is born and I have to plan my narrative to lead up to it. This becomes a major obsession with me. I think of elaborate calculations: a thousand words a day and by February first, I should complete the first draft. In order to facilitate my work I take a typewriter on hire, but after three days of tapping away it gets on my nerves, and I lounge on the sofa and write with my pen. Whatever the method my mind has no peace unless I have written at the end of the day nearly two thousand words. Between breakfast and lunch I manage five hundred words, and while the rice on the stove is cooking a couple of hundred and after lunch once again till six, with interruptions to read letters and reply to them, or to go out for a walk along the mountain path, or meet and talk to a friend.

Telephone call from Chamu to say that his neighbour, an elderly man who often used to invite him to watch the television, died suddenly of a heart-attack while shaving in the morning. Chamu and his wife terribly shaken. In the United States death sounds unreal. The man had said, 'How do you do?' from the road, as I was waiting for Chamu to open the door on the previous evening. Chamu's landlord had also died similarly three months ago. So a feeling of insecurity about Peralta Avenue itself.

With John and Biligiri, went to an Italian restaurant to eat pizza: but the atmosphere was spoilt by a debate between me and Biligiri—who was also a severe, uncompromising vegetarian like me, but who somehow protested against my statement to John that I was a vegetarian because I didn't like to kill for food. He asked whether we didn't kill the vegetable world for food, to which I said with some heat, that we don't generally uproot a tree for eating its fruit, which he hotly debated. He became very gloomy and remained silent for the rest of the day. (I fear he is very homesick and has had no letter from home.) After dinner they went to hear a lecture on linguistics, but John would not take me along, probably for fear that I might behave frivolously or utter loud, cynical remarks at the meeting.

More Joint than Food

Lunch with South East Asia Group—imposing name, actually consisting at the moment of John, Ed Harper, and one or two others.

Ed Harper, talking to someone, entered the lunch hall, at great speed with an air of one not knowing where he was going. They were preoccupied with the joint family. I heard them say, 'The joint family is . . .'

'No, I want to know its structural . . .'

'It is like this. The members—I mean the agnates—the whole thing is . . .'

'According to the original matrilineal scheme . . .' With all these idioms on their lips they approached the lunch table and took their seats. The subject was interrupted for a tenth of a second by a 'Hello' to me, as they suddenly remembered I was their guest. One of them leaned over to ask, 'Oh, here he is, let us ask him . . .' and they demanded: 'Can you define joint family?'

'Of course I can, being a member of one,' I began. 'You see it's like this, a father, mother, and sons, and then the sons and their families, all under the same roof . . .' Before I could warm up to my subject they lost interest. They turned away and were completely lost in their own talk. They kept gesticulating and talking all through the course, now and then pausing to draw a chart of joint-family organization on an imaginary sheet of paper on the table. There was someone on my right who made a few desultory observations on India—most men here had been to India and knew some aspect of it. With their preoccupation with the joint family, my lunch reduced itself to a small plate of fruit salad. Providing a lunch for me is a complicated business at any time, but it is rendered more difficult when my hosts become preoccupied with the evolution of Indian society. After they left, I went back to my room, cooked a lunch for

myself, and I could take a more generous view of the South East
Asian group after my rice and curd at four in the afternoon.

Versatile Bob

I must pause to say a few words here about a young man whom I
shall call Bob. I received a telephone call one night. 'This is Bob—of
the UCL. I want to interview you for our paper.'

'Which is your paper?'

He said something that I did not quite catch. I gave him an
appointment for next day, when there walked into my room a young
man biting a long piece of carrot. He had the usual dress and
deportment of a college student: crew-cut, pullover, some odd
trousers and a bundle of notebooks under his arm.

'I am doing features for our *Daily Californian*, and I want to
write a feature about you. I have written features about Christopher
Isherwood, Aldous Huxley, and Henry Miller, I drove down to Los
Angeles and saw them. Isherwood says that he writes only for his
own satisfaction and that he doesn't think of his public while
writing. Do you agree with his view?' I said something, and like the
reporter at Michigan, he searched for a paper in his pockets, found
one the size of a bus ticket, then vainly rummaged for a pencil, and
gave up the idea of jotting down anything. He asked, 'Is this your
first visit to this country? How do you like this country? What are
your impressions?' I answered something briefly and then asked
him, 'What made you come to me?' He had no ready answer for me.
He merely said, 'Mr Harper told me that you are a novelist from
India and so . . .'

I asked him how much he knew about my books. He knew
nothing but asked, 'Are your books available in English translation?'
I felt it would be a strain to launch on an auto-bibliography. I gently
turned the talk to other matters. I asked, 'What do you plan to do
after you leave college?'

He said, 'Well, I am hoping to become a journalist. I am a
feature-writer for our college paper, and they are very popular. I am
married. I have a little son, four months old. I and my wife live a sort

of joint-family life with my aunt, who has a big house.' At the end of the interview (mutual) he said, 'I have a car, and I would like to drive you to San Francisco, if you wish to look round there . . .'

'Why should you take the trouble?'

'I enjoy driving people . . . also if you would like to see Henry Miller I could drive you to Big Sur . . . only a hundred miles away. Shall I write to him and fix an appointment? He was very kind to me.' When he was leaving I asked him, 'How will you write the feature, I didn't see you note down anything?' He said that he had a good memory and that he could write this interview out of his head; he also requested me to give him my candid opinion of it when it appeared at the end of the week, offered to send me cuttings of his other published features and confessed at the end, 'I want to write a novel during the vacation next year.' That was the last I saw of him as a feature writer and journalist. Next I met him a fortnight later outside the grocery on the Telegraph. He had as usual a bundle of class-books under his arm, and was munching peanuts. (He must be one of the steadiest customers for the picturesque ice-cream vendor who stations himself at the Sather Gate 10 a.m. to 5 p.m. every day, crying 'Crunchie-munchies, yes come on, buy 'em, eat 'em, them's good for you'.) Bob's mouth was full as he tried to say, 'Good morning, my car is over there. I have parked it at Dwight Way, because there's no parking here at the campus. I am off to Palo Alto immediately. I have a new assignment for which I have to refer to old newspaper stacks at the Hoover Institute. I am particularly interested in seeing old copies of the *Times of India*.'

'Really? Why?'

'I am going to study the matrimonial advertisement columns in the paper so that I may get an idea of the trends in the caste system in India for the last thirty years.'

'How will you be able to get an idea of that?'

'I hear that matrimonial advertisements are popular in India and people mention what castes they prefer or no caste restriction and so forth. I am going to note it all carefully so that I may get a picture of the breakdown of the caste system in India.'

Next time we met, Bob was in the lobby of my hotel. One

morning, weeks later, he telephoned me from the desk as I was struggling with the two-thousand-words-a-day of my new novel. I went down to speak to him for a moment. This was the only occasion when he was not chewing. He must have had a surfeit of snacks. He said, 'I have just finished my examinations, and I want to know if you would like me to drive you anywhere, sir?' I thought over it, still sixty thousand words to write. I'd not have peace of mind anywhere except my desk. 'I have no time, my boy. I will call you whenever I am free.' I could not resist asking, 'What are you interested in now?'

He answered like a shot, 'I have taken Russian Collectivism as the subject for my thesis.'

I left him at that and had no occasion to see him again. I look forward to seeing the result of his versatile activities in due course, provided I knew in which walk of life to look for him at a given time.

TV

I've become a television addict. Every evening I rush through my quota of writing and prepare my dinner in order to go down to the lobby and sit down with half a dozen others and watch the television, which goes on till eleven-thirty at night. I have no peace of mind until I know the latest progress of the sixty-four-thousand-dollar question or seen a full-length film of other days. Kaplan generally informs me if there is a special programme—'Nehru is appearing in a programme at eleven', or 'Ed Murrow's special interview with—' and we finish our dinner and crowd the lobby. I return to my room at eleven-thirty. It is diverting but it spoils one's reading habits. If I have to read, it can be only after television—that keeps me awake till one-thirty or two at night.

The television personnel exude 'prosperity'—aggressively cheerful, relaxed, homely, confident, assured: knowing what you want and what others need—in cars, cosmetics, food, cigarettes, and cleansing agents. Their perpetual smile is of paradise—their gleaming hair, teeth, and knowledge are of a superworld.

Luckily for us, advertisers have not learnt the technique of projecting themselves and their ideas into our dreams; not the day ones but the night ones, when we are asleep and may completely be at their mercy, if only they knew how to reach us there telepathically.

*

'Hutchi' (a Kannada word meaning the 'crazed woman') is the name of Ed's cat. It's just like any other cat. But they like to think that their cat is slightly touched in the head. Watching it, it did nothing more than any other cat. But it's a fashion, I suppose. Remember the French girl at Madison who held the gathering spellbound with an account of the madness of her various cats, and how she took them one by one to a psychiatrist, because her husband was positive they should be psychoanalysed, and so forth. It's an affectation. Edward also said that a cat he had in Shimoga would behave all right till orthodox Brahmins came to his house for a conference in the evenings, when she'd bring in half a mouse and toss it in their midst, outraging the pious assembly. Proves the devilry of cats.

The Unforgettable

California is a state where 'morticians' abound, where mortality is constantly kept before one. On a public bench you cannot lean back without reading the inscription on the back-rest, 'No-flame cremation is our speciality. Calcification is the latest form of disposal.' Or one may read on a corner hoarding, 'Bring us your funeral problems. Sympathetic responsibility is our motto.' Or 'Funerals undertaken on easy-instalment plan.' In this atmosphere, I grew dejected when I discovered one morning a drop of blood coming down my nostril. It completely spoilt the day for me. Could hardly manage to write fifty words for the day; became a prey to all kinds of morbid thoughts. Should I leave instructions at the desk, 'If my door is not open when the room maid calls in tomorrow, please get in touch with Chamu whose telephone is—'? Spoke to Kaplan and felt comforted to know that nasal congestion was common in this part of the country. Later confessed my worries to Chetty and

Biligiri, who confessed that they too had this trouble. Greatly relieved. It is good to know that all Indians coming to this country bleed at the nose for the first six months!

The word 'prosperity' has almost a religious compulsion about it. An anthropologist friend of mine asked me, with reference to India, why we fought shy of prosperity, and why Indian philosophical thought was opposed to it, how anyone could avoid prosperity or set a limit to it.

A car for every third person is prosperity. And then an endless creation of goods, and their sales. And so a vast advertisement programme starts. Its urgency, because of competition, is so great that it invades every medium of communication. At first you may naïvely think what a wonder television is. But alas, it is only a sales-medium. Every programme serves only as an excuse for sandwiching messages about hair cream, cigarettes, soap, and automobiles; health, wealth, wisdom, and happiness, according to the character on the television screen, are to be attained only by inhaling the smoke of such and such cigarette which has the distinction of having fifty thousand filters (whatever it may mean, it prevents lung cancer, about which the medical profession has chosen to make so much fuss)—all adjectives are used in support of it, all music is subservient to it, and all acting, personality, dramaturgy, is a message-bearer.

In times of war all talent is pressed for propaganda. In peace all talent (the television could make the highest bid) is pressed for sales promotion.

I feel a violent jolt when a narrator who earns our respect otherwise suddenly interrupts his performance to step aside to say, 'I want to tell you about the cigarette which I most enjoy smoking. It is —remember—' and then he spells and repeats it. Or the tragedienne of classic dimensions suddenly goes off to say, 'You may wonder why I care for — soap . . .' and then goes on to spell the name of this profound soap. Perpetration of such a violence to the sacredness of artistic illusions makes one furious—out of that fury the following scene is written:

One Continuous Mood

SCENE: Dark night. A lonely cottage. Wind whistling outside. An old woman is warming soup over the fireplace. Knock on the door.

O. W. (Old woman): Who is it? At this unearthly hour.

Voice: Sh! Sh! Open the door, matter of life and death!

O. W.: I won't open the door.

Voice: Please, save my life. Don't delay. (Distant baying of hounds.) There they are. Open the door. (The old woman shakes her head and tries to go on with her soup.)

Voice: By the way, I can hear you drinking your soup. Remember one thing. XYZ soup is reinforced with vitamin B14. It is the only soup with vitamin B14. Remember it. B14 will knock the years out of your age.

Voice: (As the baying of dogs approaches) Good woman, do you want to see my body mangled at your very doorstep?

O. W.: No, go, go away, do not disturb me. (Suddenly the dogs are right at her door. Several voices are heard. She listens intently to the various sounds. She pushes away her soup bowl, wringing her hands.) Perhaps he really needs help . . . Oh, God save that poor man! (She tiptoes to the door, and with her hand on the latch pauses for a moment and says:) My hands are soft because I use only Gopi Flakes for laundering my linen. Gopi can also wash your silks, your sink, your utensils, your walls, your furniture, floor, carpet, shoes or automobile. In fact, Gopi is right for any cleaning job. Gopi cleans twenty-five times faster than any other detergent and costs five times less. Remember Gopi is the only one which has Blimol in it.

(At this moment the man outside hurls himself against the door and crashes in. The old woman is thrown off, but luckily supports herself by putting her hands out and catching the wall.)

O. W.: What do you mean by this?

Visitor: (who has a cloak around his head) I am sorry, terribly sorry. I will repair your door for you.

O.W.: (surveying the man) Who are you? Are you a thief or a renegade? You look fierce enough with that beard of yours.

Visitor: (stroking his beard thoughtfully and finally taking it off)

You see, it is false. My enemies are after me.

O. W.: You may rest in that corner.

(Darkness falls on the house; the man sits hunched up at the door waiting for his friends. He falls asleep and wakes up at dawn. The old woman enters.)

O. W.: Oh, you're still here! (The visitor wakes up and yawns.)

Visitor: One reason why I prefer Watterrwet Towels is that they are soft, soft like the petals of a rose. They come in seven pastel shades—one for each day of the week, packed in— (He flourishes a glittering package.)

O. W.: I have to go out for a while. (The old woman picks up her mop and bucket.) Watch that kettle. Take it down when the water boils.

Visitor: I will. (At this moment, the clatter of horses' hooves is heard. The old woman has just opened the door.)

Someone outside: Who is inside?

O. W.: (trying to shut the door) No one.

Horseman: He must be here. Do you know who he is?

O. W.: No.

Horseman: (seeing the Visitor) The rebels are busy pillaging the palace. They have announced a price—on Your Majesty's head. Let us rush away. (The old woman is aghast on hearing the word 'Majesty', and kneels down.)

Visitor: (giving her a ring) You have been good to me. Keep it. Goodbye, I must go now. (The men march out and get the horses ready. H.M. rushes out, but pauses at the door to say:) There are three reasons why I prefer Stonebreak Soap. First, it is the cleanest soap in the market. Two, it is the only soap which can make your worn-out skin glow again, and three, it never slips through your wet fingers.

(More horsemen arrive.)

King's friends: (cry in unison) We are lost, they have found us! But we will fight. (Swords are drawn. It is difficult to see who is who in this melee. You hear the clash of swords, and groans of the wounded as they fall to the ground.)

O. W.: Ah, bloody sight! In my poor cottage! (She edges her way to where the King is fighting with his back to the wall. She carries the kettle of boiling water and pours it down the neck of the man who has cornered the King; the man leaps up. The King knocks him down, kneels over his chest, ready to run his sword through him.)

King: If you are thinking of a nice birthday present for your daughter, give her a Sissy Tractor, which is the only one with a built-in Dish Washer. Run it on your field; it'll plough the earth. Set it up in the kitchen; it'll wash your dishes. No down payment, no up payment. In fact, no payment at all. Take the tractor, use it, when it's worn out, bring it back and we will give you another. Remember, for your child's birthday, a Sissy Tractor!

Fallen man: Take away your sword. I'll tell you.

King: Yes, speak.

Fallen man: About your children.

King: (with sword at his heart) Oh, what about them? Tell me, tell me soon.

O. W.: (to the audience) Bad breath is instantly abolished if you use Breatho pills; the cost works out to a quarter of a cent each hour. It's the most scientific antiodour pill ever made.

King: Oh, tell me about my children. Are they safe?

Man: They were intercepted, and they are now in our custody. If you do not surrender before mid-day they will be . . .

King: Oh stop; don't say the word.

Man: I know where they are. I'll take you there.

King: And also collect your reward; you will get your reward and I shall lose my head, h'm?

Man: (embarrassed) I suppose so, Your Majesty. For that headache that never stops, take Pancita 606. Pancita 606 gives thirty-two times faster relief than others. (The old woman bursts into tears. All the King's followers go out mutely. The man leads the King out gleefully.)

King: All our yesterdays have lighted fools their dusty way to death. One word more. Porcupine Underwear keeps you cool in summer and warm in winter. Look for Porcupine Underwear wherever you go.

Postmistress

Postmistress at the Berkeley Post office, while registering my letter: 'Gandhi! What a great man! Himself so simple, but helped the people to raise their standard of life. He created a bloodless revolution—like the Christian revolutionaries during the early years of Christian era. I've heard friends say that Gandhi was a devout Christian too. Have you states and districts and counties in your country? Population 400 million, that's a lot of population! Must be hard-pressed for space, isn't it so? What's the area of your country? We've a 100 million population in this country, but a lot of waste space in-between everywhere! The charges would be 46 cents: give me a penny, I'll give you a nickel for the half dollar. Penny! It's a survival of our British connection you know. We are one with you there: actually we are cousin-like, because we both got rid of the British.'

'Bew-da'

Religion is not a thing that anyone can openly avow—it's like one's underwear. You may make an oblique reference to it or joke about it. At the cocktail party in Lyla Jacob's house, biochemists and other such people from the Science department of the University, and a couple of Indian students who would not betray their traditional outlook. You may joke about God, but that's as far as you should go in civilized societies. 'Ambedkar, author of the Indian Constitution is dead—'

'Did he not convert one million Hindus to Buddhism?'

'What's Buddhism?'

'Followers of Buddha.' (Pronounced 'Bew-da' or 'Booda' in this country.)

Someone: 'I am all for Buddhism—'

'What does it oblige one to do or imply?'

'Nothing. You are just a Buddhist—that's all.' One of the scientists sat rolling his eyes and parodying a religious attitude, quite grotesque in a man usually grave, mumbling, 'Oh, I'm the Buddha—I see him there—I hear a knock on the door; they are coming up—I prophesy there is a female coming—Buddha in female form . . .'

Just nonsense. And then they talk about monsoons and earthquakes.

'Funny feeling when there is an earthquake.'

'How does it occur?'

'Well, God is supposed to bear the universe on his little finger, and when he changes it from the right to his left—there is an earthquake.'

'The world is borne on his head.' Someone mimed the action of such a God as he lifted the burden off and on. Laughter.

Lyla: 'I think it could just as well be that—simplifies everything. Why not so?'

Scientist: 'Nice way to explain everything. If you say God, you don't have to explain anything. Plenty of hypotheses, unquestionable basis for conclusions, you can stop halfway through an argument or data and put the rest on God. No notes or step-by-step calculations. What a saving! If I could have him in biochemistry research, it'd save us so much labour!'

'I saw Martin Luther—it was good. It seems they had to stop a television programme of it in Chicago.'

'I wonder how Catholics could tolerate it even at the beginning . . .'

'How can the word of God written three thousand years ago, be a fixed factor? "Thou shall" or "shall not" may sometimes have to be elastic . . .'

'I hope there is no Christian here,' said the scientist after another performance of God-miming. Irreverence and blasphemy are here as compelling a creed as any religious practice in a monastery.

*

Half an hour with Kaplan at the desk, discussing the fate of old people in this country. Carlton full of them, grandparents thinking and talking to each other of their sons and grandsons, and waiting all hours at the lounge, hoping for a letter or a meeting at the weekend. I was touched by the old man who brought around the framed photo of his grandson holding two large fish he had caught. The boy had bowed his head as he held the two large fish. The old man almost lifted him in the picture by the chin, so that we might see what a fine smile he could display. He explained that the boy's modesty made him look down, and so called the picture, 'Modesty in achievement,' much to the approval of the erect, deaf, ninety-year-old man who moved on measured steps all day, and who remembered India from when he was in Calcutta in 1912—'I had a watchman, outside my bedroom. I had bearers all over the house—I wonder what India is like now?' This old gentleman told me that he was writing a monumental work on the philosophy of common sense. He advocated in the book the test of common sense for all problems—it is sure to abolish not only war in the international field, but also divorce. When any conflict was imminent one had only to ask, 'Is it common sense?' and the problem would have a ready solution. He had split common sense into practical, manageable doses and had examined its application, in personal, family, state, national and international problems. He said that he was busy with it all day, preparing the final copy with the help of an editorial secretary. As we were talking, beside the glass door, people were passing in and out, but he noticed no one—his mind was all on common sense. I was duly impressed with the possibilities of his work and its application, until he said, 'I'll send you an autographed copy of my book before you leave.'

'But,' I said, 'Your book is not yet printed, is it?'

'No, one or two publishers have asked for it, but I'm still working on the manuscript.'

'How can you promise me a copy? I'm leaving in two weeks.'

'Not impossible,' he said, 'in these days when we have such good printing machinery.' So I left it at that. He looked so earnest, I had not the heart to contradict and argue with him as to how a book could be set up, printed and bound, and be ready to be autographed in fifteen days; especially when no publisher had yet seen it and the book was still unwritten.

*

Mr Woolfe: 'Countries are arming themselves to the teeth and when that happens, history has shown us, there is always a war. This part of the country is particularly bad to live in if there is a war—with its cyclotron, naval-building yards and so on. The thing to do is to quit this place. If there is a war, I'll be the first to quit. If you find a sudden gust of wind blowing in at the door and someone asks, "What is that storm?" you may say, "It's Woolfe clearing out of San Francisco."'

*

'Hi! Professor!' said the active and ever-busy, ever-smiling scholar, also a permanent resident of our hotel, whose name I never learnt, but who mentioned one night that he was working on the history of ideas—and knew Greek, Hebrew, Latin, French, and many other languages, and was also able to fix the television for Woolfe, when something went wrong with it. He greeted me with 'Professor!' and a nod whenever he saw me. My convocation and the conferring of an honorary doctorate on me by the staff and fellow-guests of Carlton deserves a whole chapter by itself. Shortly no one need be surprised if I print my cards as Doctor N; I have so got used to being called 'Doctor' or 'Professor' by all and sundry.

*

The Guatemala lady whose son is in a hostel spoke to me in whispers at the lounge.

'This whole American life is based on getting rid of parents. I sent my boy to the Berkeley college and planned to take a house and run it for him. But the university would not hear of it. And so he has been in a hostel for a year now. Already I see him changed. He does not care for me. No respect for mothers!' I have discussed all this with Kaplan, who agrees that family life should become broader and include others besides the husband-wife-child unit. People should become less self-centred. He said the improvement in nutrition and public health has produced longevity, which has resulted in the presence of a lot of old people, retired from family and profession, as permanent residents in hotels—because a son, when he marries, likes to live independently, and a modern house is so built that except the immediate family no one else can dwell in it without becoming a great nuisance.

'So, I think the solution lies in building houses with an extra suite for parents, built in such a way as to afford them privacy and independence. So, the fault is with the architects,' I say.

Metro is of the view that the old people themselves are responsible for their present condition. 'They want to be either totally independent as in a hotel room or totally interfering if they are with their offspring. They are a troublesome unaccommodative lot.' Nor does Metro seem to approve of children. He called them an unmanageable nuisance in this country. He suspected that unnoticed, they were gradually forming themselves into a 'pressure group'.

Metro bowled me over by asking, 'What is the real difference between Hindus and Muslims?' I began to say, 'Hindus write left to right and Muslims right to left. Our auspicious days are inauspicious to them, Hindus venerate cows, while Muslims feed on them. Hindus don't mind the pig, while Muslims abominate them. Hindus worship idols, while Islam forbids idolatry.'

Metro listened to it all and said, 'Still I do not see why it should lead to fighting and bloodshed.'

'That's true,' I said.

'So what is the real difference between Hindus and Muslims?' he persisted and I had to say, 'I don't know.'

*

A couple of mornings ago, an old man, standing on a pavement at Channing Way, who watched me hop across the road avoiding a Volkswagen remarked when I reached him, 'Bad enough even if it's a small car that runs over one,' and then he asked, 'From India?' followed by 'I've a daughter in India.'

'Which part of India?'

'Madras.'

'Madras! Where in Madras?'

'Her husband is in the State Department in the Information services.'

'Name please?'

'Tufty.' I was taken aback. What a coincidence to run into Mrs Tufty's family like this. I explained how well I know the Tuftys, how they gave a party for me when I left India, no longer than a couple of months ago, good friends of mine. The old gentleman was overcome with emotion; 'The world is a small place indeed,' he cried.

'I had been thinking only today how far away my daughter is—it's a far off world for us, but what a joy and relief to meet you, you bring that world so close to us. Please come for tea and my wife will be so happy to meet you.'

*

Metro was also an author living in this hotel. He had written a novel of over one hundred and twenty thousand words, working on it for five years now. He had a room in Carlton, and a job as a night clerk four nights a week at a hotel in Oakland, which gave him enough funds to maintain himself at Carlton, where he was completely lost in composing and chiselling his novel during all his spare days and hours. He showed me a few chapters and I found them rather strong—too much blood in each chapter; overloaded with corpses in deep-freeze, blackmail, million dollars changing hands, and fast driving. He had taken courses in fiction-writing, studied books on the subject, and worked unswervingly on the theories he had learnt. But still something was wrong somewhere, as he himself felt that there was too much beating-up, and the speeches of his characters sounded vapid and impossible to his ears. He asked for suggestions. I could only say that he should cut down the length by half. He considered my suggestion until he saw my own work; I lent him my copy of *Waiting for the Mahatma*, which he read at one stretch and returned to me saying, 'I think the book is weak in motivation, we don't learn anything about Mahatma Gandhi, and the narrative lacks punch.' And thus my criticism of his own effort was set off, and he felt less unhappy as he realized that I was after all a writer of weak motivations, and with probably no theoretical knowledge of fiction writing. Apart from this difference of views, we often met and went out to drink coffee and talk literary shop.

*

Having written the last sentence of my novel I plan to idle around Berkeley for a week and then leave on my onward journey. I have lived under the illusion that I would never have to leave Berkeley. Berkeley days were days of writing, thinking, and walking along mountain paths, and meeting friends. And so, when the time comes for me to plan to leave, I feel sad. How can I survive without a view of the Sather Gate Book shop, the chime of Campanille clock, the ever-hurrying boys and girls in the street below, the grocer, the laundry and the antique shop? I shall miss all the musical names of the streets—Dwight Way, Channing, Acton, Prospect, Piedmont, Shasta, Olympus, Sacramento. I shall miss all the scores of friends I have somehow managed to gather. I shall miss Lyla's voice on the telephone. When the sun shone the telephone was certain to ring and she would say, 'Isn't it a beautiful day?'

David Mandelbaum invited me to tea on the eve of my departure. Ruth had just read *The English Teacher,* and I could see how she was overwhelmed by it. She wanted to ask so many questions about it, but could not. David told me later that the book had a disturbing effect on her mind. In the hope of lightening her mind, I gave her a copy of *Swami and Friends.*

The whole of Sunday busy cancelling my original plan to leave on Monday. The whole of Monday spent at bank counter, baggage forwarding agency, and telegraph office. Late in the evening Biligiri dropped in. John came to ask if he could drive me to the airport next day, but the Vincents have already offered their help. Ed Harper came in with a box of candies to announce to me, Indian style, the birth of a son.

Frantically busy morning, because I have still not completed my packing. John and Irene Vincent come to drive me to the airport. Kaplan at the desk becomes sentimental about my leaving. John Vincent carries my bags all through, in spite of my protests. They come up to the last inch of the barrier, and hand me a hamper of fruits and candies before saying goodbye.

LOS ANGELES

Los Angeles at 6 p.m. Arrive at San Carlos. Find the room rather small—and I am not able to find a grocery store nearby. Eat sandwich for dinner and stroll down Broadway.

*

By bus to Venice to see Mrs Dorothy Jones. A critic and serious writer on filmic values, especially valuable is her study of Hollywood's treatment of foreign themes, which she did under the auspices of the Massachusetts Institute. More than everything, her helpful nature and knowledge of film studios and personalities made it easy for me to visit the film world. Met her at six o'clock in the evening at her house in that far-off place. Over an hour's journey by bus right through the heart of Los Angeles. The magnitude of Los Angeles could be realized only in such a journey. The word 'sprawling' is uttered the moment anyone thinks of Los Angeles, and one could understand the epithet now. Venice is nearly at the other end of the town and searching for Glyndon Avenue on foot proved an interesting way of familiarizing oneself with this vast city. The types of faces one encountered were all different from anything one saw in other parts of the country, starting with the gallery of old men at Pershing Square; and the Bible lecturer haranguing them '. . . I can have all the wealth in the world. But I don't want it . . . I know God gives me what I want . . .' and so on. 'I'll tell you about the Holy

Ghost . . . Recently the wise men of California said that if a certain oil company should cease, the town would become a ghost of itself . . . But this holy ghost is not a ghost like this threatened oil town . . .' He was clearly going off the rails, nobody in the least minding it. They paid no more attention to his lecture than they did to the pigeons hovering around and cooing . . .

*

Tomorrow I'm going to make notes on the road, about the bearded and other extraordinary personalities one comes across on the road. Women of tremendous beauty pass along in the crowds—and the men all look suspiciously like film toughs, and deliberately cultivated picturesque characters. A newspaper vendor near my hotel looks like W.G. Grace, the old English cricketer with his beard and peaked cap . . . He has begun to call today's evening edition, already stale, 'Thursday morning edition,' and recommends as I pass him, 'Read it; you will be well-informed if you read tomorrow's morning edition, that's what it is actually!' It is about nine in the evening. Tomorrow is still far off. Is news printed ahead of occurrence? I wonder!

*

I must definitely give Milton Singer's camera back to him because I'll never photograph anything. The very idea of photography detracts my mind from watching any scene or situation with a free mind (as a writer). I start worrying about how it will look in the view-finder, and am seized with the regret that, as usual, I've left the camera behind, or that I've carried it when there is no sun and so forth. It's all a useless preoccupation. Every place sells picture post-cards, and that should be sufficient for my record; the photographs are so much more competently taken!

*

First time in my life purchased a clock at the corner drug store. Bought a big one for one dollar odd, kept it on my table for five minutes, went down again and returned it, and bought a smarter one costing a couple of dollars more. 'For an extra dollar, sure, you get extra value, sir,' moralized the store assistant. I bought it just by way of precaution against unpunctuality with regard to various engagements ahead. At the Carlton (Berkeley), I could peep out and read the time on the Campanille tower, but here I could see nothing but dark, sooty walls when I looked out; and the view was always better curtained off.

By virtue of possessing the time-piece got up early, arranged my affairs tidily so that I had cooked, dishwashed, and was ready to meet Mrs Dorothy Jones at eleven-thirty. She was very helpful. She drew up a list of persons for me to see in Hollywood, and sat at the telephone and filled up my programme book with the address and telephone number of each person. When she saw that I had a tendency to note my engagements on loose paper she presented me with a small pocket diary, and for a start put down all my engagements in it, and handed it back to me with, 'Don't forget to look into it, first thing each day.' Drove me to Hollywood, searched far and wide, and fixed a room for me in a motel on Sunset Boulevard as a first practical step, as my downtown life at the hotel did not have her approval. After this a drive-in lunch and we went to the United Artists Corporation. Met Sidney Harmon (Security Productions), said to be a sensitive playwright and high-brow producer. He asked me a number of questions about India—from geology and population, down to individual daily life, and asked what exactly was the difference between Indians and Americans. But I have grown used to questions and never rack my head to find an answer, as from experience I find that most persons (like the Jesting Pilate) don't wait for an answer. He asked me suddenly what he could do for me at Hollywood, and when I told him I'd like to meet a producer interested in an Indian subject, he went on to dilate on the quicksand economics of the film, listed all the good films that proved a failure since the beginning, and finally talked himself into the conclusion that it would never, never pay, and nothing would ever pay in films. He quoted enormous statistics and spoke, he said, as a businessman. The recent success of *The Giant* seemed to have brought a lot of confusion and rethinking in all their production plans. One would think a big success would make everyone feel more encouraged, but I've noticed film producers are afflicted with mixed emotions when they see any picture become an abnormal success. They call a halt to all their own plans, telling each other, 'One can't survive unless one gives the public another *Giant*.' For a moment I was oblivious of my surroundings, not really knowing, whether I was listening to one of our own movie moguls in Madras, Coimbatore or Bombay. They have all the same idiom, eloquence, and monologous tendency. They will set aside everything else to drive home a point with 'You know what I mean . . .', 'You see what I mean . . .' with brief (and sometimes prolonged) interludes into the telephone. I liked Sidney Harmon and he promised to take me to the sets the next day. Dorothy suddenly remembered that she had to get back to her children and started off at four-thirty. I found my way back downtown by bus. Returned to my hotel and started out again to buy foodstuff. As usual found all the grocery shops closing. This was the third evening in succession that groceries were unavailable. Returned to my hotel to get a call from Dorothy, who gave me for my diary a number of engagements for tomorrow. I've to pack up and be ready to leave at noon tomorrow. Dread the prospect of packing again. Anyway, time to leave this, hotel—the traffic noise is getting on my nerves, and my room is so dark that I don't know whether it's night or day.

Dorothy phoned to say she would come at one in the afternoon. Frantic packing and cooking—two activities for which I am, by nature, unfit, but which are on me all the time. For brief half-hour went out to visit the library on 5th Street. It's a magnificent place on several floors with millions of books in every language in the world. At the information hall on the second floor (first floor in our reckoning), the lady pointed out to me the huge murals on the walls—showing the discovery of the coast and the founding of Los Angeles. Here and there on the niche were kept Egyptian relics of thousands of years, gifted by a local collector. Went through the fiction department and saw *The Financial Expert* and *Grateful to Life and Death*—the copies looked well thumbed and their issue cards were crammed with entries.

Hollywood

Afternoon occupy the motel on Sunset Boulevard according to plan. I'm now right in the heart of Hollywood. Call on Mr Geoffrey Shurlock, Vice President of the Motion Picture Academy who has taken over the functions of the old Hay's Office, and applies the Production Code to new pictures; he is concerned with the censoring of scripts and reels. He flourishes on his desk the *New York Times* Book Section as a thing he studiously follows and claims that he is familiar at least with the reviews of my books. He asks about Indian films and I mention *Avvaiyar*. We have many other topics coming up but at four-thirty Dorothy remembers her duty to her children—Kelley must be picked up and then her husband at his office and we leave Shurlock. She puts me down at the library of the Motion Picture Academy, which attempts to collect all literature and documents concerning films, a very thorough, comprehensive library, where one may read the accounts of films of half a century ago and all the press cuttings connected with them. I glance through an album presented by Richard Barthelmess (of *Little Lord Fauntleroy*) of old days, containing press-cuttings of his performances; including a letter of congratulations from Mary Pickford on the day of his marriage, in her own hand, with envelope preserved intact. A waft of history; the dust of time has settled on many things here. Hollywood is already building up a past, creating a tradition, and, I think, rightly too, considering the shattering impact of television at home and the trade restrictions abroad, and the general economic morass, in which, I'm assured by everybody, the trade is grounded at the moment.

Aldous Huxley

'Take the Bus No. 89 at Hollywood and Highland and come along to the very end of the line—Beachwood Drive, I'll come and take you in my car,' Mrs Huxley had phoned last night. At Hollywood Boulevard, I got into Bus No. 89. I asked the driver, 'I want to drive to the end of the line, what's the ticket?'

'Where do you want to go, pal?' he asked.

I showed him Huxley's address.

'H'm. We go all the way down Hollywood Hill. Whatever is beyond is yours to manage, OK?'

He took me in with resignation—a cheerful soul, more talkative than anyone else of his kind I've seen. He told a lady who had failed to get off at the right 'transfer' point, 'Learn to know your bus, honey.' He also spoke to girls adopting a thin piping voice: with all this entertainment, I did not notice the passage of time and felt sorry to part when he stopped at a place and said turning to me, 'Well, this is all, pal; I go back now.'

It was the beginning of a hill-road with a drug store and laundry, and a post-box. A number of cars were arriving, driven by women, myself always wondering which of them might be Mrs Huxley. As I sat there on a bench outside the store, a tall, handsome, old man, looking like Francis Ford of the old days came up and sat beside me and started talking. Pointing at the granite bastion at the entrance to the hill road he said, 'There used to be guards posted in those days to keep off peddlers and others whom we didn't want here . . .' History again within fifty years! When he learnt I was from India, he said, 'Your country! A great job it's doing to keep the peace of the world. But it's a mad world—people don't want to live and let live, that's all . . . How Britain exploited India and other countries! I'm a Canadian. Canada is the only country in which Britain's tricks did not work, although in World War I and World War II, they made us the front line in every battle! . . . I suppose they did the same thing with India too! Sixty years ago I fought . . .'

I had to leave him. 'Excuse me!' I said and abruptly went off to look for Mrs Huxley, who, I feared, might be looking for me. Very soon a small car came up—Huxley recognized me, and brought the car down to my kerb. He got out of the car asking, 'Have we kept you waiting?' Recognition was mutual and instantaneous. His house was on the hill. As we entered his gate, there was another car standing, and he said, 'I've asked Alan White of Asiatic Studies at San Francisco to lunch. He is an Oriental scholar, you'll like him.'

At the drawing room, the furnishing and upholstery was all white, with glass windows bringing in light—(I suppose in order to help Huxley move around without difficulty on account of his sight). He took me to his patio and pointed out the magnificent valley ahead. He pointed to a pot of foliage: 'It's just sweet potato—which has just burst out in such foliage, isn't it amazing! . . .' At lunch I knew he had to divide his talk between the other guest and me. They had terse references to works on Mahayana and Hinayana Buddhism, and he was rather surprised at the revival of Buddhism everywhere—and wondered if it was partly a political strategy. We spoke of Gandhi (Otto Preminger had once consulted him for a possible film on Gandhi), industrialism, and he asked many questions about India. Mescalin and the opening of the doors of perception were of course extremely recurring subjects. After the other guest left, he took me into his study—full of books and letters, and an uncovered typewriter.

'Perhaps you may want to rest?' I asked.

'Oh, no, I don't rest in the afternoon. Stay on, I may go down later and let us go together, if you do not mind it.' I had mentioned *Gayatri Dhyana Sloka* earlier in the day, in connection with his own thesis on colour perception as an aid to yoga. He wanted me to say more about it. I explained *Gayatri Dhyana Sloka* and the *Mantra* step by step, and suggested he might find more of it in Arthur Avalon's writing. He took down several of Avalon's books from his shelf and wanted me to show him the exact place where reference to *Gayatri* could be found. I couldn't find it anywhere just then, but I promised to write to him later about it.

'What books are now being published in India on tantra? Are the theatres very active? How is the younger generation? Are they conscious of their cultural traditions? No? What a pity! When two nations get together they get the worst of each other—rope-trick and such things from your country and gadgets and mere technology from the West! Isn't it extraordinary! A most fantastic piece of history. Britain's one hundred years' association with India—a company going and settling down and creating all kinds of problems at that distance! Under Mescalin, a single bar of music lasts a whole eternity. I'm not a born novelist. It does not come easily to me. I've to struggle and work hard to get it out—not like Balzac for instance through whom it just flowed; the novel form is wonderful if you can achieve it. As we grow in years, it becomes more difficult to write a mere novel—all meditation technique is just to open up our own layers of consciousness and experience—to feel the richness of awareness and not for any particular achievement or results . . .' He quoted Blake.

'Yes . . . the Perennial Philosophy helped me a great deal in understanding. I'm glad I wrote it.'

Calm, gracefully slow and careful in movement, lean and very tall, with a crop of hair which younger people might envy, perfectly shaped nose and lips—it's a delight to watch his profile: his hands and the long tapering fingers; a check jacket, and corduroy trousers, and the hand-knit tie, gave him a distinguished appearance. I sat talking in his study till he said he was ready to go out. Before starting he brought out his new volume of essays, 'Perhaps you'd like to see this, well, the first two essays are good, I think.' He drove me downhill with a promise to telephone me again. 'We must get together again before you leave,' he said.

∗

Spent Sunday in Dorothy's home at Glyndon Avenue, Venice. Kim, Kelly, and David—the youngsters—were wonderfully active. Jack, Dorothy's husband, was relaxed, in an absolutely Sunday mood. They put the chairs—rough, wooden ones—out in the yard. They showed me their guinea pigs, the fat cat, their parakeets. They thanked me one by one for a box of candies I had brought them. Jack, not a very talkative man, told me that his association with India was when he passed Madras coast at a distance of 30 miles during the War and saw a ball of fire shooting across the horizon—to this day this phenomenon remains unexplained to him;

and at Colombo they got down and searched for beef-steak, a guide promising to help them took them to a restaurant where they palmed off lamb as beef!

Afternoon they became quite active building up a fire for a barbecue—father and boys, running hither and thither and setting it up. Sally Simmons, Dorothy's friend, dropped in; she was full of knowledge, observation, and curiosity. Her hobby was watching crowds and characters. She knew Hollywood (of normal life and people, not of films) inside out. She declared that Hollywood was no longer what it was reported to be—it had ceased to be anything different from a normal town. It was a centre of oil business, aeronautic construction and electronics, rather than of mere films; all the studios had moved outside Hollywood proper. We sat round talking, eating, drinking and watching television, and it was 8.30 p.m. when Dorothy drove me back to Hollywood. Before I left, little David brought me his file of stories—he wanted to be a writer. I blessed him and hoped he would be a writer with a Book of the Month honour one day, much to the delight of his Dad, Jack.

*

Visit to Sam Goldwyn studios, arranged by Dorothy with Sidney Harmon. At three o'clock I was there. The routine phone-up from the reception desk and so forth before the portals could open. Since I was a little early, I waited in his office. Harmon's secretary, a smiling, cheerful creature, offered me coffee without sugar or cream. She explained, 'It's really very good coffee, you know,' endorsed by another visitor waiting with a portfolio under his arm. It encouraged the girl to explain, 'You know why it's so good? I make my own blend and kiss every grain . . .'

'Well, in that event, I think I'll try it even without cream, you seem to have given it the right treatment,' I said, and tried to enjoy the decoction.

'Are you hungry?' she asked next.

'No,' I said.

'I have a packet of salmon sandwich which I can give you.'

'Why don't you eat it yourself?' I asked.

'I'm dieting. I don't want to grow fat.'

I did not ask what made her carry around sandwiches which she didn't intend to consume. I just said, 'You don't look the kind that'll grow fat, but if you are destined to grow fat, no power on earth or in heaven can help you.'

'We Americans eat too much,' said the other visitor, and demonstrated it by offering to help the girl out of her salmon-sandwich load.

Meanwhile the room was getting crowded with sleek men and elegant women, all of whom nodded and said to me, 'How do you do?'

I am too experienced in the film world to take too much notice of anyone or offer my seat. It's a free-and-easy world, where there is a lot of relaxed, mutual indifference, and the courtesies of the humdrum world are neither missed nor noticed. I carried on the same technique when Sidney Harmon, whom I was waiting to see, who had been so warm and communicative two days before and had said I was to ask him for anything I needed in Hollywood, came out of the room. I just continued to sit and look away at a pretty girl who had also emerged from his room, a few minutes before. We might have been total strangers for all it mattered. He threw a brief glance at me, muttered a word to someone, and passed out of the room. I never saw him again. A new person (Public Relations?) came on to me with a fresh smile.

'Please come with me. Let us go down to the studio.'

'What about Mr Harmon?' I said, suddenly feeling that Harmon was slipping out of my ken.

'Yes, sure. He will meet us later. Shall we go down?'

'Sure!' I said, catching the spirit of the hour.

We were presently passing on to a stage crowded with people. The moment the door was shut behind me, I might, for all it mattered, have been in Gemini Studios—the same groups of people—half of them too tense and the other half too relaxed. Suddenly my guide put his finger to his lips and cautioned. It was as if we had stepped into a cave where a tiger was asleep. The tiger here

was a temperamental director of whom every one seemed afraid . . .
At a corner of the studio they were shooting a scene with Burt
Lancaster and Miss Simmons. The cameraman was pointed out to
me, in respectful, nervous whispers, as an academy winner—a
Chinaman, with his thick glasses and five-foot height who looked so
much like Ramnoth (of Gemini Studios at Madras) and moved
about like him. It made me regret for a while about Ramnoth, a good
friend and a film-associate for years, of whose death I had learnt
from a newspaper, which I opened on the plane while leaving India.

The man who guided me slipped away after handing me over to
another, who spoke to me for a while, and slipped away in his turn,
with a 'Make yourself comfortable'. I watched the endless rehearsals
and preparations for the shot and found it was all the same the world
over. The Director was high-strung and kept saying, 'Silence,
gentlemen, someone is talking . . .' like a class teacher, and every one
giggled at the fuss he made and tried not to creak their shoes. I
noticed on the set a property which intrigued me—Nataraja in
bronze . . . the ubiquitous god, whom they pick up and carry about
like some savage visiting a city and picking up an electric lamp
(without current or wiring) for a display in his jungle home. To see
Nataraja, the Shiva of India, included in the setting for a Chinese
story, being made in Hollywood, seemed to me a grotesque but
perfect international mixture. I slipped out in my turn and went back
to my hotel without a chance to say 'thanks' or 'goodbye' to anyone.

Evening dinner with Sally Simmons, and then a drive, which she
had arranged with an automobile-owning friend of hers. We went
up the hill to the planetarium and saw half this country stretched out
below, and then here and there nearly fifty miles of driving looking
around Los Angeles. We ended up at a famous ice-cream cafe in the
university village which offered seventy different ice-creams. The
menu card displayed a list of all the film and literary celebrities who
had tasted the ice-cream. While leaving, I saw at the door, a niche in
the wall and a very large Ganesha in white marble kept in it. Where
did they get it from, the god from a distant land, blessing this
ice-cream bar with prosperity! I told the manager, 'Wherever you
may have got it from, he is a god, Ganesha the elephant-faced

(because, oh, that's a big story in our mythology), who is the remover of impediments, and giver of prosperity; you probably owe your popularity to his kindness—apart from the quality of your own service.'

Unloved

Visit the famous Universal International Studios. Lunch with William Gordon—head of the international section, who feels disturbed by the attitude of the Indian government, which was understood to be hostile to Hollywood in general. Nothing disturbs film folk so much as the thought that they are not loved and admired. The Indian government is somehow averse to Hollywood. Mr Gordon projected for me *Bengal Brigade*, which was refused a certificate in India. No use attempting to find a reason for the refusal since the government itself had not given any. The producer had gone carefully through the script changing all words likely to offend Indian sentiments—such as 'caste'; 'Get out you low caste' was changed to 'Get out, you low class', but it had sounded to my ears, 'caste', until it was explained to me; in any case it didn't matter materially, since the word caste is by no means a tabooed expression. Why, why was the Government of India so inimical to Hollywood? I couldn't say. He took out huge files and showed me all the correspondence. The picture was not certified by Trinidad, Indonesia and Hong Kong, countries, which somehow accepted India's leadership in such matters. The nations of the world seemed to be marshalled against Hollywood. It was nice sitting in that well-furnished office and listening to all these problems. In no other walk of life do people arrange their office equipment so stylishly— the poorest film producer will have at least four coloured telephones and all kinds of table equipment, which the President of a nation might envy. Mr Gordon proved that India was a loser in the long run as every film producer interested in India would bring in at least two million dollars into this dollar-starved subcontinent. It was all high economics which I didn't quite follow. Ultimately Mr Gordon hinted that if the government continued its unfriendly acts, Hollywood would be driven to making pictures on India uninhibitedly, faking all the background in Hollywood, stories wildly misinterpreting India, which would certainly create box office records all over the world. I said, 'Why not?' instead of worrying about Delhi attitudes.

*

Visit to Macgowan, head of Theatre Art at the University of California. At first he mistook me for a visitor from Pakistan whom he had been expecting. He looked confused and bewildered by this slip. Personally I didn't mind. I see nothing wrong in being thought of as a Pakistani as long as I am not questioned on politics. He phoned his next-in-command to come up and join us. Before ten minutes were over, I had collected an armful of departmental literature. The next man came up and kept the conversation going. He took me round to see the departments, handed me over to the director of cinema-teaching and disappeared. This man, Richard Hawkins, proved a valuable friend. A deep friendliness abiding for three hours. I have lost all value for the duration of friendship, as long as it is good while it lasts. He showed me his film department; and then said that as he had nothing in particular to do at the moment, he would like to drive me around in his car. He took me up the hills all the way, down to the ocean, along Will Rogers Avenue, across the city, and all the way around and finally insisted upon driving me back to my hotel. He had been driving for over three hours continuously, a quiet, gentle soul, full of sensitive film values. Thanks to him I saw the entire Bel Air area, more aristocratic than Beverley Hills, Santa Monica, Will Rogers Beach and some of the hill locations of old-time movie chases on horseback.

*

At two o'clock Walt Disney studio with Dorothy and her son Kim. A guide met us at the reception, and for the next two hours, he explained everything in that fifty-six acre ground, with its twenty-six buildings and one thousand and five hundred employees, working to entertain, amuse, and make money. Television, movies, magazine publications (eight million total sales in various places of the world), articles of amusement for Disneyland. How many things! How many! What coordination! It took six years to make a picture; one million drawings made for a feature. Shot frame by frame through a stop camera. Fundamentally, it depends upon a single individual, on the creative work of an artist. The animator actually draws pictures for every stage of movement, arranges them one under another and flicks them with his fingers, muttering the dialogue and syllables in order to synchronize sound and picture. To help him in this work all the dialogue is completely recorded first, and played back. The colour store, fantastic combinations and numbers—made by Dupont (seventy odd primary colours, made into two thousand by combination), the 'Cel' painters, girls, with their own radios and earphones to while away the tedium when their hands colour-copy. A place where genius, creative play on a large scale, the toy-maker's spirit, expert organization, technology, business, specialized engineering all combine. It's so crowded and so organized that it made me wonder if there was space for Disney himself to do anything. Our guide assured us that his spirit pervaded the place—when he passed with a nod or a word, he set his stamp. He was unseen, but like God, he was pervasive. I wanted to ask which God ever possessed such business acumen. I was told that Disney's brother managed all the business. The odium of commerce is on the other Disney, not on Walt.

Shurlock brought his car and took me to the Huntington Library and Picture Gallery at Pasadena—a most attractive place (Huntington was a rail-road president) with its green lawns and park-land, looking like an English countryside—names also, such as Euston, Wembley, Oxford and so forth. Huntington Library— where one saw Chaucer's and Shakespeare's first editions, Caxton's original, and ancient etchings, woodcuts, and illuminated manuscripts, and the art gallery with Gainsborough's 'Blue Boy' and 'Lady Turner' and various other pictures one has heard of all one's life.

Reserved

The famous cemetery, made famous by Evelyn Waugh's *The Loved One*, the Forest Lawns, was the next place of visit. A whole mountain converted into a burial ground by a big business organization. Flowers on picturesque tomb-plates, lordly avenues, churches, statuary and spacious lawns, meadows, and arbours—verily a place where one might live rather than be dead in. The speciality is that you could drive in and lay a wreath. I saw one or two mourners pulling up their motor cars beside their loved ones and laying flowers (the supply of which is also a part of the business organization) on the horizontal tomb-plates. The tomb-plates do not stand out but lie flat along the sloping ground, because they save space (which is the real commodity on sale here, selling the dead space to be dead in) and do not disturb the perspective. The plates are of metal with the names of the dead engraved on them, with a nice cavity in each for sticking flowers as in a vase. Everything is provided for here. Under this Grand-Hotel-like perfection of arrangements there is no time to feel the pangs of bereavement. The sting of death is removed by business foresight. I noticed also schoolchildren picnicking in various corners of this attractive retreat. Ever since I entered California I had been seeing gigantic notices hitting one's eyes everywhere, '. . . 110 dollars assure a place in Forest Lawns', which I had taken to be some sort of Save-Our-Trees-and-Lawns campaign on a statewide scale. Now I understood that these were only advertisements of cemetery-space. The view of the city from the hills quite inspiring. At the massive iron-gates, offices of Life Insurance companies too! Geoffrey wondered how these two businesses were compatible!

And then he drove me to the Hollywood Bowl, an open air theatre, which can accommodate twenty thousand at a time, on the mountain side, where concerts are held in certain seasons, with parking space for twenty thousand cars. And back to his flat—stopping on the way to see the 'Tar-pits' at a public park, where natural tar is oozing out of the ground, where Indian cattle paths lay, and where they have dug up an immense quantity of prehistoric fossils. Back to Shurlock's room on the eleventh floor looking out over the entire city; where he made coffee for me, and we spoke of Indian castes, Gandhi, the Gita and so forth. He showed me a copy of the Gita in translation which he has read for years. Dinner at a cafe. And then he took me up a hill to show me the city view at night. We parted at 11 p.m. He must have driven me over one hundred and fifty miles today showing me the sights of Hollywood. He would not let me thank him, because he said he could not have seen Huntington Library but for me; he had been planning a visit to the Huntington Gallery and other places for about thirty years, and could achieve it only today. Great soul, silently suffering—having lost his wife three years ago; in his lovely flat on the eleventh floor, surrounded by music, books, memories and a view of the city, he tries to forget himself in his work as a censor. He is one of the most lovable and popular men in Hollywood, although in his position he could easily make himself odious to everyone.

Aldous Huxley

Another afternoon with Aldous Huxley. As usual they came down to meet me at the bus terminal. Huxley took me for a walk to show me a few places on the hills and a lake, an artificial one, which is supplying water to Hollywood, pumped up all the way from Colorado, nearly one thousand and seven hundred feet up, as he explained. He explained at length various statistics about water supply; his mind is really encyclopaedic, storing up all sorts of facts and figures, as one notices in his latest book. I have left a copy of *The English Teacher* for him to read. I explained to him some of the psychic phenomena in it, and told him about the lesson Paul Brunton taught me years ago. He explained that he was trying almost a similar experiment, but would like to try the suggestions in my book too. He cheerfully takes up any mental experiment suggested to him. We talked of Forest Lawns and he said, thinking it over, that it's so colossal and detailed that it's past the stage of being laughed at, where there are chapels, but no crucification, no cross, no suffering; only the Last Supper, but not beyond—a place where a discreet censorship is applied to death, so that no pain or suffering is indicated—these are not to be remembered; death only as a happy holiday—even adding a sort of glamour to it, as a sort of inducement to book a space in Forest Lawns; a chapel where a recorded hymn goes on; and marriages take place, immediately to be followed by a cremation. 'In this country,' Huxley said, 'you come across fantastic things side by side. At one place you'll see a huge advertisement for Forest Lawns, next to it whisky, health food, and gambling at Las Vegas, probably also some religious activities, and something else. Well, consume whisky and ruin your health, or gamble and blow yourself out or think of God, but the end is the same in any case—that may be the underlying philosophy in all this. You find things rather jumbled up, in this country.'

Mrs Huxley said when we returned home, '*Grateful to Life and Death* is a beautiful title.'

'It's the last line of my book—' I was rather surprised to hear her approval, as apart from Lyle Blair who changed *English Teacher* to *Grateful to Life and Death*, I've not met anyone to approve of the change.

During tea, which was very welcome after the walk, we were joined by —(name not clear at the moment) and his extraordinarily beautiful wife. This man continued the talk on Forest Lawns. It was rather careless of me not to have listened attentively when the visitor's name was mentioned, but I gathered from the talk that was going on that he had come to the States to direct an opera at the New York Metropolitan, that he had directed some outstanding pictures in England, and that he was eminent in the theatre world. I hoped for the best, thinking there would be an occasion for me to catch the sound of his name in due course. When we all rose to go, Huxley told him that he could drop me on the way as they were going down Sunset Boulevard and were in need of someone to show them the way. His wife drove the car, because the gentleman had found the gadget-ridden, left-hand-drive, American car they had rented for the trip, as well as the traffic rules, beyond him. They stopped the car in front of my hotel on Sunset Boulevard. I thanked them and said, 'You should come to India and make a picture.'

'I would love to; it has always been my ambition to make a picture in India. Can't we discuss it sometime?'

'I'll be in London next month,' I said.

'That will be wonderful. Why don't you give me a call when you are in London?'

'I will take down your number in a minute,' I said, the engine was running as they were in a hurry to reach a party at eight o'clock. I felt awkward to hold them up. But I had to know where I could see him again. He seemed to be a worthwhile man, who knew my books, and also a friend of Graham Greene. I fumbled for my pocketbook which I had left behind, while holding a simultaneous conversation with him and his wife. And now suddenly a police-officer on a motorcycle drew up along the driver's window. He wore a helmet and was grim-looking. He held out his hand and said, to the lady, 'Your driving license and birthdate.'

'Why?'

'You are getting a ticket.'

'What is that?' she asked.

He took out his book and started writing.

'Your birthday? Your name?'

The lady was distraught. She said, 'What has happened?'

'You turned the wrong lane.' The gentleman tried to ask a question or two and said with resignation, 'There is nothing I can do about it. Let her deal with him,' and turned away from the whole thing to me at the other window, and said, 'Please give me something on which I can write my address.' At the other window the policeman was arguing with the lady. He seemed to derive a fiendish delight in tormenting this lovely person.

The lady was saying, 'But I didn't know. . .'

'You should know the rules.'

'What is a wrong lane?'

'You shouldn't have taken it,' the officer said. He handed her a ticket. He was bawling at one window, explaining to her the traffic regulations and also what was in store for her at the law court. She was angry and kept telling him that she was a visitor, a newcomer to the country, which only provoked the man to hold out more and more terrifying prospects for her. I felt a tremendous responsibility for the whole situation. If I had not asked them to stop at Highland Motel . . . I apologized aloud, through the window, to the lady on the other side, over the head of the gentleman. She kept asking something of the grim policeman, who wore a steel helmet and looked like a Martian just landed with a ray gun in hand, out to disintegrate and atomize the citizens of this earth, and he was bawling something in reply. Her husband had completely detached himself from the whole proceedings. He snatched from my hand a journal I was carrying and wrote on it his name and London telephone number. It was a magazine Huxley had lent me to read a tough article on ESP by someone. I still could not decipher his name. I told him, 'Yes I will telephone, but perhaps you would be busy,' wondering by what name to call him on the phone in London.

'Oh, I will be rehearsing . . . you will be welcome.' The lady said, 'This is ridiculous, we are returning to New York early tomorrow.'

'Well, you will have to go later, that is all,' the policeman said.

The motorcycle pattered out. In a quarter of an hour she could start her car again, having mastered all its gadgets. They were so preoccupied that I had not the heart to say goodbye to them. On this confused note we parted.

I couldn't make out his name on the magazine cover. I telephoned Aldous Huxley and learnt that he was none other than Peter Brook, the famous British stage director. Later, when I went to London I tried to get in touch with him, but I learnt that he was busy at Stratford-on-Avon conducting the Shakespeare festival. His wife answered the telephone and said, 'Oh, dear, I can't forget that awful evening. Wasn't it dreadful! I will never go to Los Angeles again.'

*

Dr Kaplan picks me up at twelve o'clock and takes me to Columbia Pictures to meet the writer-producer Michael Blankfort—fine, sharp, friendly man, who looks like a reincarnation of Arnold Bennett, with his moustache and chin. Lunch at Naples—a famous Hollywood restaurant and pub, full of atmosphere—low, head-scraping roof, from which dangle hundreds of wine-baskets in miniature, autographed pictures of a million movie personalities, dim red light, smoke and narrow sofa seats at the tables. I have learnt to manage these luncheons—having my own food (which I call heavy breakfast) earlier in the day and nibbling salad and stuff like that at the parties, the company itself being more important. Kaplan is a brilliant wit, scholar, and conversationalist; and Michael is equal to him. Michael is good enough to inscribe a copy of his novel and give it to me, with the remark, 'If I were a painter, I'd have given you a picture, but this is all I can offer.'

Back to hotel, where Dorothy Jones comes to take me to Twentieth Century Fox. It's easily the biggest studio here. Our public relations takes us first to their chief cameraman, who explains at length their latest lens for use of wide screen and fifty-five millimeter films; and is good enough to show us some tests— amazing sweep the lens has without panning, which he demonstrates with sight boards arrayed ahead in a semi-circle—the lens takes it all in in one glance; and then close-shot also on the same principle, of any object at a distance of about seven hundred feet. He shows me several charts with enthusiasm.

'Any questions?' he asks.

'Uh, no. It's all so clear I've no questions.' It's difficult for me, in spite of my vague, general interest in technicalities, to maintain an intelligent face while he is talking. He is a man completely submerged in his technicalities, and cannot think for a minute that there could be anything else in life worth thinking or talking about. Moreover, through some initial error somewhere, I have been introduced as a novelist, screen-writer and 'producer' from India, and it's too late for me to correct the error. It gives me a chance to observe technical matters closely. Next, in the sound department, they explain the changes that the advent of the magnetic tape has brought in. I'm taken through vast, complicated recording rooms.

'You must be familiar with the magnetic—'

'Yes, of course, naturally,' I say. It's all very complex and impressive to me. Sound has always attracted me in a vague way, but I don't understand a thing about it. I manage to essay one intelligent query, suitable for the occasion.

'Are these compatible with fifty-five millimetre frames?' The question, it's a cute one I think, passes the rounds, and they say, 'Well, not exactly yet . . .'

And then we pass on to more theatres. I could probably appreciate it better if I saw something happen there. Mere technicalities bore me; and then our guide takes me to see the 'Lot'—'New York street', 'Ocean and Sky', 'French village', 'Egypt', 'Blue sea and Horizon', 'A London street', all facades used for outdoor scenes, a symbol of 'maya', as Huxley said, permanently built on several acres of ground. I'm soon out. I catch the bus on Santa Monica. The bus driver is very careless. First he shuts the door with me halfway through (some day an American is going to be cut longitudinally and only then will they alter the arrangement of doors in their buses) and next he crashes into a new Chevrolet. The cars are stopped. It's extremely calm. No police. Our driver distributes a card round to the bus passengers, 'I'd appreciate it if you gentlemen will fill this,' like a conjuror involving the audience in a trick. I look away. I don't want to be involved in anything. People get very busy writing down.

'Can you pull out your car—?' he suggests to the man whose car has been rammed in.

'Yeah,' he says and does so. If it were our country there'd be so much of speech and action and recrimination, and comments from bystanders. Here no one bothers. No argument between the protagonists, no accusations or gesticulation. They exchange notes and papers—behave like real gentlemen in an ancient duel. And then the bus is on its way again; and the car is driven off. Only sign anything is amiss being a long piece of chromium-plated metal which is flung out of the Chevrolet. People are full of praise for the driver of our bus. They have silently, unconsciously become partisans. No one likes the man whose car has been rammed in—not even himself. They mutter, 'It was a terrible piece of driving.'

I feel irritated at having to go out again at 8 p.m. I am on the brink of calling off the evening engagement. But Sally won't hear of it. She has fixed it with David So-and-so, the writer. After a hurried meal, I am out again, meeting Sally at Hotel Roosevelt. We go by bus to David's home. Find the family quietly settled after dinner—with the daughter at her homework. David is a successful screen and television writer, whose speciality is the 'western'. He is not a born writer. He does not like writing; does it only to make money—and hopes to retire, go on a holiday, and take to painting: he has adorned his walls with grotesque, obscure daubs in frames. He may be called the 'robot' writer. He is evidently very successful and in demand. Even while we were talking, producers were calling him on the phone. He looks on me, I don't know how. He views other literary work as mere prolific raw material for his screen-version, I suppose. He even mentions that most book writers indulge in a vast quantity of unnecessary writing. However, I'm happy to talk shop with him. His wife evidently has great admiration for the profession and keeps saying that the percentage of human beings that could be called authors is ever so small, while there are doctors, barbers, etc, in any number.

*

The Metro-Goldwyn-Mayer visit. The same type of talk as with the 'International' man. Difficulties with the Indian government. *Bhowani Junction* was not shot in India because the government did not give in writing an agreement that they'd make no demand on its world profits! Strange are the ways of government and films. Lunch at the famous restaurant, watching the shooting for a while by the famous George Cukor of *Les Girls*, more 'Lot' inspection, New York, French village, Sea and Forest. While crossing the lawns, a brief shakehand meeting with George Murphy—an old time actor, who says, 'You are from Mysore? I have just met a convent sister from Mysore, who is collecting funds for a high school. She and her companion: they were so charming, like a couple of birds alighting and flying away. I could not help giving a small donation because their appeal is so sincere . . . You know about that school?'

'Name?'

'Christ the King . . .'

'Oh, that is where my daughter studied, it is next door to our house, what's the name of the sister?'

'Bernadine.'

'She was my daughter's teacher.' The world has shrunk suddenly. Who could imagine in these surroundings Bernadine, the kindest of teachers and the most despairing one for my daughter's arithmetic, who often came down to see me and say, 'Oh, you must do something about Hema, the poor child needs special attention.' There was nothing I could do about it, arithmetic being as much a terror to me. To hear Bernadine's name again after all these years! Human beings get knit up in fantastic unbelievable ways, complex and unexpected links like the wiring at the back of a radio panel.

Visit Paramount Studio, which is just a repetition of other studio experiences. My guide the grandson of Zukor, called Adolf Zukor the Second, slow, timid, shy and very intelligent. He keeps saying, 'I don't know what you can see here!' He crashes into a studio where a notice saying 'Closed' is hung outside; they are shooting a scene with Lizabeth Scott and someone else.

Next engagement, visit to 'Consolidated', a hectic place, where I sit on a bench at the reception, waiting for a man to appear and take me in. There is a spring door in front of me, which is being pulled and pushed continuously—men and women, chatting, preoccupied and in a deadly hurry sweeping in and out. Those who wait at the reception are restless and fidgety, and those who move do so in a run; never was a spring door more agitated. It is a place where 16 mm films are processed and sent off to various television studios, as it seems, exactly with a minute to go for the scheduled programmes. Finally a man turns up and takes me in to show me a magnificent colour film on an Indian village made for the Ford Foundation. After the show, offers to drive me in his car to my hotel. An over-active man, who wastes a lot of my time by neither letting me go, nor keeping me company, he makes me sit in his car and dashes in and out of various buildings on the way. So that I reach my hotel late in the evening.

A telephone call at my hotel.

'Is that Narayan?'

'Yes, speaking.'

'*Namaste,* Narayanji.' I was surprised.

'Who is speaking please?'

'Kenneth McEldowney.' Another man whom I had lost sight of in Bombay seven years ago. Fantastic contacts really. He had seen my name in *Variety*, the trade paper, and had tracked me down. Years ago we should have made a picture called *Khedda* with the background of elephant-trapping in Mysore jungles, he had several reels of it taken in technicolour and wanted me to write a story around the subject. We met in Bombay, discussed plans and then kept writing to each other; a file developed, he became famous with his picture, directed by Jean Renoir, called *The River*, but the second picture never came to be done in spite of a very fat file of letters and cables growing out of it on my table. Ken McEldowney got into some contractual difficulties with the government of Mysore, thought it best to abandon the project altogether, and the loser was myself since I had already worked on a number of possible stories for him. But it had an unexpected result. I had gone through so much research into elephant-catching in Mysore forests, where herds live and flourish and are rounded up through an elaborate system of drives, that I grew interested in the subject myself, and I may possibly deserve a doctorate in elephant affairs! . . . This man telephoned me today and took me to his home in Bel Air.

'Vedanta Plaza'

In search of the Vedanta Society of Hollywood on Vine. The county authorities, having cut a freeway through a corner of the estates of the Ashram, have compensated by officially naming the area Vedanta Plaza. Hollywood is full of philosophy and yoga. At one end of Sunset Boulevard we have the self-realization centre with its own chapel, where I spent an evening listening to a sermon on 'reincarnation', where books by the late Yogananda and mystic souvenirs are sold. Young men and women were listening to the lecture on reincarnation. They looked fashionable, modern and young; one could not think they would be attracted by reincarnation, but there they were, voluntarily walking in and listening. The self-realization centre, incidentally, has at its entrance one of the best vegetarian restaurants in the United States; the first step in self-realization is good food, and that is provided for at the entrance, after which you could step in to hear a lecture or buy a book on *vedanta*. At the other terminus of Sunset Boulevard, four miles away, I saw another signboard announcing yoga lessons by appointment. Here we have 'Vedanta Plaza' officially included in the county registers—so that's where Indian philosophy stands at the present moment in Hollywood, which seems to me really a versatile place with its technology, television, aeronautics, world of illusions and world of enlightenment . . .

Swami Prabhavananda, the head of this Society, is away at Santa Barbara. His next-in-command is a young person by the name of Swami Vandanananda, who left his family in Mysore when he was seventeen, about twenty years ago; spent over ten years in Almora at the mission's headquarters in the Himalayas. Like a true *sanyasi*, as one who has renounced the world, he had not thought of his home or written to any of his relations for over a decade. But talking to me in that hall, brought back to his mind Mysore, his home in D. Subbiah Road, his aunt, uncles, and friends, and the Kannada and Tamil in which we spoke induced in him a slight homesickness, perhaps. I seem to have brought with me a waft of his old life for him. At six o'clock, he left me and went to the chapel to conduct vespers. A number of inmates assembled and sat in silent meditation before a picture of Ramakrishna and the Holy Mother. Lamps were lit, flowers and incense. The prayer went on for a long time; in that stillness, I slipped out, while everyone sat with shut eyes, and wandered in the garden.

Later the swami joined me and took me to the dining hall. There are about sixty American men and women, living in this ashram. They go through a course of studies and ascetic discipline; men and women are necessarily segregated—sometimes they change their minds and return to the mundane world; sometimes a romance develops and they wish to renounce the ascetic life and go out and marry; Swami Prabhavananda, the head of this institution, takes a very generous view of all such second thoughts and never denies his disciples their freedom of action; some stay in the Ashram for ten years, become qualified to be called 'Swami', learned, and austere and carrying on the work of this mission in various parts of the world . . .

*

With Aldous Huxley and Gerald Heard to the Los Angeles Medical College, where they address a group of medical men on Mescalin. They dwell on the deepening of consciousness as a means to helping the next phase of evolution, which must all be spiritual and mental, men having reached the peak in the material world. Mescalin and lycergic acid, are some of the drugs with which Huxley and Heard are experimenting. One memorable sentence of Huxley's in the speech, I forget why he said it, 'Alcohol is incompatible with the automobile.' At the end of the meeting, my camera goes into action and I manage to take several group photographs with Huxley and Heard. After the meeting, I stop off at Huxley's house, for tea and talk. Later they drive me back downhill at the end of the day as usual. Huxley urges me to come back to the States. I dine at the self-realization centre restaurant on the way and go back to my room for packing.

*

Checked out of my room at noon. I had grown rooted to this motel and felt sorry to leave it. The motel lady gave me a room till the evening train-time, free of cost. The whole day messed up by the hope of seeing Gerald Heard, and by an uncertain engagement with a young man I had met at the Huxley lecture, an underwater specialist. He kept threatening to come any minute from 7 a.m., onwards to take me out in his car. I had to make Dorothy wait uncertainly at her telephone, although she called nine times to find out when she should come for me. Finally, the sub-aquatic man turned up at two-thirty in the afternoon, and drove straight to a television studio because he was under the impression that that was what I wanted to do. He forgot that he had offered to take me to his house. I wriggled out of this mess; the only wise act for the day on my part being my refusal to hand him my roll of exposed negatives, which he wanted to take charge of in order to help me get them developed. Dorothy arrived at three, and immediately plunged into my travel and packing arrangements. Pack up and leave motel, seen off by the entire family who manage this motel. The old man said, 'Give my respects to Nehru—he is a sound man.'

GRAND CANYON AND BEYOND

Grand Canyon

The word grand has never had a grander function to perform. Its mighty quality is a thing that has to be directly felt, and no report at second-hand can ever convey its tremendous impact. It has versatility and modifications in its apparent geological fixity. Yes, now when one comes to think of it, the word 'fixity' could never be more misapplied for a thing created by the interaction of water and soil and rock, and mellowed by light and sun. It is a work of art by Nature—a sort of abstraction in which Nature has indulged after having passed through the phases of symmetry and perfect form. Here we have pure abstract forms, colours and chromatic scale from blue to red and grey—so well merged that you would not notice the hundred shades in it. Here are forms which defy classification. They look like South Indian temples, they look like Buddhist temples; we have before us a conglomeration of Mahabalipuram, of Hoysala architecture, various battlements and pyramidal structures, mighty ones, which not the sternest slave-drivers could ever have hoped to erect or copy; chasms, and prototypes of every architecture on earth. The resemblance of various formations to temples is so great that they are called 'Shiva temple', 'Brahma temple' and 'Zoroaster temple'. Here all religions meet and merge. It is here you feel with an unbearable agony, a mystic mood; the almighty takes his name here. Here is a performance that overwhelms us with its might.

The sun is setting and I feel it a sacrilege to be writing this instead of keeping my eyes on the rocks. It is easy to become incoherent in this presence. I noticed my fellow-passengers in the tour bus uttering involuntary cries at every turn and the word 'temple' was much heard. Those who would not notice a temple anyway involuntarily utter the word. God has shown in the most solid of things—rocks—the highest of elusive abstractions of form. Observing this I get a sympathetic notion of what abstract painters attempt to do. Far down, the Colorado winds along its muddy course, and its roar comes out muffled and softened. The chatter of fellow tourists is rather trying. But it may be remedied, I suppose, by suggesting that silence must be maintained while viewing the chasm.

Before the East lightens, to watch the Canyon is to watch an infinite void. At this hour when the sky is still starry—there are seven stars over the void—it looks like the beginning of creation itself. At first there is absolute darkness below, but if you keep looking on, gradually contours and rises become faintly visible—softly emerging to view. At this hour, with only the stars to witness (fortunately they make no noise), absolute silence reigns over the whole scene—everything is absolute here.

Fortunately all the guests in the hotel are asleep. This is one of my own private and special sights of the twilight of the night. Some whisperings rise from the depth, if you will hear them—like the echoes of the ocean one hears in shells. The light of the morning—the first shaft to bring the chasm to view again. I'm waiting for it, but, alas, the bus has already arrived to take me to Williams and end the charm.

Santa Fe

At the Williams station, we learn that the train will be late. No one knows more. There is a casualness about the railways here which I like. A train is heard to approach far away. One man runs out with a flag. The train will pass unless it's flagged down. We are all alerted. The man who stops the train for us also does multifarious things—sells tickets, writes on forms, operates the controls, holds out the mail bag, and pushes our luggage into our respective coaches.

I don't know if he can be tipped. How can one tip a station master, which perhaps he is? I don't know whether to look up on him as a porter or a station superintendent. Finally I take the benefit of the doubt, having tipped so many others.

Leaving Williams, the train passes through the deserts of Arizona for hours and hours—huge signposts announcing 'Serpent Gardens', 'Rattle-snake Farms' and such attractive places all along the way. The scene is very much like passing from Arsikere to Davangere: dry, sandy, with rusty wrecked cars everywhere.

Lamy at four-fifteen—a small flag-station with the threat of the train pulling out before you are fully out of it. A bus journey and now in Santa Fe actually.

Hotel hunting, and then to La Fonda—single room without bath for the night; sneaking up the corridor for the toilet.

Evening, having no other business, stray into a cinema.

People eat and drink too much inside the hall, constantly going out during the show to fetch noisy things to eat, and of course flirt and woo in their seats, hardly paying any attention to what goes on on the vista-vision, cinemascope, perforated, plastic, silver-screen.

At the Mexican restaurant beautiful girls in costume-skirts serving, lovely music on violin, piano and guitar, slow, soothing tunes (God knows what they are), restful yellow lights, blue star-lights and white and red painted rough wooden furniture, the smiling musicians—all this creates a fit atmosphere for eating enchilada, beans, and what not. A couple at the other table get up and dance, leaving their dinner for a few minutes and resuming it after the dance. A fat couple whom music has made oblivious, for a moment, of their bulk. Looking at them, I feel like uttering the uncalled-for, uncharitable comment, 'They keep off eating only when they are dancing.'

This morning Mr Long, Gilpatric's friend, takes charge of me. An ex-official of the State Department. It is a relief to find someone to talk to in this place. It's snowing outside. 'Bring your coat along, and let us go out,' is his first call. He has tracked me at La Fonda, which, I suppose, is a sort of a human lost-property office.

Mr Long drives me to the Museum of Folk Art and explains

everything expertly. Introduces me to a number of archaeologists for a couple of minutes at each seat. The Doctorate is back on me. It was only at the Grand Canyon that no-one called me 'Doctor'.

Santa Fe has the combined appearance of Monkombu, Krishnarajapuram, Sivaganga and Seringapatam—with its little streets and abodes made of clay and tiles; some of the bigger buildings have about them a touch of the palace of the Nawab of Carnatic at Madras—the same richness of timber and style of construction. Every bit has a romantic interest here—that foot-track might have been an Indian trail, that piece of pottery on the ground Indian pottery (in fact the great archaeological museum was started by John D. Rockefeller when he came here once and found his children picking up pottery pieces). Santa Fe has a constant flavour of this Indian background—the Indians in deliberate costumes selling souvenirs on the veranda of the Governor's palace. There is a Spanish section in the town—half the persons speak Spanish; the churches and palace of the Governor and bits of a fortress here and there still have a touch of Spain, the Anglo-American influence since 1846 evidenced by the American post office housed in an unbelievably ancient-looking, quaint mud structure. For a small place, too many influences are intermingled here. At the moment the local legislature is in session, and the hotel lobby is full of well-dressed, loquacious, self-important legislators. Mr Long is busy now, lobbying with them for securing a grant of a million dollars for a downtown museum.

'Palmess'

Our guide is an interesting man. He is OK, but for his frequent fascination for pointing out 'pumice', which he calls 'palmess'; he is somehow fascinated by the rocks. He ought to be a geologist and not a guide.

'It's all palmess—see that—it is red through oxidation, and nothing else, but if you scrape it off it's white . . . see that! That's palmess—'

Seeing that the whole mountain range surrounding us is lava, 'palmess', or whatever you call it, he ought to see the absurdity of mentioning it again and again—an average of twice every five minutes. After hours of driving through passes and canyon roads, we arrive at the Bandelier National Monument, where preserved in a well-ordered museum in that far-off place, is an amazing collection of relics of Pueblo Indians, who lived in this region about eight centuries ago. Here we have also an outdoor museum of their community village, the Tyuonui ruin, excavated in 1908; and pre-historic dwellings gouged out of the northern cliff-wall of Frijoles Canyon, one to three stories in height, with many cave-rooms in each. This affords me a delicious moment of escape into a dim, prehistoric period, although we are walking in the rain with the elevation making me gasp for breath and I feel as if I should bleed at the nose the next moment. The guide goes into minute details of the Indians' daily life. I pay little attention to his narration, preferring my own vision of the prehistoric life in this mighty wilderness of the Rio Grande Valley, traversed in some places only by trails. But the Finnish girl, who is also on a visit, listens to the guide with interest.

The word 'Indian' constantly gets mixed up. 'I had an Indian visitor,' says the guide, meaning a visitor like me; and then, 'The Indians were . . . etc.,' meaning the Navajos or the Pueblo or the Apache. The original confusion caused by Columbus still continues in speech.

On our way back our guide takes us through parts of wonderful scenic beauty: snow-filled trees, and snow-covered fields and pines stretching away on both sides. And then he takes us into the nuclear city at Los Alamos, which had been closed to the public for thirteen years. Our guide is thrilled to be passing through it. He points to the cars going ahead. 'Boys returning after their day's work—they never discuss their work even with their wives.' He indulges in an imaginary conversation between a scientist and his wife, as he is about to set forth on a mysterious mission to a testing ground. Our guide is very proud of the fact that Santa Fe was the first to be rocked by a small test atomic explosion. He hints that at Santa Fe, of all places in the country, there is an idea of what's going on in nuclear affairs. His incessant talk suddenly depresses me. A guide should talk less, because his employers are totally at his mercy in a car. It's like having a radio permanently tied to one's ears. His voice rasps and sounds worn out, like the voices of some of the over-experienced newsreaders of the All India Radio. With all that he is a good man, generous, human and warm. At the Bandelier site he would not let me approach the ruins in the rain, but insisted on clamping his own hat on my head, although he was exposing himself to the cold and revealing an incredible state of baldness.

Forgot to add that we visit an Indian village in one of the reservations on our way to Bandelier Monument, and see some houses and two women, with three children watching them bake bread. One of the Indian women goes in and brings a loaf of bread wrapped in paper, and hands it to the Finnish girl.

'May I buy it?' she asks, taking out her purse.

'No, I'm giving it to you. Please take it,' says the Indian woman, in perfect English, much to everybody's astonishment. This place just looks to me like the backyard of any home in a Mysore village. And our guide seems to be a familiar figure here.

I have seen the full swing of civilization's progress—from the cave-dwellings of Pueblo Indians to a fresh, almost wet-paint-smelling nuclear city. Enough history for the day.

Morning I get up with travel anxiety stirring in me. Various complications become evident before 11 a.m. It is all more indefinite than a reservation on the Blue Mountain Express at Coimbatore. They want me to buy the ticket, but will not confirm a journey. The air services simply feel that if I don't go fully through, I should claim a refund when I'm back at Santa Fe, and will not understand that I may never re-visit this place. The lady at the 'Indian Detour Section' (it's the travel department of the hotel) is very helpful and works out schemes for me and keeps at the telephone for hours, trying to persuade the airport to see my point of view. All is well that ends well—I get a ticket in the evening, confirmed only up to Memphis!

I have phoned Monroe Spears to meet me at Nashville tomorrow evening!

Meet Mr Long again and gently resist the various involvements he is planning for me. He tries to take me through the museum again, but I tell him definitely that I have already seen all of it; he tries to involve me in a lunch, which also I ward off, and then he gives me two tickets for a Euripides play this evening, saying, generously, 'Take a girl with you for the other ticket.'

'Where is the girl?' I ask.

'The girl who came to our house last night, I forget her name, take her along with you. She is very intelligent.'

When I plead doubt, he says, 'There is another girl—' He takes me across to a shop and introduces me to a chirpy, bright 'girl', a super-active person selling souvenirs, saris from India, and 'Madras' shirts. I wriggle out of this situation too. She informs me incidentally in the few seconds I am there that she lost a thirty-dollar sari last night . . .

I bid goodbye to Mr Long after all. Call up Mrs R— and spend the evening at her home, while my mind is all bothered about the tickets. She is a sad, forlorn creature, with two children, who keep her fully busy. She is from New York. Coming away here, after living for five years with her parents, and realizing that the children would not grow up satisfactorily under the grandparents' excessive devotion. She is a fugitive from her parents' home, having fled to the extreme end of the country, thousands of miles away, to start life anew, strange driving-force her parents must have exercised. The more pressing question is about Mr R—where is (or was) he? But I shall never know. It's snowing today as I've never seen it snow before. It's white and brilliant everywhere.

Wayfarer

Visit St Miguel's Church, 'the oldest church' in the United States. In this town one comes across too many 'oldest'. The church has three layers in excavation—of AD 1300 revealing Indian bones, of AD 1600, Spanish, and over that relics of a later period, which is all left uncovered at the altar. There is a Father showing us round and, of course, selling picture postcards and souvenirs. I notice another person, with a simpler camera than mine, trying to photograph the altar. It's his first reel and first clicking! The camera establishes a link between us.

I notice him asking the Father about a weekend 'retreat' nearby. We become friends. He is a road-engineer on his way to Los Angeles. An Illinois man going to California to seek his fortune. He arrived but an hour ago in his car, and is passing on to Albuquerque and beyond. I induce him to spend a little more time at Santa Fe. He invites me to go about with him. Find him an extremely noble-minded, sensitive young man. We go to Lamy Cathedral. In the chapel he kneels and prays. And then he goes up to an adjoining office to enquire about a 'retreat' again. I ask what a 'retreat' means. He explains that there are monastic places where one could spend a weekend in meditation all through. I suggest the Grand Canyon to him, as a place where one could meditate without any special effort.

He drives me about till one o'clock through Santa Fe and its suburbs, and joins me at lunch in the Mexican restaurant, where the girl has kept Spanish rice ready for me. She calls it pure vegetarian, but God knows what there may be in that red sauce. My companion admires the autographed Hollywood photographs that I have secured for my daughter, which I am carrying around before posting. The waitresses come over to see the photographs and all of them cry, 'Gee! What a treasure!' (Later when I go to a stationer to buy an envelope, the younger assistant cries, 'Gee, you've got real treasure. Be careful with it,' and he takes it in to show to his friends in other departments, and I overhear several 'Gees' coming from there, and the word 'Hema' spelt out aloud—it delights me to hear my daughter's name uttered everywhere!)

After lunch my friend and I part. Well, we may never meet again. We've been together for three hours in all—I feel I have spotted the finest type of human being. A brief encounter, but a rich and potent one really.

Harveyism

Harveyism consists in converting rocks, scenery, rivers, canyons, towns and atmosphere, including all their civilizations, into cash-business, by selling them to tourists. Fred Harvey is almost a legendary name here. He has built his hotels exactly in the style of each place, has a shop selling genuine souvenirs, employs dancers who execute folk dances, starts factories where souvenirs are manufactured, dresses his staff in the costumes of the place and period, and by every effort keeps up the Indian, Mexican, and Spanish qualities of everything from Grand Canyon and Santa Fe to God knows where. I fervently hope that our country may not become so utterly tourized (touristized?) that it turns all its cultural treasures and antiquities over to Harvey, although there are signs of it—seen in the number of Indian gods, who have invaded American homes, and the small slabs of carved temple-chariots that every American tourist brings home with him.

GURUKULA IN TENNESSEE

Sewanee is beautiful with its tall trees and brooks and its houses built in valleys and on mountain slopes. Sewanee is a '*Gurukula*'—a small college of five hundred boys (no girls admitted), lovely cottages, few and far apart on the hill, tall trees; in every way a most attractive little place, where it is possible to practice studies and discipline without any distraction. They do not seem to have even a cinema nearby, nor any of the allurements that grow around the mammoth campuses. The boys, by a resolution among themselves, are dressed in full suit and tie and look extremely sober (no crew-cut and fancy jersey here); the staff are all quiet and intelligent and devoted. I am a guest in the home of Professor Monroe Spears. Monroe's home is a scholar's retreat; set amidst dogwood in bloom, filled with books, music, and pictures, with no television or radio in the house, and run by the generous, ever-cheerful Betty; her little daughter Julie, the moment she saw me, promptly announced, 'I love you. I'll marry you,' but cancelled her plans in a huff three days later when I left, because she was not being taken along.

*

Up early in order to be ready for a class of boys in Monroe's college. At nine we march into his class. Monroe writes on the black board 'Assignment—R.K. Narayan'. He reads to the class Graham Greene's introductions to two of my books. The normal work of the class has been suspended. I speak to the boys on my books, the problems of a writer and answer their questions. Afternoon Monroe drives me around and shows me the sights of Sewanee, beautiful valley-views from various points of vantage, and a drive to an immense cross standing on a hillock: a memorial to the youth killed in the war of 1914-18. Evening a large party in Monroe's house. I hold a glass of sherry as a courtesy—but a sip of it sends my head reeling and I put it away. I meet here the entire society of Sewanee, and quite a number of them say how much they appreciate Tagore's writings. Nowhere else have I come across so many who mention Tagore. A lady has come wearing ivory pendants and ear-drops made in India in my honour, and feels happy when I assure her they are genuine. Betty, our hostess, has dressed herself in Indian material. This is an Indian day at Sewanee. The crowd leaves as fast as it gathers. After dinner a number of college boys arrive, and we sit in a semi-circle. I answer questions, even such a one as, 'Has the sacred cow been abolished in India?'

'Why do you want it to be abolished?'

'Food is scarce in India, we learn, would it not be better economy for people to eat beef?'

'Cows are also scarce in India, and it's better they are not eaten but allowed to provide much-needed milk as long as they can, and when they go dry we like to leave them free to live an honourable, retired life instead of killing them—just as you treat old-age pensioners who may not be active now, but who are none the less treated considerately.'

*

After lunch, to Monteagle to catch a bus for Nashville where I shall take the plane for Washington DC. The bus depot displays in its waiting hall 'For Coloured' and 'For Whites' notices. Even in the bus the white passengers are the first to take their seats. The conductor manoeuvres things in such a manner that the coloured men can get in only after the whites are seated. The convention seems to be that the last seats should be occupied by coloured passengers. White passengers blink unhappily when I get in. Each tries to cover a vacant seat next to him with an overcoat or hat for fear that I may attempt to occupy a prohibited seat and create a 'situation'. I pass straight on to where two negroes are sitting, and they make place for me. There are still four seats vacant in our row, but no one comes there. A fat white man and his short wife get into the bus on the way, but prefer to stand on their feet for seventy miles rather than sit down next to me. The short wife cannot reach the strap on the roof of the bus, and the fat husband cannot keep on his feet; they suffer hell, yet they prefer to stand and travel rather than sit by my side. At the Nashville bus terminal I see 'Coloured' and 'White' notices everywhere, and immediately take a taxi for the airport, and 'check in' my luggage, have coffee, and correct the novel for two hours, in an effort to forget the problems of human complexion.

WASHINGTON DC AND ONWARD

Bus and tram drive through the capital, which is definitely a government town, with government buildings, government quarters, government offices, and my only human contact is with the officials of Indian embassy. I cannot move around too much owing to the very cold wind freezing my ears. I wrap the muffler over my head, like an Ooty bus driver, and create a sight for everyone to gaze at! Visit Washington Memorial, Jefferson Memorial and Lincoln Memorial. This is a city of mighty monuments. This whole city is one of offices, office buildings, protocol, and office-talk. It has the stamp of New Delhi and Bangalore combined.

Washington is the cleanest city I've seen. Its one other attraction is the sweetness of its taxi service. Anywhere to anywhere, however circuitous or delayed it might be, it is just 40 cents or 60 cents according to zone, and no tips, mind you. I've found the most enchanting taxi-service on earth.

*

'I've been a barber longer than your years—I've been a barber for fifty years—starting at fifteen. I'm now sixty-five. I was in England in World War I. I've educated three sons. I have four grand-children. I have always managed to work and keep myself going. Work is my religion—you come from India? Great country—but have never been there. You are a lucky fellow to have travelled so much . . . you want your hair clipped close? I can take out anything, but never put back even one—remember that when you ask me to cut. Crew-cut! Horrible! Hopeless! I'll never never give anyone a crew-cut. I've cut hair for fifty years; I know my job. Why don't you leave that to me?. . . Well goodbye, it's nice seeing you. If you are happy I am pleased. Those who come here must always go back happy, that's what I like.' Hotel barber. All the time he was cutting, he had a cigar in his mouth. I gave him a five-dollar note, not being certain what would be the correct payment. He took a dollar and a half and returned the balance.

*

On the train to New York. Ideal time to try and read the manuscript of my novel, which I wrote in Berkeley. I try to read it, not as an author, but as a novel-reader who has picked it up for a train journey. Difficult to keep up the pretence—the book being in my long-hand manuscript; still, I manage. Well-settled in my parlour seat, I start with the first line of my novel beginning 'Raju welcomed the intrusion', and try to feel curious about further developments. I notice through the corner of my eye the passing piers, jetty, cranes, hangars, and the skyline of steel works, aluminium or plastic manufacturing concerns, oily shores and tumble-down houses, noting the heavy industrial stamp on this landscape. Still I am quite absorbed in *The Guide*, and realize with a great deal of relief, for the first time, that it does not bore. The journey takes about four hours and gives one an ideal situation for reading one's own novel for the first time.

I can only specify this part as the East Coast, was it Hudson or what river: there was one of those huge American rivers looking like the ocean—or was it the Atlantic itself? I couldn't say. Everything in this country looks like an ocean. The so-called lakes of Chicago are like the Bay of Bengal! I am no good at geographical details and I am not interested in industry, and so I can only say I passed a number of chimneys and coast lines and ships in harbour and so forth. What a contrast to other parts of the country—the Californian open spaces and hills, the mountainous green portions of the mid-west with their mighty trees and suggestion of tremendous sweep, the desert region of Arizona, the slick governmental touch of Washington, and the versatility of New York. This is a thoroughly industrial area, the one which is perhaps responsible for keeping America in prosperity and modernity. But I have not the time to brood on this scene too long, for one thing it doesn't interest me, for another I find Raju's career more inviting. We pass Philadelphia and I recollect with a sigh how many lapses I may be charged with for not answering the numerous letters from Norman Brown of Pennsylvania University, asking me to address the India Society group. He also suggested in his letter that they were starting Marathi and Gujarati studies and that my valuable opinion on those courses would be welcome. I had to write to say that they could sooner ask me to suggest a course of studies in Swahili and Yiddish and that I knew only Tamil and Kannada, and none of the other fourteen Indian languages. To which their only answer was to repeat their invitation. I put away the letter, not knowing what I should do about it. Now the brief halt at Philadelphia pricks my conscience. After seeing the Asia group in Berkeley I fight shy of such organizations anywhere. I sit back with my novel. Raju is making passes at the archaeologist's wife . . .

NEW YORK

Call Keith Jennison (of the Viking Press) first thing in the day. He invites me to lunch. When I go there, he apologizes for having made a mistake, as he already has another lunch engagement. He is happy and relieved to know that the book is finished. He, with one or two others, listens to my narration of my novel. He likes the story, and feels very hopeful for the book. My manuscript being what it is, I have to revert to the ancient system of oral story-telling. I think a story acquires an extra dimension in this kind of narration—and it's such a labour-saving device. I think an ideal situation would be where one gets a royalty for dictating at a publisher's office.

*

Snatch a snack at a restaurant. On an impulse phone Faubion, who tells me to jump into a cab and get there at once. 'Some persons who adore you are here, you must see them.' So I'm there soon, find a lot of people assembled in his house. The Bowers are absolutely overwhelming. After an hour we go to a party—where we meet Anna Magnani, the Director of Metropolitan Museum of Art, a psychiatrist, an Italian publisher's representative, the fiction editor of the *New Yorker*, and so on. We are soon in the thick of introductions. Santha and Faubion are so generous in referring to me that everyone views me with awe. It's Anna Magnani's birthday, and there is a chorus of happy-birthday-to-you and raising of glasses.

Major part of the day taken up in shifting to a room on the eleventh floor—looking out over Madison Avenue and the river of traffic there. All day in the room—letters, kitchen arrangements, and, in general, putting one's house in order. Lyle Blair turned up in the flesh. Wonderful to meet him after so many years of friendly correspondence. At first sight I know it must be Lyle and none else.

Went down to see him off and then post a letter. At the post office in 34th Street, gave the packet for weighing. Looking at the address, the counter clerk says, 'India?—Oh, how is India now?'

'Very well, thank you.'

'Things OK now?'

'Perfect.'

'Fifty cents—Oh! . . .'

'Can I put more in?'

'Sure, just a little over half an ounce—write more, put plenty more; do write to all your aunts, uncles, and companions, and tell them how do you do, it'll still cost only fifty cents. Photographs? Wonderful, go ahead . . . well, how are things at home? I mean in India. All OK? How are the new conditions?'

'Wonderful. They are doing big things in a big way there; tremendous projects, industrial schemes and so forth.'

'Oh, isn't that marvellous! Now do they make shirts and suits and machinery and things like that?'

'Yes, yes, that's just what they are doing.'

'What's that coat you are wearing? Is that imported?'

'No, made in India.'

'Really! What wonderful stuff! You mean to say they make such things there?'

'Yes, all this wool comes from Kashmir. . .' I say casually, not quite convinced within myself, and dreading lest he should go off at a tangent and start an investigation of the Kashmir issue.

Lyle Blair

Meet Lyle Blair at Bleeker Street, off Washington Square, at an address he has given. It is drizzling, but I manage to find the place and press the bell. A girl comes down the stairs and leads me to a room on the second floor (third according to the American step-counting system), where there is another girl. Lyle is expected. They know my name and I see my books on their shelves; they work in a publishing firm and are Lyle's friends. He comes in presently. He settles down on a sofa and I see him at his best—arguing, contradicting, emphasizing, and overwhelming all through whether the question be publishing, Kashmir, or anything. He has a lot of resemblance to an aggressive uncle of mine, especially when he goes into breath-taking philosophical turns. We repair to an Italian restaurant for dinner. I get an enormous plate of egg-plant fried in cheese and can eat only half of it. During the dinner Lyle declares: 'I'm terrified for your future, because you are going to be eaten up by the lions of New York; but let me tell you, in future you may do well or ill, but to have written *The English Teacher* is enough achievement for a lifetime. You won't do it again and can't even if you attempt it.'

'Why are you so arrogant that you will not let people do what they like for you? It pleases them to do something for you; please give them that liberty,' he says later.

'No, but I'd like to be able to do something in return . . .'

'You write. You've given them *The English Teacher* and that's enough. They like to do something in return. Let them do it.' And so, I had to watch his friend go down two flights and into the rain to fetch me ice cream, for which I had expressed a preference inadvertently at the restaurant.

Our discussions go on until midnight. Lyle constantly swears at a cat, which is a guest here, really belonging to someone involved in a motor accident and now in hospital, the cat alone escaping unhurt; and a parakeet which goes on pecking at its own image in a mirror creating an uproar, the cage kept out of reach of the cat on a shelf high up. Lyle calls the parakeet 'Narcissus'. The cat, like all New York cats, is fat and bloated. It can't go out; it goes to the window and keeps looking out through the glass, at the drunken and the bohemian population of the street below; Lyle who is somehow averse to the parakeet hopes that the cat will go up and make a meal of it, but it is perfectly safe here. The cat is so indolent and demoralized by synthetic cat-food that it can't spring up to the cage on the ledge. When the cat needs exercise, they give it cat's-nip to stir her into action—a small bundle of it flung on the floor makes the cat execute a variety of dances and caperings. Who discovered this? The same civilization which provides tinned food for the cat and saves it the bother of hunting mice and birds, also provides it cat's-nip for exercise—a rather comprehensive civilization. What's happening to the cat is what's happened to human beings since their days of cave-dwelling and food-hunting.

Get up at ten, and do not leave the room till five in the evening. Hear the drums of the St Patrick's Day parade on 5th Avenue, but cannot go down because I feel too lazy to dress. Glimpse a uniformed procession with band on Madison Avenue, from my window—regret that I cannot photograph it although there is such beautiful sunlight outside. I keep revising my book before lunch and after lunch—but have not progressed beyond five pages for the whole day. Every word, on examination, looks doubtful.

At five o'clock, take a subway on Lexington, change to a local somewhere and go up to Bleeker Street, which is full of tottering drunkards today, due to St Patrick's festivities. After my San Francisco experience I've a fear of being held up. Go up to Lyle's friend's house, where a fine dinner is prepared for all of us. Lyle has a terrific cold today, but is still in form.

After dinner I ask, 'When do you plan to visit India?' 'I have been there once, years ago,' he says. This is rather a surprise for me. Lyle has a tendency to unfold surprises. I ask for details. 'I knew something of the country through my uncle.'

'Who was your uncle?' I ask.

'Robert Flaherty, you know the man who directed *The Elephant Boy*, who brought Sabu to the States, etc. etc.' It is unnecessary to dwell on Flaherty's achievements at this distance, but the sequel to a mention of him is interesting. I say, 'Do you know that he shot *The Elephant Boy* in Mysore, where I live, where there are elephant-jungles all around?' And then I add, 'And I know his daughter who has settled in Mysore. I have met her a few times, and we did a feature together for a radio programme on the trapping of elephants. She was our narrator.' This stings Lyle into unexpected action. 'Do you mean to say that you know Barbara? Wait a minute. I want you to talk to her mother.'

'Where is she?'

'At Vermont, five hundred miles away. You must tell her about Barbara.' I try to excuse myself. 'Well no time for it, let us think of it later, I don't know the lady. . .' He brushes aside all my objections, and pulls me along to the other room where the telephone is. He dials the operator and cries, 'I want Vermont, Mrs Frances Flaherty.'

'Number?'

'I don't know the number. Don't insist on it.' He adopts a sudden, bullying tone and says, 'I don't know the number but I must talk to the lady immediately. I am giving you her name and address, you will have to find her number somehow . . .' And he puts down the receiver and waits till the operator calls him again and I hear him shout, 'You have the number? Fine, why do you tell me what it is? I am not interested. Give me the connection.' He turns to me and says, 'We will get the connection now. It is twelve years since we saw Barbara off. You must tell her mother about her.'

'Tell her what?' I ask anxiously. He ignores my question. He gets the connection to Vermont. It is eleven-thirty at night and it is evident that the population of Vermont has retired long ago. They are pulled out of their beds, and feel naturally anxious at being called at that hour. After a few minutes Lyle speaks into the telephone.

'I have a friend here from India who has known Barbara. He is from Mysore.' He hands me the telephone.

It is Mrs Flaherty. She is thrilled to hear about her daughter; she asks numerous questions about her, how she looks now, what radio programme we did together, and what I thought of her voice. She is overwhelmed, as she says, 'How I wish I were going with you to India to see Barbara!' Lyle feels gratified, 'You have made one soul supremely happy.'

*

Evening went out on a ramble. Never realized till now that I was living so close to the famous Empire State Building, though I have been seeing its tower every day for over a week. This is the worst of working too hard on a novel—you become blind to the tallest building in the world. Proximity makes us indifferent, although, in Laxmipuram I'd have been eloquent about it on hearing about it. Must go up sometime, but I can't bring myself to the point of joining the regular sightseers anywhere, though it ought to be the most sensible, and practical thing to do. But who cares to be sensible and practical? I may probably go back home without ever ascending the Empire State Building but then I shall have done nothing worse than any confirmed citizen of New York. I watch for a while people buying tickets and moving up to the elevator, wondering where they came from. Glance through all the tremendous 'promotion' material around. One would have thought a building like the Empire State was in no need of promotion (my little nephew at home can say exactly how high it is). But there it is. Its statistics are impressive, but I could not accept their own list of eight wonders of the world (which they display at the window—in which the Empire State finds a place but not the Taj Mahal).

Food for the Gods

Lyle Blair's party for me at Algonquin to celebrate the publication of the American edition of my *Mr Sampath*. Algonquin party room is so exclusive that only fifty guests are invited. Everyone is there, the Indian Consul General, the Australian Ambassador and his wife, the Breits, the Bowers, Gilpatric, a girl from *Look* looking like Ingrid Bergman, two priests, two publishers of paperbacks, the President of Michigan University and the Vice-President, Professor Blackman, the Viking Press, Balaraman, many men and women from the writing world, whose names I never catch, and above all the Indian delegate at the United Nations Organization, who sits in a chair and says to me when introduced, 'I am dictating my third novel to my secretary, having completed my second in eight weeks. I am surprised where all the ideas come from. In the midst of all my office work, I am able to do it. I'd like to talk to you—what is your address?' I mention my hotel and its whereabouts, which does not interest him. He says, cutting me short, 'Why don't you call up my secretary and leave your telephone number with her, so that I may get in touch with you sometime.' I leave him at that.

After the party a small, compact group stay on for supper. Two New York paperback publishers, whom we shall indicate as Mr A and Mr B, a priest, a girl in a red gown, Lyle, and myself. We have a corner to ourselves at the dining hall of Algonquin. Publisher A, sitting opposite me, leans across to say, 'I like your *Financial Expert*. It is your best book.'

'I like your *Bachelor of Arts* better; it's my favourite,' says publisher B, sitting to my right.

'William Faulkner, Hemingway, and Narayan are the world's three great living writers,' says A.

I blush to record this, but do it for documentary purposes. After the discussion has continued on these lines for a while, I feel I ought to assert my modesty—I interrupt them to say, 'Thank you, but not yet . . .' But my own view and judgement are of the least consequence and no one pays any attention to me. They brush me aside and repeat, 'Hemingway, Faulkner and Narayan, the three greatest living . . .'

'Take out Hemingway and put in Graham Greene. Faulkner, Narayan, and Graham Greene,' says Lyle.

'I don't like Graham Greene,' says one.

'Why not?' asks the priest in a kindly tone.

'His obsession with Catholic theology upsets me.'

'What is wrong in it?'

'I don't like it, that is all.'

'Come, come, you can't dismiss it so easily. You have to explain what upsets you in Catholic theology.'

From this mild beginning a veritable storm soon developed. The waiters came and went. Each whispered his or her choice in their ears. They brought the food and placed it around. The napkins were spread on laps; shining cutlery was picked up, but they were hardly put to their legitimate use; they were being flourished to add punch to arguments. Plates remained untouched. One or the other would draw the plate into position and carve a bit, but before he could stick the fork in, there would occur a theological exasperation, and up would go the knife and fork to emphasize a point or to meet the challenge. Lyle who had ordered a joint done brown, could not proceed beyond pecking at it once every ten minutes. The lady in red was the only one who proceeded smoothly with her dinner, and then of course myself. Out of courtesy I waited for a while to be joined by others, but I found my asparagus soup growing cold. The waiters were bringing in the courses mechanically. I followed the example of the lady in red and ate my food unobtrusively. I quietly worked my way through, and had arrived at the stage of baked apple pie and cream, but found the rest still at the stage of Torment, taking a morsel to the lips and withdrawing it swiftly to rebut an affront. What really stirred them to such a pitch was a thing that I never really understood. It was all too obscure, too much in the realm of higher theology, the minutiae of belief. The only thing that I caught was that publisher A was out to puncture the priest. Mr A was saying, 'Answer my question first. Could a betrayer be an enemy?'

'He has to be a friend. How can an enemy betray?' A sinister laughter followed. When it subsided Mr A said, with a quiet firmness, 'I am a much better priest than you are. Take off that dog collar you are wearing, what is that for?'

'John! John!' pleaded the priest, 'Don't lose yourself so utterly. Pull yourself together.'

'I am all right. I can look after myself quite well. It is you who needs pulling together. You are no better than the drunken, dissolute priests one encounters in Graham Greene's novels.' The priest could do nothing more than cry, 'John! John!' in a tone of tremendous appeal, and then he pointed at me and said, 'We have a distinguished guest with us tonight. Let us not insult him by our unseemly acts.' Which seemed to have the desired effect as Mr A bowed deeply to me from his seat and said, 'I apologize to you, sir, for any inconvenience caused.' The greater inconvenience was to be the centre of attention now, and so I said, 'Not at all, not at all. Don't mind me. Go on with your discussion. Please don't stop on my account.' This was accepted with gusto and publisher B turned to the priest and said, 'You have not really answered John's question.'

'Why should I? Am I bound to answer?' A fresh sinister guffaw followed this. The two publishers seemed pleased at the effect they had produced; they leaned over to each other and spoke under their breath and laughed among themselves. Lyle thought that the time had come for him to assert himself. He held his arms over his head and said, 'All are my guests here; I won't have anyone insulted at this table. Let us have this discussion some other time. Let us eat now.' This was really a sound, practical suggestion. The time was nearly eleven. Three hours had passed since the food had been served. I had noticed through a corner of my eye the progress of the night at the restaurant. All the other guests had left. The linen had been taken off all the tables. The lights had been put out, half the hall was in darkness; on the outer fringe a couple of waiters stood patiently. Cordiality was restored, plates were passed round. One heard not theological remarks but 'Did you order this chicken?' 'Oh, dear, I must abandon this soup . . . Fish! Lovely!' Everybody settled down cheerfully to eat, drew their chairs closer, rolled up their sleeves, with the exception of the lady in red and myself who were lingering over our desserts in order to let the rest catch up with us. It would have gone on well, but for the arrival of a steward at this moment and a whispered message to Lyle who had just tasted his joint. Lyle immediately cried, 'Listen friends, here is the steward come to say that Mr— the manager of the hotel, wants us to accept a round of drinks in honour of this evening . . . Please give him our thanks. Surely. Won't he join us?'

'He had to go away, sir, but he requested that you should accept his hospitality. Champagne, sir?' 'Yes, why not? There are,' he counted heads, 'six here.' 'Give him our thanks, won't you?' Conviviality was restored, but the food receded once again into the background. One or two got up to visit the wash. I was relieved to find that religion had gone to the background. When they resumed their seats, they were all smiling. 'We must really get on with the dinner,' Lyle said.

'Of course, of course,' everyone agreed.

The time was nearly eleven-thirty. I noticed less rancour now, the priest as well as the rest were laughing while arguing. I felt relieved. The priest turned to the lady in red and said, 'While all of us are talking you are silent, why don't you say something?' She merely replied between drinks, 'I have nothing to say.' She was the one person who had pursued her food and drink with a steady aim, and now she seemed a little bored. 'What can she say?' said Mr A pugnaciously. 'You are a priest, and it is up to you to talk and save our souls. Here I am asking, what are you a priest for, if you can't answer a simple question?' The priest merely looked at him, pointed at me and said, 'Let us not make fools of ourselves before him. Let us talk it over tomorrow.' 'There he is,' he said pointing at me. 'He is an Indian, he is from the East. He knows these problems inside out. It must all look childish to him. Let us shut up now. He is watching us silently. Remember he is dead sober, while we are drunk. Let us end all this talk.' At this Mr B leaned across to say to me, 'You see sir, we are a young nation, we don't know the answers, we long to have an answer to our questions.' He held his hand to his heart as if there were excruciating pangs there. 'We are a tortured nation, that is why we seek an answer. It is no problem for you really, because you know the answer to all the questions.' I had to say, 'No, I don't think I know the answers, I haven't even understood the questions, you know.' He just brushed aside my protestations. 'No, you know the answers. I know you know because your *Financial Expert* contains in it answers to all our questions.'

'Does it?' I asked, rather surprised. 'Where?'

'The last portions of the book,' he said.

'I didn't know,' I said, completely baffled.

'You wouldn't know, but we know. We can read them,' he said, and left me marvelling at the theological implications of my fiction. He came close to me and said, 'But you must sympathize with us, we are all the time struggling and searching. You must watch us closely. You don't have to do anything except put down all this conversation as you have heard it, and that will be a wonderful conversation piece. I know you can do it, because I admire your *Financial Expert*.' (I have acted on his advice and hence this narrative.)

He pointed to Mr A with a good deal of sympathy, 'His eagerness to know is very real, his enquiry is honest.'

'I must have an answer,' Mr A said, stung by this reminder. He looked straight ahead at the priest and cried, 'I insist upon your answering my question.'

'John, John, you are starting it all over again.'

'Tell him something, why do you spurn his question?' said his friend.

'We have no business to be arrogant, it is arrogance which is at the bottom of all our troubles,' began Lyle. He is ever fond of the word 'arrogance' and brings it up anywhere.

'The priest is the one who is arrogant,' Mr A cried with passion. 'What is he wearing that dog collar for, let him pull it off and throw it away.' Saying this he proceeded to attack his dinner.

At this, the priest looked at him fixedly and said, 'You have provoked me enough. I'll answer your question after you answer mine. Tell me who you are, what you are, and where you come from?' This question stung Mr A unexpectedly. He was livid with rage.

(Later, I understood that Mr A came from a part of the country which was supposed to be known for its display of bigotry.)

'It has nothing to do with my problem.'

'Gentlemen, let us eat our food,' Lyle said. The priest repeated, 'John, who are you? What are you? Where do you come from?' In answer, Mr A pushed his chair back and his plates away. 'I refuse to sit at the same table with this—priest. You are a—priest. No better than a Graham Greene character. I will say it again and again.' He turned to me and said extending his hand, 'I apologize for going, but I can't sit at this table. It has been nice meeting you. Goodbye.' He walked away.

Jackie

My handwriting generally reduces typists to a state of apathy and defeatism. After years of writing I have not yet evolved a clear system of writing. I am often asked how I write, whether I type or write long-hand—I do both. Whether typed or written, while revising I generally write between lines; sometimes there may be twenty lines of original writing, to a page, but twenty-five lines in-between, and further corrections on all the white spaces around a page. Most of this disfiguring of the page is unconsciously done, the main aim being to get through the work and put it in shape.

I had now an occasion to study my own methods dispassionately, when I tried to find someone to type up the manuscript of my new novel *The Guide*. No doubt sitting in the train from Washington, I could get through the manuscript, but I did not stop to think how it might strike anyone else trying to read the manuscript. I realized my folly only when I promised to deliver the manuscript to Viking on a certain date and began to look for someone to type my manuscript. Through various recommendations, I got a number of persons willing to take up the job, but one look at a page and they would invariably say, 'At the moment we are busy . . .' I was in despair. After trying everywhere, one afternoon, after lunch, I appealed to Faubion to help me. He said, 'I'll ask Jackie to type up your work.' He took the telephone, spoke, and said to me confidently, 'Jackie will meet you at your hotel at eleven o'clock tomorrow morning. She will do your work.'

I asked, 'She may look at my manuscript and go away as others have done.'

'She won't,' Faubion said, 'I know her.'

Next day she was in my room punctually at eleven. She went through ten pages of my manuscript and said, 'This is nothing compared to what Mr Bowers gave me when I had to type his book on the theatre. I will make a start tonight and give you about thirty pages a day. I will leave blank spaces for doubtful words.' She came back with thirty pages next day, but before proceeding with further work she noted down on a slip of paper words which had confounded her. It tied me to a routine again. Every evening I broke away from a late party with the excuse, 'I have to have thirty pages ready by morning for Jackie.'

Jackie found an added interest in the novel because the book was written in Berkeley where she studied, and she was from

Oakland nearby. What made her settle in New York? After graduation from Berkeley College, she had an ambition to join the stage, and so came to New York. While attempting to work her way on to Broadway, she had to maintain herself by freelance typing work. The frustrations in this country operate mostly in the world of arts and letters, and not in the ordinary walks of life as in our country. I cheered her up by saying that some day in Broadway I should visit a theatre, see her starring in it, tell everyone that she typed my novel once, and go backstage to greet her.

*

'Your women don't look worn out at all—they always look so soft and slow—while here all the time one has to be catching a subway or a bus, working, working. Indian women don't work? They do! But probably not much to do—sharing the housework with six other wives. I heard that an Indian husband had seven wives—all living under the same roof: one to make the bed, another to wash dishes, a third to take care of the linen, a fourth to run the vacuum cleaner, another to take the waste basket and garbage and so on; it must be a great relief . . .' says Myrtle who comes every morning to tidy up my room.

*

Jackie explains how she is enjoying typing up my novel; finds Raju's character engrossing; confesses that last night she nearly resolved to give me up, because she could not make out certain passages however much she tried. I believe she must have cried a little. But finally victory was hers, and she has managed her quota, with but three errors. I assure her that she has got through the worst patch (which I very much doubt) in my manuscript. I decide not to bother her to work over the weekend because she is planning to go to New Jersey, where she has her boyfriend. 'He is a chemist, you know, but really calm, without any neurosis, a wonderful man. He is thirty. I know I can be happy with him. He is devoted to music and the theatre and we have common interests.'

'Why don't you marry him? What are you waiting for?'

'Ah, can't decide that fast. It will take time. We are not able to make up our minds yet, about a great many things . . .'

'But don't you love each other? If you do, it should blindly sweep aside all other considerations, you know.' She merely repeats, 'Can't decide that fast.'

G. G.

Walk down Lexington Avenue, to John Gunther's house. He opens the door with the warmest greetings, and takes me inside. His wife Jane introduces me to a lady sitting on a sofa, wearing a grey gown. While we are talking Faubion, Santha and Donald burst in. After settling down, Faubion says to me, 'Tell us about your mystic experiences.' I say something evasive, but he will not let me go. I plead for time, but he says, 'Now, I want to hear, I must hear all about your mystic experience . . .' The lady in grey says something very profound and subtle. I am impressed with her talk. And then, it's time for all of us to go. I suddenly remember that I must know Balaraman's address where I'm dining this evening. I take out the telephone book on Gunther's table and fumble with it. Anthony West arrives. Santha and Faubion go out and wait for me on the road. The lady in grey goes out, but before going she comes up to me, nods a farewell, presses my arm. When I join them on the road Faubion asks, 'Can you guess who that lady is!'

'No.'

'Try.'

'No, I don't know,' I say. 'Only thing I can guess about her is that she must be continental, perhaps an artist—'

'She is Greta Garbo,' says Faubion.

We are all going to be late for our various engagements. Faubion hails a cab and bundles all of us in. Santha says, 'I'm getting worried about you. I don't know how you are going to reach Balaraman's house on West End Avenue.' As our taxi turns on Third Avenue, we see Garbo standing on the kerb, waiting for a cab. After they get off at their place, I take the taxi on and reach Balaraman's house only an hour late, but Balaraman is used to my ways and has forbearance.

*

After a couple of hours of work in the morning, lunch with Anthony West and Donald Keene at Chateaubriand. Anthony is leaving tomorrow for Japan and India. I have promised to meet him in India. Donald gives him a number of Japanese addresses. After lunch we walk down Lexington, visit a bookshop, a picture gallery and finally I go on with Anthony to the end of 80th Street. We plan to meet in Mysore (actually Anthony arrived ahead of me and was waiting for me at Bombay). At the subway, telephone Santha, and she asks me to come to their house at once. I find them celebrating Ruth's birthday (Ruth has been with them for years and helps them with housework). Numerous guests drop in. My good friend from India, Dr Narayan Menon phones from somewhere, to say that he's just arrived and will be dropping in soon. Santha says that Garbo wishes to meet me again. She called this morning to say that she wants to meet 'that man from India' again. It's a rare instance of her wanting to see anyone. She has only four friends in the world: John and Jane Gunther, Santha and Faubion.

We move to a party in someone's house. Many men and women whose names I don't catch; and a Spanish novelist, who writes in English, and who has many complaints against publishers in general. An artist from *New Yorker* buttonholes me, 'I'm looking for any system of teaching which has abolished duality.' I mention Shankara and others, but he will not accept anyone, proves everytime that a man who attacks duality is dual himself, and so forth! I waste a little time arguing with him. Faubion is ensnared in this discussion and cries out, 'Oh. Narayan, help me with an argument.' Narayan Menon arrives, but before one can say 'Hello' to him, he is cornered by this 'duality' man.

*

Ill with an attack of allergy. All day have to remain indoors. It is snowing heavily outside. All day scratching and coughing, awful life, but still keep up progress with the novel; Jackie comes and goes as usual. Evening telephone Gil and cancel an engagement at Oberlin. The thought of travel aggravates my allergy. Gil suggests a doctor. Call him on the phone. Engagement at 1.30 p.m. next day.

Rain and sleet outside. Cab to 70th Street. Doctor takes me to bits. Examines me like a mechanic looking over a derelict automobile. Stripped to the waist, I move from room to room. Screens my chest. Pricks my fingertip for blood. He is worried about an infection at the base of my lung. But assures me there is nothing to worry about. Gives me pills and an injection. He is a normal, healthy doctor, with normal aversions and suspicions about abnormal conditions. He orders grimly, 'Go back to your room and stay in bed.'

Afternoon with Gil. His wife and children are away in Washington and he is in sole charge of the house. He manages quite well, able to pick a meal at a restaurant or fix something for himself. That is not his main worry, but the white mouse, which his daughter has left in his charge, with strict injunction to keep it alive till she comes back. It is kept in a small cage in the bathroom and Gil gets quite anxious about its welfare, often running in to see it and assure himself that it is flourishing. 'Only four days more; I hope nothing will happen to it before then. Bah! what a responsibility!'

The afternoon is fine and sunny. We go out, we pass through Frick's Museum, enchanted by Rembrandt's self-portrait and the collection of Dutch paintings. People are moving east and west and along the kerb. We walk in Central Park and enjoy the sight of children at play, and finally we come to a spot where groups of men are playing chequers on park tables; it is a characteristic of New York; chequer-players in parks, on a bright day there will always be a set of players concentrating on their game and a circle of onlookers equally absorbed in the game. After this round of orthodox sightseeing, we walk back to Gil's house. He toasts a couple of muffins for me in his kitchen, and makes sandwiches and tea. We sit at the dinner table for over an hour with these. It is most peaceful and enjoyable. We wonder what to do next, and come to the conclusion that the best engagement would be to lounge in his study and talk. We go through this engagement so thoroughly that it is past nine-thirty when we look at the time again. We must have got quite drunk on a few glasses of orange juice and a great deal of conversation. Gil is one of those great souls who can give and take in conversation and his interests are wide-ranging, let us say, from Mysore to Santa Fe, touching upon all the worthwhile personalities and politics therein. I suspect that he does not let television invade his home mainly for fear that it might destroy the art of conversation.

*

It is almost a routine with me now. I keep working away on my novel till three in the afternoon and telephone Narayan Menon at Prince George's to find out if he is free. He always says, 'Most welcome, come immediately.' It is a fresh joy everyday to meet Narayan Menon, who opens the door, bows elaborately, and asks, 'What can I give you, sir?' as if we were formal strangers, and then he always gives me news of what he did since we last met—a composer he lunched with or a recording of his music, or news from home; and there is always his veena, lying on a cushion, covered with a brightly-patterned, hand-woven cloth. It brings the whole air of India into this room at Prince George's. It is a tempting instrument. Menon plays for a moment and generally hands it over to me; a few tunes in *Bhairavi* and *Kambodhi* and we appreciate each other unreservedly, and start out at about five, hail a cab and get down at Faubion's house at East 63rd street; where we invariably find a large and lively gathering of all kinds of personalities from the theatre, publishing and literary world.

G. G.

Adopting all the precautions suggested by Faubion, I am ready to meet Garbo again at lunch in Santha's house. Garbo never likes to be reminded of films or of her past association with them.

Garbo and her best friend in the world, Jane Gunther, arrive. Ruth has provided me with macaroni and cheese, cucumber sandwiches, and fruits. It is fascinating to pretend that I am not aware of the personality of Garbo but that I take her to be a commonplace woman of New York. Films and television and all kinds of shows are so much a part and parcel of our lives that one inadvertently stumbles into these forbidden topics and retreats hastily. 'When I was in Hollywood . . .' I begin, and then catch a look from Jane or Faubion and suddenly withdraw from the topic, and cover it up with something less dangerous, as Faubion threatens that if anyone so much as mentions film-life, Garbo is likely to get up, open the door, and leave unceremoniously. It is a very trying situation. I think this is a unique instance, of someone passionately craving for obscurity and oblivion, while plagued all the time by fame and immortality. For this reason we had to leave out Narayan Menon, who was very eager to join us today. He even said, 'I will stay quietly in a corner and never say a word. All I want is just a glimpse of Garbo. My memory of her is as Queen Christina, and Ninotchka and Anna Karenina; please allow me a glimpse of her.' But unfortunately he had to be told, 'Another time, please,' for it is generally observed that G.G. (as she is addressed) just shuts up, or turns back and retreats if she finds a stranger in the company.

The lunch is a success. The conversation is all about religion, mysticism, evolution, and reincarnation. G.G. asks, 'Why have we been created, why have we been made to suffer, undergo pain, and then, what is the meaning of all this? Why? Why?' Her voice as she says it is rich and modulated as if she were speaking the lines in a play. I have to find an answer because evidently she has enough faith in me to think I can give her an answer. I can only view her problem from the point of view of *karma* and the evolution of a being from birth to birth. She argues about it. The practice of meditation could probably give an answer in a flash. She confesses, 'I don't know how to meditate. What do you meditate upon?' I am generally reluctant to speak about my inner convictions, but there is no way of avoiding it now. Her enquiry is so earnest that I cannot help speaking to her about it. I have to confess to her that we are taught the *Gayatri mantra*. She wants me to repeat it and explain its meaning. She follows my words with the greatest attention; I explain to her the power of the syllable according to *Mantra Shastra*, the meditative principle, the picture of the goddess on which the mind has to dwell, the symbolism of the image, and so forth. After listening to me, she says, 'It is all too advanced for me. You belong to a nation which is highly advanced in these matters. When and how can we reach your level of thinking and understanding?'

'Sooner or later,' is all that I could reply.

'May be not in a single birth, but after a series of them, that is why we believe in a sequence of births,' I say attempting to sound as prosaic as possible and avoiding at all costs the tone of pontificality.

Time to disperse. She rises, asking me, 'Do you owe those teeth of yours to your vegetarian diet? Do all Indian have strong teeth?'

'Even the poorest have strong and resplendent teeth in our country.'

Before leaving she brings her palms together in an Indian salute.

'Where did you learn it?' I ask.

'Many years ago at Hollywood, I used to visit the Vedanta Society, and the discourses and lessons there gave me so much peace . . .' she passed on, probably disturbed at the word 'Hollywood' that had slipped from her own lips. A little later I left. While crossing 1st Avenue I saw her and Jane ahead of me. They waved before disappearing from view.

*

Rather crowded since the moment I got up at nine o'clock. I had only an hour to spare for myself. The rest of the day till midnight, handed over to others. Till one in the afternoon revised the last ten pages of my manuscript and Jackie came in exactly at one to take them away. A big burden is off my back. To think that tomorrow I shall have no manuscript to revise! Delicious thought. After disposing of Jackie, took a cab and rushed to the Indian Consul's home for lunch; it being Tamil New Year's day, this good Consul had remembered to ask me in for a South Indian meal. Back to the hotel and then on to Narayan Menon's room to play the veena. After dinner off to Faubion's for a night party, where Narayan Menon is to play the veena, explaining South Indian music to the guests.

Really a gorgeous gathering of music and theatre: Leopold Stokowski, John Gunther, Martha Graham, Edward G. Robinson, all distinguished men and women. Menon plays the veena. Edward G. Robinson is a marvellous personality. When he lights his cigar, you couldn't think he was not on the stage. He has a pleasing gruffness and drawl in his voice, and listens to you with puckered brow and a slight tilt of his head. He asks about India, wants to visit it someday. As usual I generously extend him an invitation. About his pictures he says, 'I felt so rich when I had my collection of pictures around me. They meant something to me. Now I feel really poor . . . They had to be sold owing to a stupid Californian law of divorce. Some Greek fellow has bought them. I've only fourteen left. But I'll collect again. I can't help it—but those that are gone are gone.' He lightly thumps his heart to show the pain—his voice, expression, and gestures are memorable and sad. He invites me to see his *Middle of the Night*. 'I have seen it, I think you have the problem of the middle-aged man beautifully brought out in it.'

'There is no middle age,' he declares. 'We are middle-aged when we are born, or have no middle age at all. Life is important . . . You write about the common denominator in all humanity—all nations and men are one. Your books, I am sure, will bring out the idea. Perhaps, when I travel on I shall be able to understand the same message, and carry it back with me to this country. I am not interested in curiosities, but in common denominators. I hope, when I come to India, you will help me understand the Indian mind.'

Pleasures of Indecision

Earlier in the evening helped Menon to get his air ticket for Washington. He likes to remain undecided and confessed, 'Once I've bought the ticket, I'm always racked with the feeling that I've done the wrong thing, and want to cancel the journey.' I can understand this temperament more easily than anyone else can. I decide to write a short piece on the pleasures and perils of indecision in New York.

New York is one place in the world where you cannot afford to be indecisive, whether it be the business of crossing the road at the right moment or booking one's passage for a future journey. But such decisiveness has not yet come into my nature. I like to leave the door open for a retreat at any time. And so it is with trepidation that I visit the fifty-fourth floor of the Rockefeller Foundation. The fifty-fifth is a place where the visitors are allowed to indulge in semi-dreamy talk, because it is the floor of the directors who generally put up with the vagaries of their grantees, who are drawn from all over the world and are of a varied kind. For instance, if Gil is not actually pressed for time, he is generally very tolerant and understanding of all the contradictory plans and proposals I keep making; but it won't work on the fifty-fourth floor, which I have always named the zone of stern realities. Here we have the controller to whom you have to give very concrete replies if you have to draw the funds allotted to you. The *per diem* and the travel grant and the non-taxable portion and clearance from income-tax, and so on and so forth are all very concrete and very important. The most vigilant actions are performed here. And then the travel section on the same floor, where they just ask on what day you propose to leave and where you want to go and when, and what you propose to do until you reach your home in Mysore three months later. It is extremely unrealistic for me to think so far ahead. The travel officer makes the reservations all along the way, warning me, 'Better have some reservations on hand than none . . . you may alter these things later as you go along . . . You will arrive in Zurich at 10 a.m. and leave . . .' With his pencil poised over a tablet he awaits my decision, an acutely uncomfortable situation for me. There is no such thing as making a casual statement and then building up on it little by little, knocking down a bit here, smoothing out something else there and so on. The pleasures of indecision are not permitted here. You have to think fast, precisely. And then the other room where your baggage is handled. You are directed there to an officer who can parcel anything and pack it off to the ends of the earth. Whether it is a large shipping case or the little test tube containing a serum or a mosquito (often required by the medical section of the Foundation), he is the man to do it. His greatest triumph was in the case of a professor from Mysore who had lost all his baggage, did not know where, between India and the United States. He did not have even a blade for his morning shave when he arrived in New York. He confessed his trouble to the officer, who contacted the airports all along the route and spoke long distance to everyone on earth, and within a week the professor got all his baggage back, placed in a Pullman in which he was travelling to Boston.

'I have some baggage to be sent to Mysore,' I begin.

'How many? How many pieces?'

'Maybe four,' I say.

Paper and pencil are poised ready for action now. I am rather terrified. 'I have not packed anything and I don't know.'

So I say, 'Maybe one or two more.'

'Shall we say six packages?'

'Yes.' He at once telephones someone, 'Six packages to be picked up at nine in the morning tomorrow at Hotel—' He turns to me and says, 'The truck will call at nine. Will you advise the desk clerk at your hotel?' I feel amazed at the speed of these decisions, and would like to postpone the whole thing. 'I have not packed them properly yet,' I begin.

'Oh, it doesn't matter at all. You just lock the boxes and put all the other stuff into a cardboard case . . . I will give you some twine and labels and tabs. You just tie up everything roughly and stick on the labels with your address and we will do the rest. Don't bother to pack, we will do all that. We will put them in bigger cases, waterproof and seal them, so that you will receive them all intact at your end. Leave it to us. OK?' This speed does not suit me. I begin, 'I have just come to find out about these things from you. It will be quite a while before I leave, the date is not settled yet. As soon as I am able to know the date, I will see you again.' He says, 'Any time you are ready, you just give us twenty-four hours notice.'

'Yes, yes,' I say in a businesslike manner. 'Thanks a lot,' and I leave the fifty-fourth floor with the greatest relief at having put off so many decisions. The practical men on this floor may perhaps be wondering how I ever got through any place at any time at all. I am as surprised, but as I write, I am back at home after visiting most of the countries I planned to visit and all my baggage has arrived intact.

March of Dime

Having nothing definite to do, I decide to walk without aim as I often do in Mysore. Up 5th Avenue to 63rd Street, watching shop-windows, crowds and the flux of New York, and back to my hotel through Madison Avenue. At Vanderbilt Square a man says, 'Hot chestnuts sir, very good.' I have always been curious to handle and taste chestnuts which I have only read about. He takes them from over a brazier and gives me a packet. 'Twenty-five cents, sir.' A handful, for the same money you could buy a first-rate dinner in our country. I try to taste them, cracking their shells and eating them on a public highway, wondering how it may strike New York citizens, but they are a generous lot, who do not mind an active chestnut-muncher walking in their midst. A young man in a heavy coat, a few yards behind, stops every passerby and says something. I want to know what he is saying to everyone, and slow down till he comes up alongside. I stare at him with so much interest that he sidles up to me.

'Can you spare a dime?'

'Why?' I ask.

'I need it,' he says. He would rather walk slowly while talking than stand in one place. I realize that he does not like to be noticed. I adjust my pace. He looks quite respectable; his shoes are sound, his coat is good, his hat is quite sightly. Quite a presentable young man.

'What would you do with a dime?'

'What does one do with money? Buy myself food, I suppose, that is all.'

'You look young and strong. Don't you do any work to earn?'

'Sure, off and on. I do some work. I was a truck assistant and got off the job only two weeks ago because I was sick and in New York Hospital. I am just coming out of the hospital.'

'Can't you find another job?'

'Yeah, sure I could. But,' he lowers his voice further, 'I am the sort that can't stick in one place long. Rolling-stone sort you know.'

'Why can't you stick in one place?'

'Well, that's how I am,' he says philosophically.

'How do you manage then?'

'Like this.' I understand that in other words he is a born vagrant who is pleased to be so—rather a rare specimen in a place like New York. I gladly part with a dime for the pleasure of seeing this rare specimen in New York, and he goes off. Before leaving I tell him, 'If you hate to work and would prefer to risk living on charities in the streets, you should be in our country, where such a life is understood better.'

Loose Coins

One of the minor skirmishes that I was engaged in daily with Menon was in the matter of tips. He was of a liberal disposition, but I always felt that he was overdoing it. He seemed to set aside ten dollars a day for tips alone. It was of course his own business, but I felt that he was responsible for creating a bearish tendency in the tip market, and was also creating a social order consisting of good-tippers and mean-tippers, in which (latter) category I feared that I would be thrown . . . Not that I don't want to give a legitimate tip where it may be due, but this man's habit of scattering coins somehow oppressed me. Every day I protested against it. He tipped even where it was not expected and surprised many a tip-receiver by suddenly darting at him with a quarter dollar. He believed in tipping not less than a quarter each time, and multiples of a quarter—fifty cents for a cab ride that cost thirty, one dollar for lunch and so on; twenty-five for someone who flicked the dust off his coat and said, 'How do you do, sir?', twenty-five for someone who said at the door, 'Another nice day h'm.' My impression was that since the moment of leaving his room (no, even before leaving his room: he parted with cash when his breakfast tray was removed), going down the elevator, crossing the lobby, and passing through the door, he handed coins to whoever looked at him. He asked a hall porter, 'What time does the train for Washington leave?' (which, in any case, he was not taking), and when the man brought a reply, he handed him a quarter. He handed a quarter to the elevator boy when he said, 'Nice day sir,' or 'How are you this morning?' and of course the doorman who whistled for a taxi got his share; not to mention the usual quarter dollar for caretakers of his coat in various buildings. He paid enormous tips all through lunch and dinner, and I need not explain what he did with his cash when he travelled in a train: the porter got three times his legitimate charge of twenty-five cents per bag, and of course every time the train attendant peeped in to ask, 'Did you want anything, sir?' he got his dues.

This was absurd. I felt that my friend was carrying it too far. It induced in one a peculiar view of the American currency. If Menon's practice was carried to its logical limit, none of the loose coins one got in the country was ever meant for one's personal use; all of them were for giving away. The coinage seemed to be so devised that you could not keep it. Starting with the smallest coin, let us say the one-cent piece: it is just there to help you to find out your weight. At every street corner, drug store, and subway there are automatic machines to show you your weight, for tuppence you may have your weight and fate indicated simultaneously (as they say, 'Wate and Fate'); the five-cent piece is for automatic machines once again, you can get chewing gum of any sort for a five-cent coin, Kleenex tissues, or anything in that line; the next coin is the dime, ten cents has a specialized and restricted function as it is useless for tips. (I heard an old cab-driver, reminiscing, refer to a millionaire of half a century ago, who took a cab-ride every day to his office, as 'that bastard was a dime-tipper'.) But the dime has its functions. It is used mostly for wayside telephone conversations. Any other coin that is put in obstructs operations and will not stay in. (In quite a number of instances, I have discovered a quarter dollar slip out the moment the receiver was lifted, left there no doubt by some hasty dime-less phone talker.) Not knowing what to do with it, I would often ask the operator about it and she would say, 'Put it back please, thank you,' which I did, but I was not sure if it stayed there long. The dime is also useful for provoking juke-box music in cafes. The quarter dollar has its functions; it is the basic tip for cabs, train service, shoe-shines, and of course the basic fee for the red-cap railway porter, and if you don't have to go shamefaced you must add a quarter to it. After all, these coins seem to belong to the public and have an impersonal touch about them, and Menon seemed to be right in disposing of them at that speed.

Whether a tip has earned the complete approval of the recipient or not may be judged by the taxi driver's saying before leaving, 'Watch your step, sir,' instead of just pulling up the meter flag and starting off. So also the elevator boy: when he says, 'Watch your step,' you may be sure you will be expected to remember him when you leave. He does not expect a tip every day, he is more practical minded. You are under his constant scrutiny, you can never go away without his knowledge (you may venture to use the steps occasionally, but not again and again if you live on the fourteenth floor), and he expects you to settle his account when you leave. My friend Menon, we may judge his popularity by this, was the one person who was repeatedly told wherever he turned, 'Watch your step, sir.'

The big fifty-cent piece is the most coveted and admired coin among tip-collectors. But it combines with in itself, unlike the lesser coins, both personal and impersonal utility—that is you may occasionally use it to pay off a charge and also say, 'Keep the change.'

The dollar bill is the only currency which is meant completely for your personal use, which means that you may keep it until you are obliged to change it into its components. Once it is split into components, you lose your hold on it; it becomes again something for Menon to distribute. It is a fact that everyone is aware of, as one may easily judge from the fact that even the surliest bus driver gives change for a dollar without a minute's hesitation. Nowhere else in the world do you get so much cooperation for changing a higher currency into a lower one. In our own country every bus displays prominently the notice: 'Please tender exact fare, don't ask for change.' In the United States you have only to hold out a bill and the driver's fingers travel automatically to a number of little cylinders on the dashboard, and draw out dime, quarter and fifty, as if they were drawing milk from the teats of a cow.

After visiting Paris and Rome I came to the conclusion that New York has the most equitable system of tip-collecting. The morning coffee and a small roll costs 300 francs plus forty-five in tips in any Paris hotel, and then there is a final addition of fifteen per cent to the total bill when you leave, for what are called 'service charges'. You are generally told that you don't have to pay further tips beyond this, but someone or the other keeps greeting you significantly in your hotel, like the elevator-boy in a Rome hotel who kept asking whenever I was closeted with him, 'Well sir, I am going off-duty at eleven tomorrow; what time are you leaving? I would like to say goodbye to you.' I found a number of others too wanting to say goodbye to me, and I asked the manager whether I was expected to pay further tips beyond what had been collected in the bill. He said, 'Not at all necessary, sir, but there are some guests who like to give, and in that case we don't interfere, sir.' This meant tips twice over—once in the bill and again without the bill. 'Oh, it does take such a long time for all that to be divided and come to us,' wailed my bellhop, when we discussed the subject.

In London the system is gradually coming, but they are very gentle about it and the scales are also very modest. About sixpence for a short run delights the London cabman, and a shilling for longer runs. When I displayed forgetfulness once, the cabman said, 'This is the exact fare, sir! Perhaps you wanted to add sixpence, sir?' Gentle beings.

In our own country tips are not inevitable, and the technique of collection is neither systematic nor standardized, although an extra eight annas now and then will certainly earn the undying gratitude of any railway porter or barber. I wonder if Menon, after his return home, finds his pockets unbearably heavy with loose coins.

'Finis'

As always happens while completing my revision of a manuscript I think I worked from ten in the morning to ten in the evening continuously—Jackie walking in for an hour or two in the morning, afternoon, and evening, to put in the corrections on all the four copies. Painful, boring job, but there is nothing one can do about it. At ten-thirty on a Thursday night, we finish work on the manuscript. What a joy! I see Jackie off at the subway on 4th Avenue and return home to sleep. Friday, delivery of the manuscript to Keith Jennison as promised. We celebrate with a lunch. Later Faubion insists upon opening a bottle of champagne, when I meet him at his house to announce the handing over of the manuscript to Viking.

*

Ravi Shankar's sitar recital at the annexe of the Museum of Modern Art, before a distinguished gathering of musicians, composers, music critics, and above all lovers of music. On Ravi's request, Narayan Menon and myself leave our chairs and sit down on the carpet, Indian fashion. Many others follow this example, and sit on the carpet. Although it is difficult for anyone to sit down in a suit with shoes on, they put themselves through this trial as a tribute to the music from India. Ravi explains to the gathering that in India the convention is to openly express one's appreciation of a recital all through its course, that the proximity of the listener and his reactions, such as little cries of delight and even the nodding of the head, are vital to an inspired performance, and that he misses it in this country where the convention is for listeners to sit still, maintaining a sort of grim silence throughout . . .

Ravi has brought incense sticks from India and has lit them in a corner. He has spread an Indian carpet on the dais, and has dressed himself and his accompanists in *dhoti* and *jibba*. Against this background providing the colour and fragrance of India, he plays pure classical music which transports the audience—establishing the truth of the matter that the highest form of music transcends boundaries and classifications. The atmosphere of India is further authenticated by a large cockroach which peeps out from under the platform . . .

Passing down a street in Greenwich Village, suddenly come upon Circle-in-the-Square Theatre, and peeping down its doorway I see Jackie sitting at a table, unrecognizable in a resplendent evening gown. I was used to seeing her in her working clothes. She has reason to dress herself festively today. She tells me in-between answering telephone calls and selling tickets for Eugene O'Neill's *The Iceman Cometh* that she is engaged to Jerry, who came down from New Jersey in the afternoon and proposed at lunch. As we are talking, all sorts of people are passing in and out, and she has to answer a dozen enquiries every minute. I leave her for a while and go out for coffee, come upon a bookshop where I see a copy of Santha's book offered at half a dollar. I take it, the bookseller regretting that he did not demand a bigger price when he learns that I know the author and intend to get it autographed.

I go back to Circle-in-the-Square and instantly recognize Jerry as he waits for Jackie to come out. They celebrate their engagement at a restaurant, with me as the sole guest. After that a walk through the Washington Square observing the loungers, and chequer-players on the park bench. They drop me at Helen Hays theatre where Faubion has got me tickets to see Eugene O'Neill's *Long Day's Journey into Night*—story of a southern family disintegrating through dope, drink, niggardliness and sloth, continuing to disintegrate, and doing nothing about it. I seem to get nothing but disintegration to watch whenever I go to a theatre, beginning with *Macbeth* which I saw some time ago. Thanks to Paul Sherbert I saw *Orpheus Descending* a couple of days later. Again it concerns personalities who have gone to pieces.

*

With Menon to old Greenwich by train in response to Ann Laughlin's invitation to visit her home. An hour's journey and we are in Connecticut country, a retreat lasting a whole afternoon, from the bustle of New York into an ancient home set in vast grounds, surrounded by apple trees in bloom, brooks, and the greenest of lawns, with the enchantment occasionally broken by the flight of jet planes overhead.

*

Menon takes me to a Chinese restaurant to meet Cartier-Bresson and his wife. Cartier-Bresson wants to see the work of an Indian photographer, and explains his philosophy thus, 'The camera is a limited instrument. It is the photographer who makes it a living medium. He should watch his subject, and take it. Composition is a sense of geometry actually; the quality of life and its expression must be caught accurately. Facial expressions are things like clouds which float by. They change from moment to moment and are gone before you know it. You can never say, smile again, please—it can never be done. Human expression is fluid, ever-changing, evanescent. For instance, your expression as you say, "Is that so?" can never be repeated, or be the same again. I don't know how to say it. But I'm looking for a photographer who doesn't imitate the West, but has an Indian quality. He must watch, run around, and catch big events in an original way. Twenty photographers will be clicking the subject, but it's not that that I have in mind. The photograph must show where he (the photographer) is, what he does and how he searches for the right, original situation.'

G. G.

Lunch at Santha's—other guests: Greta Garbo and Jane. Garbo was delighted when I accepted a cigarette from her; and called out to everyone to watch my performance. She showed me her diary of engagements to prove how little she was wanted. She peeped into my pocketbooks and exclaimed, 'Ah, telephone numbers and addresses everywhere!' She was lively and talkative. She took out her own diary to show me the entries, 'I have a bad hand, forgive me. I'm ashamed to show it, but see these—so many blanks; and these names are my doctors—the one who operated on my foot, my dentist—and the other is a beauty parlour man. Nobody is interested. Nobody calls; you see how blank my pocketbook is!'

'If only you wanted—' I said.

She said she was going to the south of France for a vacation; where her only activity, day in and day out, would be to pick up pebbles in the garden, collect them in an old bucket and fling them over the wall. And then she recounted her early story of how a young man was very devoted to her at one time. But she always wore an outsize men's sweater, and never bothered about her appearance. It came near a marriage proposal. But the young man's mother said to Garbo, 'Won't you dress prettily like other girls of your age? How well you would look if you took the trouble!' G.G. was so hurt by the implications of this remark that she walked out of their house and never saw the young man again.

After lunch we part, G.G. saying, 'How I wish we could stop time from moving and always taking us on to a moment of parting! Goodbye.'

Short Essays II

Narayan wrote these essays for the Hindu *and other periodicals in the 1950s, 1960s and 1970s. Written when he was at the peak of his career and widely regarded as a master storyteller, these pieces represent various aspects of Narayan's engagement with post-Independence India.*

TOASTED ENGLISH

IN AMERICAN RESTAURANTS they call for 'toasted English', referring to English muffins which, though being made in America, now retain 'English' as a sort of concession to their origin. The same may be said of the Americans' language too. They too went through a phase of throwing out the British but retaining their language and letting it flourish on American soil: the resultant language is somewhat different from its British counterpart; it may be said to have gone through a process of toasting. One noticeable result of this toasting is that much of the formalism surrounding the use of English has been abandoned.

In America, they have freed the language from the stifling tyranny of the Passive Voice. Where we would say ceremoniously 'Trespassing Prohibited', their signboards, as I noticed in the parks of Berkeley, merely say 'Newly Planted, Don't Walk'. Or 'Absolutely No Parking' leaves no room for speculation, and no motorist need spend too much time peering out and studying the notice. In a similar situation our authorities are likely to plant a twenty-line inscription across the landscape to say 'Under Municipal Act so and so this area has been reserved, etc. etc. and any vehicle stationed thereon will be deemed to have contravened sub-section so and so of the Motor Vehicles Act, etc. etc.' I saw on many American office-doors just 'Do Not Enter'. The traffic signs at pedestrian crossings never mince words; they just say 'Go' or 'Wait'. In a

Hollywood studio I was rather startled to read, 'Mark Stevens—Keep Out'. Mark Stevens is a busy television personality who does not like to be disturbed by visitors. Incidentally it left me wondering why, if Mr Stevens did not like interruption, he announced his name at all on the door! But it is one of the minor mysteries that make travel through that country so engrossing.

The 'toasting' of English has been achieved through other means also. Americans have evolved certain basic keywords which may be used anywhere, anyhow, words which have universal, multi-purpose use. I may make my point clear if I mention the example of the word 'check' which may safely be labelled the American National Expression. While the British usage confines it to its bare dictionary definitions, the American uses it anywhere, this expression being so devised that one may blindly utter it and still find that it is appropriate for the occasion. 'I'll check' means 'I'll find out, investigate, examine, scrutinize, verify, or probe.' 'Your check' means your ticket, token or whatever you may have to produce. 'Check room' is where you leave your possession for a while. 'Check girl' is one who takes care of your coat, umbrella, or anything else you may leave in custody. 'Check in' and 'Check out' (at first I misheard it as 'Chuck Out' and felt rather disturbed) refer to one's arrival in a hotel and departure therefrom. And there are scores of other incidental uses for the word. If you are ever hard up for a noun or a verb you may safely utter the word 'check' and feel confident that it will fit in. 'Fabulous' is another word that is used in that country freely, without much premeditation. Of course everyone knows what fabulous means, but American usage has enlarged its sense. I heard a lady in Wisconsin declare, 'Oh, those cats of mine are fabulous'—meaning that they were eccentric. 'Oh, So-and-so, he is fabulous!' may mean anything from a sincere compliment to an insinuation that So-and-so displays a mild form of charming lunacy.

O.K. or okay is another well-known example. It is the easiest sound that ever emanated from the human vocal chords. Everyone knows how comprehensive its sense can be. 'Okay' is a self-sufficient word which needs no suffix to indicate any special respect for the listener; it can stand by itself without a 'sir' to conclude the sentence.

In this respect it is like 'yeah' which seals off a sentence without further ado. 'Yes, sir' or 'Yes, darling' are conceivable but 'Yeah sir' or 'Yeah darling' is unthinkable. 'Yeah' is uttered in a short base-of-the-tongue grunt, which almost snaps any further continuation of a sentence. 'Yes' involves time as the sibilant could be prolonged.

The refinements of usage in countries where English has a bazaar status are worth a study. On a London bus you will never hear the conductor cry, 'Ticket, Ticket'. He approaches the passenger and says, 'Thank you', and on receiving the fare says again, 'Thank you, sir'. I found out that one could calculate the number of passengers in a bus by halving the total number of 'Thank yous' heard. In any western country if a receptionist asks, 'Can I help you?' it really means, 'Have you any business here, if so state it.' Or it may mean 'Evidently you have wandered off into a wrong place, go away.' A man who wants to pass you always says 'Excuse me', while he may with all justice burst out, 'What do you mean by standing there gaping at the world while you block everybody's passage? Stand aside, man!' When you send your card in, the busy man's secretary appears and whispers in your ear. 'Would you like to wait?' Though the tone is one of consultation, you have really no choice in the matter. The thing to do is not to answer the question but say 'Thanks' and look for a comfortable seat in the waiting-room, although you may feel like saying, 'No I wouldn't like to wait. I have other things to do.'

The time has come for us to consider seriously the question of a Bharat brand of English. As I've said in my essay on 'English in India' so far English has had a comparatively confined existence in our country—chiefly in the halls of learning, justice, or administration. Now the time is ripe for it to come to the dusty street, marketplace, and under the banyan tree. English must adopt the complexion of our life and assimilate its idiom. I am not suggesting here a mongrelization of the language. I am not recommending that we should go back to the days when we heard, particularly in the railways, 'Wer U goin', man?' Bharat English will respect the rule of law and maintain the dignity of grammar, but still have a swadeshi stamp about it unmistakably, like the Madras handloom check shirt or the Tirupati doll. How it can be achieved is a question for practical men to tackle.

HIGHER MATHEMATICS

THERE RECENTLY APPEARED a news item that a profound mathematical discovery has been made, a solution to a problem that has been bothering the minds of mathematicians for half a century, something that will build a 'mathematical bridge' between the forces within the universe as a whole and the forces within the nuclei of the atoms. Any news that mentions the atom becomes suspect these days. I only hope this does not mean that belligerent folk are going to be in possession of a new weapon; a combination of figures and symbols with which to paralyse the thinking powers of an enemy nation. Apart from this, I view the news without emotion. This mathematical discovery may thrill some people, but it leaves me cold. Mathematics is a matter of constitution. It is like music. Some people are tone deaf and often wonder how any adult could go on sitting in a hall for three or four hours, tolerating the noise and gesticulations of a singer. In the same way I am, if I may coin an expression, 'figure-blind'. My mind refuses to work when it encounters numbers. Everything that has anything to do with figures is higher mathematics to me. There is only one sort of mathematics in my view and that is the higher one. To mislead young minds by classifying arithmetic as elementary mathematics has always seemed to me a base trick. A thing does not become elementary by being called so. 'A rose by any other name would smell as sweet.' However elementary we may pretend arithmetic to be, it ever remains puzzling, fatiguing and incalculable. There was a fashion in the elementary school in which I read to prescribe a book in which the sums were all about English life. The characters in the problems were all John and Joan and Albert, and the calculations pertained to apples and the fares of hansom-cabs. In those days we saw apples only in coloured picture-books and we never understood what hansom-cabs meant. We were used to dealing in mangoes and *jutkas* and bullock-carts, and the payments were not in farthings or pence, but in rupees, annas and pies. While wrestling with the problems in this book I was always racked with the thought that perhaps I could solve the sums if they dealt with Indian life. Fortunately, in answer to this prayer, we soon had sums dealing with the interminable transactions of Rama and Krishna. But I soon found that this did not make things easier for me. The problems remained as tough as ever, and my wit and calculations remained defeated. My constant preoccupation was with the last section of the text book where one found the answers to the problems. Every time I did a sum I turned to the last section with trembling and prayer, but I always found there a different figure from what I had arrived at laboriously. The disappointment reduced me to tears. A sense of hopeless frustration seized me each time I referred to the answers in the printed book. I sometimes wished I had been born in another world where there would be no mathematics. The whole subject seemed to be devised to defeat and keep me in a perpetual anguish of trial and error. I remember particularly that the sections which made absolutely no sense to me were called 'Practice'. The teacher decreed 'Find out by Practice' etc. and the intelligent boys of the class at once drew three vertical lines and did something or other with them. I never understood what they did with those and why it was called 'Practice'. To this day I have no idea what it is all about. I also remained oblivious to the intricacies of stocks and shares and discount, these I viewed as the worst snares ever laid for a human being. I had a fear at one time that I might have to spend the rest of my life in a high school, arithmetic acting as a barrier to my exit; but in every young heart at this stage there arises a hope of redemption, through algebra and geometry. It might only be a delusion to think that drawing a circle within a triangle (or is it the other way) could be easier than calculating $3\frac{1}{4}$ and $7\frac{7}{8}$ of something or other, or that the anonymous hooded figures of algebra were easier to tackle than quantities of mangoes and percentages. Anyway, one got out of high school with a feeling of escaping from a concentration camp, the greatest virtue of university education seeming to be that unless one chose one need not go near mathematics.

I don't think years have improved my outlook or equipment in regard to mathematics, although as a grown-up I am not supposed to give out my real feelings in the matter. I have to keep up appearances before youngsters. So that the other day when I found my nephew (who has evidently imbibed my tradition in mathematics) literally in tears, sitting at his desk and chasing an elusive sum, I told him patronizingly, 'Well, there is no use shedding tears over mathematics. If you read the sum correctly and think it over calmly, I am sure you will get the answer. The thing is you must not be in a hurry. You must be very calm, I tell you. At your age, do you know how we were managing it?' And I told him what I fully knew to be a cock-and-bull story about my prowess and industry in this subject. He asked, 'Won't you help me do this sum?' I looked at it critically. It was something about profit and loss. As I gazed at the sum, the answer suddenly flashed on my mind. I casually turned to the last page to see if my answer was correct. It wasn't. I gently put down the book, telling the boy. 'Well, of course. I can do this sum but, you know, my "working" will be different: it won't be much use to you. You must do it in the way it has been taught in your school; moreover, you must learn to depend upon your own effort. Otherwise you will not learn.' I hastily moved out of the pale of mathematics.

TAXING THOUGHTS

THE UPPERMOST THOUGHT in anyone's mind today is, 'What new taxes shall I wake up to, tomorrow?' Of course this is a very unenlightened attitude to adopt. In a modern welfare state with such complex and well-defined aims as are generally to be noticed, the least that any person could do to show his appreciation of the troubles that his rulers take, is not to grumble at the notion of taxes. In an ideal State, according to any tax-deviser, the moment a budget is announced there will not be *hartals,* protest meetings, and acrimonious exchanges in Parliaments, but rather processions, public thanksgiving, and prayers. Every normal citizen will cry in joy, 'What a privilege it is going to be to pay a rupee more per yard for every cloth I buy! How grateful am I that I am going to pay an anna extra for every matchstick I strike! Oh, why don't they tax my breath also at so much per lungful! I am happy and proud to be a taxpayer.' He may even go to the extent of telegraphing his representative in Parliament, 'Pray suggest Finance Minister increase my income tax fifteen annas in rupee.' Following the proceedings in Parliament he will demand to be told not why there are so many new taxes but why there are so many glaring omissions in the budget speech. For instance why have they not thought of a four-anna levy on every bunch of coriander leaf in the market, which ought to yield three crores?

This is only in the nature of a vision and is hardly likely to be realized in the near future. But let us hope that the speed of political enlightenment will be such as to enable us to witness the transformation within our lifetime. But as things are, it must be very depressing for our tax-devisers to note the public reaction. It is so because people have developed a selfish tendency: they are more preoccupied with private finance than with the public one. Public finance, of course, in the view of any statesman, should take precedence over every other kind of finance. But the private citizen has not yet got over the dark and uncivilized habit of thinking that his own finance is all-important and should be left untouched. He hates all association with tax. Income-tax upsets his digestion, excise levy affects his sleep, something else frays his nerves, and the multi-point sales tax is an abomination and a nightmare to him. He indulges in dreams of a tax free universe. This is the normal constitution of a citizen, and how could any State run its administration and carry out its plans, with such a psychology always there to neutralize its efforts? We have to admire the pluck and sense of duty of persons who pilot the ship of the modern State. Public administration is becoming a costly business; river-valley schemes, railway links, cultural projects, national theatres, building new radio stations or transferring old ones to new places, all these are activities to be paid for not in thousands but in lakhs. It is no one's business to suggest, 'Why not hire a building for the national theatre instead of constructing one at a cost of seventy lakhs? Why not hold the assembly in the old town hall instead of raising a new building at a cost of sixty lakhs? Why not let cultural activities wait? Why not leave the old radio station where it has been making its noise all these years?' The typical public agitator is likely to put all these questions to his rulers, but he will be dismissed with the succinct statement, 'It has all been decided upon already.'

I read somewhere that in ancient times the prestige of a kingdom depended upon the number of taxes it was able to levy on its people. It was very much like the prestige of a head-hunter in his own community. The ruler who had not the wits to devise enough taxes was considered to be weak and spineless. And so we read of seventy-eight different taxes in an ancient State. Birthdays and death-days were taxed alike. The most lucrative tax was the one levied on any person found swinging his arms while crossing certain streets of the capital; in certain other streets tax was levied on folk with their arms folded across their chest or locked behind. By the operation of the law of averages all citizens were caught one way or the other. This was based on the principle of the pincer-movement in taxes; taxes should leave no one out. If you taxed every false tooth worn, you should assure yourself no one went scot free by displaying a sound set of thirty-two teeth. It ought to be covered by the provision that whoever displayed sound dentures beyond certain years should pay a certain sum into the treasury. A creative mind can extract a tax almost out of anything.

My pet phobia is that some day the tax authorities may suddenly realize that while they are sufficiently penalizing those who move in motor cars and other vehicles, those who walk do not contribute anything to the treasury. To remedy it, they may suddenly say that every declared walker must submit a statement of the mileage covered on foot. This is likely to produce a very large figure for tax purposes. I walk five miles a day, one-hundred-and-fifty miles a month, one-thousand-eight-hundred miles a year, and nine thousand in five years. Now let the experts calculate what it would mean in terms of revenue!

EVEREST REACTIONS

IT WAS THE youngest member of the household, Thumbi, now twelve years old, who came in with the news. He had gone out a little while earlier. It was his habit to go out and keep dashing in every little while with reports of Test scores, saucers, traffic accidents and other such matters. Today he came in crying, 'Everest has been conquered. They have reached the top.' People thought he was joking. Although generally an accurate reporter, occasionally, perhaps when he felt that people's interest in living was flagging, he tried to rouse them with stories of dacoity or arson in the neighbourhood, stories that would not bear a moment's scrutiny. Such tales would make the elders sit up and ask where he heard them and so forth, and the young man would go away pleased that he had succeeded in stirring his elders from their torpor. This seemed to be such an occasion. Thumbi tried to run away after declaring the conquest of Everest, but he was caught by the wrist and asked to explain.

'Where? Where? Who told you about it?'

'Got it over the radio in the next house.'

'Next house! How often have you been told to keep to your books and not loaf all over the place in the sun?'

'I was studying all afternoon and went out only for a moment to listen to the radio at the next house.'

'What has happened to our own radio?'

Finding that the subject was getting unnecessarily twisted, the young man declared, 'Everest has been climbed and that is all I know.'

'Don't be absurd!' cried his elders. 'Who has been telling you this cock-and-bull story?'

'I knew long ago that it would be climbed,' said Thumbi.

The elders groaned. 'How could it? How could it be? It is impossible!'

'Tensing and Hillary have done it,' said the well-informed boy. He was delighted with his own success in impressing his elders. He added casually, 'They also find now that the height of Everest had all along been mistaken. It is about a thousand feet more than what it was thought to be.'

'Impossible! Who has been putting ideas into your head?' cried the elders.

'How do you know all this, boy? It was only yesterday that we heard that the assault was to be given up.'

'But there it is,' said the precocious boy triumphantly. 'Hillary and Tensing . . .' The elders took in the news with a sort of gloomy resignation. This was a piece of news for which the world had waited for a century or more and now, instead of arriving in a spectacular manner with a fanfare of trumpets, it was reaching them through Thumbi—that habitual purveyor of news titbits.

Soon they had to accept it for a fact. For the rest of the day, they were bandying about expressions such as cwm and col, no two persons agreeing on the definition of these expressions or their origin.

Their reactions were interesting to watch. Somehow there was a general sense of disappointment at the fact that Everest had been conquered. It would have been so nice to have left Everest as an unassailable part of the earth. Said one, 'It is not good to think that human beings have conquered everything under the sun. It does a lot of good to the human spirit to feel that there are still many things beyond our reach. Human beings should not become so proud.'

Said an enthusiast, 'A masterpiece of planning. It restores one's faith in human endeavour. Clear-headed planning is the most difficult thing to achieve. I challenge anyone here to plan a journey to Tirupati and get through it without having to alter it half-a-dozen times on the way.'

'It depends,' said another, 'on inaugurating the whole thing at the right moment from an astrologer's point of view. The secret of success lies in getting the horoscope of the persons concerned and fixing the time accordingly. If it is done accurately it will solve ninety per cent of the difficulties of any undertaking.'

'And so no marks for preparation, knowledge, study, and scientific application and so forth?'

'Even a study becomes successful only when it is begun at the right moment. I am sure they must have avoided *rahukalam* and other inauspicious moments while beginning their arrangements. I am going to write to Col. Hunt to send the horoscopes of the members of the expedition and also to tell me the exact hour at which they started their preparations. Astrology is a great science, sir.'

'Now that they have made a start,' began another, 'I believe going to Everest will become common. It may almost become a holiday resort. It is going to be difficult to come across a person who has not had a holiday on Everest.'

'With so much ice,' said another with a business temperament, 'suppose they find some means of quarrying all that ice and sending it down! It will revolutionize the cold-storage industry completely. Ultimately it may become necessary to rehabilitate the members now attached to refrigeration and air-conditioning industries.'

'Whatever geographers might say,' said another, 'we cannot help feeling that Everest is in India. Even Tensing, do you know, is an Indian?'

'I won't be happy until I hear that an Indian expedition has planted its flag on Everest,' said another.

'How are you sure that someone is not already at it? By logical methods we can do many things: we could climb the highest peak without any special equipment. There are more things in heaven and . . .'

'Oh, stop, stop. I won't hear that quotation again. I am tired of it.'

Further discussion on this subject was stopped when Thumbi burst in in his usual lightning manner with the announcement, 'My friend's father who had gone out hunting last night, it seems, has bagged five tigers simultaneously . . .'

RICE AND HOSPITALITY

AFTER YEARS OF rationing, once again we see rice on the pavement, sold like any other commodity. For the first time these many years the rice dealer is willing to exhibit his stock and solicit custom. Apart from other benefits this will probably mean the reinstatement of the virtue of hospitality in our homes. In those days of juggling with fractions of ounces on ration-cards, when a guest arrived, one's first thought was, 'Oh, God! How shall I provide the calories for this man?'—a most demoralizing line of thought. The depth of degradation was reached when one was obliged to print on marriage invitations the legend 'Please bring your rations along'. Of course no one would take it literally but if a food inspector suddenly burst upon a group of diners he would see that the food regulations were being honoured—just a party of thirty consuming their own rations, while the wedding host provided them only a place to spread their leaves about. It was sometimes feared that an over-zealous inspector might check the number of leaves thrown into the garbage bin. I don't think food auditing was pushed to that extent but it must be admitted that the host in a marriage party always felt nervous and advised his helpers to remember to bury the dined-off leaves deep and out of sight. And then the manner of inviting guests to rise for dinner was itself conducted with an air of intrigue. While the music went on, the host went round and unobtrusively whispered in the ears of his guests of honour: 'Get up, will you?' The guests would leave their seats without a word, and with the air of men assisting in an assassination, vanish from the assembly and reappear half-an-hour later chewing betel leaves. This whole makeshift smoke-screen was an extremely distasteful procedure to every sensitive soul. If a man was heard to cry out, 'I would rather let my daughter remain unmarried than go through this,' the sentiment could well be understood, seeing how important a place hospitality occupied in our scheme of life and how the celebration of a marriage was looked upon as an occasion when a man could make himself host to the entire town.

Fortunately all this is past. Now those who have daughters to marry may be heard to say, 'Fortunately there is no problem about rice now; only I must find the bridegroom. If I know how to get at him I could have the marriage done within twenty-four hours.'

*

Rice has brought back to our homes the lost hospitality. The doors of our 'guest-room' can be thrown open again without trepidation.

I met a foreigner who thought that the guest system in India worked on some such procedure as the following: a guest gave a month's advance notice saying, 'I shall be there between such and such a date; I shall be leaving again by such and such a train.' This supposition attacks the very basis of hospitality, its greatest charm being the element of surprise in it. In a household that practises the truest form of hospitality it is unnecessary to give any intimation of arrival. Giving a forewarning would be viewed as an unnecessary strain put upon a guest. A guest must have enough confidence that his sudden appearance on the threshold will not cause a nervous shock or a heart-attack, and that it will be taken with casual ease and even joy. The slightest consideration shown will look magnified in the eyes of a true guest. He may find no place other than the cement *pyol* abutting the street for sleeping in, but he will speak of it as if he had been provided with a four-poster and eiderdown, and a softly-curtained magic chamber for his repose at night. He may find that his hostess has served him only diluted buttermilk, and a most inedible piece of vegetable, but he will arise from his dining leaf with the air of one emerging from a banquet and call his host a man who takes a peculiar delight in watching the discomfiture of an overfed guest. The host for his part would say, 'I don't know if I have left you half-starving,' after actually serving a thirty-course dinner. Such a verbal exchange of courtesy between a guest and a host is a social necessity. The word *upacharam* means merely the verbal aspect of hospitality and the most important. A man may have neither milk nor sugar nor coffee powder at home but he must enquire, as soon as he has a visitor, 'May I give you coffee? Or would you prefer a little milk with sugar?' And the genuine guest will always reply, 'I just had everything. Even if you tempt me with a thousand sovereigns you cannot make me take a drop.'

*

The true host must know how much hospitality he should really exercise on a guest. So much depends upon the guests themselves. Some guests feel extremely uneasy if they are fussed about. They like to be left alone. A host must take a guest on his own terms. Some, especially those involved in a marriage celebration, like an excess of fuss. Even if the distinguished man is seen to be bursting with food it is the duty of the host to enquire: 'You don't look quite well. Are you on a diet? If I may provide you some special fare, please tell me.' A lapse in this regard is seldom forgiven, and many a marriage alliance has nearly been shattered on account of it. The true host walks on a razor's edge. An excess of a sense of hospitality is not a good thing either. A man I know is so eager to have guests that he nearly misbehaves when someone passes through the town without stopping at his house. It has embittered all his associations so much that in a few years' time, I fear, he will have no friends left. Hospitality is a sacred virtue, but has to be practised with circumspection, care, and in the right degree.

RECEPTION AT SIX

NOT TOO LONG ago the South Indian marriage was a five-day celebration. Festivities went on day and night. It was great fun, the chief entertainers being the newly-wed couple. It was all very well as long as there were child marriages or near-child marriages. As civilization advanced the old type of festivity and fun became unacceptable. The bridal couple were not of the age to face all this tomfoolery. In fact the bridegroom uttered this word a great deal! He looked askance at every ceremonial and punctuated it with, 'Why all this tomfoolery?' He liked to give an impression of being sophisticated and extremely modern-minded; and this being the one occasion when people listened to the words emanating from him with every show of respect, he indulged in a rather free commentary on the irrationality of most of the functions going on around him. At this the priest and the elders begged him to put up with their eccentric ways, promising to abbreviate the proceedings as far as possible: the bridegroom grunted and let them go on. But he drew the line somewhere, and it was where the old type of wedding fun was concerned. He refused outright to go in a procession or amuse his audience in any manner and discouraged giggling children from gathering around him; but it took away from the whole function all entertainment. People were invited, and when they gathered together some excuse had to be found to keep them on for a while. In order to achieve it, there began to appear at the bottom of the invitation card the legend: 'Reception 6 p.m.'

Now it is a well-established institution, and no one needs to be told what it is all about. In fact the complaint is that it is too well-established. The business part of it is well-set: festoons of lights, arrays of folding chairs, a musician on the dais; and tea and cool drinks in one corner, and the couple safely placed on a sofa facing (somehow) both the dais and the auditorium. Invitees arrive at the other end and proceed along in a variety of walking styles, stumbling over chairs, extending their hands towards the bridegroom and bestowing a simpering smile on the bride. To save the visitor all this strain, stage fright and awkwardness, there is now the considerate practice of stationing the couple at the entrance itself, where the visitor may shed his good wishes and possibly presents, and go forward, spot out his friends in that wilderness of folding chairs, and enjoy himself. But at this point it is worth asking: does he meet anyone and get all the expected enjoyment out of the situation? It is a delicate point. Actually it seems as though one has little to do in the place after one has thrown a smile at the bride and bridegroom. The visitor feels restless and bored and waits for a chance to clear out. At the time he received the invitation he told himself, 'I must attend the reception, otherwise so and so will be wild with me,' a piece of self-flattery. And so he presents himself under the decorated entrance in due course. The master of ceremonies is of course there. The invitee runs up to him with 'You see, I could not come earlier, what happened was . . .' He does not complete the sentence, the other is not listening, he is busy bestowing a smile of welcome on the next visitor and then on the next, as invitees are pouring in in an endless stream.

It is evident that the man, the chief host, has been meeting and has had to be nice to too many persons since the beginning of the day, greeting and welcoming on a mass scale, and it has rather worn him out. Full of sympathy and understanding, the invitee, the man who considered himself his particular friend, proceeds to relieve him of his presence and drifts to a nearby chair, exchanges some banalities with someone in the next chair, takes to bits some nondescript buttonhole flower given to him at the gate, smells the back of his hand and notes the scent of sandal paste, and tries to listen to the music. But there is too much babble. He notices the master of ceremonies officiously leading a VIP to a chair in the first row, saying something agreeable all along the way. The invitee who has so far engaged himself through his own efforts, suddenly realizes the futility of the whole business; he feels that there is a lack of cohesion somewhere and that he need not have come here at all. If he is a hardened, happy-go-lucky type and manages to catch his host's eye again, presently he finds himself in a group drifting towards a dining chamber, but if he is the retiring sort he leaves unobtrusively, snatching the paper bag with coconut at the gate, and melts into the night. It is likely that when he meets his friend the host again, many many days later, he may be asked, 'How is it that you did not attend the reception at our house the other day? I remember having sent you an invitation!' And he must have a suitable answer ready, which is neither untruthful nor too offensive.

BRIDEGROOM BARGAINS

THE STOCK Of the bridegroom is rising again. He is again displaying bullish tendencies. It must be a heartening situation for the speculator who has been nursing the stock for a little over two decades. I heard an optimistic father declare that next to investment in housing, whose value can never go below a certain level, the most secure 'gilt-edge' is a son who is unmarried. All that is advantageous in the case of a father with a son naturally turns out to be otherwise for one with a daughter. It may be put down as a safe axiom that the satisfaction felt by the father of a girl is in inverse ratio to that felt by the one with a son. It is naturally so considering that one is a seller and the other a buyer; and matrimony today remains a seller's market. The father of a girl always prays that matrimony should cease to be any sort of market, and that he should be in a position to say, 'My daughter is a priceless possession I have had with me for sixteen years now, I don't know how I am going to be without her. She is invaluable as far as I am concerned and even if you pay me a price of ten lakhs, I would still feel unhappy to part with her, and so I am not selling her; I shall give her away provided you satisfy these two conditions. I must have a confidential report from one of the daughters-in-law of your house, on the outlook and conduct of the elders at home, and I want a psychologist to examine your son and give him a certificate of soundness.'

The reality of course is otherwise. The parent who has groomed a son properly, so that he sweeps the honours in all examinations and has been selected for an administrative career, is the actual dictator of prices today. This market was temporarily dull, or nervous, owing to various political causes, when the Indian republic was newly established, and there was some uncertainty in the services, when the system of recruitment and prospects were undefined. Old values were falling and new ones had not risen. In that brief period trading was cautious. It was an interim period when one heard a bridegroom's bargain agent declare, 'Dowry! Never. We don't want anything. We care for only a good alliance, all else is secondary. We don't want any dowry, but since you are pressing it on us, it is enough if you give us something to meet our actual expenses.' This 'something' might mean anything from eight thousand to twelve thousand rupees, most of it supposed to be utilized for defraying the expenses of travel of the large army of relatives and friends accompanying the bridegroom. The bad word *Varadakshinai* was avoided; instead it was called expenses. But now it is a sign of returning confidence that the word is coming into vogue once again. One might note a new directness in demands. The demands today for an eligible bridegroom are beyond the wildest expectations of a former generation. Says the bargainmaster of the prospective prize boy, 'I want a cash dowry of forty-five thousand rupees and a motor car.' This is a new trend in bargains, this addition of a vehicle to the cash dowry. If the girl's father thinks that he can palm off a second-hand 8 HP to 10 HP, he will be told presently, 'My son has to maintain his status, you know, and he must have a car big enough to seat at least six at a time; and you know he is a very sensitive boy, he is very keen on these things; he has an aversion to driving any car manufactured earlier than 1953.'* Some may throw in along with their other demands a refrigerator or a radiogram, as an afterthought, explaining, 'You know my boy likes ice cream,' or 'You know he is a great music lover.' The poor man, the would-be father-in-law of the boy, is too timid to ask, if the young man was so fond of ices or music, why he should have waited so long to provide himself with these amenities; but he cannot speak out since, to repeat the position, he is in a seller's market. It almost looks as though the inspiration for these demands is derived from the

---

*   This essay was written in 1959.

advertisements of crossword competitions, which sometimes make special seasonal offers of a phenomenal cash prize plus a car plus a refrigerator plus various other inducements. The poor man sadly reflects whether he should hold out so many inducements along with his daughter in order to make her acceptable. The limit was reached I think recently in a case where, following the announcement of the competitive examination results, the hopeful father of a daughter knocked on the door of a successful candidate, whose father opened the door and asked not whether the girl was good looking or accomplished, but whether the man was prepared to buy an 'A' type house in Gandhinagar for himself and his wife, in addition to other items to be mentioned later.

I don't think there is going to be any effective way of abolishing dowry, the victim himself being often an abettor. If it is made illegal, a black market is likely to evolve from the repression. I often think a sales tax may be levied on the transanctions involving a bridegroom, but this may again be shifted on to an already overburdened father of a girl. So it is just as well that we recognize the institution and work out a table of payments and presents which will provide at a glance what liabilities a would-be *sambhandi* is likely to incur: first class in competitive examinations: Rs 45,000 plus a 20 HP motor car, model not earlier than October 1953; engineering graduate: Rs 15,000, jeep, plus a miniature locomotive in solid gold; MSc (nuclear physics): Rs 15,000 plus five acres of land containing thorium, lignite, etc.; pilot with 'A' certificate: cash, plus a helicopter for private use; third class BA, without any property: Rs 5,000 plus a bicycle or an autorickshaw (if he chooses to make a living out of it). Marriages are, of course, made in heaven, but they are a business in our part of the universe, and why not run it on efficient lines?

THE ELECTION GAME

THE FEVER OF elections which seized the city during the first half of this month has noticeably subsided. The posters on the walls are already discolouring and peeling away. The loudspeakers have been packed and stored away. Slogan-shouters and lecturers are recuperating in silence and whispers. Superannuated automobiles which had been kicked into temporary activity as beasts of burden to carry loudspeakers, placards, demonstrators and what-not, have limped back to their workshops. A lassitude has come over the city, similar to the feeling one experiences on the day after the fair. The meeting places where thousands gathered every evening and where thundering speeches were heard are deserted and the normal lounging by the local cows has resumed there. Now the interest of the public is all in watching the results to know who has gone up by thousands and who is going down by hundreds. People are becoming aware of the subtleties of the English language; everyone discusses the difference between 'unseated' and 'defeated'.

Viewed as a large-scale rehearsal for political life, I feel, apart from other considerations, this election has been a great success. When the principle of adult franchise was adopted, there were many doubts whether it would be practicable in a country like ours, where only three or four out of a hundred could spell their way through an election manifesto. But it looks as though they have got over this difficulty by not depending too much on the written word but on the spoken, or rather the shouted word; and irrespective of whether a particular candidate has won or lost or spoken sense or nonsense, the activity itself has been a success if it is viewed as a means of political education. Now even persons whom one would not normally associate with a sense of authority discuss (as they halt for a moment in *paan* shops or bus-stands) whom they will have the country ruled by and whom they will not. It seems as though a sense of sovereignty has been roused even in the most insignificant of us.

One notices that children too have adopted electioneering as one of their games. I know of at least one fellow called Ramu whose house was in the proximity of an election-meetings ground. It was great entertainment for him while it lasted. He used to be the first to arrive and take his seat even when the dais was just being put up. He studied in a school nearby but his mind was far away from his studies. When events of tremendous consequence were convulsing the country, it was not the occasion to talk about the Gulf Stream or the Great Mughals or speculate what would happen if a number of persons could do a piece of work in a certain number of days. He had put away his notebooks and homework, with the intention of taking them up again the moment the country settled into its normal routine. He went about the house always mumbling 'vote for this' or 'vote for that . . .' echoing all the slogans he had been hearing all day in the streets. When he went over to the next house to meet his friends he plunged into a game of demonstrations and counter-demonstrations. On the eve of voting Ramu and his friends spent long hours not only in vigorous demonstrations but also in excited discussions.

'My father has promised to take me too for voting,' said one.

'Nonsense. We won't be allowed to go there; it is only for grown-ups.'

'You are young. It seems anyone can vote, didn't you hear what they said in the meetings?'

'Not everybody, only tall persons will be allowed to vote.'

'No. It is all wrong. What about our geography master? He is our height and I know he is going to vote.'

'What is a vote like?'

'My father said it is made of paper.'

'What is its shape?'

'We are not allowed to see it.'

'I am going to slip in somehow and see what it is like. They are going to have it after all in our school. . .'

'You will be handcuffed if you go there, it is against the law to try and see a vote. Don't you see how many police they have kept there?'

'I don't care if the police take me. I am going to get in there and shout "vote for Mango Mark".'

'Why Mango?'

'Because I like mangoes.'

'I will go and outshout you there. I will cry "vote for X".'

'Why X?'

'It seems when he becomes a minister he will abolish arithmetic and make cricket compulsory.'

Needless to say when the elders went out to cast their votes, they left the children behind much to their chagrin, which increased when the elders came back and displayed the little dot on their fingers. It made a little girl called Kamala very jealous, and she vowed, 'See if I don't get my vote very soon. And when they put that dot on I will tell them to place it between my eyebrows . . .'

THE UNSEEN SHOP

THERE IS THE modern legend of a stranger to the city who stood at a bus-stand for hours scanning every bus-sign, finally asking a passer-by which bus would take him to the Black Market. We generally pretend to be amused at his plight, but secretly feel that we too should like to be told a little more about this black market. We should like to see what sort of super- (or sub-) men people it. It is no doubt a morbid attraction, like the instinct to peep into an operating theatre. We cannot help it. Our waking hours are too full of reminders of its existence. It is an all-pervading evil. It is so subtly constituted that it can hardly be seen. Elaborate government machinery is set up to track it down. An elaborate code of ethics has developed out of its presence: people are good or bad according to the colour of their transactions.

The common man may be forgiven if he, in his innocence, sometimes visualizes the black market as a paradise. He is sorely tried in many ways, and he may be allowed to exercise his fancy a little. The Black Market Puram is to this desperate soul a world of fulfilment. He visualizes it as a vast, well-stocked, though subterranean world, where narrow streets criss-cross, and muffled men move about stealthily like shadows, for they dare not show their faces. But how well-filled all the shops are! Here he finds everything from A to Z. A certain talcum powder which disappeared years ago can be had here in any quantity. It stays here in protest against government interference in regard to its price. Do you want that glucose, the lack of which took someone to the edge of the grave? Here it is, piled up to the ceiling. Foodstuffs, finery, clothes, motor cars (one never thought a huge thing like an automobile could be tucked away thus), black gram, and medicines. It is a world of bewildering assortment.

This stygian market, B.M. as it is affectionately known, is a monster left behind by the Second World War. Apart from its obvious evil effects, it is responsible for a certain pathological condition of mind. Because of its perceived presence, everyone is lusting to possess dozens of articles now. Everyone is constantly thinking of something that is not available. One never thought before that this particular carminative for the infant stomach or that brand of soap or that milk-food or tonic could become a matter of life and death. In other days, a man passed by these things indifferently. If somebody at home insisted upon it, he retorted, 'As if we could not live without these things!' But now as he passes the shops he looks hungrily at the shop-windows, and if a display of any precious brand of stuff catches his eye he is ready to jump out of his tram or bus.

And there are those who make capital of this fixed devotion. They are again a type produced by the war. The magic sentence 'I know where to get it' is an Open Sesame for them in society. To a man of this type, the greatest pleasure is to have people running after him. Nothing is so pleasing to his ears as such words of despair from another as 'I don't know where to find such and such stuff'—whereupon he promptly comes forth with the assurance 'I can manage it.' He spices his assurance with a significant wink and smile. He likes to view himself as a saviour of his fellow men.

B.M. owes its birth to the War God but owes its continued flourishing condition to Red Tape. Taking an instance, though it may sound fantastic, a person urgently requires a little ginger for a *sradhha* at home. If it is a very strictly controlled commodity he will probably have to apply to the Director of Pungent Articles at Delhi in a prescribed form which is to be had on application. This Director may turn him over to the Regional Controller, who will probably intimate that it is not in his jurisdiction but in that of some other person, who may demand an attestation from the Registrar of Births and Deaths before he can agree to take any action in the matter. If the person is an ordinary man he will stand aghast at the orgy of paper-filling that confronts him, not to mention the amount of time and energy consumed in the task, and so when a cheerful soul comes round to say 'I can get you . . .' he just steps into the trap and keeps the cycle going.

It is a world disease. It has given a touch of absurdity to our very existence. I recently read in an English paper, 'Mr A was fined £250 on each of four summons—two for conspiring to obtain and supply edible oil and eggs and two for obtaining oil and eggs without a permit.' And again, 'Mr X, of Hampshire, was fined £100 for conspiracy with regard to eggs.' I saw in another paper a photograph of a society gentleman with a long broom in hand sweeping a public street—punishment awarded for blackmarketing: a possible model for all countries: one should be forced to keep clean either the market or the market-place.

ON FILMS

THERE WAS A time when films were disbelieved. Those were days when the magic lantern held its sway in darkened halls. A dusty beam of light falling on a patch of lime-washed wall, the voice of the lecturer coming through the darkness, explaining anatomy or travel, a baton waving before the static projection . . . You might or might not have grasped all the explanation emanating from the lecturer, but it easily held you in a spell.

Then we heard one day that a thing called 'bioscope' had arrived. We were told that pictures moved and gesticulated. It sounded like a cock-and-bull story at first. 'A moving picture! Don't you believe such things. It can't happen here,' argued the wiseacres till they saw it with their own eyes. The bioscope had arrived at a place called 'Electric Theatre' off the Harris Bridge. We travelled in a *jutka* one day to see the wonder. In the theatre we sat eagerly watching the screen in front of us. The hall darkened and figures appeared. We were shown a gentleman coming downstairs, picking up his hat and stick and walking out, a cobra swaying its hood, a lady opening her parasol and strutting in the sun, two boys jumping over a hurdle, and an automobile of that year's make coming towards us—this gave us the greatest thrill since the motor car seemed to come off the screen into the auditorium. People screamed in excitement at this part of the show. The lights were switched on, and we were asked to move out and make place for others waiting outside. This bioscope drew a lot of attention and became the talk of the town. People with an enquiring mind asked, 'How do they do it?'

At the next stage we were shown stories on the screen. A story ran into twenty-four parts, with six parts shown each week. A hero, a heroine, an important document constantly changing hands, and endless chasing and tormenting of the heroic set. The hero was not the unbuttoned-throat-rumpled-hair-lovelorn-crooning-type which Bombay films have popularized in recent times, but fulfilled the orthodox definition of a hero—fearless, strong, and noble. He knocked down his opponents with bare fists; he withstood an attack from a dozen persons at the same time; he underwent ever-multiplying crises for the sake of the document constantly slipping away into enemy hands and the heroine clung to him through every situation. Each instalment was shown for a week and cut off at a critical point where the heroine, bound hand and foot, was about to be pushed under a band-saw or an oncoming express train. As you anxiously watched the situation the picture faded out and a caption came on to say, 'Was Pauline crushed under the merciless wheels or did she escape? See in the next instalment at this theatre.' We bore the suspense and lulled our curiosity for a whole week and turned up at the same seat for the next instalment. No doubt the film was not yet very highly evolved: people walked about in a sort of jittery manner and a certain tremulousness was evident in all their movements, and most of the time we had to watch their lips and guess what they might be saying to each other. We thought it wonderful all the same. And then the big news came one day. 'They are showing Krishna Leela!' It seemed unbelievable. It was all very well to make a film in America, but to venture on it here, in this country! But the fact was there. We saw Krishna being born or Harischandra surviving his evil times.

The bulk of the population liked to see only our own tales and our own actors on the screen although the intelligentsia said 'Oh! I have never seen an Indian picture.' A cleavage occurred very early in life between the class which would see an Indian picture and that which would not see one. The film producer named the former his paying public and the latter the intelligentsia. This word is very much in use in film-production circles. It means one who would see an 'English' picture rather than an Indian one, who sneers at the sight of gods on the screen, who has contempt for sword-fighting heroes in velvet costumes, and who constantly asks 'In which period have you set the story?' This man is obsessed with 'anachronisms'. 'What is an anachronism anyway?' asked a gentleman who had made a film of pre-*Ramayana* times. The man of the intelligentsia replied, 'You have shown a rattan easy chair in the *rishi's ashram*, with the young hero lounging in it. That is an anachronism.' 'Nonsense!' snapped back the gentleman, 'What is your proof that there were no easy chairs in those days? You probably think that we alone have the brains to make them. Anachronism! There is no such thing.'

*

The big news of this fortnight is the publication of the 'Film Enquiry Committee Report' which is a dry title. Instead they could have called it, 'What is right with Indian films and what is wrong?' The answer to the first question is, as discovered by the Committee, that India stands second in the world as a film producer, 275 pictures produced each year represents a capital of 400 millions, and 600 millions see the pictures every year. Nothing that concerns the film world can ever be in terms other than millions. It makes us proud that we have climbed on to the second seat in this world of million counts. But the satisfaction is purely quantitative and statistical. When the next part of the enquiry is taken up, 'What is wrong with our films?', many depressing facts come to light and we seem to be assigned the very last place in the world of motion pictures. On this aspect the Committee speaks with the tongue of the intelligentsia and concludes with a recommendation for the formation of a statutory body called the Film Council, 'which will enforce standards of quality to make the film a purveyor of culture and an instrument for healthy entertainment.'

*

I had a friend once who was full of artistic theories and notions. He was exasperated by the aping and vacuity that he saw in most films. He said, 'The only way in which our films can be improved is to float a company and collect at least one crore of rupees.'

'And make pictures?'

'Oh! No. Buy up every picture produced as soon as it is available and put it out of sight. After all people make pictures only in order to make money. Our company will give back the capital plus the profit. One crore will be thrown away but it will save a very large public from cultivating a corrupt taste. We must have a nation-wide organization for buying up every picture produced in this country.'

STREET NAMES

IN THE INDIA of post-1947, the most marked feature is the passion for changing names of streets, towns, parks and squares. Our men in authority seem to have come to the sudden conclusion that old names, like old clothes, are not good. We must first understand that a street is not born with a name. It is given one, say, by a donor who financed something or the other or a municipal councillor who had the pluck to manoeuvre his name into it, or the first gentleman who dared to take his residence there. Through a street name one often seeks to immortalize a personality. This immortality, however, is more imagined than achieved. In the fancy of the man whose name is given to a street the public, as he thinks, will stop to ask every time the name board is seen, 'Who is this Shri XYZ, after whom this place is named? Must have been an outstanding personality to have his name gracing this locality.' But actually usage is deadening. However grandly a name might have been devised, it is hardly noticed after some time. A minister, of course, might have presided over the function and might have unveiled the name with his own hand with a speech dwelling on the importance of streets in the Five Year Plan, and the important role played by Shri XYZ in the nation's life, with garlands slipping over heads, and with nearly a public holiday thrown in. But with all this, it is unfortunate but true that in course of time every passerby will see the name of Shri XYZ but will not bother to know who he might be.

Generally speaking, a name grows up with a street and no one bothers to think what it might signify. All the significance is forgotten in the very first week following the naming ceremony. The friends and members of the family of the man may remember it for some time, and feel a glow of pride whenever they see it or think of it. But even they will get used to it in course of time, and they, as well as everyone else, will look at the name coldly, till it sheds all its significance and association, and the name stands by itself on its own authority, a pure name. This may not be so tragic after all. It is only a name which acquires a status, independent of all its associations and significance, that could be said to possess real vitality. For years I have been seeing a certain Ramaswami Street. Till this moment it has never occurred to me to question who he might be. It may refer to an eminent local personage, or a national figure, or an unknown, forgotten municipal councillor, or a bullock-cart driver who fell off his seat, or a first-class mathematics student who was denied a seat in engineering and stood on his head till his grievance was redressed. None of it is remembered when the name is uttered; it is just Ramaswami. No one could ever associate the street with any other title. Ramaswami becomes the street. It begins to sound almost like a common name, something like door, chair or bottle, and no one bothers to analyse why these have come to be named so. No one goes into the origin of these terms. They are just accepted as they are. When a proper name becomes common as a common name, then it may be said to have vitality, if not immortality. People must not bother to ask who was that person.

While proper names are thus reduced to insignificance, think of the actual common names which somehow come to pass. No one gives them a thought. Katcheri Road never provokes any one to ask, 'Whose *Katcheri*? Vocal or instrumental or what *Katcheri*?' It's just accepted. Or Salai Street or Solai Street never provokes anyone to demand the sight of the lush vegetation that the appellation conjures up in one. There is above all the instance of Broadway. I do not think anyone has so far demanded that the irony of this term be ended and that the place be given its rightful name. It is accepted without question, not because of its rational association, but because it seems to have grown up with it, however meaningless it may be. And of couse there is the classic Barbers' Bridge (which I hope now is not going to be changed to Bharat Bridge or something similar).

There must not be too much rationale in the naming of a street. This is just where members of municipal bodies and perfervid patriots go wrong. They attempt historical aptness or the righting of a historical wrong. This is generally seen in changing foreign names. Smith Lane, for instance, is always in danger of being attacked by righteous-minded persons. Someone will suddenly discover that Smith was an odious colonial administrator and transform the lane, with every pomp, to Jagadguru Lane. Apart from confounding a familiar, used landmark, it only achieves one object: it gives an extra-job to a signboard painter. If the authority thinks that it is likely to gratify the Jagadguru, he is grievously mistaken. The Jagadguru can well afford to ignore this honour. He has reached an eminence where this honour cannot in any way be taken as an addition to his glory. Nor, on the other hand, is this change likely to make the ghost of the old despot go pale with shame and remorse. Even if it does affect the ghost, would it be legitimate to achieve the end in a country nurtured on *ahimsa,* the essence of which is that we should not hate our enemies, much less our dead enemies? On the contrary, the despot's name should be left untouched just to show how his despotism has proved futile in the long run. Acrimony, contemporaneously or in retrospect, can have no place in a nation nurtured on *ahimsa.* And will you remember, you passionate changer of street names, the tradition thus started by you may be continued by someone else coming to your place later, whose views may be different from yours? He may take down the very names which you put up with such veneration now, elevate his own candidate and give out an equally rational explanation for it. And then what is to happen to the man who tried to find his way about the town depending upon familiar landmarks?

RED-TAPING CULTURE

'CULTURE' IS A vague expression, employed widely and understood in different ways, but it is handy and sounds respectable. Like the quality of mercy it's twice blessed—blesseth him that gives and him that takes. No one would, normally, demand a definition of the term. In my college days, I remember a professor of cultural history saying on the very first day, 'What is culture? We know agriculture, sericulture and apiculture or any blessed culture with a prefix. But just "culture" is an elusive term. We teachers have to manage somehow, according to our own inclination and equipment; a seasoned archaeologist can create culture with pieces of pottery, coins and beads dug out from under layers of ancient dust. We historians have to base our conclusions on the labours of sycophants at the courts who chronicled for their survival the glorious deeds of ancient despots. Social anthropologists have developed their own jargon based on field studies, kinship charts, and so forth. It is all a laborious and indefinite pursuit and one has to sympathize with culture-dealers who try to give a shape to an abstract something.'

Where academic professors have to labour hard for mining culture, the bureaucrat takes it in his stride (especially after 'culture' has become State property), and he can deliver neat, categorized packages of culture tied in red-tape. Presently, there may come up an imposing edifice named Culture Bhavan in Delhi. One may look forward to hearing the following conversation at the enquiry counter.

'Yes?'

'I want culture.'

'Instant or regular?'

'What's instant?'

'For personal and family purposes. Regular is for export. Fill up the yellow form if you want folk . . .'

'What's folk? Aren't we all folks? Who is in the special category of folk?'

'No time for any discussion. You will find all the relevant information in the folder—study it carefully and come tomorrow—if you are interested in bronzes, fill the red form—you'll have to produce I.T.C. Certificate and export permits . . .'

'What's I.T.C?'

'Read the folder—all forms should be completed in triplicate. Write your father's name in full and your mother's maiden name . . .'

'But they are no more . . .'

'In that case, file their death certificates with your application. After it is processed, we will work out an estimate—and subsidize a part of it in pursuance of our policy to encourage private effort.'

'If our countryside dances and entertainments are performed out of their context and background, will they not look grotesque and unconvincing, against, say, the Eiffel Tower? Secondly, how can bronze images be uprooted from the shrines where they are installed with so much ceremony? Will it be proper?'

'Are your doubts genuine?'

'Yes, sir.'

'Then you should go to the Doubts Clearance Cell on the third floor and present your doubts in writing . . .'

'More forms to be filled?'

'No, no. You may write on blank paper on one side—only a notarized attestation will be needed for your signature . . .'

'One more question please! What will it cost me?'

'A crore or two—more or less. Don't bother about it at this stage. However, if you have financial questions, go to the fourth floor, but remember, the lift is out of order.'

*

Following last year's Humour Conference in Hyderabad, I suffer from a growing anxiety that some day humour may become nationalized and packaged. A Central Circular may emanate on the following lines:

Confidential: To all District Heads:

It has been found desirable to compile a roster of humorous men in our country. You are requested to submit a list of jokers, clowns, buffoons, raconteurs, and wits in your area.

All officials should immediately realize:

(a) That they are part of a humorous community and conduct themselves accordingly, the policy being that laughter, rather than grimness or gloom, makes for efficiency in public service.

(b) Humour is the natural entitlement of every citizen, rich or poor, and must begin at the grass-roots and spread into a broad spectrum.

(c) Elitism and subtlety must be minimized, if not discouraged. Humour must be aimed at the weaker sections and similar categories who may be in need of immediate relief.

(d) Spontaneous laughter may be generally authorized but care must be taken not to be misled by every grin and simper.

(e) Minimal infrastructure with staff in appropriate uniforms (for grading and inspection of the quantum of available humour) must be built up without delay. Budgetary proposals for this purpose must be submitted for allocation of grants under the general heading 'culture'.

FAMILY DOCTOR

I FEAR THE grand old institution of 'family doctor' is now gone. I say 'doctor', rather than 'physician' or 'surgeon', since no one ever bothered about such distinctions in the good old times. 'Doctor' was a generic term without a category or classification, and also the family doctor of pre-War years lived up to our expectations of his being an all-round healer.

That was before medical science developed complex branches. There was little popular writing on health, disease and sudden mortality: too much information has now created hypochondriacs who suspect the worst at the least symptom of pain and rush to the doctor for an opinion, who cannot help suggesting, 'Why don't you go through a complete check-up and see me again?' The man appears again before his doctor in due course, clutching a sheaf of documents and papers, like a habitual litigant at a lawyer's office, to be assured by the doctor in most cases, 'You are fine. Nothing to worry about.'

The present-day doctor has to make sure that he has scientific backing before pronouncing an opinion. But the old family doctor gave the same cheerful verdict spontaneously, intuitively, without much ado. Probing and scanning being unheard of, he had to depend for diagnosis on a stethoscope, thermometer and a flashlight, and probably a spoon to hold down the tongue for examining a throat. Also, by tapping the abdomen and chest with two fingers, he could judge from the subtle resonance what might be right and wrong under the skin. His final advice would be, 'Avoid buttermilk and drink plenty of water,' or he might sit down and write a prescription, perhaps in Latin, with an air of one composing a sonnet, to be interpreted only by the pharmacist later, who would fill an eight-ounce bottle with a colourful mixture labelled properly. A bazaar doctor of my acquaintance, whose clients were mostly villagers, wrote his prescriptions in not less than twenty minute lines and then turned the sheet sideways and wrote also on the margin while his patients looked on solemnly, in profound admiration.

Tablets and antibiotics in aluminium strips were unknown in those days. In case of pneumonia, I remember fermentation with what seemed to be warmed-up horse manure (judging from the pervasive odour) was recommended. For eye trouble, which is nowadays handled by specialists with extreme delicacy, our doctor would just turn up the patient's eyelids and rub on silver nitrate every morning while the patient groaned and squirmed. Occasionally, in an emergency, the doctor would also hold down the patient and incise an abscess with a scalpel and soak the wound in tincture iodine while the patient screamed and cursed and tried to knock down the doctor. However, relief was definite in most cases, achieved through an unflinching faith in the family doctor and the doctor's faith that we would not so easily crumble or collapse, which speaks for the hardihood of the human constitution.

There was an indefinable quality and sustenance in the relationship between a doctor and his patient, which is missing today. Nowadays every doctor is hard-pressed for time with an unrelenting 'Kumbh Mela' crowd at his door night and day. The doctor-patient relationship has become literally mechanical. At a busy doctor's establishment, you will come face to face with the doctor, if at all, only at the end of a long journey through a number of secretaries, technicians and assistants.

I have come to this conclusion after a recent experience with an ear specialist after a great deal of importuning over the phone. At the waiting hall, by the time my name was called, I had finished reading cover to cover several old issues of a ladies' journal heaped on the table. I presented myself at a ticket window. On the other side a lady was sitting and questioned me as to what was wrong and took down dictation while I narrated my troubles through the grill. Next, I was ushered into the presence of the doctor who studied my card, examined my ear and gestured to me to follow his assistant. I found myself in a chamber of electronics. The operators seated me on a stool and turned switches off and on after fitting an ear-phone to me, and finally produced a chart on graph paper. Back to the doctor, who studied the chart, handed me a printed message which just confirmed that I was having an ear problem, but assured that it was inevitable at my age, and concluded with the advice that I take B-Complex daily. I wanted clarification on some points in the printed message but I realized that the next patient was already breathing down my neck. And 'I came out by the same door as in I went', my head throbbing with unasked questions.

COFFEE WORRIES

FOR A SOUTH Indian, of all worries the least tolerable is coffee worry. Coffee worry may be defined as all unhappy speculation around the subject of coffee, as a habit, its supplies, its price, its quality, its morality, ethics, economics and so on. For a coffee addict (he does not like to be called an addict, the word has a disparaging sense, he feels that we might as well call each other milk addicts or food addicts or air addicts), the most painful experience is to hear a tea-drinker or a cocoa-drinker or a purist who drinks only water hold forth on the evils of drinking coffee. He views it as an attack on his liberty of thought and action. Even a misquoted Parliament report (as it recently happened) on the coffee policy of the government can produce in him the gravest disturbance, temporarily though.

It is not right to call it a habit. The world 'habit' like the word 'addict' has a disparaging sense. One might call smoking a habit, one might call almost everything else a habit, but not coffee. It is not a habit; it is a stabilizing force in human existence achieved through a long evolutionary process. The good coffee, brown and fragrant, is not a product achieved in a day. It is something attained after laborious trials and errors. At the beginning people must have attempted to draw decoction from the raw seed itself or tried to chew it; and then they learnt to fry it, and in the first instance, nearly converted it into charcoal. Now people have developed a sixth sense, and know exactly when the seed should be taken out of the frying

pan and ground, and how finely or roughly it must be ground.
Nothing pleases a normal man of South India more than the remark
'Oh, the coffee in his house is excellent. You cannot get the like of it
anywhere else in the world.' Conversely no one likes to hear that his
coffee is bad, although the truth may be that the powder he has used
is adulterated, the strainer has let in all the powder, and there is every
indication that they have (a horrible thing to do) added jaggery to
the decoction. In this instance the thing to appreciate is not the coffee
itself but the spirit behind it. South India has attained world renown
for its coffee and every South Indian jealously guards this reputation.

Coffee forms nearly thirty per cent of any normal family budget.
The South Indian does not mind this sacrifice. He may beg or run
into debt for the sake of coffee, but he cannot feel that he has
acquitted himself in his worldly existence properly unless he is able
to provide his dependents with two doses of coffee a day and also ask
any visitor who may drop in, 'Will you have coffee?' without fear at
heart. This is the basic minimum for a happy and satisfied existence.
Here and there we may see households where the practice is more
elaborately organized, and where coffee has to be available all hours
of day or night. There are persons who call for a cup of coffee before
starting a fresh sentence while writing or conversing. Perhaps all this
may be too much. These are likely to come under the category of
addicts, but their constant demand is understandable. No man asks
for a fresh cup of coffee without criticizing the previous one. 'It was
not quite hot . . . It seemed to have too much sugar. Let me see how
this is . . .' It is only a continuous search for perfection, and let no one
spoil it by giving it a bad name. Anyway, it cannot be called an
addiction since anything that takes on that name brings forth evil
results. Coffee has produced no bad result. It is supposed to spoil
sleep, but there is a considerably growing school of thought that it is
very good for insomnia. For one person who may say that coffee
keeps him awake there are now at least three to declare that they can
have a restful night only when they have taken a cup before retiring.
All moralizing against coffee has misfired in this part of the country.
'Coffee is a deadly poison, you are gradually destroying your system
with it, etc.,' declares some purist. He may lecture from a public

platform or on a street corner but people will listen to him with only a pitying tolerance, with an air of saying, 'Poor fellow, you don't know what you are talking about, your don't know what you are missing. You will still live and learn.' In course of time this prophecy is fulfilled. Many a man who came to scoff has remained to pray. Coffee has many conquests: saints, philosophers, thinkers and artists, who can never leave the bed unless they learn that coffee is ready, but not the least of its conquests is among those who came to wage a war on it.

FIFTEEN YEARS

LANGUAGE HAS BECOME a profoundly embarrassing subject nowadays. The thought of it gives a peace-loving citizen a pain in the neck. I mean it with particular reference to the English language. An average citizen today is in the position of appreciating the language but not wanting it. We are not so far away from the time when people used to say as a matter of prestige, 'He speaks perfect English', and a bride who could write her letters in English and who could claim to have read Scott and Dickens was considered fully accomplished. In the matter of employment, too, a young man who could draft an English letter with ease and confidence stood a better chance of being employed than the one who was proficient only in his regional language. And there were people who didn't know English, and who said with a sigh, 'If I had only learned English I would have conquered the world . . .' This may not be a very comfortable memory for anyone now, but it would be false to pretend that such values did not exist at one time. However, various causes, practical, political, etc. have demanded the abolition of English from our midst. It is almost a matter of national propriety and prestige now to declare one's aversion to this language, and to cry for its abolition.

But the language has a siren-like charm and a lot of persistence, and (if we may personify it) comes up again and again and demands, 'What have I done that you hate me so much?' The judge does not lift up his head for fear that he might weaken. He assumes the gruffest tone possible and says, 'You are the language of our oppressors. It is through you that our nation was enslaved, and it is only through you that the people were divided, so that those who were masters of English could rule others who didn't know the language. Your insidious influence wrought a cleavage in our own midst . . .'

'You speak very good English.'

'Well, well, I won't be flattered by it,' says the judge. 'All of us are masters of English, but that proves nothing. You are the language of those who were our political oppressors. We don't want you any more in our midst. Please, begone.'

'Where shall I go?'

'To your own country . . .'

'I am afraid this is my country. I fear I will stay here, whatever may be the rank and status you may assign me—as the first language or the second language or the thousandth. You may banish me from the classrooms, but I can always find other places where I can stay. I love this country where:

Full many a glorious morning have I seen
Flatter the mountain tops with sovereign eye,
Kissing with golden face the meadows green
Gilding pale streams with heavenly alchemy.'

'That is a beautiful Shakespeare passage. However, I cannot allow the court's time to be wasted in this manner. You have a knack of beguiling the mind with quotations. I forbid you to quote anything from English literature.'

'Why are you dead set against me, sir? I have a fundamental right to know why you are throwing me out, under the Indian Constitution . . .'

'But it doesn't apply to you.'

'Why not?'

'Because you are not an Indian.'

'I am more Indian than you can ever be. You are probably fifty, sixty or seventy years of age but I've actually been in this land for two hundred years.'

'When we said "Quit India", we meant it to apply to Englishmen as well as their language. And there doesn't seem to be much point in tolerating you in our midst. You are the language of the imperialist, the red-tapist, the diabolical legalist, the language which always means two things at the same time.'

'I am sorry, but red tape, parliament and courts have a practical purpose in having a language which can convey shades of meaning and not something outright. This reminds me: have you got the criminal and civil procedure codes in the language of the country now? And have you standardized this language of the country? I remember the case of humble author who got his English works translated into Hindi but later had to put away the manuscripts in cold storage.'

'Why?'

'He had the translations done by a pundit who appeared to him very good. Not being very proficient in the language, the author accepted what the pundit said as gospel truth and thought that the translations were unimpeachable. But when he showed the manuscript to others, one set of persons condemned it for being too full of Sanskrit words, and another set condemned it for being full of Urdu words. Not being able to decide the issue himself the author put the manuscript out of sight. The moral of this story is . . .'

'You need not concern yourself with this problem. We want you to go.'

'You probably picture me as a trident-bearing Rule Britannia, but actually I am a devotee of Goddess Saraswati. I have been her most steadfast handmaid.'

'All that is beside the point. Even if you come in a sari with *kumkum* on your forehead we are going to see that you are deported. The utmost we shall allow you will be another fifteen years . . .'

'Fifteen years from what time?' asked the English language, at which the judge felt so confused that he ordered, 'I will not allow any more discussion on this subject,' and rose for the day.

TO A HINDI ENTHUSIAST

YOU ARE NATURALLY devoted to the language which is as natural to you as swimming is to a fish. But you do not realize that a dry-land creature like me cannot step into the water with the same confidence. Aquatic competence (even more so amphibian competence) can be acquired only with hard practice. Practice implies time. Time alone can mature certain things. You feel fifteen years is a long enough time. In a matter like the nation-wide adoption of a language you cannot fix a time-table in advance. You cannot command a tree to put forth fruit on such and such a date. You cannot stop the waves on a seashore, as King Canute ably demonstrated long ago. One may multiply instances and analogies, but the point is really this: ripeness is all, as Shakespeare has said somewhere. Ripeness cannot be forced by a government order or even by the recommendations of a commission. You cannot coerce nature, and the rooting and growth of a language is a natural process. You must first shake off the notion that the time element is all-important. It is not. It can be altered, the more easily because it is in the Constitution. Do not look so outraged at this suggestion. You know as well as I do that any Constitution worth its name must be amended, if not forgotten.

Do not imagine that I underrate the urgency of the question. That the country should stir itself from the spell cast on it by a foreign language is a point that anyone will readily grant, although personally I think otherwise. For me, at any rate, English is an absolutely *swadeshi* language. English, of course, in a remote horoscopic sense, is a native of England, but it enjoys, by virtue of its uncanny adaptability, citizenship in every country in the world. It has sojourned in India longer than you or I and is entitled to be treated with respect. It is my hope that English will soon be classified as a non-regional Indian language.

You have perhaps a suspicion that we in this part of the country are not sufficiently devoted to the cause. Let me assure you that we are in dead earnest and putting forth our best efforts. Our homes resound with Hindi declensions night and day. The domestic atmosphere is fully Hindi, let me assure you. South Indian womanhood, at any rate, has lent the cause its unstinted support. It may be that the men here are not showing equal competence or application for the task. It is because they are still entangled in the sordid business of working for a living and do not have the time or the energy for mastering a new language, but our women are forging ahead with single-minded devotion. Their zeal has made men nervous. Multi-lingualism is threatening to invade our homes too. Women flaunt their Hindi with undisguised glee; men do not understand a word of it. Presently we may need interpreters in every home for the efficient management of home affairs. The women's zeal is such that men, in their selfishness, sometimes wonder if they will attend to anything else at home, a rather unprogressive fear. Women do attend to both home and Hindi. As the season of *Visharad* or some such examination approaches, it is a common sight in any household to find the lady putting in twenty-three hours of study, all the while carrying on all her routine domestic activities. While her left hand holds open the textbook under her eyes, her right hand prepares the meal, washes the clothes and rocks the cradle. The indications are that presently an average South Indian housewife will prove an adept not only in Hindi but also in the use of a single hand for various purposes. I could not help asking a certain lady why she went through all this travail. She did not say that she felt it to be a national duty or that she hoped to be recruited to the IAS, but simply, 'I find it interesting, that is all.' This is what I would like you to note. Leave it to our good sense and pleasure and nothing will go amiss. It is not necessary to hold threats to your fellow men who, after all, belong to the same civilization. It is odious to be told, 'You will not get your salary or your ration card unless you speak this tongue or that.'

Here are my tips if you want Hindi to flourish in this part of the country:

Do not send us postal stationery with Hindi inscriptions on them. At the moment it only puzzles and irritates us, and wastes a lot of our time as we try to divine where to write what. Form-filling, even with the old money-order form with its payee and remitter (instead of receiver and sender), has been a trying business, always making one pause to wonder whether one was a payee or a remitter, but with Hindi text on it, it is becoming just impossible to get through any business at a post-office counter nowadays. It is childish to imagine that by sending us Hindi forms you are making us more Hindi-conscious. Shall we supply your post offices with forms and stationery printed in Tamil, Telugu, Malayalam and Kannada? That would at least give this whole business a sportive and reciprocal touch.

Secondly, try to make your textbooks attractive, not only in content but in format. I may say without fear of contradiction that some of the Hindi textbooks I have seen are the shoddiest specimens of book production in the world. The *Rashtrabhasha* deserves a more dignified dress. Flimsy newsprint pages, thin, coloured covers, smudgy blocks of indifferent drawings and a stiff price are the components of a Hindi textbook as far as my observation goes. It should be possible to spend a little more on paper and production, seeing that every book of this kind has an assured sale of several thousand copies each year. Remember that half the charm of English was engendered by the manner in which its schoolbooks were produced, at least in the old days. I still keep with me an old Nelson Reader, nearly forty years old. I still get a peculiar delight out of turning its pages: its exquisite coloured frontispiece showing some London bridge and river and towers in a fog, its thick and smooth pages, its typographical excellence and, above all, its carefully selected content with relevant black and white pictures, all these have in a subtle and unseen manner helped the language in this country.

CURIOSITY

IF I HAD the time and the resources I should soon be starting an organization called SPC. This is an age of multitudinous abbreviations. The United Nations Organizations have appropriated most of the letters in the alphabet. If someone says, 'I am working on behalf of NAAF which as you know is a branch of EEZF,' we do not bother to know what it means. We are getting used to many abbreviations in daily life. I feel that I might add, without anyone noticing it, just one more to this wealth of abbreviations. Mine is going to consist of only three letters: SPC—Society for the Promotion of Curiosity.

One of the saddest developments in recent years is the attitude we are adopting towards curiosity. It is one of the undesirable results of urban standards of social life. One is supposed to be behaving properly as long as one does not display any curiosity towards another. I think we have been misled by the old saying, whatever may be its origin, 'Curiosity killed the cat'. It is possible that the cat owes its nine lives to this virtue.

The old type of question that an aged lady puts to a stranger, 'How many children have you? What is your husband's salary? How much has he saved?' is one of the most spontaneous acts on earth. The modern tendency is to shudder at such 'personal' questions. What question is worth asking unless it be personal? When it is discredited, naturally, a lot of coldness creeps in, and all intimacy and warmth goes out of human relationship. When two persons meet, they are obliged to talk of the weather, Test-scores, ministerial crises and such other impersonal matters, and waste precious hours of existence. When all topics are exhausted and there is nothing more to speak about they suppress the yawn (bad manners to yawn openly), and look bored. In spite of all the suppression that sophistication decrees, one's instinct keeps clamouring inside one all the time. One may outwardly be engaged in discussing political questions with a friend, while really wanting to know what are the latest antics of that pugnacious brother demanding a share of the ancestral estate. One might spend an hour elaborating trade statistics while one would rather ask what fee the friend took to get through such and such a case; one might discourse on comparative religion while one would rather ask of one's hearer if so and so and his wife are still quarrelling like wild cats and if not, why not? All this is tabooed in polite company. This is one of the reasons why club-life has become somewhat dull nowadays. Members disappear into the cards room or billiard room or sit morosely reading weekly papers in a corner. There is no scope for free conversation in any club nowadays. Here and there we may see a small group talking, but there is nothing in their talk which is not found in the day's papers and known to one lakh persons already.

It seems to me that the old town planning was based on the principle that curiosity must be kept alive. Rows and rows of houses stuck side by side, thin partition walls through which you could follow all the conversation in the next house, and narrow streets which made anyone passing thereon conspicuous, were some of the features of corporate life in our country. Every house in the street knew what was happening in every other house, what the postman had brought there, who the visitors were that came in a big car, or how much so and so had borrowed from his uncle. No one could flaunt suddenly his prosperity or suffer adversity without everyone being aware of all the reasons for it. This system has its own advantage. 'Disclosure of income' is the greatest headache for the income-tax department at present. Their present difficulty is mainly due to the voluntary abstention from curiosity which has been in practice for a long time now. That the income-tax department still has faith in human nature is borne out by their latest request calling upon anyone to disclose any one else's income without any fear or reserve.

It is only through curiosity that children learn to understand the world around them, it is only through curiosity that artists and writers gather material for their work, it is only through curiosity that science has progressed. If Newton had ignored the fall of the apple as an unwanted personal question pertaining to the tree and the apple, mankind would probably never have known of gravitation.

RAMBLES IN A LIBRARY

A FIT OF spring-cleaning seized me once. I made a start with our ancient library at home. This is a respectable word for a book-museum, left over by an earlier generation. It was situated in a neutral territory of the house, in which nobody had any special interest, and persons while passing on to their rooms cast a glance at the back of the books standing there three or four deep, in shelves which were ten feet high. We were so used to this sight that we took it casually, as if these were a part of the wall. We borrowed any book we wanted from the Public Library, and never disturbed the books on these shelves. They were a respectable heirloom and nothing more. The shelves ached with their loads. Hundreds of volumes gathered for nearly half-a-century through varied means of book-acquisition: books bought, borrowed, and left behind by other book-lovers. Complete works of Milton, Tennyson, Browning and other poets, Sheridan's plays, Moliere, French Revolution, Kant's *Critique of Pure Reason;* several Sanskrit volumes whose titles we were not fit to lisp, and Tamil books. There was a whole shelf filled with the textbooks that an earlier generation had read as children, youths and then as adults. Every book was there—from the colourful red-backed Nelson Primer to *Paradise Lost* and *Macbeth* in college editions with pencil notes in the margin. I felt an admiration for the preserving capacities of our forefathers. A look at them in a mass, and we understood the cultural history of our country for half-a-century or more, the root and branches of our cultural growth and the mixed sap coursing through them.

It was nearly twenty years since anyone went near those books. What was the purpose in keeping them there, I wondered. Even confirmed, accepted, junk-hoarders mention only seven years as the time-limit for an article. It must be used by that time or flung away. But these books! They collected the dust of other days, and harboured all kinds of vermin. It was a house with many mansions for any sort of insect which might care to come up and settle: wasps and silverfish, mosquitoes and bright-hued beetles had established themselves securely among these volumes.

I stayed the duster for a moment and reflected. Why let them stay here at all? But it seemed sacrilege to touch any of them. If any volume was to be removed, what was to be the basis of selection? Certainly not their innate worth, or worthlessness. This element could not weigh at all, for the bulk of them were works of the highest quality, already enthroned as classics. Who was I, a petty library worm, to sit in judgement over them? The only standard to adopt now would be to consider whether a volume looked well or ill. The dullest volume, I decided, would be allowed to stand if it kept itself presentable. Though untouched by human beings for a long time, most of them seemed to have been well used by the book-worm, who had criss-crossed several rows of books end to end with his deep and devious tunnels.

It was evident that with the best of intentions in the world, and with every respect due to them, they could not stay. I brought in a basket, and put into it all the volumes that seemed worn out. I believe I apologized to their authors mentally promising that their works would soon be replaced in new, modern editions. There are persons to whom an edition, mellowed by time, is precious. But this luxury has to be sacrificed when classics crumple at a touch, or exude such minute dust that in turning those leaves, you tempt providence and go down with cold and cough for a week.

The basket filled up very fast. And very soon another large basket had to be called for. A Milton in microscopic type in double column, an album of European views, an obscure orator's collections, several novels of Bulwer-Lytton, and a thick book called *Indian Social Revolution,* dated 1870, challenging every kind of orthodoxy of those days.

There was some space left in the second basket. I looked about for something more that could be put in. I noticed a *Social History of India* on a top shelf, a stalwart volume over a foot-and-a-half high, and half-a-foot wide with all kinds of gilt decorations and a coat-of-arms on the binding. It had a frontispiece portrait of the author himself—a colonel of the Company days, who had evidently a lot of time to spare and a willing amanuensis at hand. I read a few pages and realized what it was: it was more a record of the gentleman's views on Indian history, geography, and sociology and anthropology or anything else that caught his fancy—written probably on the heels of Macaulay's scheme of Native Education, as a sort of supplementary study. It had in green ink the name of an Englishman's library, a second-hand bookshop's stamp and someone's inscription of presentation for someone else. Who were all these? And resting so well, disturbed neither by men nor by insects.

After the baskets filled up, I wondered what I should do with them: The only reasonable and practicable course would have been to give them away to someone, who might be willing to relieve me of them, and add a reward for his trouble. But I said to myself vaguely that I might need them again some time for urgent reference; and at the back of my mind was also a vague hope of selling them off to any fool willing to part with cash for literary dust. In this uncertainty, I brought in a ladder, put it up against a loft in another part of the house and hauled up the baskets to that region where rested a hundred oddments waiting for a second chance in life: broken locks, boxes without lids, canvas chairs minus canvas, tin boxes, and skeletons of umbrellas—it was a veritable charnel-house of all objects which should have been flung into the garbage heap long ago.

Six months later when I went up the loft again, I saw no traces of the books, nor of the basket. I noticed in their place only a great colony of white ants, moving about, looking extremely well-fed. They had consumed not only the classics without leaving a trace behind but also the baskets. Apparently they had waited all their life

for this chance. All the other objects in this place being mainly of
iron and teak, they had all along been waiting for something on
which they could set their teeth and they had made a thorough job of
it. The only book relic on the spot was the gilt coat-of-arms of the
Colonel who had written the *History of India*. This somehow
seemed to have proved distasteful to the white ants, and though they
had devoured the hefty volume with its binding board, they had left
the coat-of-arms intact like a badge.

AT AN AUCTIONEER'S

ONE MORNING, STROLLING along the marketplace, I passed by an auctioneer's shop. So far I had never stepped into an auctioneer's place, always feeling that I could never succeed in getting what I wanted there. The clamorous competitiveness of an auction crowd usually frightens me. For instance, how often have I passed a fascinating writing desk in teak in that shop but have not dared to go and ask for it because I know I shall be told, 'For auction, not for sale', although I am ready to pay a fancy price to be spared the pains of bidding.

On this Sunday I stepped into the shop. 'Stepping in' is not the right word, for on an auction Sunday the shop bursts its boundaries and overflows into the street, and the traffic obligingly detours on such days.

A variety of objects were dumped together. Writing desks, mirrors, bedsteads, perambulators, parts of a cycle, flower vases, a gramophone, a set of Scott's novels in an ornamental book-case, pictures, paintings, photos, and heaven knew what else.

Looking at these I wonder how they have found their way here. This seems to be a most poignant place on earth—where men are separated from their possessions. What is the story behind that double-cot? Where are its occupants now? Surely it must have gone as a gift from a father-in-law. What has happened to its owners? Have they parted in silence and tears or have they become bankrupts or have they become too prosperous to care for this cot? That single cot. Where is the man who slept on it? At this point I notice a man going round the double-cot muttering, 'If I can get this! It only needs a slight retouching and polishing. My son-in-law will be asking for one, very soon, I know he won't mind a used one if it is good. In these days . . .' By his look I know he is going to secure it whatever happens. No man visits an auction but with an iron determination. I have imagined such a gloomy background for this cot that I send up a silent prayer for the continued happiness of the new couple who are going to acquire it. That perambulator, that high-wheeled, gawky apparatus is the only object which does not convey any unhappy impression. The very person for whom it had been bought might be auctioning it now. But who will buy it? No modern child will ever consent to be perched so high . . . I notice a grizzly tinsmith poking into it critically. I suspect he wants it more for its wheels, which may be put to entirely unexpected uses such as working bellows or turning a screw.

There are all kinds of pictures lumped together in a corner. Excited and exaggerated splashes in oils and watercolour, portraying waterfalls, mountains, forests, and rolling seas. What despair drives artists or art-lovers to discard masterpieces in this manner?

There are one or two large-sized group photos of very ancient times, judging by the heavy turbans of the sitters and by the side-whiskers of the European district judge or whoever he was sitting at the centre. One wonders how these pictures will interest anyone now. As I stand pondering over it I notice a person scrutinizing them. I cannot resist asking, 'What use are these to you?' 'Frames and glasses and the mounts! We can pay any price for them now,' he says callously. What a festival they must have made of that day of photographing! This is a chamber of disillusionments. Yet the attraction of an auction is irresistible for some persons. I can speak with certainty for at least one—an opthalmic surgeon who would rather miss a patient than an auction sale. He has the instinct of a hunter in this matter. He watches the auction advertisements with a wary eye and is present at every auction in the city. He is wealthy, and his spacious bungalow chokes with unnecessary and varied furniture, radio sets, gramophones, and automobile parts. He has sometimes paid three times the ordinary price for some pieces (often duplicated). He will not miss for anything the thrill of bidding and outbidding, and he sets apart a thousand rupees a year for this joy. The members of his family naturally protest and try to hold him in check both for reasons of space and finance. But he has his own technique of dodging them just as he dodges his patients on a Sunday.

To the Englishman his home is his castle—as long as he occupies it—but on the eve of his departure it is turned into an auction chamber. The motley may walk in and out at its ease, sit on the couch, turn the gramophone handle, doubt the soundness of the springs of any mechanism, and question his taste in books. He turns over his entire possessions, from dinner table to a safety pin, for sale. No man could shed his possessions more thoroughly. Till a moment ago it looked as though he cherished these articles and would defend them with his life. But at a moment's notice he brings them under the hammer—all the knick-knacks and furniture he had gathered around him during a lifetime. There is a touch of cheerful renunciation about it.

It was in tune with this sentiment that the gramophone at the auctioneer's sang. It was a tiny miserable model full of creakings and unwanted noises and the music came through a pink funnel but it made up in speed what it lacked in clarity. It stood on a rattan table with a dozen tired-looking records by its side. The table, the records, and the gramophone had come from different sources, though here, at the auctioneer's, they were united in a common purpose. Someone was grinding its handle, and someone else was putting the records on, in spite of the prolific warnings everywhere that said DON'T TOUCH. Through its raucous gurgle and shrill I recognized the voice of a musician who usually charged two-hundred-and-fifty rupees for a performance. He no doubt sang at top speed now, but nonetheless the song said '. . . All the eye-filling, eye-gladdening objects around us turn to dream and dust . . . Wherefore possessions?' It was a fitting song for the occasion, though difficult to discern through the babble of the crowd, and the beat of the tom-tom of the fellow sitting half on the edge of the lot.

PRIDE OF PLACE

ONCE I MET the wife of a writer, who let out a cry of disappointment on reading the announcement of the Nobel Prize for the year. She said, gloomily, 'Once again it has happened!'

'What?' I asked, sympathetically.

'I expected that at least this year they would give the prize to my husband. Again he has missed it.'

I made the appropriate sounds of sympathy—suppressing the obvious remark that perhaps the judges did not share her admiration of the man's worth. 'Do you know why?' she continued. 'Because of XYZ who has a big voice in the Committee and who is prejudiced against North Indians.'

'Oh! I never thought the people of Sweden would ever notice the difference between North and South Indians. What is the reason for XYZ's prejudice?'

'If you don't mind my being frank—because he has a South Indian friend who advises him on all matters.' She hinted that as long as XYZ had a voice in the Committee, and listened to the advice of a Ramaswami, Subramaniam or Venkataraman, the Nobel Prize was destined to go to Italians, Russians or the French, rather than to a North Indian.

To counterbalance this view I have my friend, a teacher of physics. He is up-to-date and original—I have to take his word (or perhaps his wife's) for it, as I have no knowledge of physics and no means of understanding his attainment. It is his constant refrain that he should not be 'rotting' in a miserable hole in south India—('South is being neglected, I'm one more evidence of it,' he always says)—his rightful place would be the head of one of the research institutions on a salary of Rs 2,000 or more, but he will never get there because science is a preserve of North Indians, and no one from South can get in there even if he holds appreciative letters, as this gentleman does from Sir or Doctor So-and-so of Cambridge who is always urging him to get out and do something to claim his share of recognition.

In Bombay, my friends advised me, 'Why do you want to go to Calcutta? It is an awful place. They never remove dead dogs from the streets.' At Calcutta, my friends said with one voice, 'I can't stand Bombay. When I go there for a meeting, I take the first plane back. Bombay is colourless, sophisticated and arty-crafty.' In Madras, one hears, 'Delhi is all right for a trip, but I cannot understand how people can go on living there. My son is employed in Delhi, but he says the vegetables there are insipid. Poor boy was always keen on brinjals from our native village, which, even some Americans have remarked, are the best in the world. I know some people at the Secretariat. I am trying to get the boy a transfer to Madras. He is not happy in Delhi!' I have heard a Punjabi businessman say, 'Engage a Madrasi! Not unless I am in a mood to commit suicide. A Madrasi will sell me under the counter if I am not watchful.'

*

Generalization about a whole slice of the country is a common habit. 'Oh, Bengalis! They are all . . . etc.,' or 'Maharashtrians are as a rule . . . etc.,' or 'Madrasis, you know what they do, all are . . . etc.' It is as if a whole population, several million men and women, were all type-designed or were pressed through a particular mould and tarred with a particular brush, like the figures turned out by the toy-makers of Kondapalli. Every person assumes the role of an expert sociologist who has made a scientific study of human behaviour and motives and could speak with authority about others, but the data gathered is mostly uncomplimentary, always underlining craftiness, stupidity, unreliability, slothfulness and so forth.

Prejudice is only the other side of the medal of pride. The mind plays tricks at all times and at no time more than when one talks boastingly of one's own ('native') place: the food, its flavour, spicing, the scenes, the roads, the flowers, and the general quality of life and cultural attainments are unmatched. This condition particularly afflicts an expatriate. He suffers doubly. He longs for a place he can't get to and hates the place where he has chosen to spend his days. The paradise one speaks of is geographically impalpable. At first, one speaks of a whole place of several thousand square miles as the paradise on earth; if you question further, it shrinks down to a part of the country one lives in, and then to a street, and a corner of the street; and all 'other points of compass' are inevitably contemptible.

Even adjoining cities, such as Mysore and Bangalore, to take an immediate example, have antagonistic temperaments although they come under the same State administration and partake of the same culture, separated only by an eighty-five-mile concrete road, which you can cover in two hours; and yet what a difference! Strangers who have passed through, inadvertently say, 'I was in Mysore,' when they mean Bangalore! This sort of slip distresses a true Mysorean and a Bangalorean equally. For the shades of prejudice between the two cities are not mere gradations in a chromatic scale but well-defined conflicting colours. In the shops of Mysore if any commodity is unfairly priced, and you ask for an explanation, pat comes the answer: 'It is all due to Bangalore, where they have put up the prices.' The Bangalorean thinks, 'God, nothing will prosper in Mysore. People are too sleepy and impossible. Once, when I was in Mysore, I tried to get a plumber to fix the tap in my bathroom and for fifteen days no one turned up. In Bangalore . . .'

Bangalore hotels, taxis, water supply, and the colour and composition of *masala dosai* are categorically disapproved of by Mysoreans. 'Mysore is dull' is balanced by 'Bangalore is getting so congested that it will choke itself one of these days.' If a Mysorean admits certain deficiencies in Mysore, he'll always trace them to the fact that it has no spokesmen either in Delhi or in Bangalore, most of the ministers (at least till recently) being men of other districts, which is the reason why Mysore is without a train connection to the South through Chamarajnagar-Satyamangalam (a distance of only forty-five miles through an oft-surveyed track), an airport, a broadcasting station, and a broad-gauge track. No one in authority has any feeling for Mysore. There is also a comforting view adopted sometimes that Bangalore is a sort of filter keeping out undesirable industrial elements, leaving Mysore to live in its pristine glory.

In every state, there is one particularly important town or district or city which claims for itself outstanding merits. In Madras State, this role is assumed by Tanjoreans. Every Tanjorean is convinced that there is some peculiar merit in the soil of Tanjore, in the waters of the Kaveri (blind to the fact that the Kaveri flows through several miles of other territories too) that produces geniuses in mathematics, Carnatic music, Bharat Natyam, civil service, architecture, sculpture, wit, wisdom, Sanskrit grammar, and Tamil eloquence. One wonders if anything worth a mention is left for other parts of this state since it included twenty-four other districts at one time. The answer is, 'It is enough if others learn to appreciate our good things.' The other districts don't yield the point without a fight and say, 'Most of these accomplishments you catalogue are at least one century old. What have you to claim within the last two decades, please? Is your city clean, roads passable, houses modern; is there anyone in science or arts who can claim recognition within the last decade, let us say?'

'Oh, Tanjore is neglected, because the Minister in charge of development is from . . . district, and has starved this area. What can we do? We cannot get even ordinary water supply. All the funds are diverted elsewhere.'

The 'One World' idea was mooted by the late Wendell Willkie. We need not aspire for it yet. Let us make a start with the thought that we belong to one country and are not living in the midst of strangers. North, South, East, West, are relative terms. Even the Himalayas are south of some other place; and the extreme point of South India could be viewed as north by a Sinhalese.

HOUSES, HOUSES

IT MAY BE stated as a safe axiom that a house destroys human nature, tears up human relationships, and is generally responsible for much deterioration in human conduct, if it becomes a business between two persons. Under that condition they never remain just two persons but are transformed into two parties. One would never have thought that such a noble institution as a house could ever become such a disruptive force, but it is in keeping with the times when many noble objects have debased themselves in various ways. Till about 1942 we were never conscious of anything special about houses. They were just there—one went in and out of them. One shut the doors and opened the windows and did all the normal things one generally likes to do with houses. But now a house means troubles all round. If there are fifty thousand houses in a city you may be sure that there are at least fifty thousand different worries and troubles. It is all very well as long as not more than one party is involved in it. But it is like saying that cricket is a fine game and a safe one provided not more than one is involved in the playing of it. The cricket simile is not just a chance mention. There are many ways in which cricket and houses compare. In both one aims a missile at another, leaving him to guard himself with the narrowest possible shield, with every chance of being knocked out.

The contending parties may be a landlord and his tenant or a house-building enthusiast and the man who undertakes to build it for him. The trouble is that the days of perpetual landlords and perpetual tenants are gone. We have known times when a man occupied a house and paid a rent for it all his life, and nobody bothered about it. But that is all over now. Everyone knows why it is so, and it is not necessary to elaborate the point except to remind ourselves that now this relationship is being administered by the rent-controller. When a tenant finds it impossible to remain the protégé of the rent-controller any longer, he moves to another house, if it is available (which remedy is in the nature of a lull in the battle and not to be mistaken for peace), or tries, if he has the hardihood and the money, to build a house of his own. This is indeed a hazardous undertaking. In fact, actually a jump from the frying pan into the fire. Later this man will have many introspective moments to decide whether he is really happier for rushing into the arms of a house-builder whose tactics seem often incalculable and baffling from those of a landlord who at least had the virtue of practising a familiar technique. The whole trend of this activity was admirably expressed in a crystallized form by a friend of mine who once said that the Final Bill (so-called), the House-warming, and the first hearing in a court, usually, coincide for most people. It is not necessary to go into details now since the causes, symptoms, and the course of this disease are well-known. Heartburns, disillusionments, shocks, cold despair, nervous tremors, impossible rage, and an unshakable conviction that one is being let down and persecuted, are some of the observable signs in a man stricken with the building disease. Everyone knows about it and has heard about it. All that we must ponder over is if there is any record in human history of the same pair, namely the house-dreamer and the house-builder, coming together again for a second transaction.

Even when all things are nicely settled, I don't think a house leaves one in peace. We have complicated our lives. It was enough in other days for men to have a little privacy, a little shelter, and a few comforts, and a few ornamentations; men did not demand too much of their houses. But now we seek too many facilities in a house. The first thing seems to be to keep up a general pretence that one got up from bed radiant, dressed, groomed, and was in every way fit at the breakfast table. It is a noble attempt, no doubt, but involves architectural modifications. It means that each bedroom should have a bathroom. This sounds simple enough, but the man who seeks to accomplish it will really find himself engaged in strange quests. It is understandable when we remember that nowadays a man's good sense, taste, and capacity are indicated not so much by what he does with his front hall as by what he has done in the bathrooms. In spite of all expense and trouble he may still find himself far away from perfection. In these matters opinions are widely varying. I have heard people remark with a shudder, after inspecting a house, 'Did you notice that towel-rail! . . .'

Electricity is another headache. It is not enough that a bulb hangs down and sheds its light. There are a dozen fine points to be observed: the wiring must not be seen, the bulb must not be seen, and the light itself must not be seen. They call everything 'concealed this' or 'concealed that' where electricity is concerned (which object, if logically followed, is best achieved by short-circuiting the entire system), and everything that is sought to be concealed costs four times the one left open. A lamp-shade has not only to obstruct the diffusing light rays but has also to proclaim the house-owner to be a man of sound taste and finances. But it can at best be only an attempt. Approbation of our fellow-men is not so easily obtained—whatever may be the expense one has put oneself to for its sake. Unless it is a saint who has been taken round to see a new house, most normal men think that many items in the new house seem unnecessary, extravagant, garish, and in bad taste, which they neither feel nor say. If a man says what he feels, he will probably be thrown out; if he doesn't it puts an undue strain on his conscience. Anyway, it doesn't appear to be a healthy state of affairs. I never fail to sigh whenever I see one of the good old houses, the type we see in what is sneeringly called 'Moffusil Places'. It is the house with a few walls and a single roof sloping down and covering the entire structure. Here is an example of a house built without undue worry or fuss, something that grew out of bricks, apparently without the aid of an engineer or architect. Traditionally speaking I don't think there has been much distinction between a builder and an architect in our country. I wonder if more than five per cent of the public are aware of the functions of an architect. Most people are likely to confuse him with the contractor or with the engineer—neither of which a true architect is likely to appreciate. It is as if you did not see the difference between the sonnet-writer and the compositor who put it into type. An architect is in the category of an artist rather than an artisan. He dreams and theorizes and calculates: this is why a house-owner feels less perturbed when dealing with the contractor who is plainly mercenary, than with the architect whose idioms are strange, complex, abstract and concrete at the same time. The architect constantly says, 'I will have this' or 'I will not have that', 'Your house must have horizontal lines', 'Your house must have vertical lines'. He may declare that the house must merge with the landscape or that it must stand out in contrast. He may love symmetry or he may adore a deliberate asymmetry; he may want all corridors to diverge or he may demand that they run parallel, he may declare the rectangular outlook a curse on buildings, he may champion all hexagons and what not. The result may terrify the prospective house-owner, especially when he finds that the architect has a clear-cut definite outlook in these matters. He may accommodate the novice's notions ultimately but only with contempt and resignation. Here again is a possibly explosive situation, where the human relationship is likely to strain and snap.

A house in construction is a meeting-point of many minds and faculties: engineer, labourer, financier, architect, etc. etc. and eventually perhaps a doctor, preferably a nerve-specialist who can put the house-owner back into shape at the end of it all. But there is this satisfaction for any man who undertakes the task: even a mighty institution like the central government fares no better when it tries to build houses. We have more than a hint of it in the news item. '"The Government of India considered that it would not be in the public interest to disclose the findings and the recommendations on the working of the 'pre-fab' housing factory in Delhi," said the Health Minister in Parliament today . . .'

CASTES: OLD AND NEW

I FEAR THAT foreign observers of Indian life would feel frustrated if the caste system should completely disappear from our country. They will have nothing left to talk about. The caste system has always offered a convenient handle for foreign observers. In my opinion, next to Russia, India is the most visited and the most commented-upon country in the world. I am afraid that the abolition of caste will affect the tourist traffic, on which so much anxious thought and discussion is being bestowed at present. If a notice should be put up at Santa Cruz aerodrome or on the Gateway of India announcing, 'There is no caste system in this country,' I believe many a tourist would turn back home with the feeling that he has been cheated of legitimate entertainment for which he has paid a heavy fee in the shape or air or steamer fare.

Once a visitor from a far-off country called on me. When I asked her what I could do for her, she replied, 'I should love to take Indian coffee in Indian style.' This was an understandable request in this part of the country. After coffee she said, 'Now I want to see the caste system. May I see it in your house?' I blinked for a while and then told her that the caste system was not a curio in a glass-case to be displayed on request. 'Then what is it?' she asked, cross-examining. I explained, throwing into my sentences a proper sprinkling of such words as *varnashrama*, *dharma*, etc. She was properly impressed. 'What caste are you?' she asked. I told her. She would not believe it. 'You can't tell me that! If you were really a

Brahmin you would not have drunk coffee with me, don't I know so much?' I felt that there was some justice in her observation, and explained to her how the caste system was disappearing in our country and how our national aim was to create a casteless society. She was aghast. 'What, no more caste system!' She looked as if I had told her that the Himalayas were soon be shifted to another location. Presently, she asked, 'What will you give us in its place, for people like us who come thousands of miles to see you country?'

'Perhaps fertilizer factories, river valley projects, hydroelectric . . .' She would not allow me to finish my sentence. 'I have seen all kinds of factories and projects in all parts of the world. I don't have to come to India to see them. I would not have taken all this trouble to come here if I had known there would be no caste system. I wish I had known it earlier.' Then, out of sheer pity, I took her to a Sanskrit college: there she saw people wearing tufts and caste-marks, wrapped in colourful shawls, sitting on the ground and reciting their lessons. She took several photographs of the classes at work, and then told me, 'Now show me where the other castes are. I want to photograph the entire caste system.' 'Why?' I asked her.

'I have signed an agreement with a lecturing organization to tour America and lecture on the caste system in India.' She went away greatly pleased, and I am sure she has gone through a heavy lecturing programme. I do not know whether she abused or complimented this country on this subject, but anyway it brought her here.

We hear that several thousand tourists are likely to visit India in the coming year. In the interests of this traffic, would it not be advisable to start a model caste-system village, kept in full swing, if need be with a subsidy from the tourist department?

The old caste system is wearing away, no doubt, but who is to check the development of new castes? Breathes there a man, except a saint, with soul so dead that he does not attempt to show off his learning, possessions, contacts, and so forth? The reason why a certain person adopts the nursery-picture-bush-coat seems to be, not that he could not secure any other cloth, but that he attempts to remove himself from a group wearing bush-coats made of non-spectacular material. I recently learnt that among bush-coat wearers there are twenty-five sub-sects. Among motor-owners there are said to be forty different sects, depending upon the length of the whip-like aerial on the mudguard, the variety of little plastic birds stuck on the glass inside, and so on. New lamps for old seems to be the law of life. Old or new, lamps serve the same purpose. It almost seems as if all change is illusory. We seem to be repeating the same set of old things. But under a new guise and a new denomination. It would be an interesting pastime for anyone to observe and classify the new castes that are springing up all around.

THE NEWSPAPER HABIT

THE MORNING PAPER in the city (and possibly the afternoon one in the mofussil) has grown on us as a habit. There are many whose vision of paradise is a high and soft cushion, long couch, and a newspaper to which one is accustomed. It is not enough that some newspaper is read but it must be *the* newspaper. Everyone has his own taste in this: some persons like to be dragooned by strong headlines, and some like their paper to leave them alone, ever suspicious of anything that is clamorous. The advertisement pages too are a source of great delight. The variety of life that is presented therein gives one the same pleasure as going through a crowded bazaar; here is one asking for a suitable person for some job, there one demanding a place under the sun, here a car for sale and there someone trying to dispose of a house or a horse; jobs to be filled up, jobs to be had, lawyer's notices to defaulting debtors or of ex-parte proceedings. It is indeed a composite reflection of the world. It gives one reclining in his couch the feeling of being in the thick of life and the same sensation as of pacing before shop windows.

The man-in-a-hurry glances at the headings and summary and puts away the paper for a thorough study later in the day; but unless he is a tyrant before whose dark moods humanity quails, he is not likely to find the paper again. The daily paper gets buffeted about in the house and rests, if at all, in bits in the various corners of a house. It is one of the causes of the numerous minor skirmishes that occur in a normal household everyday, but so far no one has been able to enforce a general code of observance in regard to the handling of a newspaper at home. The boy of the house will always detach the sports page, the young lady cannot help tearing out ruthlessly any portion of the paper that interests her: it may be anything— beauty-tips or about a pudding or the weather conditions in Simla or the birth of a baby in a royal household. It is no use the zealot crying out, 'Oh, keep the sheets neatly folded back so that others may also read.' It becomes a routine statement to which nobody pays any attention. There is a widespread belief that every copy of a newspaper belongs to all humanity irrespective of who pays the subscription. Its boundary certainly is not limited to the doorsteps of the house on which the newsboy drops it. There are people always on the alert for the arrival of the newspaper in the next house. In harmony with this condition there is the subscriber who is so tolerant that when he wishes to see the day's paper, he sends a messenger around to investigate its whereabouts in the neighbourhood, and resigns himself to it if the hardened borrower sends back word that he has still not finished reading the paper. Often this good man will have to content himself with reading day-before-yesterday's issue. For it must be said that while we cannot always get at the latest issue, the one a few days old turns up spruce and tidy a dozen times during a search. This constant turning-up of an old issue may drive some mad with rage till they snatch it up and fling it out of reach on to a loft, but the man of patience may accept it as a design of fate and take it to bed with him.

. Personally I must confess I am not thrilled by the usual news items, however important they might be. Not for me the obvious excitements. I keep an eye on the politics of the country and glance through the messages pouring forth from ministerial quarters, but the real delight for me is the news tucked away, printed in small type, without a heading. It is this type of news that stirs in me the profoundest reflection. As an instance, some days ago, I read a three-line news item at the bottom of a column, used as a space-filler, which said, 'Turbans will be one of the prizes which the government of India proposes to give to successful farmers in the crop competitions. This item is estimated to cost the government Rs 2½ lakh.' Now I gazed upon this item with the profoundest interest. It was like looking into a smooth-faced crystal with its polished surface. Now, I wondered, what made the government select the turban for a gift, and not some other item of dress? When did they learn that our farmers were fond of turbans? How many turbans could one buy for two-and-a-half lakhs of rupees? Anyway, actually, who thinks up these things at New Delhi? Are they going to give the Mysore lace-turbans or the Punjab ones or the Poona style? What will they do to secure turban-cloth in the present textile position? Is it a sign that the textile position is improving and that the black-marketeers have been successfully choked and buried? It stirred up in my mind a most pleasing picture of the Indian peasant. He wore a loin cloth, his body was bare and was baking in the sun, his feet were unshod while he patiently walked behind his plough, but his head was resplendent with a turban that was placed there by the minister with his own hands . . .

This is only an instance to show how I read a newspaper. I fear it is an extremely subjective experience. I hope everyone will perfect his own technique of drawing the subtle essence out of every item of news he reads.

THE POSTCARD

IN A FICKLE and fluctuating world, the postcard alone has retained its identity, though a victim of a sort of caste system operating in the world of letter writing. I have heard people say, 'I never write on a postcard nor accept one, but tell the postman to take it back . . .' I am sorry to say that such snobs will not hesitate to use a whole sheet of crackling note-paper for a couple of lines of acknowledgement, and ceremoniously tuck it into a parchment envelope.

I must confess that I too was guilty of ignoring the postcard for years out of a cowardly feeling that it might offend the receiver. But suddenly I had a flash of illumination the other day, of all places, at the Bangalore airport, having driven a hundred miles to catch a plane for Delhi at noon which didn't show up even at five p.m.

At the counter, the officials sounded grumpy and scowled as if the passengers had cast some sort of a spell and immobilized their Air Bus. The public address system was not of much help either—it kept up a series of throaty growls which did not add much to our information; a black board at the Enquiry evidently bore a message for us but chalky writing on rubbed-off chalky writing demanded a kind of scrutiny for which my eyesight was not equal, especially when a hundred others were also going through the same drill. And so I was forced to slip into a state of semi-coma and resignation.

Nowhere on earth could weariness overwhelm one as at an airport 'wait'. For a while you enjoy the spectacle of fellow passengers, burdened with baggage and restless children, looking for seats or in various attitudes of abandonment in the lounge. Presently one tires of looking at the same set of faces round after round, tires of the bookstall and the restaurant, gets bored with the funny comments on air travel everyone is uttering and concludes that this is perhaps a foretaste of purgatory while the gods take their time to decide whether to send one to hell or heaven.

It was in this state of mind that I peeped through the little window at the post office counter. The man on the other side asked, 'What do you want?'

On an impulse I said, 'Postcards, please.'

'How many?'

'Ten.'

And there it was. I sought a secluded corner and settled down to write, and addressed and dropped the cards into the mail-box, thus clearing arrears of correspondence weighing on my conscience for months. I bought more cards and dashed off greetings, congratulations and condolences, on a mass scale, in flight. Since that day, I have set myself up as a promoter of the postcard.

Among its advantages: You don't have to be longwinded on a card: you could write a one line note to your correspondent and be done with it. No one will mind it. On the other hand if you choose to be expansive, you can write two hundred words on the back of the postcard and one hundred on the space in front, through measured, careful calligraphy. In olden times our noble ancestors wrote only on postcards. They filled a card without wasting a hair-breadth's space. Starting from a millimetre margin on top with 'Safe' or '*Om*' etched minutely, they progressed, line by line, and then also in the half-space on the address-side right down to the bottom edge of the card—thereafter the card was held breadthwise and all second thoughts were crammed along a slender margin, as also blessings and the signature.

Marriages were no doubt made in heaven, but were translated into earthly terms only through postcards. Marriage proposals were initiated and conducted through an exchange of postcards: the 'bio-data' of the principals, their background and lineage, extending to four generations, the disposition of the stars, as well as complicated negotiations relating to dowry, silver, gold, brass, stainless steel, and silks, and specifications of the dimensions and quantity of *murukku*, and details of wedding and travel arrangements were all satisfactorily concluded on this humble stationery. Nothing ever went wrong, and thousands of couples lived happily ever after.

The chief merit of a card is that it circulates in an open society. No secrets are possible. Everyone could know everything about everyone else in a family and anyone's business became a matter of general discussion, comment and advice. Even the postman used to be aware of the contents of a card before delivering it. If some auspicious event was taking place at a particular address, such as a birthday or a betrothal, the postman would delay the delivery of any unpleasant news. In my boyhood at Puraswalkam (Madras) over half-a-century ago, we had a postman, an old man in a red turban and khaki uniform, called Thanappa. When schools closed for summer, on any day we could anticipate his announcement from the door, holding out a card, 'Periamma, your daughter in Bangalore is coming with the children on the tenth of this month, so get ready.' Or to a young student who had his lodging in our house, 'You have failed again! No wonder. I see you always at the street corner gossiping. Why don't you study properly, instead of wasting your time, with your father worrying so much about you in the village.'

Correspondence has been a matter of despair for me and equally so for my correspondents. I generally put off answering letters while I wait for the arrival of the typist and other propitious conditions. Dictation, scrutiny of the draft, and all the labour of sealing, glueing and stamping, terrifies me, and I put off answering letters as far as possible. Now it is all changed. With a postcard, all intermediary activities are abolished. You just dash off a line or two, turn it over, write the address, and drop it in any wayside postbox. It is pilfer-proof. Nobody has any use for a used postcard.

Lastly, by confining oneself to postcards and avoiding the more expensive postal stationery, one may defeat the aim of the budget-framers, who seem bent upon mopping up your cash. The 'hike' (what a popular but hybrid expression, of petro-dollar parentage) in postal rates may be nullified by writing only a postcard for every occasion. You may carry on thus safely, until the government wakes up and levies a 'surcharge' (or would it be a 'cess'?) on every word beyond a free allowance of twenty. If that happens, further action would still remain in your hands. Don't write letters. Avoid all correspondence.

As I am closing, a card arrives, on which I see a red seal indicating that this is the centenary year of the postcard (1979). It is sheer coincidence. I had no idea of it when I began this essay. May the postcard continue to serve us for centuries to come.

THE LOST UMBRELLA

I REALIZED AT about eleven in the night that I and my umbrella were parted. While returning from my evening walk I had stopped by at a little shop for buying cloves. It did not seem a particularly appropriate moment for this transaction, as the Sales Tax department had descended in strength on this particular shop, and an inspector and his minions were swarming around the counter. The shopman who was normally genial and communicative could do no more than throw a hapless simper in my direction, over the shoulders of the officials hemming him in. It was like a class in zoology practical with enquiring minds crowding over a disembowelled specimen on the table. There could be no doubt that it was an inauspicious hour for replenishing one's stock of cloves. No one in that shop was free to look at me, every hand being pressed into service for propitiating the gods with offerings of day-books, stock-registers, and ledgers. But I preferred to wait: the cloves of this shop were reputed to be genuine 'Zanzibars'—any connoisseur of spices knows what it means, cloves of ebonite shade, sheeny with oil, and each perfectly designed in miniature like a Greek column supporting a four-pointed cupola. A quarter of this pristine specimen placed on the tip of the tongue would be enough to sting and to tingle the nervous system. At other shops cloves looked anaemic, enfeebled, and tasted like matchstick. This was the shop for cloves. It is human nature to have faith in one shop rather than another; going out to buy something becomes not just a casual act but a profound undertaking. The same brand is displayed everywhere, the same labels are arrayed on the shelves; you could pick up the articles you need anywhere but still the matter is not so simple. Even if one's favourite shop fails to hold the price-line too tautly, still one prefers it, for various reasons, to an officious cooperative store. Among the multitudinous *avatars* of our government, the latest one is that of a shopkeeper. I wonder if the red-tapist at the counter is going to appreciate the psychology of an average shopper and treat him with the considerateness he is accustomed to at his favourite shop. People on their side have no reason to expect that multistoreyed, multi-purpose supermarkets and mighty 'price-line' holding establishments will ever do better than our State Banks, Telephones, Airlines, Railways, Cooperatives, Corporations, or Coffee Boards, where a customer is reduced to the rank of a supplicant or petitioner, unless he proves influential or aggressive in one way or another. The ordinary man, the unknown soldier in civic life, the meek one—blessed though in the next world—has enough trials in the present one, and whose only source of power is the single vote to be revived and cast quinquennially, would prefer his accustomed shop.

I waited hoping to catch the shopman's eye, deriving meanwhile what entertainment I could from watching the Sales Tax operations. In a state of mild beguilement I hung up my umbrella on an awning-rod projecting from the shop doorway. I have recently got into the dreadful habit of unconsciously hanging up my umbrella on any projection, leaving my spectacles and pen on any available ledge, and half my time is spent in searching for something. I waited, hoping that the Sales Tax men would leave but they seemed determined to outstay me at the shop; so I left. At eleven in the night I remembered my umbrella and immediately drove back to the shop. The shop was shut and deserted. I examined the awning-rod for any trace of my umbrella. After an uneasy night of sleep, I went to the shop again just when the shopman, who still looked battered and dazed from his Sales Tax encounters, was unlocking the door. He complained, 'There was such a big crowd to watch last evening's *tamasha,* anybody could have walked away with your umbrella. Even the Sales Tax people carry away articles from shops, rather forgetfully I think.'

I have filed a detailed complaint with the police, fully describing my lost property, in case they want to identify it in the hands of some gentlemen who unfurl a new umbrella every night and perambulate around the clock-tower at the market offering a bargain to the crowds. I myself propose to frequent the clock-tower and watch like an FBI agent. The police officer who took my complaint happened to be a reader of my books as well, and was overjoyed to see his author in the flesh. I have no doubt he will do his best for me. Meanwhile, I turn a searching look on every umbrella handle hooked on any arm in the streets, sometimes hurrying up close to the side of any that may appear suspicious but most of them on scrutiny prove un-American—that is, no push-button, automatic opening (in order to facilitate the opening of an umbrella with one hand while the other is holding the loaded grocery bag, evolved specially for a coolie-less society).

Even supposing that I noticed my umbrella in someone else's hand, how could I claim it? Invite him to the police station? Or shadow him to his address and hurry back to tell my inspector friend, or just snatch it back? What would happen if I found it in the hand of our local wrestler, who might have negotiated for it at the clock-tower or got it from an admirer happening to visit the clove shop last evening soon after I left? Fresh and unsuspected phases of the problem unfolded themselves to me every minute as I planned the strategy to retrieve my umbrella.

Finally, I think, I should fall back on philosophy. In a country where ninety-five per cent can't afford an umbrella, I have enabled some poor creature to shield himself from the sun and the belated monsoon. (I only hope he knows how to open my umbrella without dismembering it.) Our *shastras* enjoin upon every individual to perform umbrella *daan* on every possible occasion. The bridegroom's umbrella on his wedding day is just as important as the one given on less auspicious occasions to the priest as a possible insurance against inclemencies in the next world for a departed soul. An umbrella is a highly-prized possession. An umbrella devotee will not hesitate to cover the black cloth with white cloth, as a reinforcement, and carry his umbrella into the innermost sanctum of a temple, unable to leave it out of sight even for a moment, or nurse it on his lap while listening to great music. No one takes amiss the words of warning or caution uttered by one who is about to lend an umbrella. In England, the sleek silk umbrella rolled to a rapier, could almost be a part of an Englishman's limb, while he walks down Regent Street holding it a few inches away without touching the ground or his person. In America, that automobile land, they are terribly casual and indifferent; when the wind becomes sharp the man just thrusts his umbrella into a trash-can on the roadside, and hails a taxi. Unthinkable in our country, where the umbrella-repairer is regarded as a saviour and sought after. The American economy may be termed a 'throw-away' one, since mending is a millionaire's privilege costing ten dollars an hour, while ours is based on a Cherish and Mend philosophy.

On the fourth day of my loss I am feeling actually elated being filled with a sense of redemption. Forty years ago, I acquired an umbrella as someone else has done four days ago at the clove shop. My first umbrella must have belonged to one Mr Bettiah; the man coming in to deliver an invitation had left it hooked on our gate and later must have looked for it everywhere else.

LOOKING ONE'S AGE

HONESTLY SPEAKING, ONE is never satisfied with one's own photograph, the feeling always being that it could have been better. One puts the blame on the photographer, light, some unexpected distraction that brought on that stunned expression, and so forth.

Photographers advise their subjects to look pleasant, casual or unconcerned. But nothing helps. Among facial expressions a smile is the most risky one to adopt. 'I never realized how ghastly I look till I saw that snapshot of mine taken when I was supposed to be smiling,' confessed a friend to me recently. 'One feels sympathy for a world that has to go on looking on this face.' The only consolation in this is that it is mutual and universal. The feeling is one of uneasiness in any case, whether one thinks that one's photograph might have been better or worse. No photograph can be said to be perfect: it always overstates or understates one's personality. One's thoughts are either, 'I wish I deserved the compliment the photographer has paid me!' or 'What a bother! This man has caught me while I am simpering like a moron.' I have met very few persons who have the hardihood to hang portraits of themselves in their studies or at the entrances to their homes.

A photographic impression is perhaps the most fleeting of impressions. A photograph caught in a fraction of a second is valid only for that fraction of a second. Even as the spool is being wound the personality changes. In this sense a mirror can hardly confirm what a camera presents. I do not refer here to the young person who gets into the habit of deep contemplation of his or her own features with due appreciation of the reflected image, but of a normal person on whom Nature has started her operations unmistakably.

One goes on living in a fool's paradise, visualizing oneself as one used to be, never acquiring a sense of reality, always blaming the photographer or the mirror for anything that may seem uncomplimentary. If others do not give out the actual state of affairs, it might be because they are considerate or have not noticed the changes. This state continues until one day someone, whom one has not seen for a long time, turns up, and exclaims, 'I say! It took me time to recognize you. I thought it was someone else, possibly your uncle.' 'Why? Why?'

'Oh, you have . . .' he hesitates, 'you used to be so slim and your hair probably was not so grey.' However indifferent one might be, there comes a time in everyone's life when one hears it for the first time. Depending upon the type of person to whom it is addressed, it comes as a shock or a pleasant surprise. It is not everyone who is likely to feel depressed at the thought that he has lost his original youthful apprence. It is only an abnormal person who will cling to a vision of himself as he was years before. Most persons, after they get over the initial surprise, will settle down and accept the position with a good deal of cheer. That is how Nature has intended it to be taken. Within reasonable limits one ought to look one's years. There is a certain propriety about it: that girth is inevitable at that age or that degree of greyness. To be rosy-cheeked, curly-headed and slim at fifty! You have only to think of this picture to realize how incongruous it could be. It would be in the nature of an insult to the age, as unacceptable as attaining the rotundity and baldness of middle age at eighteen. Nature seems to have arranged it all with great forethought. That receding forehead, that greyness at the temple, that filled-in shape are all divinely ordained, and succeed in producing a wonderful picture of serenity and wisdom, and lend weight to the personality. I have come across persons who are bothered by their youthful appearance: that shock of youthful hair, that smooth chin, that unwanted slimness are greatly distressing, especially when the man has to keep up an appearance of authority or pugnacity in order to get some work going. He attempts to remedy the deficiency by nurturing fierce whiskers or by wearing heavy black-rimmed glasses, masks which are expected to overawe an onlooker.

It is good to acquire the appearance that one's age warrants and to know how one strikes others, without any feeling of shock or surprise. This thesis, however, is intended mainly for men and not for women, about whose psychological reaction in these matters I dare not speculate.

A PICTURE OF YEARS

HE IS PAST eighty. In his own home there are a great many corners, which he has not visited for years and years now. It is seventeen years since he climbed the staircase. He has lost all recollection of what the upstairs rooms look like. They are all being occupied by his sons, grandsons and grandnephews. They seem to be stamping their feet there all the time, the din they make all through the day! It keeps his nerves on edge, as he dwells in his corner down below. He has a long cane chair placed in a corner of the hall passage, with a window behind him through which he can see the street, but that is a minor consideration; he likes to be here because he can watch the movements of the entire household without moving himself. He watches; that is the only activity which his condition permits him now. He watches the young children going off to school early in the morning, he watches his granddaughters dressing and decorating themselves, and the other women-folk running the household. He sees his eldest son rushing up and down at office time, and the stream of visitors who pour in to consult him professionally. He finds he has a word to say to everyone that passes near him, only they do not stop to hear him out fully. Half-finished sentences throughout. He has so many unfinished sentences, trailing one into another that he feels perplexed and worried. He often wonders, 'Why can't they settle down and listen to what I have to say? Where is everybody hurrying away? In those days—' Those days! How long back? It seems like five hundred years ago. They were more restful in those days. They stopped and listened while one spoke; phrases issued from one's lips, fuller and slower; one sat down for food and went through it with a zestful calm. Not that there were no offices or law courts to attend then. He did stand before a mirror and wind a turban round his head, every day after breakfast, and then climb into his bullock-cart and was off to the court. The pace of life was more in harmony with human capacities. One went to the court rather leisurely, perhaps, but the judge would never be there earlier. But it made no difference. One returned home laden with money. If necessary, one continued one's work while eating, washing, or undressing: the clients followed about everywhere, talking and talking: the office table was not the only place where business was done; and one even slept off in the middle of a talk and it did no one any harm. With all this there was no lack of earning, no lack of health and industry. Clients held on for a lifetime, he built this huge house and a dozen others, and he reared and brought up nearly a hundred souls. Looking at him now they perhaps think that he has always been like this, not worth a moment's pause. The entire family, quite a population of all ages and both sexes, flourished under his care and guidance in those days. The education of some young men here, a suitable match for a maiden there, extricating someone from a financial or legal entanglement, and so on: every question ultimately drifted down to him for handling. His wisdom. His wisdom, instinct, and judgement, served for the entire family, and they were none the worse for it. But nowadays one notices everywhere an aggressive notion of independence. The youngest boy of the house, seven years old, to the eldermost member of the family, his own son bordering on sixty, everybody thinks he is qualified to judge and act for himself. You may tell the youngster every day not to carry his fountain pen to school, but only slate and pencil, but he persists and loses one pen every week. Why does his father indulge all his fancies! In those days, even if they studied in MA, they never possessed fountain pens. He himself would not have had one, but for the fact that his father-in-law bought him one for Deepavali. That was as it should be. Fountain pens, watches, and rings were not playthings but precious gifts given or received on rare occasions. But now, the youngest fellow has a watch on his wrist. It is all foolish luxury. They do not know how to bring up children.

He thinks that he used to be very strict in his days, but it is only a trick of memory. The person against whom he complains now, the present head of the house, used to receive ten rupees every time his father went out of station. The old gentleman does not remember now how he once prolonged his stay in another town because he heard that a pedlar would be arriving next day with a wooden horse on wheels, the sort of thing the youngster had been demanding so long. He has no recollection of it now. The only person who could bring it back to his mind is his wife, but she is not here. That good soul left the earth a dozen years ago, a piece of memory which hurts even at this distance. This is the worst of living to an advanced age. One sees the fingers of death too often, plucking up a life here and a life there. He has lost count of all the bereavements he has suffered in life: friends, nephews, children, and elders.

At this point, however, he feels less bewildered by death than by life. As years advance gradually, unnoticed, the swing of existence narrows down: the orbit of movement shrinks visibly. Till sixty he walked six miles for recreation, went round the tank, and visited the market once a week. Next the excursion was confined to a visit to the third street, and then up to the bungalow gate, and now he never steps beyond the veranda. He feels dazzled even at twilight, under an open sky. His boundary is the bench on the veranda, an ancient twelve-legged piece of furniture which he acquired in his younger days. No one goes near it, but it is his favourite piece of furniture. All through the day he is in eager expectation of moving on to it in the evening. At four he seizes his staff and moves on to the bench. He sits there watching the street. He stops almost every hawker who cries his ware in the street and calls him in; he has a feeling that he is helping the household with its supplies. Very rarely does he find himself in agreement with the price quoted; he finds the prices at least ten times over what he used to pay in his days. Or if, by rare chance, the price is acceptable, he finds it again a great source of worry; he has to undertake an excursion back to his room, get through the maze of old furniture there, and open the drawer in which he keeps his cash. This activity cuts badly into his evening.

His great joy is when a neighbour, an old friend, occasionally drops in for a chat. This man is very vivacious, and much stronger, though of the same age. He visits all parts of the town and acts as a sort of compendium of information of persons and places. The gentleman sees the world through him. On the days he arrives, the old gentleman prolongs his stay in the veranda by half an hour. Otherwise, normally before the twilight is gone, he gets up and hobbles back to his room. In a few minutes, he sits in a corner of the hall with his eyes shut in prayer, his fingers turning the rosary. He does not open his eyes for nearly half an hour, although the children return home from play, shout and create a din over their books, and their home tutor comes and drowns their voices. At his dinner time he goes in, calling everyone to join him. But no one heeds his invitation and he eats alone. He has had a lonely dinner for years now.

After he has been in bed, and slept and dreamed for hours, he opens his eyes and still hears voices in the house. He picks himself up with difficulty, goes to his threshold and cries, 'Why are the lights still burning? Such noise even at midnight!'

'It is not midnight, it is only 8.30 now, grandfather,' corrects the youngest child, and he goes back to his bed. He is up before 3.00 a.m., and wonders why everyone is still asleep. 'Something wrong with all their time,' he mutters to himself, resigning himself to staying in bed for an hour more.

Later Essays

These essays were written during the 1970s, 1980s and early 1990s, and provide rare glimpses into Narayan's private world. Also included in this section are some of the longer essays Narayan wrote on topics that were significant to him.

INDIA AND AMERICA

THE SILENT MOVIES of the Twenties were the main source of our knowledge of America when I was growing up in Madras. We had a theatre called the Roxy in our neighbourhood. For an outlay of two annas one could sit on a long teakwood bench, with a lot of others, facing the screen. When the hall darkened, there came before us our idols and heroes—hard-hitting valourous men such as Eddie Polo and Elmo Lincoln, whose arms whirled around and smashed up the evil-minded gang, no matter how many came on at a time, retrieved the treasure plan and saved the heroine who was on the verge of losing her life or chastity. The entire saga as a serial would be covered in twenty-four instalments at a rate of six a week, with new episodes presented every Saturday. When Eddie Polo went out of vogue, we were shown wild men of the Wild West, cowboys in broad-brimmed hats and cartridge-studded belts, walking arsenals who lived on horseback forever chasing, lassoing and shooting. We watched this daredevilry enthralled, but now and then questioned, when and where do Americans sit down to eat or sleep? Do they never have walls and doors and roofs under which to live? In essence the question amounted to, 'After Columbus, what?'

In the Thirties, as Hollywood progressed, we were presented with more plausible types on the screen. Greta Garbo and Bette Davis and who else? Ramon Novarro, John Gilbert and other pensive, poignant or turbulent romantics acting against the more versatile backdrops of Arabian deserts, European mansions and glamorous drawing rooms.

Our knowledge of America was still undergoing an evolutionary process. It took time, but ultimately one was bound to hear of Lincoln, Emerson, Mark Twain and Thoreau. The British connection had been firmly established. The British way of life and culture were the only other ones we Indians knew. All books, periodicals and educational material were British. These said very little about America, except for Dickens or Chesterton, who had travelled and lectured in America and had written humorously of American scenes and characters—after accepting a great deal of hospitality, and dollars of course. This seemed to us a peculiar trait of Americans—why should they invest so heavily in foreign authors only to be presented as oddities at the end?

After World War II, the Indian media focused attention on American affairs and personalities and we became familiar with such esoteric terms as the Point-Four Plan, Public Law 480, and grants and fellowships, which in practical terms meant technical training and cultural exchanges. In the post-War period, more and more Americans were to be seen in India while more and more Indians went to America. Americans came to India as consultants, technicians and engineers and to participate in the vast projects of our Five Year Plan. We noticed that Coca-Cola and Virginia tobacco and chewing gum were soon making their appearance in shop windows, and American bestsellers in the bookstores. For their part, Americans displayed on their mantelpieces Indian bric-a-brac of ivory, sandalwood and bronze. Academicians from America came to India to study its culture and social organizations, as did political scientists (unsuspected of having CIA connections), and returned home to establish departments of South Asian Studies in such universities as Chicago, Pennsylvania, Columbia and the University of California at Berkeley. Some American scholars of Sanskrit, Hindi or Tamil are unquestioned authorities, and a match for the orthodox *pundits* in India.

Americans working in India adapted themselves to India style with ease—visited Indian homes, sat down to eat with their fingers, savoured Indian curry, wore *kurta* and *pajamas,* enjoyed Indian music. Some even mastered Indian music well enough to be able to give public concerts at a professional level before Indian audiences. Such colleges as Wesleyan and Colgate started regular departments of Indian music. Young Indians began applying for admission to American institutions for higher studies or training.

My first chance to visit America came when I was offered a Rockefeller grant, which enabled me to see a great deal of the country—perhaps more than any American could. By train from New York to the Midwest and the West Coast, down south to Santa Fe, then through Texas to Nashville and Washington and back to New York, where I spent a couple of months. The more cities I saw, the more I was convinced that all America was contained in New York. For more than two decades I have been visiting New York off and on and never tire of it. I could not send down roots anywhere in America outside of New York. An exception was Berkeley, where I stayed, in a hotel room, long enough to write a novel. From my window I could watch young men and women hurrying along to their classes or hanging around the cafe or bookstore across the street. I divided my time between writing and window-shopping along Telegraph Avenue or strolling along the mountain paths.

When the time came for me to leave Berkeley, I felt depressed. I could not imagine how I was to survive without all those enchantments I had got used to. The day's routine in my hotel on the fringe of the campus, the familiar shops, the Campanile, which I could see from my hotel window if the Bay smog was not too dense and by whose chime I regulated my daily activities (I had sworn to live through the American trip without a watch), and the walk along picturesque highways and byways with such sonorous names as Sonoma, Pomona and Venice. Even the voice of the ice cream vendor who parked his cart at Sather Gate and sounded a bell crying, 'Crunchymunchies, them's good for you,' was part of the charm.

On the whole my memories of America are happy ones. I enjoy them in retrospect. If I were to maintain a single outstanding experience, it would be my visit to the Grand Canyon. To call it a visit is not right; a better word is 'pilgrimage'—I understood why certain areas of the Canyon's outcrops have been named after the temples of Brahma, Shiva and Zoroaster. I spent a day at the

Canyon. At dawn or a little before, I left my room at El Tovaro before other guests woke up, then took myself to a seat on the brink of the Canyon. It was still dark under a starry sky. At that hour the whole scene acquired a different dimension and a strange, indescribable quality. Far down below, the Colorado River wound its course, muffled and softened. The wind roared in the valley; as the stars gradually vanished, a faint light appeared on the horizon. At first there was absolute, enveloping darkness. But if you kept looking on, contours gently emerged, little by little, as if at the beginning of creation itself. The Grand Canyon seemed to me not a geological object, but some cosmic creature spanning the horizons. I felt a thrill more mystic than physical, and that sensation has unfadingly remained with me all through the years. At any moment I can relive that ecstasy. For me the word 'immortal' has a meaning now.

The variety of college campuses is an impressive feature of American life. One can lead a life of complete satisfaction at any campus, whether Berkeley or Michigan State or tiny Sewanee in Nashville. Any university campus is a self-contained world, with its avenues and lawns, libraries, student union, tuck-shops, campus stores and restaurants. I spent a term or two as lecturer or Distinguished Visiting Professor or Very Distinguished Visiting Professor in various universities. Whatever my designation, it seemed more an opportunity to enjoy the facilities of a campus in comfortable surroundings, among agreeable and intelligent people. The duties I was expected to perform were light—give a couple of lectures and be accessible to students or faculty members when they desired to meet me. I have found campus life enjoyable in all seasons—when the lakes froze in Wisconsin or the snows piled up ten feet high in Michigan, during the ever-moderate climate of Berkeley or springtime at Columbia.

If I were asked where I would rather not live, I would say, 'No American suburban life for me, please.' It is boring. The sameness of houses, gardens, lawns and dogs and two automobiles parked at every door, with not a soul in sight nor a shop except in a nine-block stretch containing a post office, firehouse and bank, similar to a hundred other places in the country. Interesting at first, but monotonous in the long run. I have lived for weeks at a stretch in Briarcliff Manor, an hour's run from Grand Central Station. I could survive it because of the lovely home of my hosts and their family, but outside their home the only relief was when I could escape to Manhattan. The surroundings of Briarcliff were perfect and charming, but life there was like existing amidst painted cardboard scenes. I never felt this kind of desolation in New York at any time, although I have stayed there for months at a time, usually at the Hotel Chelsea.

New York takes you out of yourself. A walk along Fifth Avenue or Madison or even 14th Street, with its dazzling variety of merchandise displayed on the pavement, can be a completely satisfying experience. You can visit a new ethnic quarter every day—German, Italian, Spanish, even Arab and Chinese; or choose an entertainment or concert or show from the newspaper, from page after page of listings. If you prefer to stay awake all night and jostle with a crowd, you can always go to Washington Square or Times Square, especially on a weekend.

At the American consulate the visa section is kept busy nowadays as more and more young men from India seek the green card or profess to enter on a limited visa, then try to extend their stay once they get in. The official has a difficult task filtering out the 'permanent', letting in only the 'transients'. The average American is liberal-minded and isn't bothered that more and more Indian engineers and doctors are snapping up the opportunities available in the US, possibly to the disadvantage of an American. I discussed the subject with Professor Ainslie T. Embree, chairman of Columbia University's history department, who has had a long association with Indian affairs and culture. His reply was noteworthy. 'Why not Indians as well? In the course of time they will be Americans. The American citizen of today was once an expatriate, a foreigner who had come out of a European or African country. Why not Indians too? We certainly love to have Indians in the country.'

The young man who goes to the States for higher training or studies declares when leaving home, 'I will come back as soon as I complete my course, maybe two years or more, but I'll surely come and work for our country—of course, also to help the family.' Excellent intentions, but it will not work out that way. Later, when he returns home full of dreams, plans and projects, he finds only hurdles wherever he tries to get a job or to start an enterprise of his own. Form-filling, bureaucracy, caste and other restrictions, and a generally feudal style of functioning waste a lot of time for the young aspirant. He frets and fumes as he spends his days running about presenting or collecting papers at various places, achieving nothing. He is not used to this sort of treatment in America, where, he claims, he can walk into the office of the top man anywhere, address him by his first name and explain his purpose. When he attempts to visit a man of similar rank in India to discuss his plans, he finds he has no access to him, but is forced to meet only subordinates in a hierarchical system. Some years ago a biochemist returning from America with a lot of experience and bursting with proposals was curtly told off when he pushed open the door of a big executive, and stepped in innocently. 'You should not come to me directly. Send your papers through proper channels.' Thereafter the young Indian biochemist left India once and for all, having kept his retreat open with the help of a sympathetic professor at the American end.

In this respect American democratic habits have rather spoiled our young men. They have no patience with our Indian tempo, whereas the non-Americanized Indian accepts the hurdles as inevitable *karma*. An Indian who returns from America expects special treatment, forgetting the fact that the chancellors of Indian universities will see only other chancellors, and top executives will see only other top executives, and no one of lesser position under any circumstances. Our administrative machinery is slow, tedious and feudal in its operation.

Another reason for a young man's final retreat from India could be a lack of jobs for one with his particular training and qualifications. A young engineer qualified in robotics spent hours explaining the value of his speciality to prospective sponsors, until eventually he realized that there could be no place for robots in an overcrowded country.

The Indian in America is a rather lonely being, having lost his roots in one place and not grown them in the other. Few Indians in America make any attempt to integrate into American culture or social life. Few visit an American home or a theatre or an opera, or try to understand the American psyche. An Indian's contact with Americans is confined to working with his colleagues and to official luncheons. He may mutter a 'Hi' across the hedge to an American neighbour while mowing the lawn.

After he has equipped his new home with the latest dishwasher and video and his garage with two cars, once he has acquired all that the others have, he sits back with his family and counts his blessings. Outwardly happy, he is secretly gnawed at by some vague discontent and aware of some inner turbulence or vacuum he cannot define. All the comfort is physically satisfying, he has immense 'job satisfaction', and that is about all. On weekends he drives his family fifty miles or more to visit another Indian family to eat an Indian dinner, discuss Indian politics or tax problems (for doctors, who are in the highest income bracket, this is a constant topic of conversation).

There is monotony in this pattern of life, so mechanical and standardized. India may have lost an intellectual or an expert, but it must not be forgotton that he has lost India too—and that is a more serious loss in the final reckoning. The quality of life in India is different. Despite all the deficiencies, irritations, lack of material comforts and amenities, and general confusions, Indian life builds inner strength. It is through subtle, inexplicable influences, through religion, family ties and human relationships in general—let us call them psychological 'inputs', to use a modern term—which cumulatively sustain and lend variety and richness to existence. Building imposing Indian temples in America, installing our gods therein and importing Indian priests to perform the *puja* ritual and preside at festivals are only imitating Indian existence and could have only a limited value. Social and religious assemblies at the temples in America might mitigate boredom, but only temporarily. I have lived as a guest in many Indian homes in America for extended periods, and have noticed the ennui that descends on a family when they are stuck at home.

Indian children growing up in America present a special problem. Without the gentleness and courtesy and respect for parents that—unlike the American upbringing, whereby a child is left alone to discover for himself the right code of conduct—is the basic training for a child in India, Indian children have to develop themselves on a shallow foundation without a cultural basis, either Indian or American. They are ignorant of Indian life; aware of this, the Indian parent tries to cram into his children's little heads every possible bit of cultural information during a rushed trip to the mother country.

Ultimately, America and India are profoundly different in attitude and philosophy, though it would be wonderful if they could complement each other's values. Indian philosophy stresses austerity and unencumbered, uncomplicated day-to-day living. America's emphasis, on the other hand, is on material acquisition and the limitless pursuit of prosperity. From childhood an Indian is brought up on the notion that austerity and a contented life are good; a certain otherworldliness is inculcated through a grandmother's tales, the discourses at the temple hall, and moral books. The American temperament, on the contrary, is pragmatic. The American has a robust indifference to eternity. 'Attend church on Sunday and listen to the sermon, but don't bother about the future,' he seems to say. Also, he seems to echo Omar Khayyam's philosophy: 'Dead yesterday and unborn tomorrow, why fret about them if today be sweet?' He works hard and earnestly, acquires wealth and enjoys life. He has no time to worry about the afterlife, only taking care to draw up a proper will and trusting the funeral home to take care of the rest. The Indian in America who is not able to live wholeheartedly on this basis finds himself in a halfway house; he is unable to overcome his conflicts while physically flourishing on American soil. One may hope that the next generation of Indians (American-grown) will do better by accepting the American climate spontaneously; or, alternatively, return to India to live a different life.

MY EDUCATIONAL OUTLOOK

MY EDUCATIONAL OUTLOOK had always differed from those of my elders and well-wishers. And after five or more decades, my views on education remain unchanged, although in several other matters my philosophy of life has undergone modification. If a classification is called for I may be labelled 'anti-educational'. I am not averse to enlightenment, but I feel convinced that the entire organization, system, outlook and aims of education are hopelessly wrong from beginning to end; from primary first year to PhD, it is just a continuation of an original mistake. Educational theories have become progressively high-sounding, sophisticated and jargon-ridden (like many other subjects aspiring to the status of a science), but in practice the process of learning remains primitive. In the field of education, the educator and the educatee seem to be arrayed in opposite camps, each planning how best to overwhelm the other.

In my boyhood, the teacher never appeared in public without the cane in hand. I used to think that one's *guru* was born clutching a cane in his right hand while the left held a pinch of snuff between the thumb and forefinger. He took a deep inhalation before proceeding to flick the cane on whatever portion of myself was available for the purpose. I really had no idea what I was expected to do or not do to avoid it. I could never imagine that a simple error of calculation in addition, subtraction or multiplication (I never knew which) would drive anyone hysterical.

I notice nowadays a little girl at home always playing the

school-game in a corner of the veranda, but never without a flat, wooden foot-rule in hand, which she flourishes menacingly at the pupils assembled in her phantasmagoric class-room. On investigation, I found that the cane, being discredited, has yielded place to the foot-rule, especially in 'convent' schools. The foot-rule has the advantage over the primitive birch of mauling without marking (which could count as an achievement in torturing technique) and it also possesses the innocent appearance of a non-violent, pedagogic equipment. A modern educator, naturally, has to adapt his ways to modern circumstances, and put away obsolete weapons. The flat-scale is employed only at the primary stage: at higher levels of education, torments to a young soul are devised in subtler forms progressively: admissions, textbooks, and examinations are the triple weapons in the hands of an educator today. In June every father and son go through a purgatory of waiting at the doors of every college. Provision of seats planned in a grand musical-chair manner keeps every applicant running frantically about, unless, as in certain well-geared technical colleges, the parent could make a bid in the style of a competitor at a toddy auction of old times. Five thousand rupees for an engineering seat is considered quite reasonable nowadays. I recently met a hopeful father who had just written a cheque for ten thousand rupees for two sons in the first year BE in a certain college. He is a businessman fully aware of the debit and credit value of his action, and must have undertaken the financial sacrifice after due consideration. Those that cannot afford it have to queue up in the corridors of colleges, hunt and gather recommendations, plead, appeal, canvas, and lose weight until they find (or do not find) their names in the list of admissions. At the next stage the student will once again queue up, beg, beat about, and appeal—for textbooks this time (especially if it happens to be a 'Nationalized Textbook', which may not be available until the young man is ready to leave the college). Finally the examination. In a civilized world the examination system should have no place. It is a culmination of all sadistic impulses. Learned commissions and conferences meet and speculate why young men are always on the verge of blasting street lamps and smashing furniture. In technical language it is known as 'student indiscipline'. It has always amused one to note the concern the problem causes and how it always ends in woolly, banal resolutions such as: students should be given compulsory military training, asked to perform compulsory rural service, and compulsory what not. Students should keep out of politics (a great many others ought to keep out of politics too; in any case, it's too late to suggest this as students were inveigled into politics not so long ago in our history). The real wrecker of young nerves, however, is the examination system. It builds up a tension and an anxiety neurosis day by day all the year round, all through one's youth, right into middle age (for some). I remember the desperate nervousness that debilitated me from January to April every year. After four decades, I still jump off my bed from nightmares of examination. I feel convinced that the examination system was devised by a satanic mind. The anxiety and sleeplessness, the gamble over possible questions, the hush-hush and grimness of the examination hall, the invigilators (the very word has a Grand Inquisitorial sound) watching like wardens at the gallows, the awful ritual of breaking open the seal of the examination papers, the whole thing now appears ridiculously ritualistic and out of tune with a civilization in which man is capable of taking a stroll thousands of miles above the earth towards the moon.

If I became a Vice-Chancellor, my first act would be to abolish all secrecy that surrounds question papers. Instead of permitting wild speculations or, as it happens nowadays, advance sale of questions in the black market, I would take advertisement space in newspapers and publish the questions in every subject, adding under each a credit line: 'Set by Professor So-and-so'. I would not hesitate to announce with courage the names of those who are going to evaluate the answers and decree failures and successes. I would add a postscript to every question paper: 'If you cannot answer any of the above questions, don't despair. Remember your examiners are not infallible and may not do better if placed in your predicament. Your inability to answer will in no way be a reflection on your intelligence. We apologize for the embarrassment. Also remember, if you expect a first class and do not secure even passing marks, don't rave against your examiner, he is also a human being subject to fluctuating moods caused by unexpected domestic quarrels or a bad digestion just when he is sitting down to correct your papers; also, not being an adding machine, occasionally he may slip and arrive at 7 while totalling 8 and 3. Please forgive him.'

At a certain university in America I met an advanced soul. He taught Political Science. One month before the annual examination, he cyclostyled (or 'xeroxed') the questions and distributed them among his students, who thereafter spent nearly twelve hours a day in the library in the 'assigned reading room'. I described to him our habits of hiding the questions till the last moment. He remarked, 'Why on earth keep the boys in the dark over questions that after all concern them?' I explained, 'We believe in mugging up; on an average 200 pages per subject, and fifteen subjects in a year. One who can demonstrate that he can recollect three thousand pages in the examination hall will be considered a first-class student in our country, although he need not understand a word of what he reads, or remember a syllable of what he has read after the examination. The whole aim of our education is to strain the faculty of memory . . .'

'Your system must have been devised before Caxton, when there was no printed book, and handwritten books were chained and guarded. Memory is not so important today. Our need is for more libraries and multiple copies. The only condition I make for my boys is that they spend at least six hours a day in the library a month before the examinations, and while writing their answers I permit them to refer to the books. My only condition is that they should write their answers within the given time.'

In my college days, I had a professor of history, who said, 'It's a pity you have failed. If you didn't know the answer, you could have written any answer you knew; if you didn't know anything of the subject, you could just have copied the question paper. If you couldn't do even that, you could have told me and I would have given you marks.'

'I didn't know you were an examiner, sir.'

'What a pity, they ought not to keep it a secret. All our troubles are due to it. After all, you have listened to my lectures for a year and that's enough.'

I had another professor from Scotland who taught us English; an enlightened soul, who marked a minimum of 35 per cent on all papers, and raised it on request. He was accessible, and amenable to reason and even to bargaining. He would ask, 'What marks do you expect to get?'

'Sixty, sir.' He would pick up the answer paper, glance through it, shake his head ruefully. 'I have given you the minimum, of course, but I'll raise it to 40.'

'Sir, please make it 52, I want at least a second class.'

'All right. I hope your interest in literature is genuine.'

'Undoubtedly.'

Oh, but for this noble soul, I'd never have passed in English.

Here is an instance of memory without intelligence. A story of mine called 'Attila' has found its way into Pre-University prose in a certain university. I had a chance of learning how questions on the story were answered. A few answers were just line-by-line reproductions of the original, but nowhere could I see that they had realized that the story was about a dog. I was even asked once, 'When did Attila do all that you describe? I searched European history and the encyclopedia, but nowhere do I find this episode mentioned. What is the source of your information, sir?'

Two more gems to conclude this piece:

'R.K. Narayan was a romantic poetess who died in 1749.'

Long after getting his BA Degree, a person met his old teacher and confessed, 'I am sorry, sir, I never knew till today that Lady Macbeth was a woman.' Another teacher was asked, an hour before the literature paper, 'Is *King Lear* a tragedy or comedy, sir?'

I mention these without comment. If our educational system is not to continue as a well-endowed, elaborately organized, deep-rooted farce, a remedy must be found immediately. I dare not end this on a note suggesting crisis, as before the ink on this sentence dries, academic experts and ministers of education are likely to pack up and leave for New York, Rio de Janiero or Toronto, in accordance with an almost superstitious belief among our leaders (in all fields) that when there is a crisis at home the thing to do is to buy a round-the-world air ticket and leave.

CROWDED DAY

SOME YEARS AGO I attended the opening ceremony of the Air-India terminal at the Kennedy airport in New York. The Air-India PRO was keen that I should attend it. Thirty limousines were engaged to transport the guests to the terminal from the Air-India office on Park Avenue. We would take off at ten and return to the starting point after lunch. I pleaded, 'But I'm a vegetarian.' 'Don't worry, many of our guests are also vegetarians. But if you were not strict, you could enjoy it. J.R.D. is bringing special items—tandoori chicken, etc. Most of our guests are looking forward to the special luncheon. You don't have to worry, we'll take care of you.'

J.R.D. Tata was there, and after his speech proceeded to cut the ribbon—when a terrific squeal startled the distinguished assembly, for the scissors he held had slightly nicked the finger of a charming airhostess who held the ribbon. J.R.D. said, 'Terribly sorry. With a pretty face before me I could not help it.'

After this unusual inauguration we trooped upstairs to the assembly hall. Waiters bearing trays of titbits and drinks were going round. Not knowing what was what, I let the trays pass, and stood aside with folded arms. My PRO friend sidled up to whisper: 'We are proposing a toast . . . Take a glass and raise it with others . . .' I picked up a bowl with 'beaded bubbles winking at the brim', resembling Spencer's soda water of other days. The PRO whispered: 'It's only champagne, absolutely safe.' I sipped when others sipped. It tasted slightly sour. I circulated around with the glass in hand, touching its rim with my lips now and then. Whenever its level went down, the eagle-eyed waiters refilled it. I didn't keep count, but spent over an hour chit-chatting, nodding and smiling at all and sundry.

Buffet lunch was ready at another section of the hall. I saw nothing I could accept among the delicacies spread out. J.R.D. Tata had not brought anything for me. It was two o'clock when I realized that there was going to be no lunch for me. I spotted the PRO far off in a group, busy helping some guests. I went up and asked, 'Where do I find the vegetarian stuff?'

'Oh yes, let me find out . . .' He returned after investigation, 'Some sandwiches, over there—I'll get you some.' When he brought me a plate of sandwiches, I took a bite and realized that it was something soft and rubbery and mustard-tasting. I asked a waiter, 'What sandwich is this?' 'Maybe ox-tongue, sir . . .'

I hurried down and out to find a spot to spit it out, and then saw no reason to stay on; but found transport to take me back to Manhattan. It was nearing three. I realized that it was time for my next appointment, at the United Nations. A friend had secured me a pass to watch a debate on Kashmir between M.C. Chagla and Zulfikar Ali Bhutto. The hall was packed but I found a comfortable seat and felt drowsy; rousing myself with an effort I wanted to get up and shout, 'Less noise please, you bore me.'

Bhutto's retinue was large and I wanted to ask, 'Mr Bhutto, is it necessary to have an army of file bearers? Chagla is managing with less.' I found it difficult to follow the proceedings. With the earphone on and fiddling with different buttons at my elbow, I amused myself for a while listening to the simultaneous translations of the speeches in French, German, Spanish and so on. In no language did it make sense. Officious men were hurrying up and down carrying papers to their bosses seated in the front row. I was not impressed, 'This is all a show. All actors, 'comedians' as Graham Greene called them. No more of this.' I got up abruptly and made my exit. I was hungry. I went in search of T.J. Natarajan, who was my friend, philosopher and guide in New York. He was in his office. He suggested, 'Why don't you go to the Meditation Room while I finish some work?' The Meditation Room, a little soundproof chamber with a few chairs placed facing an abstract granite sculpture under a ray of light, used to be my retreat whenever I happened to visit the UN building, but now I was in no mood to meditate. I explained my predicament to my friend. 'Let us go home,' he said at once.

We took the train for Roosevelt Avenue and reached his home. I managed somehow to travel all that distance and then walk from the station to his house. He understood what was wrong with me and said, 'These parties are not for people like us.'

After dinner I felt normal, well enough go back to Hotel Chelsea on West 23rd Street. I woke up at ten next morning and realized that I had slept with my shoes on. The day ahead was crowded with engagements. I took off the shoes and moved towards the kitchen to make coffee. When I walked, I realized that my legs did not belong to me and the directions were slightly confusing. Still I resolved to go through the day's schedule.

My first engagement was at the Time-Life office, for a conference with the *Life International* editor, Cal Whipple, who had commissioned me to write a piece on Mahatma Gandhi. We were meeting in order to discuss and settle its final shape. Four more editors arrived and sat around. The discussion started. 'What we are proposing is a comparison with Nehru, whose social philosophy is so different from Gandhi's. Do you think it's possible? You will have to rewrite the Gandhi piece which we have in hand . . . Gandhi believed in the spinning wheel, while Nehru said factory chimneys were his temples . . .'

'Yes, yes, of course,' I said mechanically. I found it irksome to be sitting up and talking. Suddenly I asked, 'Cal, would you mind if I lie down on the couch over there, while you gentlemen discuss the details?' They were taken aback, but Cal said, 'Certainly . . .' I moved over to a couch and stretched myself comfortably, and listened to their talk, pretending to participate in the discussion from my recumbent position. The discussion, however, fizzled out. The others left. Cal alone remained in his chair and asked, 'R.K., what's the matter? Are you not feeling well?'

'My head is OK, but since this morning, I find my legs acting in a funny manner.'

'What have you been up to?'

I explained, and added, 'I took just a little champagne.'

'How little?'

'I can't say, they kept refilling the glass.'

'Oh, I understand now, it is a hangover in simple language. Go back to your room and sleep it off. We will meet again.'

I went down and sat on the bench in the Plaza where a fountain was playing. I took stock of myself. That day was important. I had a series of engagements. My first task would be to reach the Pathe Theatre for a preview of *The Guide* in English. Pearl Buck was coming all the way from Connecticut, Tad Danielweki who directed the film would be there, and also some film critics. The preview was in order to trim up the film before showing it to the exhibitors.

I sat there on the bench wondering how to reach the theatre. My great inclination was to flop down anywhere and sleep it off as Cal Whipple had suggested. My legs seemed to function now but were not very steady yet. Foolish of me to have yielded to that invitation. My immediate resolve was never to accept any invitation for any opening ceremony or closing ceremony anywhere on earth, and never to accept even a glass of water from anyone. People were likely to drug me.

Champagne which appeared innocent like distilled water was but a time-bomb. One would be safer probably with known plebian drinks, which made one tipsy right at the start, but this was a dangerous drink with its delayed action. I was reduced to this foolish state and wasted everyone's time, neutralizing a conference on Gandhi and Nehru while lying inanely on a couch.

I asked myself, 'Am I a Man or Mouse? If I am the former I must possess a mind which should take control immediately. I need only the will-power to get up and walk.' I got up, determined to remain firm on foot. Should I move to my right or left? If I turned right I could reach my hotel, go up the elevator and seek comforting oblivion in bed. If I turned left I could reach Pathe Theatre.

I took out of my pocket Tad's letter and checked the address. 'Walk down the avenue and turn right and left again, and go on and on till you see the "Pathe" signboard.' I had no idea how far to go, but I started out determinedly, Robert Frost's lines echoing in my head, 'Miles to go . . .' I was determined not to give in to negative thoughts, and tried to erase from memory yesterday's lapses. I walked past several 'Walk' and 'Don't Walk' signs. Now I felt eighty per cent normal and presently a hundred per cent when a sudden cloud-burst drenched me to the skin.

When I entered the preview theatre I was feeling fresh and buoyant. Pearl Buck and the rest were astonished to see me enter like the Rain God. The screening started immediately. Dev Anand and Waheeda Rehman were uttering sentiments and sentences for which I was not responsible. I accepted this *Guide* as a bastard offspring of my novel. Being in a forgiving mood and cool-headed, I let it pass without a fight. I knew that the picture was just glossy nonsense. What if? Without argument or controversy, I quietly slipped away, while Pearl Buck and others were discussing strategies for winning the Oscar or Grand Prix at some film festival with their version of *The Guide*.

My next halt was at the Indian consulate where M.F. Husain was exhibiting his latest paintings among which a portrait of myself was included. I had given him a sitting the previous week, but when I saw the portrait, I had remarked that I didn't look like myself. He had smiled at my lack of taste and replied that I wouldn't know my real self. I left it at that and adjourned to a room for recording an interview for a radio broadcast.

After the usual questions, which I could answer while asleep, the interviewer asked, 'Are you pleased with the film version of your *Guide*?'

'No,' I answered clearly, 'but anyhow they were good enough to retain the title of my story, the rest is their very own . . .'

TEACHING IN TEXAS

A TEACHER FEELS proud when he finds an occasion to say, 'So and so is (or was) my student.' It is not important what sort of a teacher he might have been—whether a sadist or an inoffensive kind. Whatever the type, he feels an inner glow when uttering the magic phrase '*My* student'.

I enjoyed the luxury of this sentiment for four months when I spent a semester as a visiting professor at Austin, University of Texas. When I received the proposal first it seemed impossible since I do not have the scholarship or the discipline required for the task. But the offer was attractive and I love to visit America on any excuse. Formerly, at different times, I had visited four universities as a Distinguished Visiting Professor, but that was different. On those occasions only my 'distinguished' presence was required, one lecture and a couple of informal sessions with students now and then, but no routine task.

But now at Austin I was being employed as a member of the faculty with specific duties. I felt rather frightened. I had to talk on subjects such as 'Religion and Caste in the Indian Novel' to the undergraduates and 'Indian Writing in English' to graduates. It took me time to understand that 'graduate' meant our 'post-graduate' and 'undergraduate' meant our 'graduate' or BA level. Following my acceptance I was asked to formulate courses of study for both the classes. Also I was asked to produce a special list of 'recommended reading' and 'required reading' for the students. I was again puzzled.

I had never been too methodical in my reading, though at one time I pored over a simple 'Outline of English Literature' and attempted to read a couple of books from each literary period—plays, poems and essays—starting with Chaucer. After that I read whatever came my way including literary periodicals such as the *Times Literary Supplement, John O'London's Weekly* and *T.P.'s Weekly, Bookman, Encounter, London Mercury,* purely for pleasure without any aim or purpose. Now to prescribe material for academic purposes seemed a terrific responsibility. Also they wanted the lists immediately to enable them to order books well in advance of my arrival.

With the help of a friend, I managed to send off through fax an imposing list of books, which included some of my own. I had had a brainwave at the last minute to suggest in one of my letters:

> I wonder if I may teach my own novels and short stories, explaining their genesis and my technique of utilizing the material I gather from my own surroundings, as the main course.

It seemed to me more practical than plodding through other writers and interpreting them. Dr Lariviere, Director of the Asia Center, welcomed my idea with the rider that I should include one or two other Indian writers for comparative study as required by the university regulations. So I added to my list Mulk Raj Anand's *Coolie* and *Untouchable,* Raja Rao's *Kanthapura,* U.R. Ananthamurthy's *Samskara,* and Anita Desai, and managed to draft courses of study for both the classes.

Although I had never read any book with the purpose of extracting any philosophical or social meaning, now in a classroom, when I started talking about a novel or a story, I discovered new dimensions in it, apart from character, incidents and construction. I elaborated the theory that there could be no such thing as *absolute* fiction; any fiction must have its source (even if it is not visible at first sight to the naked eye), in some pattern of life, whether you call it fable, allegory, ballad, or cock-and-bull story. I developed this theory in the classroom day after day, the inspiration being the young eager listeners looking up to me for knowledge and noting every word down faithfully.

The teacher's chair exercised its own magic—like the throne of Vikramaditya of our legends. Even an idiot spoke inspiredly when he ascended its thirty-two steps and occupied the seat, although when he came down, he was again dumb and dull. So from my seat I explained the evolution of 'The Caste System in India' and spoke of 'untouchability' although the phrase sounded, as I explained, absurd (there being no such word as 'touchability'). But the term somehow came into existence in Indian society, till Mahatma Gandhi made it his mission in life to fight it and banned the term 'untouchables', whom he called instead 'Harijans', meaning 'God's children'.

After this preamble lasting a couple of days, the story of *Untouchable* by Mulk Raj Anand made sense to the student who read the novel and came back the following week well prepared, asked questions, and wrote papers on the theme in its various aspects, based on the novel.

To complete the picture of the caste system at the other extreme I took up Ananthamurthy's *Samskara*, which describes high-caste orthodox Brahmin society, with its rigours and taboos, in a plague-ridden mountain village in a Karnataka province. In between, I explained, there lay whole gradations of social order, which formed the framework of the caste system. (Naranappa, a Brahmin cast out of society for his apostatic ways—drinking, meat-eating, and associating with low-class women—dies suddenly, and his body lies in an untouchable colony. The whole village is exercised over the question as to who should dispose of the body and how. Many *Shastras* are scrutinized by the leader of the community, and orthodox committee meetings are held, while the body is rotting. Finally, an untouchable woman who loved him takes charge of the body and arranges for its cremation.)

There are many subtle points of sociological interest in the story, which gave much scope for discussion in the class. Out of it came a number of papers the students wrote on the theme. This was again followed by questions, and then discussion among the students themselves. I could judge the result of my method from the papers they submitted from time to time, choosing the themes themselves from the text. I found the papers edifying and could gauge the kind of impact a serious novel could have on a reader with an enquiring mind.

I recommended also three of my own novels and several short stories. I had never imagined the existence of any social, ethical and philosophical implications in my stories till the students called them out and debated among themselves, and then chose the themes for their papers. I had warned them from time to time, 'Because I am the author sitting here, explaining my own work, a rather unusual situation, please don't hesitate to attack the book and the author as frankly as you please.' Thus I had to face and parry remarks such as, 'You have made Rosie in *The Guide* guilty of adultery. Couldn't she have remained chaste and faithful to her husband and still pursue her art? Do you approve of adultery?' 'Why are the women characters in your stories so spineless?' 'Is the wife in *The Dark Room* a typical Indian wife? She seems to be only a slave of Ramani, not his wife.' 'In *Malgudi Days,* your stories are all about down-and-out persons. Why didn't you choose to write about better lives?'

I would give some reply which came to my mind on the spot, and which might be rejected by one and accepted by another and result in a seminar with several points of view emerging. This would go on for three hours, as on Mondays I had to steer the graduates through a three-hour period. When it was proposed, I resisted the idea. 'How can I lecture for three hours? It will exhaust me. I can't speak for three long hours. I am used to radio broadcasting and such, which take up less than twenty minutes—less than 2,000 words if I wrote them beforehand.' Lariviere was very tolerant. He said, 'For this particular hour on Monday you may have to speak for fifteen minutes just to initiate a subject and then you will find that it develops into a seminar with the whole class participating and managing it. You will find three hours gone without your noticing it.' He was right.

I found this particular Monday session engrossing and rewarding while I just watched and listened between three and six in the afternoon. Lariviere had said to me earlier in his letters, 'Ours is only a suggestion. Nothing is rigid, remember. You may develop the courses and your teaching method as you think fit.' It was this kind of elasticity and absence of bureaucratic rule that charmed me most. I was also given the choice of either holding a final examination or not for the graduates. I had graded their papers from time to time and saw no reason to hold a final examination. In the last week when I announced, 'No examinations,' I received thundering cheers from the whole class, while realizing thereby my lifelong ambition to abolish the examination system, and all the unnecessary tension that kills the joy of living in young people.

ON FUNNY ENCOUNTERS

LITERALLY A NODDING acquaintance I come across on his motorcycle when I go out for a walk. I do not know his full name, nor have any idea of his features since his helmet covers his brow, but we never fail to greet each other, although he generally flashes past at thirty kilometres.

Today, he suddenly applied the brake, pushed his vehicle along to a side of the road and waited for me. In Mysore, as was in ancient Greece, many worthwhile encounters take place when people meet at a street-crossing. We don't mind stopping to exchange the news of the day, and discuss and deplore the state of affairs in general. I am quite used to this practice and appreciate its value—saves a lot of mutual visiting and all the labour involved. Nowadays such encounters have become more frequent for me—especially after Doordarshan exposed me in their 'Newsline' programme. People stop by to say, 'I saw you on TV,' and then ask for details of the modalities of a TV production.

During the week after the Presidential announcement of my nomination to the Rajya Sabha, people stopped to cry, 'Congratulations! Great honour to us!' and after I mumbled a thanks, a question as to when I'm 'joining'. I always say something and continue my journey.

But today, the motorcyclist stood beside his vehicle after hoisting it on its stand, and seemed determined to congratulate me rather elaborately. So I slackened my steps. After so much preparation on his part it did not seem fair to pass him by.

'Congratulations!' he cried, and held out his hand.

'Thanks,' I said, responding with a warm grip. First time I was getting a close view of his personality, although the goggles he wore covered half his face.

'When are you reporting for duty?' he asked.

I did not know the answer myself.

'You should do it immediately,' he said. 'From the moment it is announced you become an MP and are entitled to free calls on the telephone. Otherwise you will be paying fifty paise a call unncessarily.'

'I don't mind it,' I said.

'Why not?' he argued. 'Why should you not enjoy all the benefits? Will you be given a house?'

'I have no idea,' I said.

'I'm sure you will be given a house,' he said, apparently more informed than I was in such matters. He looked triumphant at the fact that he could tell me one or two things.

He paused, and said suddenly, 'Could you refuse this nomination?'

'What a question! Why?'

'When I heard the announcement, I got a funny feeling,' he said.

'Perhaps you thought the Government was out to amuse you?'

He ignored my quip, but went on with his own thoughts. 'How can you live in Delhi, bundling up everything here, and living all alone in Delhi?'

He looked quite panic-stricken on my account. It was as if I were being banished to the heart of the Sahara. I was touched by his solicitude (though it was unwarranted). I said placatingly, 'I'm used to it, often visit Delhi on some committee business . . .'

'What committee?'

I explained the nature of the committee I served on.

He clicked his tongue and made a sound which can only be indicated by the letters 'Pshaw'. He added, 'Committees! Committees! Don't I know about them—you nibble glucose biscuits sitting around an oval table, sip tea and collect your air fare . . .'

'Are you a member of a committee by any chance?' I asked, feeling it was time I put in a question from my side.

'I have a boss who goes to Delhi five times in a month and I know what he and others do . . .'

I felt relieved that he was straying away from the Rajya Sabha nominations. Perhaps he also realized it and returned immediately to the subject.

'I can't imagine you living in Delhi. I get a funny feeling when I think of it.' Once again this man was using the word 'funny' and I resisted the impulse to ask him to define 'fun' and 'funny'. But I left it at that.

He suddenly said, 'If you have decided to go, be sure that you are not cheated—you will be entitled to a house, free travel, etc., and other amenities, make sure you get them all. After all, we tax-payers support you, and I'm keen . . .'

I asked, 'When I secure them all—will you cease to feel funny?'

'No,' he added, 'I'm not sure, after all, this is not your line . . .'

'What do you suppose is my line?' I asked.

'You are after all a journalist and story-writer, and you must stick to your job.'

'Do you know of any of my books?'

'I'm busy from late morning till night and have no time to read. But my wife reads a lot of novels and such things and tells me about them. I'm interested in you as a neighbour and I want you to progress . . .'

At this point I felt outraged at this man's patronizing talk. I said, 'Perhaps you were going on some business. I shouldn't stop you.'

'You are not stopping me. I stopped myself because ever since I heard the announcement I have had a funny feeling . . .'

Once again that 'funny feeling'!

'May I know what your policies and plans are going to be? As a tax-payer I'm entitled to know. Will you do anything useful such as getting us broad-gauge, airport, railway connection from Chamarajanagar to Satyamangalam—problems plaguing us for fifty years? Will you do anything about it?'

'I'll bear it in mind,' I said loftily.

'Yes, you'll promise, of course, now, but will do nothing about it once you step in there. Don't I know our MPs!'

At this point I cautioned him, 'Are you aware that if you comment recklessly abut MPs you are likely to be hauled up for contempt and may face a jail sentence? Now kick your starter and be off before you do yourself any damage.'

THE TESTAMENT OF A WALKER

THERE ARE PERSONS who have no ear for music, being tone-deaf; others who have no eye for art, who may in a sense be called 'colour blind'. In a similar category, I am impervious to the subtler values in a car. To me an automobile is only the means to an end; I am satisfied if I am provided a seat and four wheels that can roll, and I am blind to all other points in a car. In spite of this constitutional defect, by a quirk of fate I came to own an 'imported' car, flashy and full of sophistication, which caused ecstacy in every auto-pundit who saw it. 'Ah! Recessed handle!' would cry one. 'Look at this steering, manoeuvrable with a flick of the finger! Push-button glass-raiser! Floating seats! Multi-coloured speedometer! Ah, controlled air-conditioner! Tape-recorder and digital alarm with calculator!' They would examine my dashboard panel admiringly, although I never understood at any time the purpose of most of the buttons, switches, and gadgets, and found it safer to leave them alone. The air-conditioner which was supposed to make one's journey free from dust, and heat, and noise, was switched on, during the ten years I used the car, for a total period of thirty minutes, which worked out to less than three minutes a year. Whenever the air-conditioner was on, the windows were to be closed; which inhibited my driver, whose habit was to show right or left turn by thrusting his arm out, who, when the glass was raised, constantly hit it with his fist. He was also in the habit of gesticulating at erring pedestrians and addressing them volubly in passing; now he felt constricted, encapsulated, and tongue-tied, and drove morosely.

Also, I think, he was conditioned to driving to the tune of the rattle and roar of other vehicles beside, behind, and ahead, and without such accompaniments he could not proceed with any confidence.

I lack automobile sensibility and do not regret it. I have a strong belief that man's ultimate destiny lies in walking, which is why he is endowed with a pair of legs, which can operate without petrol or gears. It is this philosophy that leaves me indifferent at the mention of any petrol 'hike' (a hybrid term, which seems to flourish in oil). I know that the hiking will culminate where it can't 'hike' any further (that will be at a stage where it may cost a thousand rupees to travel one kilometre), and man will rediscover the use of his feet; when that happens oil wells will overflow into storm drains or stagnate for want of takers, and petro-civilization will have become defunct. The most ambitious work I have been planning for years is to be called *Testament of a Walker*. The title has been ready for decades although the book may never be written, considering its boundless scope and ramifications. Whether written or unwritten, the philosophy is deep-rooted in me. Time was when I walked ten miles a day morning and evening (Mysore being ideal for such an occupation) and even now, I continue the habit on a lesser scale, wherever I may be, and in any season. If I am compelled to stay indoors through bad weather I can still get the mileage out in my veranda though I may be presenting an odd spectacle pacing up and down like a bear in his cage. For a fanatic of this sort the possession of a car is an anachronism: and especially the acquisition of a sophisticated imported-make, an irrelevancy and a nuisance.

Among the things I value are privacy and anonymity—both are lost when I allow myself to be carried about in a gaudy car. It is like sitting in a *howdah* on elephant-back and hoping not to be noticed.

In a compact city like Mysore (where everyone can meet everyone else at will), my movements became known to the whole town and someone or other would remark, 'Ah, you were at the store this morning' or 'I saw you going down the Market Road.' No harm, normally speaking, in such observation or enquiry; but in my case it leads to complications, and embarrassment, since I generally avoid all public engagements and invitations with the excuse that I will be away at Bangalore (100 miles) or Madras (300 miles) or Delhi (1,000 miles) depending upon the persistence of the man asking me. Apart from all this, I was in constant dread lest my driver should feel inspired to test my car's special virtue of being able to attain a speed of one-hundred-and-sixty kilometres from zero, within two minutes. At the workshop I could not help noticing the battered remains of many cars which had tried this facility on our roads. Our mechanic blithely explained, 'No problem. We can always bring them back to shape. Part of our job. Nothing is impossible. Insurance will take care of our bills even if we have to charge thirty or forty thousand for repairs. So why worry?'

Since my car was of a special pedigree, it was inadvisable to allow any ordinary workshop to open the bonnet. The accredited workshop with mechanics, wielding special tools, was a hundred miles away at Bangalore. For any attention I had to drive a hundred miles every time.

At Bangalore a team of experts would stand around and pronounce their verdict. 'Engine mountings need replacement, if you want to get rid of the 'dug dug' sound which is bothering you; one of the front shock absorbers must be replaced, better while you do it replace the pair so that your tyre wear will be uniform, otherwise your steering system will be damaged.' After their diagnosis, they would direct me to the one and only establishment, this side of the Vindhyas, which stocked imported spares, an exclusive shop catering only to the elite. They could toss across the counter anything you wanted from a little screw to a whole engine, at a price fit, indeed, for royalty still on their thrones. A customer entering this shop was expected to be lofty-minded and discreet enough not to question the price but part with his cash with an air of amused nonchalance and even benevolence.

I began to fear that at this rate (I was obliged to visit the workshop every other week to shed my savings), I should soon reach the brink of bankruptcy effortlessly. I seemed to have let myself into a strange world peopled by a class of high priests and voodoo men, the workings of whose minds I could never fathom, but who still held sway over me.

Two cyclists collided and fell on my car parked in front of the hospital, and smashed the parking light on the left side. It could not ordinarily be replaced in this country. The elite shop could produce one if I was prepared to pay two thousand for the piece. My mechanic suggested why not I visit New York and pick it up there. I had to remind him as gently as I could that he was talking nonsense. Then he examined the damage closely and declared: 'Oh, yes—only the glass is broken—we will fabricate a cover in plastic—though it may be difficult to get the curvature of the original—I will try—' Briskly, he unscrewed the whole assembly and left. He was away from the workshop for ten weeks on sick leave. When I met him again and enquired about the parking light, he looked puzzled and said, 'I remember I gave it to you. I needed only the measurement of the socket. Please check if it is at home in Mysore . . . As a rule I do not like to keep such things with me.' No further reference was made to the subject. It was impossible that both of us could be right. One of us must surely have suffered from hallucination; either myself seeing a vision of his taking out the light with the words, 'Let me keep it for safety—otherwise the boys in this workshop may steal it—' or he had an illusion of handing it over to me with the appropriate words.

That settled it. I was appalled at the thought of all the travail I had undergone and the expense, and considering that actually I had no use for a car, having no office or outside engagements, and was using it only to catch it at the end of a long walk—it seemed to me the most thoughtless thing I had done in my life to have acquired this car. I decided to be rid of it, lock it up in the shed as soon as possible to turn my energies again to writing stories.

I am not the sort of person who would enjoy getting under the car on a Sunday, as is the case with a friend of mine, who generally spends his leisure hours under his imported car, having no trust in any mechanic or workshop in our motherland. All his time is spent in collecting spare parts from far and near; he has succeeded in piling up enough stock to assemble a couple of new cars if he so desires. Whenever it becomes necessary, he strips his car bare, cuts away a diseased part, and grafts a new one. At such moments he speaks like a surgeon specialized in heart bypass and kidney transplants. I admire his competence, though I cannot accept his advice, which generally runs on the following lines, 'Don't give up your car—the thing to do is to be on the lookout for a similar model, buy it at any price and then you could transfer all the necessary parts from one car to another. It will work out cheaper that way. Ultimately you can sell away the shell of the remaining car to any fellow who is planning to set up a wayside tea-stall, or you could convert it into a little garden house in your own compound.'

A MATTER OF STATUES

ALTHOUGH THE MOTIVE for installing a statue is a solemn one, I find statues in general rather comical. There is something ludicrous in stationing a figure permanently in the open, in sun or rain, night and day, in a frozen attitude of benevolence, heroism, or contemplation.

I never look at a statue without thinking, here is a perfect instance of human miscalculation, the crown of the would-be immortal serving only as a bird-perch if not something worse. Within a couple of years of unveiling, people cease to notice the statue, and never look up at it. Time and usage having successfully rubbed off all significance, the statue might as well be a mound of rubble or a rusty tar-drum abandoned on the roadside.

Laxman once suggested in a cartoon detachable heads for all statues. The idea seemed to be that when an old hero yields place to a new one, on account of change of values or a dimming of public memory, you will only be investing in a new head with a device to screw it on, after unscrewing the other one, which could be stowed away in a museum vault or in a time-capsule, for future reference or even a possible restoration if the old head should regain public esteem. This will mean a great saving of national resources, through a sort of recycling of the existing pedestal and torso, which form the major part of any statue. The main concern at this stage should be to fit the head on a relevant torso, keeping in mind the broad distinction between a civilian and a soldier in their respective dress and departments. However, it will only be a matter of detail, easily adjusted, with a certain amount of planning and forethought. Thus we may also save the labour of moving a whole statue, when necessity arises.

Now and then certain historical causes may create a sudden uproar against a long-standing statue, with demands to move or remove it. I remember the Neil Statue Satyagraha in Madras, about fifty years ago. Colonel Neil stood at an important crossing on Mount Road, surveying superciliously the native population flowing past. That was the heyday of imperial rule. In the wake of our national struggle, there was an outcry against the Colonel followed by *jathas* and *satyagraha,* and not all the police *lathis* and arrests could stem the forces out to topple this tyrant, who 'dressed in brief authority' had left a hideous record of oppression. British rulers had installed the statue with a dual purpose: to immortalize their hero and also remind Indians to behave themselves.

Finally the public did succeed in dislodging the statue and putting it away in a cell in the museum. But not every statue is likely to end that way. Most statues, as I have already mentioned, are ignored and thus survive according to a natural law which says that a statue less noticed has a greater chance to survival. Along the same Mount Road at the northern end looms over the landcape a figure astride a horse. The details on the top portion are obscured by the height. Normally one noticed only the pedestal which rose to over fifty feet above sea level, and beyond it the figure of a flamboyant equestrian probably flourishing a lance or sword, I am not sure. It was so high that kites and vultures normally circling in high heavens glided down to rest on the shoulders of this gentleman.

It was just known as Munroe Statue, no one bothered about its history, or could stop at that point in Mount Road to gaze upward. However once it attracted much notice, when a canard was started that an eagle had dropped a necklace of gold sovereigns over its head. Enormous crowds gathered around the statue, and naturally the police also had to be there to prevent possible attempts to climb the statue. People stood about shading their eyes and looking up for hours.

If any statue could be imagined to nurse within its stony heart a craving to be stared at, here it was fulfilled. But a reaction set in, presently official moves were afoot to eliminate the statue, as a traffic hazard, though not for political reasons. The corporation invited contractors to demolish it, and found it would cost over a lakh of rupees to demolish the pedestal alone, and then there was the question of how to dispose of the statue once it was taken down. It was rumoured that even Whitehall was consulted whether they would be interested in acquiring it for the British Museum. Finally the corporators decided to leave it alone, and made a virtue of necessity by cultivating a lawn and flower-beds around it.

Sometimes the identity of a statue becomes a matter of controversy, mostly due to indifferent workmanship. While statue-making is an arduous and difficult undertaking, it is also a most hazardous one. Often the statue-maker has to build up from a photograph and oral descriptions of one who may not be in our midst; a living person normally would not think of his own statue. I say 'normally', since I remember an exception, a chief minister who supposedly spends a part of his day helping his statue-maker shape him in marble; obviously he does not wish to risk being ignored or forgotten when his term of office is over. ('It is not for myself, but I want my philosophy and the principles for which I have fought remembered,' he is quoted.) He is a busy man but never too busy to keep an eye on his statue-maker. Whether he has also chosen a site for it and intends to preside over its unveiling are 'classified material', and hence my information is limited.

I think it is better to have a self-approved statue in any place than a controversial one. In Mysore we have a certain marble statue installed about ten or twenty years ago to honour the memory of a pioneer journalist, complete with his long coat, turban, and upper cloth, but passersby, particularly the younger generation, do not recognize him as such but think the statue represents a composer, who lived till recently and was a familiar figure in our city. Having had occasions to see them both, I cannot blame anyone for taking one for the other, mainly due to the height of the statue. The veteran journalist possessed a tall, imposing figure as I remember; but the composer was short and stocky, and the statue is made to the latter specification.

Height must be a grave problem for any statue-maker; while features could be studied in a photo, the exact figure of a person can only be guessed. I remember another case where a deadlock arose between the promoters of a statue and the sculptor over the question of the height of the subject; the sculptor was charged with making the worthy gentleman look absurdly short and stooping. It ended in a protracted litigation, with the statue lying prone in the sculptor's backyard, all parties involved in the affair being gone.

Portraits are simpler. The subject sits before the painter and can express an opinion, which may not be accepted. Once a portrait painter asked me to sit for him. When he finished his work, I did not think the portrait looked like me; but the artist brushed aside my objections with, 'You would not know, but that is how you really look, it may not be what your mirror shows; but I see your soul and portray it.'

I suppose the painter was right; few of us can have a correct impression of our own personalities; the only exception I can think of was a friend of mine, a vice-chancellor, who asked me to tea one evening. After tea he took me along to his library, switched on the light and said 'See there—' pointing at a large, gorgeous, colourful portrait of himself on the wall in a red academic gown, one hand resting on a tall flower stand, and the other clutching a scroll. He had lit up the frame brightly though not tastefully. As he stood there entranced and bewitched by his own portrait, I did not know what to say and so remarked: 'I suppose you will present it to the University?' 'Oh no, why should I?' he said, 'I have paid for it in hard cash. It is mine, and it goes where I go, that is all,' with an air of finality. When I subsequently learnt of his retirement and death a few months later, my first reaction was to speculate on the fate of that portrait.

HISTORY IS A DELICATE SUBJECT

THE ONLY LATIN I know, *De mortuis nil nisi bonum*, meaning, 'Of the dead, nothing but good', has always seemed to me an unsound philosophy although implying tolerance and forgiveness, and based on the hypothesis 'Death sanctifies and canonizes'. I am not able to accept this notion, which seems to be the result of sentimentality and confused reactions in the face of death. An honest obituary should be possible. One must not hesitate to say: 'Sorry to report of So-and-so's death: he had some good points and several unholy traits too. We need not go into details now, but suffice it to say that the cooperative institution to which he had stuck all his life by hook or by crook may function hereafter in a better way and benefit the public.' Or 'Very sorry. He was after all a harmless crackpot and would not have hurt anyone even if he had continued to live . . .'

'Of the living too, nothing but good' is a corollary if the man is powerful and can afford to engage the services of a first-rate PRO. The ancient rulers employed court chroniclers whose sole business was to record unceasingly their master's virtues and valour. Much of ancient history, I suspect, is derived from such sources.

I have myself observed in the days of Palace Durbars, when His Highness stepped down from the throne to move to his chambers, he was escorted by uniformed attendants crying, what they called parak—'Glory and victory to this Emperor of the World, the unvanquished, undefeatable one etc., etc. . . . .' It was a formal cry, of course, and I don't think that any Maharaja in his right mind ever believed a word of it. But its significance is there, and its origin is in history. Every ruler, according to the court chronicler, became the supreme lord of the earth, having vanquished other rulers, whose chroniclers also made a similar claim. If there were three neighbouring kingdoms, each claimed that he became supreme after defeating the other two. As result, all history became just a record of bloody encounters and extravagant heroic claims.

I am happy that someone is taking a second look at all history. But I feel uneasy that a committee is prescribing how to write the new history which, I fear, is likely to produce history made to order again: a true historian must have the hardihood to call a spade a spade and present it instead of wrapping it up in gold foil.

I love to study history, but with a lot of distrust. In our college days we read British historians. We found the postage-stamp size portraits of kings and governors dotting the pages of our text-book charming, and the writing itself competent and readable. One did not doubt the veracity of their statements and conclusions at any stage, until a young professor, in an aside, announced one day, 'There was neither Black, nor Hole, nor Calcutta,' referring to Siraj-ud-Dowlah, the ruler of Bengal who was supposed to have packed in a jam his prisoners of war, leaving them to suffocate in a small room. The same professor also disproved that certain Muslim rulers who were supposed to have demolished temples and proselytized with fire and sword, were actually tolerant and endowed temples. And thugs and bandits actually were freedom-fighters—guerrilla fighters of those days.

Ancient history was also part of our study. The Vedic and Indo-Aryan period was taught by a specialist who entered the classroom in flowing academic robes, carrying a load of source material in his arms. While we sat up expectantly, he turned the leaves of heavy tomes and read out, 'In those days men rode on horses and women ground corn and sometimes wove mats,' in a tone of profound discovery. 'They do it even today, what is historical in it?' one felt tempted to ask. He then continued, turning the leaves of another tome. 'Here we have evidence that all those ancient cities had a wonderful drainage system . . .' 'Where is that skill gone?' one felt like asking, while the professor went on to announce from yet another voluminous document, 'They buried the dead, and sometimes cremated them too.' One began to suspect that the historian was desperately trying to squeeze information out of obvious and puerile data and from broken pottery, and thus made ancient history a vulnerable subject.

I found it all bewildering. One did not know what to believe. History is a delicate subject, the slightest falsehood could poison the whole body, like the invasion of bacteria in the human system. There are many sources of confusion for the historian, and many misleading paths open to him.

While we felt that British historians were unreliable, I heard the remark from a British scholar, 'Indians have no sense of history, no scientific attitude.' More was in store for me when he explained tritely, 'One must learn to view history as a continuum, a resultant of an endless process of Challenge and Response,' which probably conveyed some esoteric message only to other historians.

A future historian will have more headaches than any of his predecessors. The plethora of memorials and statues and news reports, often contradictory, will bewilder him. The cartoonist's version of a minister's manner of speech and form and intentions, and the portrait of the same man by his PRO are likely to be conflicting, and succeed in paralysing the historian's judgement. He may also conclude that the country had more ministers than ordinary citizens, similar to a certain Lichchavi republic of ancient days which is said to have had nine hundred and ninety-nine kings—perhaps for a population of one. He may state from a study of photographs that ministers stationed themselves before microphones all the time expect when they went up in helicopters to survey disasters, when they wore looks of profound sympathy.

The future historian's greatest headache, however, will be reports of celebrations of death anniversaries and birth anniversaries. He won't be able to make out how the twenty-fifth Memorial Day of a particular person could be followed, shortly, by the 105th birthday of the same person. The future historian will probably say, 'Normally, a person can either be living or dead but not both; we can only assume that in the later twentieth century somehow they had perfected the art of resurrecting certain very important persons, so that they continued to exist without any time limit, and the days of their death would be mourned publicly, without in any way lessening the joyful celebrations of their birthdays.'

SORRY, NO ROOM

AT THE PORTALS of Heaven, he stood forlorn. The guard would not let him in. When the man identified himself, the guard scrutinized a long scroll, and shook his head, 'You are perhaps ahead of your time ... The chart relating to you has not come; nearer the time of your scheduled departure from Earth they'll send it. You are far, far ahead of your time. Why are you here?'

'Because I'm dead, I suppose, that's all ...' The angel became thoughtful ... 'I've no power to admit you immaturely. What happened? You are not expected to be dead yet.'

The man began to explain: 'For years I was unaware of my body or its functioning, but you know there is a dreadful habit among mortals of making a fuss over each other's birthdays. My children bestirred themselves on my sixtieth birthday. In spite of my protests, they combined to organize elaborate rituals, ceremonies, *pujas* and feasting on the day I reached sixty. My wife and I were garlanded and made to pose for photographs like newly-weds. During the rituals, they emptied on our heads gallons of holy water collected from all the rivers, crowded round us suffocatingly, and deafened us with chants, greetings, chatter and loud music. Further, they planned to bundle us off on a second honeymoon. But this part of the programme had to be dropped, all that dousing of holy water brought on cough, cold and fever; we were bedridden after the festivities. My wife, being younger, recovered and was on her feet again in a couple of weeks, but I became an invalid. Our doctor had to examine me daily, and later, four different specialists at different parts of the day. I had no interests other than anticipating the doctors' arrival. Each doctor ordered a particular test on me to be carried out, only by his favourite pathologist, and my waking hours thereafter were spent in going round proffering samples of my excreta and blood and what-not to the analysts. In a short while, a nice portfolio had developed detailing every inch of my inner mechanism and chemistry.

'"Avoid sugar," said one doctor. "Avoid salt," said another. "Avoid hot water," "Avoid cold water," "Drink plenty of water," "Avoid smoking," "Smoke in moderation," "Avoid alcohol," "Drink in moderation because sudden change of habit may produce symptoms of withdrawal," were some of the expert suggestions; also observations such as "Overweight," "Underweight," "Eat less," "Eat heartily." I got rather muddled and my normal routine of life was soon gone. I fell into complete disarray as I tried to respect and fit in all the advice and suggestions into a logical pattern. I had no time for anything but attending to the repairs and patchwork of my dilapidated system, in addition to a weekly check-up to certify, it seemed to me, that I was a living creature.

'The accumulation of vials, injection tubes and tablet cases grew into a little hillock at a corner, as the portfolio of my health reports swelled to the size of an abridged edition of the *Mahabharata*. At the stated hours my doctors came in one by one, and briskly turned the covers of the portfolio, pored over the papers and left, without so much as a glance in my direction, muttering, "Nothing serious, but be careful and relaxed." An impossible combination.

'At last I found a physician who said, "Nothing wrong with you. It's all purely psychological. Throw away all the medicines. Say to yourself constantly, 'Day by day in every way I'm getting better and better,' and then leave it to nature."

'Nature? "No sir, nature has no use for the likes of me. She would sooner see me in my grave," I said, quoting a classical hypochondriac. However, I gave nature a trial, and here I am as a result.'

The angel said, 'I'm definite I cannot let you in. Try the other gate.'

*

The lost soul hesitated at the other gate as it led to Hell, but feeling
that that would be preferable to drifting in mid-air like a fluff of
cotton wool, he presented himself at the portal, which was guarded
by an angel with slightly forbidding aspect, who barred his way once
again for the same reason as before, there being no notice of his
arrival. When he explained his predicament, the dark angel took out
the records, double-checked them, and shook his head, 'Impossible.
Admission here is more difficult than at the other place. The
standards here are much stricter, being reserved for VIPs from the
world of politics, diplomacy, and business (while the commoners are
sorted out and sent elsewhere). Here we have to be careful with the •
VIPs. They hate to be crowded or inconvenienced in any way.'

'Being used to comforts at all times, how do they manage here?'

'That's no problem. They have a knack of having their own way
everywhere, and live quite comfortably here.'

'But the chastisement and chastening processes which are
reputedly the purpose of this region?'

'That's only a formality here. Not for them the rigours.
Although they are put through all that in a routine manner, the
purging of sins is gradual and in agreeable doses. We apply a system
called "Tempered Torment," "Cold Branding," and "Cushioned
Flogging"—but all that is a formal procedure once a day. On the
whole they are at peace with themselves and do not want a change.'

'Let me in,' pleaded the lost soul.

The angel considered his appeal and said, 'I could at best put you
on the waiting list. Sometimes a vacancy occurs through a freak
cancellation or absence and if you are around we can fix something.
Till then go back to Earth, to your familiar haunts.'

'No, no, there they will think I am a ghost and chase me off.'

'In that case why don't you float around the galaxies, or better
still get on to one of those satellites—and you'll be near enough to
Earth too, and maybe you could also communicate with your kith
and kin.'

JUNK

OF LATE MORE and more of my time is taken up, not in reading, writing or contemplation but in searching for something desperately: could be a life-saving tax-receipt, diary, or a key-bunch. Whatever it may be, at the moment of your need it seems to be irrevocably lost, to be followed by a prolonged mood of frustration and hopelessness. After repeatedly experiencing this unproductive, pathological state, I have come to the conclusion that it is all due to one's tendency to accumulate irrelevant odds and ends, which are not necessary either for one's welfare or wise living.

A rough listing of my treasure, I decided, would be the first step in any campaign to tidy up my surroundings. Four tape-recorders in different states of disrepair, a movie camera not taken out of its leather case for ten years or more, and all kinds of accessories, spools, and reels, a handful of nickel-cadmium cells guaranteed for ten years but dead in the first week itself, battery-chargers (only in theory), assorted ballpoint pens, transistor radios under a vow of silence, calculators which defeat all my calculations, and so on. The list is extensive. One picks up thoughtlessly all sorts of things at an airport duty-free shop or a discount store during one's travels, stands sheepishly and sleepily at the customs at an unearthly hour of arrival, and brings them home. Ultimately when their novelty has worn off all that stuff is entombed in a large cupboard.

The *Oxford English Dictionary* defines 'junk' as 'worthless stuff, rubbish'. I would extend the definition to cover all possessions that have lain in a cupboard untouched for any length of time. The need of the hour seems to me a new phrase 'de-junk', and a revolutionary programme arising thereof. For a start I ought to empty my large cupboard without compunction; but one takes time to ripen to this philosophy. 'Ultimately of course,' I say to myself. 'But immediately let us make a beginning with lesser stuff.'

And so a whole afternoon I devoted to this task. Carrying around a large basket, I visited every nook and corner of our ancient house. Under the staircase, I discovered an armful of bathroom fittings left by a plumber a year ago with the verdict, 'Completely worn out, throw them away.' Still preserved out of a mad belief that they could be reconditioned. A less frequented corner of the terrace yielded broken light switches, holders, bits of electric wires, and several unidentified porcelain and bakelite objects. From the garage I collected brushes, paints, cylinder-kits and brake-kits and fan-belt and hose-pipe and what not, dismantled from my car and replaced with new parts from time to time.

I filled up my basket with all the junk I could gather that afternoon, and tipped it over the compound wall on the northern. side, beyond which lies a sort of no-man's-land. Once over the wall, I didn't care what happened to it. It might be picked up by others or sink underground after the rains, sink deeper and deeper into the bowels of the earth until dug up by a future archaeologist who may plan to reconstruct a picture of our civilization from a study of the oddments.

After the hardware comes the software junk. Extreme sophistication in packaging techniques has brought about a condition in which a container or a wrapping appears more attractive than the content. Long after the perfume is gone, you keep the bottle for its peculiar shape and the golden top, as also all kinds of little tubes with screw-lids, aluminium containers with air-tight covers and cartons. Day by day such a collection is bound to grow in both volume and kind. If one does not wake up in time one is likely to be crowded out of one's home, a situation similar to the one visualized by Bernard Shaw when he said that the Dead would crowd the Living out of this earth some day if the custom of burial continued indefinitely.

My greatest burden, however, is paper. Every other day three waste-baskets under my table get filled up. A variety of gratuitous information from foreign missions, advertisement, appeals and announcements that don't concern me, seminar papers, and thundering manifestos, and above all cyclostyled letters which begin 'Dear Friend' and end with a facsimile signature. I consider cyclostyled letters an abomination and will not look at one even if it's from the noblest Akademi in the country.

I have said nothing about the literary litter which is special to my profession. Before a piece of writing is ready for the printer it has to pass through phases of 'growing pains': a page of printed matter may leave behind four 'unprintable' ones. I am not one of those gifted men who generally claim, 'Once I finish a piece of writing, I never have to look at it again, not a syllable to be touched.' This is the writer who perhaps could straightaway dictate his magnum opus to the linotype operator without its having to go through the intermediary stages of paperwork. But an ordinary writer not so endowed has to write, rewrite, correct, tear up and begin all over again and write on the margin and in between lines before he can present the composition to his editor. After the final copy is mailed, whether of a long work or a short one, the residue in the shape of manuscript, typescript, galleys, and final proofs, clutter the desk until they are pushed away to yield place to fresh litter.

Side by side with the proliferation of junk I notice nowadays a hopeful development. A young fellow with a sack over his shoulder, slowly, watchfully perambulates along the edge of our street picking up litter and stuffing them into the sack. I view him as my saviour, often invite him in, and empty my baskets directly into his sack.

OF AGE

AS THOUGH ONE grew up every day attached to a mercury column indicating the day, hour, and minute of one's age, a gentleman keeps asking whenever I have the ill-luck to run into him during the evening walk (his good point being that he is also a fervent walker), 'If I am not inquisitive, what's your age?'

'Always on the wrong side,' I say.

'Are you older than me? How is it you are going about without a stick as I do?'

'Perhaps I don't have one,' I say, and he walks away greatly puzzled. A few days later he crosses my path again—this time in a park on a narrow path without any scope for a detour and escape. He greets me and begins, 'If I am not inquisitive etc. . . .' and I have to say, 'You are definitely inquisitive—I told you my age last week and I couldn't have grown very much older within a week . . .'

'But you didn't tell me your exact age . . .'

'Oh, add one week to the "wrong side" which is my age, and you will have the latest figure.' He looks crestfallen and passes on. I notice him farther off the path stopping another acquaintance of his—perhaps again to say, 'If I am not inquisitive . . .'

I do not bother about my years, but a lot of others seem to be worried about it. I have no idea what I look like, how I appear to others, my use of a mirror being confined and limited to a few minutes while shaving in the morning. It seems to me from the questions asked of me that I look decrepit and pitiful, stooping and ambling and shuffling along somehow, leaving others to marvel at the feat. I have continuously to dodge enquiries after my health. Formerly if someone wanted to open a conversation, 'What are you doing now?' or 'How is the family?' would be the line of enquiry. But nowadays even the most sensible person begins with, 'How is your health?' and is satisfied with any answer I may give. The question is so casual and habitual that it need not be answered in any detail. You are not obliged to explain, 'My blood-pressure this week is —, sugar percentage in blood and urine is —, my weight has gone up but I assure you I am taking necessary steps . . .'

'How is your health?' is in the same category as the 'How do you do?' you hear when an introduction is taking place. Only a naïve simpleton would answer 'How do you do?' with, say, 'Alas! I have not brought my bio-data and health certificate—may I run up and fetch it?' while shaking hands.

Health is a preoccupation nowadays—even when there is no need for concern. It cannot be otherwise. We are being continuously bombarded with information regarding all sorts of disasters and diseases, accidents and warnings. Subconsciously everyone is keyed up and apprehensive and naturally view those advanced in years as freaks of nature if they are seen moving about freely.

*

The dialectician in our company objected to the saying, 'God helps those who help themselves.'

He explained, 'It is no credit to the Almighty that He should commit an act of redundancy by going out to help one who is competent to help himself. On the contrary, God's help may be needed for one who is such a blunderer or idiot that he cannot direct a spoon to his mouth. It is only this type that needs a constant pilot at his elbow to direct his spoon, so to speak.

'Or is God like the banker who is prepared to give you a loan if you give him twenty-five per cent of what you need, which seems to be based on the philosophy that one may attain wealth if one is rich enough! Or does the saying mean that God will watch the self-helper

to gauge how far he can struggle to achieve something, and at some
point take charge like a manager, and leave the man to sit back and
grow lazy and fat? I wonder where this God-helps-those etc. idea
originated! The more I think on this, the more I am confused.'

PICKPOCKETS

DURING A TRAIN journey recently (where else could it be?) I came across an original thinker sitting next to me. After half-an-hour of silence, he suddenly asked, 'Have you ever had your pocket picked?' I cast my mind back and said: 'Yes, years ago. I was strap-hanging in a bus going from the market to Laxmipuram in Mysore when I suddenly realized that I had lost my Parker pen with its glittering gold cap and I couldn't imagine what I could ever do without it, as it had been with me for nearly two decades. Of course I looked about and must have seemed so stricken that a man standing next to me asked: "Lost something?" When I explained, he just lifted his left foot slightly and produced, like a conjuror, my pen from under his toes; and jumped off the bus before it approached the police station at the next stop.' 'Wise fellow!' commented my train companion. 'He knew when he should make himself scarce—in all my experience this is the first time I've heard of a pickpocket restoring an article. He was a noble soul—so are most of them. I have made a special study of pickpockets—one thing I admire about them is that they are gentle and non-violent; in their profession they have to practise untouchability—that means, in substance, non-violence—although we hear instances of a knife being flourished when a pickpocket is cornered. By and large they are harmless, and they rob you only when you invite them by flaunting your purse or a pen over your breast pocket especially in these days of "bush-coats", the invention of which has encouraged this particular social malaise. What prevents you from having button-up flaps for your pocket or as in earlier days keep your things in an inner pocket. Nowadays it's a piece of vanity to display a glittering pen clip or a leather purse over your pocket, or parade a bulging hip-pocket over a T-shirt. If your tailor can redesign your dress, particularly the pocket, the pickpocket will automatically cease to be and you may rest assured that no World Federation of Pickpockets will ever protest. However my mission in life is not to encourage but to rehabilitate the pickpocket. For it must be agreed on all counts that a pickpocket exercises a delicate skill. You cannot deny that his sensitive fingers could be put to better use—such as thrumming musical strings, working delicate embroidery or knitting, and even minor surgery, with proper education and training. His genius for painless extraction must be utilized, his presence or pressure is no more than that of a butterfly flitting past. I have appealed to the government to permit me to meet pickpockets serving their term in prisons, talk to them, and conduct classes for them regularly. I hope to educate and rededicate this class for constructive work. But before I start on this mission I'd urge pickpockets to observe certain restraints and codes. First and foremost, every member of their Society must take an oath to observe a strict holiday on the first of a month, when most people get their salaries. It is heart-rending to watch a family man discover the absence of his purse just when he is about to pay the bill at the provision store after parcels are made up. 'God, how am I to manage this month—food, rent, children's school fees, electricity bill to be paid on the fifth, insurance premium to avoid penalty—and scores of other commitments!' This painful situation must be avoided. I hope to achieve results in that direction. I shall also urge the LIC to devise some kind of insurance against pocket losses for the citizen. Next, a pickpocket should also vow never to use a razor blade to slash pockets. It's unsportive: in the category of using Folidol to hunt a tiger. A pickpocket should at least return important documents and papers found in a wallet. I learn that in New York, pickpockets generally drop passports, social security cards, insurance certificates etc. into the nearest mailbox; and this admirable practice must be followed in our country also.'

When his station arrived, the monologist hurriedly got up, held out to me his card, saying casually, 'Any donation, whatever the amount, will be welcome at this address to promote our cause,' and left. Later I patted my pockets to make sure that this reformer was not an adept himself. The contents of my pocket were intact. I realized he was only a zealot or messiah looking for a cause to champion.

MONKEYS

I HAVE A partiality for the monkey. My earliest associate was one Rama (as I have described in *My Days*), a slender yellowish creature with the face of an angel, with whom I was on talking terms. He was my only companion in childhood, in my grandmother's home at Number One, Vellala Street, Purasawalkam. (Now the building is gone, to make way for a modern 'complex'. Fortunately, the massive brass-studded street door which must have been pushed and pulled a million times during its century-old existence alone was saved, and acquired as a memento by a friend.)

To go back to Rama, he lived in a cabin in the garden at the end of a long chain with a leather-band around his waist. As soon as I came home from school, I released him from bondage and kept his company, taking care not to let go his waist-band. He nestled close to me as we sat on the threshold and watched the traffic in the street.

We quietly commented on the scene passing before us: 'See those sweets—why don't you hop across and snatch the red coloured *mittai*—one for you and one for me . . .?' I suggested once. 'Done,' he replied, 'If only you will let go your hold.' On one occasion when I acted on his advice, he not only sprang away and toppled the tray of the vendor, after gobbling up the sweets, but roamed the neighbourhood, creating quite a stir, till he was caught two days later—but that is another story. The point I am trying to make is that the monkey was an ideal companion, an agreeable conversationalist, and listened to my remarks and narrations (mostly about my class teachers at the Lutheran Mission) with grave attention. He was capable of speech at a wavelength which I alone could catch.

Now, after countless decades, I have retained my faith and interest in the monkey. When I notice on my walks along a trunk road, a family on treetops, chattering and hopping about, I wish I had not lost, through inevitable adulthood, the receptivity I used to possess in childhood. Now I can only speculate on what they are saying. When I watch a big group in their hierarchy of male and female and juniors perched in their proper ranks, while the leader goes through the agenda for the day, with an attendant picking off fleas and ticks from his coat, I can almost hear him say:

'It's a pity we do not have an all-India identity. We still think of Mysore Monkey and Madras Monkey, Tirupati Monkey or Benares Monkey, and never of a moment talk of the Indian Monkey. We must strive for an all-India federation from which we should, naturally, exclude chimps, gorillas and orangutans, none of which possess a recognizable tail; being almost human in gestures, postures and movement, they are actually bipeds. We must be positive and make it universally understood that they are not our class—let them learn human speech and get merged in their society. As far as we are concerned, we will state our own hopes and demands as follows:

'First, we must thank human beings for becoming aware, after all, of the importance of trees. We welcome their Grow More Trees ideals, and support them heartily unlike the shortsighted cattle and goats (and their human keepers) which display irresponsibility and won't allow a sapling to grow in peace. Humans should, in addition to growing more trees, also pay attention to the kind of tree planted. They must be discouraged from planting conifers, eucalyptus and even casuarina trees which provide neither shade nor accommodation, nor nourishing fruits. We must urge upon the authorities the importance of cultivating fruit-bearing trees which grow to a desirable height with spreading branches. Orchards must, of course, be encouraged, and mango, guava, jambu and berries of many kinds must be cultivated. Human beings must be made to realize that God created fruits exclusively for our benefit and not for their consumption; they should be satisfied with corns, cereals and such stuff which they cultivate for their nourishment. Man has made fruit-cultivation a commercial activity, which must be condemned. They guard their orchards fiercely; there are instances where they have shot our kinsmen with double-barrelled guns and have caused indescribable tragedy and hardship in some families which happened to camp in certain orchards. One way in which a recurrence of such tragedy could be prevented is to make the humans realize that we are the descendants of the great god Hanuman who humans worship with fear and faith. As a protective measure let us adopt the emblem of Maruti—although there are partisans among us who revere Vali and Sugreeva. I cannot welcome such mischievous attitudes. After all, Vali and Sugreeva are controversial characters in the *Ramayana*. Vali was guilty of appropriating his brother Sugreeva's wife and driving him out of the kingdom, for which he was punished by Sri Rama, and Sugreeva himself has displayed certain weak points, but we need not go into all that now. Hanuman alone stands, pure and serene like the Ganga at Gangotri, and we shall adopt him as our protector from gunmen. Until humans firmly realize, without any doubt, that fruit is God-given food meant for us, we should keep away from orchards and content ourselves with food from roadside figs and berries.

'We on our part should also observe certain disciplines and restraints so that humans may get confidence in us and feel that we could co-exist with them. We must not invite trouble by slipping in through any open window and creating panic in a household. We must not frighten schoolchildren, even for a joke, and, above all, our compatriots who dwell in temples like Tirupati or Benares must not take undue advantage of the sanctuary by snatching away fruits and offerings from unwary pilgrims. The kind of warning posted on temple pillars, "Guard your Bags and Spectacles" should be viewed as a discredit to our tribe. At our next meeting we shall formulate a precise code after consulting our cousins dwelling on other trees.'

GOD AND THE ATHEIST

AT THE ROUND table the talk was all about atheism and faith. The dialectician was in his element. If anyone in the company sounded religious, he at once championed the atheist and vice-versa. And finally we arrived at a stage where the antagonists were brought together face to face.

The atheist stood in the presence of God who was enthroned and radiant. He turned to his visitor questioningly. The atheist said, 'If you are omniscient, as your followers claim, you should know what I am. It is a test. I do not know how to address you, sir; should I say "Your Almighty"?'

'Oh, no. The second person pronoun will be adequate.'

'I do not remember my grammar. What is second person pronoun?'

'Y-O-U; I cannot afford to forget my grammar. I do not have the freedom an atheist enjoys.'

'Oh, you know me, though I have not announced myself!'

'I don't have to be told. I hope I have passed the test.'

'Let us now go on, with your permission, in the manner of a press interview.'

'Excellent idea. Only you cannot have my photograph. I am not opaque, nor photogenic.'

'It does not matter, we have enough portrayals for your worshippers. Now, first of all, I want to know if you have really created the entire Universe.'

'How does it seem to you?'

'Rationally viewing it, the Universe and all that it contains seems to be self-created through various evolutionary processes and molecular actions. Where is the need for a Maker, like a potter, to give shape and colour to things?'

'The potter at least can smash up his handiwork if he is not satisfied. But I cannot do it.'

'Oh, come on, what about the catastrophes, calamities, holocausts one sees all around?'

'Most of it is man-made, and the others are caused by . . . we need not go into all that now. Normally the Universe is stable, stars run their course without bumping into each other, you can calculate with precision, as your almanacs prove, the movements and career of planets. Only human beings are unpredictable. They are ready to pounce on and exterminate each other individually or as groups, communities or armies. In all creation, human beings alone display so much ego, aggression, and greed. On the other hand, animals, birds and other creatures naturally practise a philosophy of "live and let live". Even beasts which kill for food attack only when they are hungry. But man will attack, pillage and grab and jealously hold on to it, whether it be food, money or territory.'

'Why is it so? You are the creator and you should know.'

'Creatures which follow their instincts do less damage than man, who exercises intelligence.'

'Why did you endow man with intelligence?'

'As I told you it is all built-in, to use your popular phrase. I have no control over the mind of a human being, which he is free to exercise for any purpose; and that is the trouble. I sometimes feel, watching human antics, that I am like an author whose characters have jumped off the page and are running wild. But I do not have the freedom enjoyed by your author who can tear up the page and dismiss the characters.'

'God, your flights into philosophy are unconvincing. I would prefer a down-to-earth talk.'

'Down-to-earth? Very well. On Earth you create a lot of commotion in my name. There can be nothing more absurd than the bloody feuds over nomenclature and over the label to hang around my neck, each asserting that such and such alone is my name. Champions of God have perpetrated unspeakable cruelties on anyone suspected of heresy, which is a convenient term applied against anyone voicing an unorthodox view. At one time in your history, scientists and thinkers have been tortured for the sin of declaring that the Earth is round and revolves round the Sun—this was considered an ungodly statement. Save me from my champions, I say, but to whom am I to appeal to, considering the evil generated by my followers who have provoked holy wars and perfected instruments of persecution? I feel atheists have done less harm, although fanatical in their own way.'

'Thank you, God, for your down-to-earth talk.'

'Only remember that the planet you live in with its problems is just a speck compared to the rest of the Universe I have to mind. Goodbye. Are you now convinced of my existence?'

'Not yet. How am I to be sure that our talk is real and not just a piece of self-deception?'

'What does it matter, what difference could it make?'

ON VED MEHTA

SOME YEARS AGO Ved Mehta (our distinguished man of letters, settled in New York) was almost my neighbour when I occupied an apartment on East 57th Street. He was on East 58th Street. He was planning a profile of me for the *New Yorker* magazine, which brought us together. When we met he would gather information and biographical data about me unobtrusively. He had lost his vision when he was three years old through an attack of meningitis. When he was fifteen, he was sent to the Arkansas State School for the Blind, where he was trained to develop alternative faculties such as touch and hearing and memory. He benefited from his schooling to such an extent that he was able to pursue an academic career, with distinction both in America and England. In his company one never noticed his handicap. He moved about freely without carrying a white walking-stick. He managed to gather details of my life day by day, in a subtle manner without obvious questioning, and in due course produced a ten-thousand-word masterpiece entitled 'The Train Arrived in Malgudi' for the *New Yorker* (later included in his collection of essays, *Johnny Is Easy to Please*).

He was uncannily sensitive and alert. In those days I was addicted to chewing betel-nut and carried a stock in a little tin container. Once when I took it out of my pocket, he asked, 'Narayan, what is that rattling noise?' I handed him the tin box. He ran a finger lightly over it to gauge its dimensions and asked, 'What colour is it?' sniffed its contents, remarked, 'Spiced with cardamom and cloves, I suppose,' and returned it to me. Later, I found my addiction described in his essay, with the size and colour of the little tin container mentioned.

While crossing a street he stopped on the edge of the kerb when the 'Don't Walk' sign came on. He explained to me that he was guided by the vibrations he felt underfoot when others walked or stopped! Whenever I visited his apartment, he offered me coffee after warning me not to follow him into the kitchen. In fifteen minutes he would emerge with a tray of coffee and toast. The articles in his kitchen were arranged with such mathematical precision that by stretching out his hand he could pick up whatever he needed—coffee-maker, marmalade, toaster, cutlery, cups and other things, and he knew also the position of the electric switches for the gadgets in the kitchen.

He reviewed books and corrected proofs. He had his desk at the *New Yorker,* where he worked regular hours and beyond. William Shawn, editor of the *New Yorker,* admired his writing and provided continuous secretarial help in relays. Books were read out to him, as also galley proofs, word by word including punctuation marks; he dictated corrections and checked them in subsequent proofs. He wrote not only stories and sketches but also on technical subjects. Once he was away for a couple of weeks to study a desalination plant somewhere, and then wrote a detailed report as a *New Yorker* feature.

In his company one forgot the fact, or rather failed to notice, that he could not see. He had developed compensatory faculties, which enabled him to perceive, understand and implant in memory, every detail of his surroundings.

One evening he had tickets for a play and invited me to join him. When we came out of the theatre, he analysed and discussed the play all through the evening. He attended parties and recognized everyone by voice, also entertained at home, selecting and mixing drinks for his guests from a cocktail cabinet.

When we last met, he lived uptown on Fifth Avenue, on the eleventh floor of an apartment. When he started out he carefully locked the door, never misplaced the key, walked down the passage to the elevator, crossed the hallway, summoned a taxi, reached his office on the eighteenth floor of a building on West 25th Street, all by himself without the slightest error at any point of his passage, even on a bleak day when a freak weather in April had left a seven-foot pile of snow on the New York streets. A marvel, whom I cannot forget, though I have lost touch with him.

IN THE PHILIPPINES

ONE SEPTEMBER EVENING I landed in Manila from Hong Kong, with
no idea of what I was going to do, with no notion whatever about
Magsaysay. At the airport they detained me, offering a chair in a
corner of the hall. After all the passengers had left, the officer
beckoned me to approach him. He studied my passport page by
page, comparing the photo with the person standing before him and
then asked, 'Why have you come here?'

'To write on . . .' I said, and explained my mission. At the
mention of Magsaysay, he relaxed his grimness. He was in khaki
uniform with colour strips on his chest. It looked as if he had the
authority to knock down or imprison anyone entering his country.
'Is anyone coming to meet you?'

'I don't know.'

'Go up and look if anyone has come to receive you.' I walked up
to a wall he indicated, which was perforated. I peered through the
circular holes in the wall and saw in the darkness shadowy figures
outside, all Filipinos, naturally.

I pretended to look for someone and returned to the officer. 'No,
no one has come.'

'What will be your address in Manila?' I blinked, not being
prepared for so much cross-examination. He became more and more
suspicious, and treated me like a spy or an illegal immigrant. The
hall was deserted, all the passengers who had arrived with me had
been cleared. I asked him in a fit of desperation, 'Why are you

holding me up like this?' He did not reply. 'I should like to reach my hotel. I've travelled a long way,' I mumbled.

'Which hotel?'

'I'll find one.'

'Any idea where?'

'Look here,' I said finally, 'I have come to write a book on your late President Magsaysay . . .' The mention of Magsaysay, again, at once changed the atmosphere; he became solicitous and called up someone and ordered him to book a hotel and a taxi for me. 'You are a Narayan? Any relation of Jayaprakash Narayan?'

'In a way, all Narayans are of one family . . .' I said casually.

*

I was in the dining-hall of the hotel—an attendant came to say, 'An inspector from the health bureau is waiting in your room, sir—' I hurried up to my room on the first floor. An officer had made himself comfortable in a chair by my bed. He said, 'I didn't want to wait in the lounge.' I did not want to question him. He wanted my passport and air ticket. He asked, 'You have passed through Calcutta? Your health certificate, please.' He looked at it and said, 'You had cholera inoculation. That's good. Still, you will please present yourself at the Bureau of Health at ten tomorrow morning.'

'Why?'

'You have passed through Calcutta—Bengal is a cholera zone. We may have to quarantine you—'

I protested and explained that I had only been at the Dum Dum airport.

He ignored my explanation and asked, 'Have you brought any foodstuff?'

'No,' I said brazenly, hoping he would not turn round and notice the three Horlicks bottles filled with spicy mixtures and pastes, to be mixed with plain rice, which my sister had insisted upon my taking with me. He was, for all his grimness, an inefficient fellow, who did not have the sense to turn round and notice the Horlicks bottles, though he said menacingly, 'If you have brought any foodstuff we'll have to confiscate and destroy it. If you make a false statement, the consequences will be serious.' After he left I rearranged the bottles behind a pile of clothes.

The next afternoon a taxi took me to the Bureau of Health, a place swarming with seekers of health certificates, inspectors, and quasi-medical men in imposing martial uniforms. I was led to a hall where the Chief Officer was seated at an enormous table, with a world map covering the entire wall at his back. The map was studded with coloured buttons. He addressed me straightaway, without preliminaries, 'How are you feeling?'

'In what respect?'

'Health, only health. We are not concerned with other problems you may have . . .'

'My health is fine,' I said boastfully.

'You are from Bengal?'

'No, I am from Mysore . . .'

'Mysore? Mysore?' he muttered, turning round to locate it on the map.

'Ah, here it is,' he pointed a baton at a patch on the map and asked, 'You notice the buttons there?'

'Yes.'

'What colour do you find them?'

'Yellow,' I said, wondering if I was also being tested for colour blindness.

'Yellow indicates plague and possibly also jaundice. We get information of public health from every part of the world through the WHO reporters every hour,' he said with a glow of omniscience.

'So what?' I could not help exclaiming.

'We have to guard against carriers—especially from other Asian countries and Africa.'

'Terrible continents,' I cried.

'Glad you agree with me . . .'

'But Mysore is a large state . . . so large that your report cannot apply to the whole state—it is bound to have sickness of some sort here and there in a village thousands of miles away from everywhere.'

'We have to go only by WHO reports.'

'One more thing. Now I am not coming from Mysore but from Coimbatore.'

'Oh!' He turned his neck to locate Coimbatore. 'You see the purple buttons—that means malaria and cholera.'

'Is no part of this planet safe according to WHO?'

'True, true, I am glad you appreciate the situation . . .'

I wanted to announce, 'I am not here to spread pestilence and decimate the population of the Philippines,' but suppressed it and said, 'My mission is to collect material and write a biography of your late President Magsaysay . . .'

'Ah, he was a great leader and a wonderful commander.'

I did not want to question him whether Magsaysay was ever an army commander. I had heard of him only as the President of the country. He added, 'I was in the NMC and took direct orders from him.'

He assumed I understood what NMC meant, and I only said, 'That must have been a wonderful experience for you.'

'When I heard of his death, I went into mourning, for fifteen days—even when my father died, our mourning period was only six days.'

As a result of this palaver, he showed me a concession that although I was a risk factor carrying deadly germs around, he would not order me to be quarantined, but keep me under observation for nine days. I could stay in my hotel, but had to show myself at the bureau every afternoon and report my health.

The journey was tedious, walking every day to the health bureau and the fort. I had to sit before the Health Officer, face the world health map, answer routine questions and then return to my hotel, and stay in my room. It was not an hour safe for a stroll, as the manager had warned, 'Don't go out, down the Dwight Way or along the beach—lot of freelance gunmen around at this hour, or taxi men who will take you downtown to places, where they will strip you of everything, including your pants.'

In support of this warning, whenever I stepped out of the hotel, a car would always come up in slow gear beside me, the driver asking,

'Do you want a girl?' and taking out a photo from his pocket. 'She is a beauty, sir, who will give you anything. She is not a whore but from a respectable family, a schoolteacher. If you do not like her, see this photo—or this one you may like—or this one—' He'd take photo after photo out of his pocket. I averted my head and walked off briskly.

To digress: the streetwalkers of London accosted you, softly and seductively, whispered while you passed down Piccadilly, Curzon Street, or Soho, 'Come on, darling, let us make love—' While on a stroll with Graham Greene after dinner he would always advise, 'Don't be rude to them, just say you are not interested.'

In Rome I experienced a different kind of approach. At a restaurant table a girl would materialize and take her seat by your side, and demand, 'Give me drinks.' After that, 'I want dinner. You want to come with me after food?'

One evening, a young man kept following me while I was returning to my hotel. 'May I take you to a night club, sir? You will enjoy it, plenty of beautiful girls who will give you anything. My name is Marco, sir, why won't you let me take you to nice places?' He followed me importuning. Finally he asked, 'Why won't you let me help you have a good time?'

'Because my wife will be waiting for me in the hotel—she will feel lonely and upset if I don't return to the hotel.' At once he apologized, 'Excuse me, sir, if I have bothered you.'

'Not at all, Marco, you are doing your duty, nothing wrong if . . .'

'I am glad, sir, you understand me. I don't like this profession—during the day I work hard at the Olivetti factory which is not enough for my living, so after office hours I have to work again till midnight to earn enough money—but I'll not stay like this. I am learning English and have applied for immigration and plan to go away to Canada and do farming—that's my ambition, sir.'

'Good luck to you. Be a good farmer, Marco, and good night,' I said, when we reached my hotel.

INDIRA GANDHI

I NOTICED A brief entry in my diary dated 10 March 1984: 'Promised PM a set of my books autographed, Heinemann Collected Edition.' Mrs Gandhi had remarked during our meeting that day, 'People take away books from my library and never return them. I don't have any of your books now.' I used to send her hardcover editions of my books for her library, which was stocked with a wide range of literature both in English and French. She was in the habit of reading far into the night, as I learnt, even when she carried files home.

Now to my profound regret, I realized that I had failed to keep my promise, not out of forgetfulness but through a habit of postponing things. I had hoped that I could take the books personally on my next visit. My next visit happened to be in May, but without the promised books in hand, and that turned out to be my last interview with Indira Gandhi.

Normally, once a quarter, some committee meeting or other would give me an excuse to visit Delhi. I can't really pretend that we achieved much at those meetings in Shastri Bhavan or any other Bhavan. We assembled around an oval table and carried on discussions, nibbling biscuits and sipping tea or (impossible) coffee, while also gently working our way through an agenda. At the end we dispersed amidst a general babble of How-do-you-do, Must get-together-sometime, How-long-in-Delhi, and so forth. Apart from the committee business, the trip itself had a value: I enjoyed the scene and air of Delhi and above all meeting people. Sometimes, during one of those visits, I could also call on Mrs Gandhi. If my friend Sharada Prasad mentioned to her that I was in town, she would always find a little time for me, even if only a half hour, at her office in the Parliament House or in the South Block. She suggested once, 'Why don't you come home? You have not seen my grandchildren.'

She was a dedicated grandparent, and anticipated with a quiet joy rejoining the family at the end of the day. Once she remarked, 'I don't really mind the long hours at the office, but the worst of it is that some days the children are asleep when I go home.' I met her in March at her residence, when she was about to leave for her office and she suggested that I go along with her. From the car she called Sanjay's child to come up for a ride with her, and explained, 'I don't have enough time for this child. He has temperature. I don't know why.' She kept feeling his brow all the time. In the brief journey between her residence and office, she somehow managed to keep up her conversation with me and also with the child, pointing to him the trees in bloom and birds along the way. After reaching the office she sent the child back home with many words of caution and also told him, pointing to me, 'You know this uncle writes very interesting stories.'

She was generally calm, gentle, and cheerful, and never displayed any sign of strain or irritation. Only once did I notice that she was agitated and upset. Three or four years ago at about eight in the evening she noticed a long window in the drawing room open, which gave on the fateful lawn bordered with dark shrubs and a wicket-gate beyond. She almost shouted at an attendant, 'Who opened this window? Shut it immediately.' She calmed down presently and remarked, 'Sometimes they are very careless.'

I really had no definite purpose in seeing her, I had no requests, or comments to offer, or political interests. We discussed mostly books and the environment, and problems of urban development. She admired Mysore for its natural charms, and was concerned how long the special quality of life and atmosphere there would last with the industrial developments around.

She was highly critical of the film version of my novel *The Guide* and never ceased to wonder why I had permitted all that distortion. She was critical of my version of the *Ramayana* too, 'Your *Ramayana* is very readable, of course, but one misses in it details and the poetic grandeur of the epic.'

Some years ago, during a visit to the South, she had gone to see the Kamakoti Acharya. Later, when I referred to her *darshan*, she explained, 'Some of my friends in Madras persuaded me to call on the Swami. They took me somewhere and made me sit on a bench in a narrow passage, and wait for a long time, with a well in front of me. It was uncomfortable, sitting on that bench. Eventually the Swami appeared on the other side of the well. We remained in silence looking at each other across the well. My friends whispered that I should seek his guidance for any problem I might have. I really had no questions but they pressed me. So I put to him a very long question in English. I spoke to him of the travails, sufferings, and hardship of our countrymen since the beginning of history, and asked why it was so and what would help. He listened attentively but gave no reply since he was under a vow of silence—but I felt I had an answer. There were no words of course but it did not mean there was no communication.'

Our first meeting was in 1961 when I was taken by my friend Natwar Singh to Teen Murti in order to call on Jawaharlal Nehru after I had received the Sahitya Akademi Award on the previous evening. Nehru came downstairs and received the book I had for him, talked casually for a few minutes and left, saying, 'I am sorry I have to go, but . . .' He hailed across the hall, 'Indira, here is Narayan. Look after him. Give him coffee and breakfast and talk to him.' She took charge of me, led me to a table and organized an exquisite breakfast of fruits and toast and porridge and above all very good coffee. She put me at my ease in a few minutes and soon we were discussing a wide range of subjects. She was gracious and informal, and continued to be so, unvaryingly, all through the years I have known her.

In May she gave me an appointment at her office, but the security proceedings seemed to be unusually elaborate. Finally, after a series of checks, I was taken to the waiting hall adjoining the PM's room, which was crowded. I despaired how long I might have to wait to get my turn. But presently an officer came in looking for me and said, 'Please follow me.'

Indira Gandhi left her office table and moved to the sofas in a corner, and showed me a seat. 'More comfortable here,' she said. 'Quite a crowd is waiting in the other room, some of them look like ministers,' I told her. 'Actually, they may be ministers,' she said laughing, 'and may be full of problems too. I have to give them a lot of time . . . sometimes all I can do is to give them a hearing . . . Anyway, let that not bother you, they will wait.' She was more leisurely today than ever before and was lively in her talk.

I said, noting mentally how frail she was looking, 'The Punjab situation must be a big strain.' She remained in thought for a moment and said, 'Yes, undoubtedly it is.' And changing the subject asked, 'Is any other novel of yours being made into a film?'

I mentioned *The Financial Expert* which was recently produced in Kannada. She said, 'I want to see it, Doordarshan should be able to present it sub-titled. I hope it's better than *The Guide*.'

Apropos nothing she suddenly announced, 'When I retire, I really do not know where I will live. I don't own a house anywhere . . .' When I took leave of her, she said with a laugh, 'Your brother is hard on some of us, you know!' referring to Laxman's political cartoons. 'Oh, he is made that way, he could be equally hard on himself and on all of us too,' was all I could say.

CRUELTY TO CHILDREN*

IN THE STRESS of the concerns of the adult world, the problems or rather the plight of children pass unnoticed. I am not referring to any particular class but to childhood itself. The hardship starts right at home, when straight from sleep the child is pulled out and got ready for school even before its faculties are awake. He (or she) is groomed and stuffed into a uniform and packed off to school with a loaded bag on his back. The school-bag has become an inevitable burden for the child. I am now pleading for abolition of the school-bag, as a national policy, by an ordinance if necessary. I have investigated and found that an average child carries strapped to his back, like a pack-mule, not less than six to eight kgs of books, notebooks and other paraphernalia of modern education in addition to lunch-box and water bottle. Most children on account of this daily burden develop a stoop and hang their arms forward like a chimpanzee while walking, and I know cases of serious spinal injuries in some children too. Asked why not leave some books behind at home, the child explains it is her teacher's orders that all books and notes must be brought every day to the class, for what reason God alone knows. If there is a lapse, the child invites punishment, which takes the form of being rapped on the knuckles with a wooden scale, a refinement from our days when we received cane cuts on the palm only. The child is in such terror of the teacher, whether known as Sister, Mother Superior, or just Madam, that he or she is prepared to carry

---

* Narayan's maiden speech as a Member of Parliament delivered at the Rajya Sabha in 1989.

out any command issued by the teacher, who has no imagination or sympathy.

The dress regulation particularly in convent schools is another senseless formality—tie and laced shoes and socks, irrespective of the climate, is compulsory. Polishing a shoe and lacing it becomes a major task for a child first thing in the day. When the tie has become an anachronism even in the adult world, it's absurd to enforce it on children. A simple uniform and footwear must be designed and brought into force and these should be easier to maintain.

After school hours when the child returns home her mother or home tutor is waiting to pounce on her, snatch her bag and compel her to go through some special coaching or homework. For the child the day has ended; with no time left for her to play or dream. It is a cruel, harsh life imposed on her, and I present her case before this House for the honourable members to think out and devise remedies by changing the whole educational system and outlook so that childhood has a chance to bloom rather than wilt in the process of learning.

Other areas where the child needs protection is from involvement in adult activities such as protest marches, parades, or lining up on roadsides for waving at VIPs; children are made to stand in the hot sun for hours without anyone noticing how much they suffer from fatigue, hunger and thirst. Children must be protected and cherished, which would seem especially relevant in this year of the Nehru centenary. How it is to be done is upto our rulers and administrators to consider—perhaps not by appointing a commission of enquiry, but in some other practical and peaceful manner.

TABLE TALK

I BEGIN TO doubt my wisdom in buying a TV set, investing ten thousand rupees for the luxury. Now I want my money back, if the Ministry will take it and give me bonds, even if they are non-convertible until my great-grandson celebrates his thousandth moon. Here in Mysore we receive only the National Programme which means mostly Hindi programmes for five hours at a stretch, which one sits through hoping that at least the next item may make sense. Profound and prolonged interviews, features and reports, not to speak of entertainment, are fed to us in massive doses but in a language which though pleasant to the ear, conveys no meaning. After prolonged exposure extending over months, I have come to understand only two words—*samachar* and *samapt*. To be shut up in a little room with a loudspeaker blaring used to be an ingenious form of political torture in certain European countries at one time, now to be compelled to sit through a prolonged session listening to an unintelligible language seems also a torment, though in a lesser degree. Someone seems to have hit upon it as a brilliant strategy: 'Anti-Hindiwallas won't accept Hindi, is it? All right. We will deal with them. Force-feed them. Subject them to a barrage, and they will inevitably come round. How do circus animals begin to understand and perform? Only through repeated auditory attack. How can anyone not understand Hindi? Sheer cursedness—opposed to National Integration. Anti-Hindiwallas hope to hang on to English by pretending not to understand Hindi, that's all. Down with English.' As a result of this philosophy, we have to sit before our TV every evening through the *Krishi* programme, various serials, and another and another, with forbearance, without understanding a word, sometimes wildly guessing the meaning. Even thus, some of the programmes have become our favourites. We have grown used to certain personalities appearing on the TV screen, and watch and try to extract some sense from their gestures and antics and the noise they make. Each one on this side of the TV screen in the family circle interprets the goings-on in his or her own way. The most respected linguist in our midst is the lady of the house who, years ago, studied Hindi and attained *Visharad Rashtra* status. She was preparing to scale further heights of *bhasha* until the Government of India came down with a declaration of language policy, which caused public disorder and the lady gave up her academic pursuit promptly. Now she has forgotten whatever she had learnt, but remains our sole interpreter in the TV room. One of us may ask, 'Who is this new character?'

She will say, 'O! That is the smuggler's cousin.' 'No, he seems to be the second son of the *Hum Log* family. How did you get the idea that he was a smuggler?' Another may say, 'That man in the embroidered *kurta* looks like a smuggler.'

'Somehow you seem to conclude that anyone wearing an embroidered shirt is a smuggler.' Or the next question may be: 'What is that girl saying, when her elders are discussing her marriage?'

'Actually that girl is the wife of the smart doctor and they were all discussing their holiday plans.'

'But the doctor is a bachelor—'

'He is not. Did you not notice the girl at his side on the sofa?'

'She was only a patient waiting to show her tongue.'

Thus go on our speculations, until a welcome advice be heard: 'Next programme will be the news in Hindi. Let us switch off and go in for our supper.' And so we avoid the news in Hindi since we will be seeing the same VIPs and conferences in the English news also. We avoid Hindi news not only because of its obscurity but also the deadly monotony of delivery. However, when the English news comes, we realize that we are no better off. Once again monotony from grim newsreaders who look desperate and in a hurry to reach the last line of the script within the allotted time, and grin with unconcealed relief, only when they say, 'Good night'. However, young ladies who announce the coming programmes carry it off, though they lisp and sigh and whisper and drop sibilants rather than words. No one minds anything they do because they are invariably charming, which dissolves it all.

I will end this with a few constructive hints:

- Let us have English subtitles and summaries of stories. That way Hindi will be gradually understood and in the years to come you may find us on par with, say, our fellow citizens in Madhya Pradesh.

- As a gesture of reciprocal courtesy, North Indian stations should telecast national programmes also in Tamil, Telugu, Malayalam, Kannada (by turns, of course) five hours each day, three days in a week. Thereby we shall achieve national integration.

- Fanatical avoidance of English is unnecessary and absurd, also against the spirit of Jawaharlal Nehru's promise to us. In a *Janavani* programme recently, should not the lady (who I presume was a Minister of Health from the eminent seat she occupied) have had the goodness to give intelligible advice to a Madrassi who narrated a long tale of woe of his experience in a hospital. He had had an accident and had to go through a major operation at the hospital, and later had to go through a series of further operations, owing to some mistakes in the handling of his case at the first stage, and then he had to undergo prolonged treatment for a variety of infections acquired at the hospital ward from linen, food and surroundings. The Minister appeared to give him a patient hearing, but vouched no direct reply. She suddenly turned to the officer and spoke volubly in impeccable Hindi, leaving the complainant, as well as us, guessing. She might probably have ordered the immediate liquidation of the poisonous hospital. Or she might have said, 'Let the wretch learn Hindi before presuming to criticize our medical services. Meanwhile keep the file pending until the man approaches us again properly.'

PERMITTED LAUGHTER

I SUPPOSE ONE may now look back with relief on the passing of a phase of our existence when every journalist in the country was menaced or manacled unless he wrote what he plainly saw was nonsense or, worse, untruth. Day after day the editor, the publisher and the feature writer had to hold their breath and await directions from an individual who might be decent and intelligent in private life, but who had to function as a censor and could survive only by a show of extreme mindlessness and pugnacity.

A deadly monotony had seized our newspapers and the distinction between one newspaper and another was lost. All papers and journals sounded alike, as if they had been drilled to sing in a chorus. But the reader would not be taken in—he glanced down the column mechanically and distrusted every word in it. Even such a serious matter as shots being fired at a candidate during an election campaign left him unmoved and he just commented, 'Oh, it is just another piece of fiction put out for some purpose. Wait till tomorrow and you will know why.' The average citizen was convinced that day by day he was being fed on exaggeration, half-truths, quarter-truths and mini-truths, if not lies; and he steeled himself against their influence.

*

Those who were responsible for this unholy situation, however, fell victims to their own falsehoods. Into the citadel of authority no other kind of report penetrated except what they liked to hear, often a feedback of the stuff they themselves had generated.

In ancient times, as the dramatists have presented it to us, it was not unusual for a king to question his minister from time to time without putting even his nose out of the window: 'Are we getting three rains a month unfailingly?'

'Yes, of course, Your Majesty.'

'Our subjects continue to be contented and loyal?'

'Yes, undoubtedly, Your Majesty.' Whereupon the king switched his mind off state matters and returned to his domestic pursuits. An extreme instance of this condition I read about in history: One Ganga Raja, ruler of Sivasamudram in AD 16, was playing chess in the harem and casually enquired what the uproar that reached his ears meant, and was told by his minister, 'Oh, a lot of noisy children are playing outside the palace gate.' The king continued his chess game until the insurgents reached his chamber and cut short his chess game as well as his career.

What a censor will not realize is that truth cannot be kept hermetically sealed under a lid. It will be out in all sorts of unexpected ways like a blob of mercury pressed under one's thumb.

It was in the above context that I viewed Laxman's cartoons, banned during the Emergency, bearing out my hopeful statement to him in the dismal days that he would survive his censor.

VAYUDOOT

VAYUDOOT IS MUCH in the news today. Two years ago I had the honour of inaugurating the service at Mysore with garland, speech, tea and biscuits. The inauguration was spectacular but the arrangements for the flight seemed casual and unconvincing. There was no sort of runway within sight—only a grass field with cattle grazing peacefully, around a little cottage which is called 'Mandakalli Aerodrome' and which resembles a one-roomed forest inspection bungalow, with a tiny toilet in a corner. We the citizens of Mysore have been agitating for over three decades for an 'adult' airport. We have put forth excellent reasons why Mysore should be included in the air map: every week Mysore receives several thousand visitors and tourists, who come by bus or train, and Mysore is a venue for frequent conferences, meetings, seminars and academic activities—these and other reasons are reiterated from time to time by august bodies such as the Chamber of Commerce, Rotary, the Lions, City Corporation, and so on, but without effect. 'Mandakalli' remains what it was thirty-five years ago.

The Dornier can take in only eighteen passengers at a time, but the congregation has the appearance of a milling crowd in the mini-hall, with all kinds of makeshift arrangements for checking in the passengers. The tiny toilet at the corner serves for security-checking of women passengers, while the men are frisked and searched before an assembly of onlookers.

After the speeches and photographs we march towards the Dornier, which is sitting prettily on the grass field, white and looking like a magnificent cow grazing. We climb a couple of steps grasping a rope for hand-rail, and occupy our seats. So far all is well and comfortable—until the engine is started and that seems to be the end of one's auditory facilities. I have never experienced such a monstrous assault on my eardrums before or after. I have no choice but to bear it until we land in Bangalore after thirty minutes. For more than ten days, the tremor of my eardrums persisted, necessitating several visits to an ear specialist. Later I wrote a detailed letter to the Minister for Civil Aviation of my experience in the Dornier. Perhaps we were on the threshold of a brand new National Malady: 'Dornier Syndrome'. Days passed, but there was no sign of an acknowledgement from the Minister. I was not surprised, but felt guilty of squandering a couple of hundred words which I could have put to better use professionally.

Later at Parliament, I came face to face with Mr Jagdish Tytler and mentioned my letter to him so far remaining unacknowledged. He had no idea of what I was talking about. I repeated the essential part of my letter wherein I had suggested that while they were at it, they should make the Dornier cabin soundproof in order to save our ears. He showed no symptom of following my speech; I thought I was mumbling inaudibly and wondered whether I should raise my *sruti*. While I was speculating thus, he turned on his heels and vanished.

The Dornier stands cleared by the Safety Board—now, as it seems, to the extent of assuring us that the door will not fall off again in mid-air, as it happened during a flight from Delhi.

As far as I am concerned, I decided that my inaugural flight in a Dornier would be my final one too, when I heard that after the inauguration ceremony the service had to be suspended for some days, owing to the engine catching fire in one place, the propeller getting out of commission another time, when according to rumours, a poor loader got entangled in it, and some other mishap another day. Fortunately the mishaps and snags occur only on the ground, and not at 7,000 feet. Perhaps that is what the Safety Board's certificate means!

ON WALKING

I HAVE BEEN all my life a walker. I used to walk along the tree-shaded trunk road leading out of the city of Mysore, in every direction, on the roads leading to the forests of Bandipur or Karapur, from my home in Laxmipuram, or amble along the base of Chamundi hill through rugged paths, reach Lalitha Mahal Palace on the East horizon and return home after nearly five hours of walking, brooding, thinking and making plans for my future or my writing, usually on weekends or during those years when I failed in my exams and studied privately, without having to attend classes, for next year's chance (which I considered a blessed state as it left me in a state of unalloyed freedom).

My father, though a disciplinarian and a strict headmaster of our high school, did not mind what I did; he didn't have faith in the educational system. He left me free to read whatever I liked out of the school library. Wandering about morning and evening, I felt intoxicated by the charms of nature. The air was clean and pure, the avenue trees were in bloom. In the evening I walked about two or three miles around the Kukara Halli Tank, listened to the soft splash of wavelets on the shore and watched the display of colours in the western sky. I do not mind repeating what I have said earlier in my essays, that the sunset in Mysore is unique and not seen anywhere else in the world.

I went round the tank and then sat on a bench on the bund. A little farther off, on another bench, I could see Venkatappa, a distinguished artist of Mysore who arrived at about 4.30 in the afternoon every day and watched the sky all evening, well past dusk, and then rose to go. He wore a white dhoti and a coat over it, crowned with a turban; an umbrella was tucked under his arm in all seasons. He sought no company, was content to commune with the sky till the last splash of colour vanished.

He was a bachelor and a recluse, was dedicated to painting, a genius who sought no patrons or admirers, a totally self contained man. He has left several watercolours, paintings which are to be seen at the Jagan Mohan Palace Gallery and at Bangalore. He had a few friends who were on visiting terms with him and who saw his pictures in progress and listened to his veena, as he was also devoted to music. I am straying away from my original theme, which was walking, and which includes landscape, which in turn includes stars and the sky and the lake and Venkatappa rapt in watching the wonderful spectacles. People knew him only at a distance, which he maintained all through life. Though considered a recluse, it seems to me he was more hermit-like.

At sunset I too moved; cobras were said to crawl out of the crevices in the pile of rugged stone forming the bund. I walked to the marketplace to jostle with the crowd. In all, morning and evening, I must have walked ten miles a day without any reckoning or purpose in walking. I walked because I enjoyed it and had the leisure. While walking, my mind became active and helped my writing.

I kept up this pace for years wherever I happened to be—although nature was not the same everywhere as in Mysore. That charm and abandon could not normally continue owing to new responsibilities and changing routine, but I continued my walking as a habit wherever I might be—until last year when I fell ill and had to stay in a hospital for a few weeks. When my condition improved, I was permitted to walk again in regulated doses. 'You may walk up to that cottage number 24, with the nurse's help . . .' And then, 'Be sure to walk for ten minutes exactly, from your bedroom to the hall in your home.' As I progressed, I was permitted more time—thirty or forty minutes in the park. I have lost the habit of walking in the street, dodging the scooters and autorickshaws and the potholes and pitfalls so strictly preserved by the Corporation. Nowadays, I walk in the park near my home both in Madras and Mysore, arriving there in my car.

The park is a world in itself. Here you see a variety of motives in operation. The men who walk for athletic reasons, not a few, seem to be in training for the Olympics. Jogging, running, with upraised arms or swinging them in windmill fashion, stopping in their tracks to bend down, stretch or kick imaginary balls, jumping high and low, with not a care for others in their path. For me these Human Windmills are a terror.

Those who are here on medical advice are easily spotted from the style by which they carry themselves, pushing forward as if punishing themselves for all the years of stagnation and neglect. Some of them walk as if chased by a tiger, heaving, panting and perspiring. The doctor must have advised, 'Take a brisk walk, don't slouch or amble long.' And they practice an unaccustomed exercise. There is always a group of older men seated on the bench on the lawn, perhaps *vanaprasthas,* talking of old times and current politics and comparing one another's health.

Young couples sitting in remote corners, in the shelter of bushes, conversing in whispers, their backs turned to the public. Day after day they sit there, I get very curious to know what they are saying. Of course, there must be an affirmation of each other's dedication, devotion. It can't go on being repeated a thousand times day after day *ad nauseam.* They must have other things to talk about: their homes and parents or the hurdles in their way.

I would give anything to understand them, I wish them well and success to their romance. I know the whispers will cease ultimately, once they become man and wife. You can't go on whispering all your life. There will come a natural phase when you will shout at each other in the course of an argument or spend long pauses of silence, sitting in two chairs and staring ahead at a wall, a tree, with no subject left for conversation. All that could be said has been said, followed by an unmitigated, pregnant silence. A perfect attunement and communication of minds has been attained where speech is superfluous. In Kamban's *Ramayana* when Rama and Sita are left alone after the wedding, they remain silent, having nothing to say. The poet explains, 'Those who were always together eternally as Vishnu and Lakshmi and separated only a moment ago have no need to talk.'

A couple come and part at the gate and move in opposite directions without uttering a word, reminding me of Byron's line: 'When we two parted in silence and tears.' Fresh young couples are however cheerful and relaxed, commenting on flowers and plants and smiling all through, especially if they have a toddler with them.

Students sit in little groups here and there. Cheerless and grim, anxiety writ large on their faces, desperately making up for wasted months. I sometimes enquire what they are studying and what their hopes are. They do not seem to mind the disturbance. Sometimes I ask to see the book in their hands. They are always glad to be interrupted. Last week I looked through a book that they were trying to 'mug up'. It was a bazaar 'guide' to English Prose for BA. Leafing through I found my name listed in the contents with two stories included. The stories were paraphrased, annotated in Tamil and summarized in English.

Two thousand words of my composition reduced to twenty words expertly, with definitions of 'difficult' phrases and possible questions and answers. The young men, the examinees, found this tabloid presentation more clear-headed and acceptable than the original. With these, they might also attain a First Class in English. I wondered for a moment if I should declare my authorship of the two stories, but I returned the glorious guide to them and passed on, not being sure if they could bear to see a live author and also because I was not sure I could answer if they questioned me on my stories, as they were likely to be more up-to-date with the subject.

THE ENEMIES

WE ARE IN the habit of honouring the memory of personalities who have served society in some role or other—patriots, poets, scientists, engineers, inventors, saints, composers and so on, and who have deepened and enriched human experience in different ways. I was once on a committee of All India Radio, the agenda at a particular meeting being to commemorate regularly the services and achievements of national heroes. As a first step we tried to compile a list of names, and realized soon that we had before us over six hundred names to honour, which meant six hundred hours of broadcasting even if we allotted one hour a day for this programme. The proposal seemed unpractical and was turned over to the care of a sub-committee and was lost sight of.

Later my thoughts proceeded in another direction. Why not compile a directory of enemies of society? This enemy does not rob or shoot, but invents something which causes damage and destruction, unintentionally though. For example, the man who first got the idea of polishing floor tiles created a disastrous fashion, a potential cause of damage and misery. The biped is precariously balanced on two slender supports, which have to bear an increasing load as one grows older. In childhood one keeps tumbling a great deal but recovers quickly from bruises on elbows and knees, but the adult whose foot slips cannot recover so easily, and then at an advanced age even a slight skidding may prove deadly. Observe an orthopaedic clinic, and you will have an idea of the number of fractures of hips and thighs that occur each day, after a fall mostly in a bathroom. It is suicidal to polish the bathroom floor and to fit therein a shiny porcelain bathtub in which you will have to progress at the pace of a tightrope walker. I remember the instance of the missing host when the *griha pravesam* ceremony was in full swing in a new house. He had skidded while emerging from the tornado shower over the bathtub. The bathroom door was ultimately broken open and the master of ceremonies rescued. We need not go into unhappy details, but suffice to say that he was immobilized for a year. A dazzling bathtub and a mirror-finish flooring are a deadly combination. It is surprising that those who build fashionable houses prefer to live dangerously all life. I hear frequently, 'Everything is ready, but for the floor-polisher who is delaying . . .' When I hear that I feel like bursting out, 'Keep him off please, for heaven's sake, and may your limbs and joints remain intact when you come to live in your new home.'

Now to turn to another kind of enemy: he does not contrive to trip you up, but tries to destroy you from the top by shattering your eardrums. In this category the inventor of the air horn must take the first place. If I have to erect a statue in order to demolish it later to mark my protest, I'd choose the inventor of the air horn for the honour. It is the least wanted invention at a time when we seem to be seeking protection from 'noise' all day, in all places. No invention is more uninvited and pernicious. The damage it does to your eardrums is incalculable. When a bus or lorry screams past one's path or at one's rear while driving, the noise attacks, shatters, squashes and deprives one of all judgement and paralyses all thought and conversation and concentration; and it takes a quarter of an hour at least to recover from its effects, and then comes along the next one screaming off the previous one, and so on in a succession.

Young men who pull out the silencer from their motorcycles must also be enrolled in the blacklist. There are enough laws and regulations to prohibit all such evils, but they are not enforced in our tolerant society.

The man who invented the loudspeaker must also go into the blacklist. One is thankful for the police regulation in Madras banning trumpet speakers through which organizers of ceremonials spread film music and political harangue night and day, sometimes far into the night. When the suppliers of loudspeakers went on a strike for a day recently as a protest, no strike was more welcome. One felt like shouting, 'Keep it up for ever.'

The World of the Writer

At various times during his long writing career, Narayan penned down his thoughts on the curious predicament of the Indian writer writing in English. Taken together, the pieces in this section provide a fascinating overview of the business of writing from one of the modern masters of the art.

RELUCTANT GURU

WHEN I ACCEPTED an invitation to become a Visiting Professor at a certain mid-western University, I had no clear notion as to what it meant. I asked myself again and again what does a Visiting Professor do. I also asked several of my friends in the academic world the same question. No one could give me a concrete or a convincing answer and so I contented myself with the thought that a Visiting Professor just visits and professes and if he happens to be in the special category of 'DVP' (Distinguished Visiting Professor) he also tries to maintain and flourish his distinguishing qualities. Well, all that seemed to suit me excellently.

I had plunged into the role after warning my sponsors in the initial stages of our correspondence that I was a mere novice in academic matters and that it'd be up to them to see that I did not make a fool of myself on their campus.

So, on the first morning, I reported myself at the English Department of the University. The Chairman of the Department who had arranged my visit was a distinguished scholar and critic, who, among other things, had also made a detailed, deep study of my writing.

I asked him what I should do now and he kept asking in his turn what I would like to do, the only definite engagement for the day he was aware of being that I was to be photographed at two o'clock. I sat brooding.

'Yesterday this time, Bangalore . . . Bombay . . . Rome . . .

London . . . New York . . . or was it the day before? Time gets lost in space.' I was still jet-dazed after thirty-six hours in the air.

He called up his secretary and told her, 'Here is Narayan. Please give him a room where he can feel comfortable, meet people or read or write as he may like. Please also find out if any of the English classes want him, and schedule his visits.' So on the first day I had nothing much to do except pose outside the building for a photographer against the signpost announcing 'English Dept'.

Most of the days following, I was left free to walk, think, or read, and generally live as I pleased.

The secretary busied herself and ultimately produced a time-table for me. She would telephone me in my room to say, '11.35 tomorrow, Professor —'s class at — hall—'

'Where is it?' I would ask, slightly worried how to locate it in this vast sprawling campus and reach it in time, punctuality being my nightmare.

'It's on 52nd and anyway you don't bother about it. A car will come to fetch you.' She arranged it all with precision and forethought, not demanding more than a couple of hours a week of my time in the coming weeks.

On stepping into my very first class I felt startled, as it consisted of elderly women, each one holding a copy of *The Guide* in her hand.

I was pleased no doubt at finding my book in so many hands, but I also felt uneasy. If they cross-examined me on my book, I should feel lost; they had the advantage over me of being up-to-date with the details of my story. I stiffened into a defensive attitude, and became wary, as I took my seat.

I was also struck with their enthusiasm—elderly women who doubtless had their families, homes, children and grandchildren (one member was eighty-six years old) to mind, but who still found the time to take a seat in a class-room and study English literature, which was how my book was classified.

I sat wondering where to begin and what to say. But luckily for me their regular professor who had fetched me, eased the situation with an introductory speech, and straightaway invited the members of the class to ask questions. This is always a good method as it gives an audience something to do instead of sitting back, passively watching the speaker's predicament. One member asked as usual whether I had based my novel on some actual experience or if it was pure fiction. A familiar question, which I generally answer evasively, since I myself do not know; and also I don't see how it should make any difference to the reader. Next question was if the town Malgudi (the setting of my novels) was imaginary or real. I played the ball back by asking what was the difference between the two. Next I was asked if India was full of saints, and whether the hero of *The Guide*, who is mistaken for a saint, and later compelled to become one, was typical, and if my novel itself was 'typical' of India (typical—did it imply that my readers expect the majority of the 550 million citizens of India to go through a phase similar to the one portrayed in my novel?). I had to repeat here, and later, everywhere, that a novel is about an individual living his life in a world imagined by the author, performing a set of actions (up to a limit) contrived by the author. But to take a work of fiction as a sociological study or a social document could be very misleading. My novel *The Guide* was not about the saints or the pseudo-saints of India, but about a particular person. I do not think that my explanation carried any conviction as they continued to ask in every class, outside the class, at the quadrangle, the university centre, the roadside or anywhere, the same question. Added to this the city newspaper took a special interest in my visit and featured me and my work. A reporter interviewed me, and tried to elicit my views of life after death, which happened to be the theme of my novel *The English Teacher*. I was asked if I believed in death. I was asked if I thought it possible to communicate with spirits. I was asked if I had seen a ghost, if I was prone to mystic experience. I answered the questions candidly, emphasizing the fact that I wrote fiction. When the interview appeared in the paper I found it charmingly written but over-emphasizing my mystic aspect! This led to a very complex situation for me during the rest of my sojourn on that campus. More and more people began to ask, 'Do you believe in mysticism?' 'Can anyone practise yoga?' 'What are the steps to a mystic state?' The words—mysticism, metaphysics, philosophy, yoga and ghost contacts—all came to be mixed up. At first it was amusing but day after day when I found people on the campus looking on me with awe and wonder, perhaps saying to themselves, 'There goes the man who holds the key to a mystic life!' I began to despair how I could ever rise to that sublime level. Apart from the students, I realized that even some of the staff members were affected by this notion. A senior professor of the English Department approached me once to ask if I would meet her students. I agreed, since that was the purpose of my sojourn on the campus. Nearer the time of the actual engagement, I met her again to work out the details. 'What am I expected to do in your class?' I asked.

She replied promptly, 'My students want to hear you on Indian mysticism.'

I told her point blank, 'I know nothing about it.'

'That shouldn't matter at all,' she said.

'Of course it matters a great deal to me. When I go to a class I should like to speak on a subject which I know or at least have a pretence of knowing. I do not wish to parade my ignorance in a class-room.'

She seemed to think that it was an extraordinary piece of diffidence on my part and said encouragingly, 'Please, half-an-hour will be enough. You can tell them anything you like about mysticism, just for thirty minutes.'

'Not even for half-a-minute. Why did you commit me to this engagement?'

Her answer was startling, 'Because they have demanded it. They want you to talk on Indian mysticism.'

Two points emerged from this conversation:

(1) The word 'demand' arising from the students' side as to what was to be taught. (2) Mysticism.

These were the real pivotal points on which the entire academic situation seemed to revolve. I heard later that the students' representatives met the faculty members in order to specify what they wished to be taught in the class-rooms. They wanted to brighten up (and also broaden) English literary studies, with a lot of interesting, though not relevant, additions to their reading lists. This was the basis of their demand for Indian mysticism from me. I had a chance to observe how some teachers were trying to rise to the occasion. I knew a couple of young men from India, doing their post-graduate course in English, also holding assistantships, who spoke on a different theme each day to their students. One day it'd be Fitzgerald's translation of Omar Khayyam, another day Ramakrishna, or Vivekananda, a third day on Yoga or the theory of incarnation, a fourth day on Buddhism, and on the fifth back to English literature. It was amazing with what agility they managed all this, while the seniors pored over 'black literature' and tried to include it in their talks, discussions and seminars. In all this process there was an apparent widening of knowledge, but it actually produced shallowness. I could not help wondering if all this show of adaptability and resilience on the part of the teacher was not creating an amorphous, diffuse academic climate and if they were not becoming responsible for creating a set of hollow minds, echoing the mere sound of book titles, and regarding themselves as being versatile. Finally I questioned them, how in such a world of hotchpotch studies any examination could be conducted. I realized immediately that I was sounding hopelessly antiquated, as promptly came the reply that the examinee could frame his own questions and write the answers. I did not know if this was a universal practice or only peculiar to this university. Or if this particular Indian lecturer was joking about it. In any case, I found that these two young men were extremely popular. One of them grew a tiny beard and the other left untended his nape-draping tresses, and both looked and sounded so convincing as versatile semi-(demi)mystics that they were keenly sought after by their students. Their weekends were crowded with social activities, in addition to a regular schedule of dating. I asked, 'What is dating? How far does one go?'

'It depends, anything from sitting around eating and drinking to making love,' came the reply.

I asked, 'What of the responsibilities after dating?'

They replied, 'None. I and my friend have decided not to go steady under any circumstances, but marry only in India after we get back.' I visited their apartment and found it bare, with a few rolls of mat on the floor, and books all over the place. I suppose there was an aroma of incense. One of them constantly said, 'I am much interested in Yoga and am teaching my boys Yoga.'

I asked him, 'Have you studied Patanjali's *Yoga Sutra?*'

He looked a little bewildered and said, 'Not yet but I will . . .' He finally said, 'What does it matter what I read or teach? Whatever book I may recommend they will read only Vatsyayana's *Kama-Sutra.* The campus book store can hardly keep up with the demand, boys and girls devour this book and seem to know nothing else about India, nor care.'

Whether through *Kama-Sutra* or mysticism, India is very much in everybody's thoughts, particularly among the American youth. And this was not a passing phase or a mere affectation. I realized presently that there was much validity in this search and I met many young men here and there, invited them to my room, and answered their questions about India. I give here a composite report of my talk to various persons at different times.

Young friend (I said), perhaps you think that all Indians are spiritually preoccupied. We aren't, we have a large background of religion and plenty of inner resources, but normally we also have to be performing ordinary tasks, such as working, earning, living and breeding. In your view, perhaps, you think that in an Indian street, you can see bearded men floating about in a state of levitation. Far from it. We have traffic, crowds, shops, pimps, pickpockets, policemen and what not as in any other country. We have our own students' agitations—but they are for different causes, sometimes political, sometimes personal and sometimes academic, and sometimes inexplicable. Your opposite number in our country would not be wearing beads and beards and untouched long hair as you do (how smartly your Barbers' Association withdrew a rather rash resolution to increase the rate for a haircut from 2.50 to 3 dollars!), but tight pants and coloured shirts and 'Beatles' crop-cut. The Indian student would not normally bother about eternity, but about his immediate employment prospects after graduation. You have to realize that unemployment among the educated classes is a grim reality in our country; and a young person has to overcome this deficiency before aspiring for the luxuries of a mystic state.

Of course, you are fed up with affluence, gadgets, mobility and organization, and he is fed up with poverty, manual labour, stagnation and disorganization. Your search is for a 'guru' who can promise you instant mystic elation; whereas your counterpart looks for a Foundation Grant. The young person in my country would sooner learn how to organize a business or manufacture an atom bomb or an automobile than how to stand on one's head.

As a matter of fact, if you question him, you will find that our young man has not given any serious thought to Yoga and such subjects. Perhaps at a later date he may take to it when his more materialistic problems are over and when he begins to note that it's quite the fashion in your part of the world. At the moment the trend appears to be that he is coming in your direction, and you are going in his. So, logically speaking, in course of time, you may have to come to India for technology and the Indian will have to come to your country for spiritual research.

The belief in my spiritual adeptness was a factor that could not be easily shaken. I felt myself in the same situation as Raju, the hero of my *Guide* who was mistaken for a saint and began to wonder at some point himself if a sudden effulgence had begun to show in his face. I found myself in a similar situation. My telephone rang at five o'clock one morning and I scrambled out of my bed. The man at the other end announced himself as a scientist, a research scholar, and said, 'Do you know what has happened today? The Chairman of our department summoned us and announced that he was not going to renew our assistantships next term, which may mean that I cut short my stay and return to India. Do you know if this will happen?' I could not understand what he was saying or why. I even wondered if I might be listening to a telephone in a dream!

'How should I know,' I asked and added, 'but my immediate curiosity is to know why you have thought fit to call me at this hour?'

He answered, 'Don't you get up at four for your meditations? I thought that at this hour, you'd be in a state of mind to know the future.'

Evidently this scientist had caught the general trend in the atmosphere. While I could appreciate an average American's notion that every Indian was a mystic, I was rather shocked in this instance, since I expected an Indian himself to know better. But here was this young man from India convinced that I was an astrologer and mystic combined. He dogged my steps. Although he gave up calling me at dawn, he followed me about with requests to impart to him the secrets of my attainments, to show him the way, to tell him whether he was destined to get his doctorate, whether his wife's impending confinement (in India) would be safely gone through and so on and so forth. Actually, after lunch one afternoon, he took me aside to ask, 'What should I do to get a glimpse of Goddess Kali? Will she appear before me?' in the tone of one who was trying to know the TV channel on which a particular show would be coming. When I denied any knowledge of it myself, he just looked pained, but he also looked determined to get at me ultimately when he would gather in both hands all the secrets of meditation, astrology, and spiritual powers that I now kept away from him, for reasons best known to a 'guru' of my stature.

THE PROBLEM OF THE INDIAN
WRITER

ALL IMAGINATIVE WRITING in India has had its origin in the *Ramayana* and the *Mahabharata*, the ten-thousand-year-old epics of India. An author picked up an incident or a character out of one or the other and created a new work with it, similar to Shakespeare's transmutation of Holinshed's *Chronicle* or Plutarch's *Lives*. Kalidasa's *Shakuntala* (fifth century AD), one of the world's masterpieces, was developed out of an incident in the *Mahabharata*. Apart from this type of work, many ancient writers dedicated their lives to the rewriting of the *Ramayana* or the *Mahabharata* according to their own genius. Tulasidas wrote the *Ramayana* in Hindi, Kamban in Tamil, and Kumaravyasa wrote the *Mahabharata* in Kannada. Each of these authors devoted his lifetime to the fulfilment of one supreme task, the stylus with which he wrote etching the stanzas on dry palm leaves hour after hour and day after day for thirty, forty or fifty years, before a book came into being. The completion of a literary work was marked by ceremony and social rejoicing. Economic or commercial considerations had no place in a writer's life, the little he needed coming to him through royal patronage or voluntary gifts. The work was read out to the public assembled in a temple hall or under the shade of a tree. Men, women and children listened to the reading with respectful attention for a few hours every evening. A literary work lived not so much through the number of copies scattered over the world as in the mind and memory of readers and their listeners, and passed on by word of mouth from generation to generation.

These traditions were modified by historical changes. Let us skip a great deal of intervening history and come down to British times. The English language brought with it not only a new type of literature but all the world's literature in translation. New forms such as the novel and short story came to be noticed, revealing not only new artistic possibilities for a writer but also stimulating a new social awareness. Our early stories dealt with impossible romance, melodrama and adventure on one side and on the other exposed the evils of certain social customs such as early marriage, the dowry system, suttee, and caste prejudices. Many of the realistic novels of this period are in effect attacks on the orthodoxies of the day. They suffered from didacticism, but there remained in them a residue of artistic quality, and many books of the early Victorian years survive as novels and stories although their social criticism are out of date.

Between then and now we might note a middle period when all that a writer could write about became inescapably political. There came a time when all the nation's energies were directed to the freeing of the country from foreign rule. Under this stress and preoccupation the mood of comedy, the sensitivity to atmosphere, the probing of psychological factors, the crisis in the individual soul and its resolution, and above all the detached observation, which constitute the stuff of growing fiction, went into the background. It seemed to be more a time for polemics and tract-writing than for story-telling.

Since the attainment of Independence in 1947 this preoccupation has gone, and the writer can now pick his material out of the great events that are taking shape before his eyes. Every writer now hopes to express, through his novels and stories, the way of life of the group of people with whose psychology and background he is most familiar, and he hopes it will not only appeal to his own circle but also to a larger audience outside.

The short story rather than the long novel has been the favourite medium of the fiction-writer in India, because, it seems to me: (1) the short story is the best-suited medium for the variegated material available in the country, (2) the writing of a short story takes less time.

A writer who has to complete a novel has to spend at least a year's labour on it. This complete surrender is something that he cannot afford, since most writers write only part-time while they have to be doing something else for a living. Fiction-writing as a full-time occupation has still to be recognized. For that what is primarily needed is a sound publishing organization. Before considering this, however, I have to mention one other factor—that is, the problem of language. The complexity arising from this can be better understood if we remember that there are fifteen languages in India in which writers are doing their jobs today in various regions. Every writer has to keep in mind his own regional language, the national language which is Hindi, the classical language Sanskrit (this is often called a 'dead language' but dead only as a mountain could be dead) and above all the English language which seems nearly inescapable. Some of the regional languages are understood only within limited boundaries and cannot provide more than a few thousand (or even a few hundred) readers for a book. A really livelihood-giving sale for a writer can be obtained only on an all-India basis. That being so, whatever may be the original language of the writing, the urgent need is to have an organization, a sort of literary clearing-house and translation service, which can give a writer a countrywide audience. As conditions are, there is no general publishing in this country. There are several publishing firms but they are only concerned with the manufacture of school-texts, which alone, by diligent manoeuvering, can give a publisher (and incidentally his author) a five-figure public. It must also be admitted that on the other side all is not well with the public either. A certain amount of public apathy for book-buying is depressingly evident everywhere. An American publisher once asked me how many copies of my *Bachelor of Arts* (in the Pocket Book series costing a rupee and eight annas) sold in my own town (Mysore). I suggested two hundred as a possible figure.

'What is the population of your town?' he asked.

'Over two hundred and seventy five thousand.'

'How many among them can read a novel like yours?'

'At least five thousand,' I ventured.

'How many among them know you personally and like your work in general?'

'Probably all of them and many more.'

'How many among them could afford to pay a rupee odd for your book.'

'Perhaps all of them!'

'In that case what prevents five thousand copies being sold in your own town rather than two hundred?'

I could not answer the question. I am still thinking it over. I think it is for experts in the trade to discover a solution, and when that is done, a major obstacle in the fiction-writer's way in India will have been removed.

*

In a well-ordered society there should be no problem at all for a writer. It should be possible for a writer to dash off a book in six months and see it automatically reach his reader, thus enabling him to enjoy a few months of rest, holiday and reading so that he may begin a new book at the end of it. How well should a society be ordered before this can happen? What are the things that a dynamic reformer should undertake before he can create congenial conditions in which fiction-writing may flourish?

The writer of a novel is afflicted with peculiar problems. For one thing, the novel is a comparatively recent form in our country and though people have taken to the reading of novels in order to while away their time it never occurs to anyone to ask seriously who writes them. It never occurs to anyone that no novel may be available for entertainment or instruction unless the author is kept in working order. What are the things necessary to keep this man in working condition? All sorts of amenities are devised in order to solve the difficulties of all kinds of workers. Even journalists, hitherto the most neglected of men, have come to state their aims and demand their welfare conditions. But the novelist has as yet no code of social existence. The trouble is the novelist has not attained a vocal status.

The first problem of a novelist is that he must live without too many harassments and distractions. It is necessary that he should arrive at a sort of compromise between his inner life and outer life. A writer's life is a subjective one, and it may not always be feasible for him to discharge his duties competently, as a captain steering the ship of family in the ocean of existence. Though he may be unexcelled as a writer of fiction, the facts, the hard-headed facts of life, may prove beyond his powers. I mean by hard and harsh facts such activities as balancing the budget, looking after dependents, calculating various things and so forth. He is likely to make grave errors of calculation when dealing with numbers, not because he does not know addition and subtraction but (his mind being all the time in the realm of fiction) because his cash in hand may appear exaggerated in value. He is likely to acquire the satisfaction warranted by the possession of 10,000 rupees when all that he has on hand is fifty rupees. This is rather a disproportionate way of dealing with figures but that is how he is and no one can help it. It is not a realistic manner of living and tackling the problems of life but what can he do, he is made that way, it is the only manner in which he can live and work. This creates peculiar difficulties for those who have to live along with him. However realistic a writer he may be he is likely to prove to be the most dreamy of persons on earth, and the demands of practical life may prove bewildering if not actually distressing to him, and against this he always needs something like a cushion between him and crude realities. I don't know what kind of organization could achieve this purpose but if something could be done to relieve him from the necessity of running a family, paying off bills, meeting creditors, and other such odious and devitalizing occupations, he will do his work in peace and the public may ultimately feel gratified that it has more books to read.

To understand this implication fully one must first have an idea of the method of his work. The novelist has to live close to life and keep himself open to its influence if he is to prove successful as a writer. His mind must pick out the material from life, shape it and use it. He is likely to be always busy planning the next chapter. Whether he is the type that sits down methodically to dash off a fixed quota of work each day, or whether he is the one to seize upon his work and go through it in a frenzy without a pause, the actual time of sitting down at one's desk can never be an indication of the quantity of work involved. Whatever may be the actual time spent at his desk, he is always busy. His mind is always at work. There is no such thing as finishing a piece of work for the day and rising from his seat with a free mind. There is no end to the work till the novel is completed, and if one remembers that a novel takes a minimum of 80,000 words, one may understand the labours involved. Many persons ask me whether I have in mind all the details of a novel beforehand, whether I work out an outline, or how a novel comes into being at all. I wish I could answer that question with precision. I know one thing, when I sit down to write I have no more than a vague idea regarding the outcome of the day's work. It would be not far wrong if I said that my fingers on the typewriter probably know more about what is coming on than my head. It is perhaps no compliment to myself, but I do not intend it to be. The details of what I write each day, when I am at work on a novel, work themselves out. This means that one's subconscious self should have a lot of unimpaired freedom. Writing a novel is both a conscious and unconscious occupation; it is something both of the intellect and something superior to the intellect. That means the mind should be left completely free to continue to exercise itself at all levels. The intellect portion of it pertains mostly to technique and expression, and not to the ultimate shape of the thing, though there is always a possibility that the novelist has some idea of the shape of things to come, and to that extent his mind is burdened.

When he sits down on a certain day to begin a new novel, it must be understood that he is undertaking a task which will virtually chain him up for months to come. Even if he is a fast worker, apart from the actual writing it may bind him down for nearly two years. And then he has to spend a few months revising the manuscript, because it always seems to be incomplete and not quite satisfactory. Here revision means watching over 80,000 words and their punctuation, while trying to test the validity and worth of every word. I say nothing of the misgiving that may suddenly assail one about the sense of what one has been writing. It is always there and may involve the scrapping of months of work. Let us grant he has satisfactorily settled all the mechanical details of his work, and has parcelled off the manuscript to his publisher. This is his happiest day. He feels like a schoolboy who has written his last examination of the season, looks back with a shudder on his days of drudgery and looks forward to a happy summer vacation ahead. Now, how far can this author afford to keep away from writing after his two years of labour? If he is to be in a fit condition to give the world his best again, he must rest and recuperate while giving time for the spring of his inspiration to well up again. For that it must be possible for him to afford to rest: the work that he has done must reach the public and must be accepted by the public. When all is said and done it is only public support that can sustain an author. It is important that his work should appear in the bookstalls and that the public must show enthusiasm for it. This alone can help him to live by his best work. This alone can prevent his preoccupation with pot-boiling activities, whereby he pumps himself dry and goes on producing third-rate stuff when he ought to be resting. What exactly can give him this freedom? It is that state of society whereby the publishing activity is organized so well that a good book reaches its readers without delay. From this point of view the novelist in our country suffers greatly. As I've said earlier there is not a general publishing business here as in other countries. There are few publishers who are interested in publishing, advertising and getting the work of a new writer. For this cooperation from all is required, from the press which must make new books known through its literary columns, booksellers who must keep the book in stock, and more than anything else a responsive and appreciative public which buys the book. I use the word 'buy' deliberately. It certainly connotes a different activity from reading, which may be done with borrowed books. It may give an author a vast reading public without any relief or reward. A book-buying campaign must be started on a nationwide scale. Buying books and building a home library must become a citizen's duty, which will have the double advantage of both rewarding the labours of the author and providing a general atmosphere of culture in every home.

ENGLISH IN INDIA

WHEN I WAS five years old I was initiated into the mysteries of letters with the appropriate religious ceremonies. I was taught to shape the first two letters of the alphabet with corn spread out on a tray, both in Sanskrit and Tamil. Sanskrit, because it was the classical language of India, Tamil because it was the language of the province in which I was born and my mother tongue. But in the classroom neither of these two languages was given any importance; they were assigned to the most helpless among the teachers, the pundits who were treated as a joke by the boys, since they taught only the 'second language', the first being English as ordained by Lord Macaulay when he introduced English education in India. English was taught be the best teacher in the school, if not by the ruling star of the institution, the headmaster himself. The English Primer itself looked different from the other books in the school-bag with its strong binding and coloured illustration, for those were days when educational material was imported and no one could dream of producing a school-book in India. The first lesson in the glossy Primer began 'A was an Apple Pie' (or was it just Apple, I don't remember), and went on to explain, 'B bit it' and 'C cut it'. The activities of B and C were understandable, but the opening line itself was mystifying. What was an Apple Pie? From B's and C's zestful application, we could guess that it had to do with some ordinary business of mankind, such as eating. But what was it that was being eaten? Among fruits we were familiar with the mango, banana, guava, pomegranate and grape, but not the apple (in our part of the country), much less an Apple Pie. To our eager questioning, the omniscient one, our English teacher, would just state, 'It must be some stuff similar to our idli, but prepared with apple.' This information was inadequate and one popped up to ask, 'What would it taste like? Sweet or sour?' The teacher's patience now being at an end, he would say, 'Don't be a nuisance, read our lesson,' a peremptory order which we obeyed by reciting like a litany: 'A was an Apple Pie.' We were left free to guess, each according to his capacity, at the quality, shape, and details of the civilization portrayed in our class-books. Other subjects were also taught in English. We brooded over arithmetical problems in which John did a piece of work in half the time that Sam took . . . if they laboured jointly, when would the work be completed? We also wrestled with bushels of oats and wages paid in pounds, shillings and pence, although the characters around us in actual life called themselves Rama and Krishna and handled rupees and annas rather than half-crowns and farthings. Thus we got used to getting along splendidly with unknown quantities in our studies. At a later stage, we read and enjoyed the best of English prose, overlooking detail in the process of enjoying literature. Chaucer and Ben Jonson, Pope and Dryden, Boswell and Goldsmith and a hundred others became almost our next-door neighbours. Through books alone we learnt to love the London of English literature. I have a friend, an engineer, who happening to visit West Germany on a technical mission, took off a fortnight in order to go to England and see the literary landmarks. His literary map included not only Keats's house at Hampstead, but also the amphibian world of the Thames bargemen described in the stories of W.W. Jacobs; he tried to follow the trails of Oliver Twist and David Copperfield, and also obtain, if possible, a glimpse of the comfortable world of Soames Forsyte; nor could he overlook the Drones Club mentioned by P.G. Wodehouse. He rounded off the trip with a visit to Stratford-on-Avon and the Lake District, and returned home feeling profoundly happy. Some time ago a more scholarly work appeared—entitled *My English Pilgrimage* by Professor Sadhan Kumar Ghose—wherein one could find a methodical account of a devoted scholar's travels in search of Literary England past and present.

In our home my father's library was crammed with Carlyle, Ruskin, Walter Pater, and double-column editions of Wordsworth, Byron, Browning and Shakespeare. My father enjoyed reading Carlyle and Ruskin, and persuaded me not to miss them. For his sake I read thirty pages of *The French Revolution, Sartor Resartu*s, and *Miscellaneous Essays;* twenty-five pages of *Marius the Epicurean*; a hundred pages of Fielding and Thackeray, and skipped through a dozen novels of Sir Walter Scott. We also read many European and Greek classics in English translation. We relied on the *Times Literary Supplement, Bookman, London Mercury, Life and Letters,* and the book pages of the weekly journals, for our knowledge of 'contemporary' literature. We enjoyed the literary gossip generated in a society dominated by Shaw, Wells and Chesterton. We were aware of not only what they wrote or were about to write at any given time, but also what they thought of each other and how much they earned in royalties.

For an Indian classical training begins early in life. Epics, mythology and Vedic poetry (of Sanskrit origin and of tremendous antiquity) are narrated to everyone in childhood by the mother or the grandmother in a cosy corner of the house when the day's tasks are done and the lamps are lit. Later one reads them all through one's life with a fresh understanding at each stage. Our minds are trained to accept without surprise characters of godly or demoniac proportions with actions and reactions set in limitless worlds and progressing through an incalculable time-scale.

With the impact of modern literature we began to look at the gods, demons, sages, and kings of our mythology and epics, not as some remote concoctions but as types and symbols, possessing psychological validity even when seen against the contemporary background. When writing we attempted to compress the range of our observation and subject the particle to an intense scrutiny. Passing, inevitably, through phases of symbolic, didactic, or over-dramatic writing, one arrived at the stage of valuing realism, psychological explorations, and technical virtuosity. The effort was interesting, but one had to differ from one's models in various ways. In an English novel, for instance, the theme of romance is based on a totally different conception of the man-woman relationship from ours. We believe that marriages are made in heaven and a bride and groom meet, not by accident or design, but by the decree of fate, the fitness for a match not to be gauged by letting them go through a period of courtship but by a study of their horoscopes; boy and girl meet and love after marriage rather than before. The Eternal Triangle, a standby for a western writer, is worthless as a theme for an Indian, our social circumstances not providing adequate facilities for the Eternal Triangle. We, however, seek excitement in our system of living known as the Joint Family, in which several members of a family live under the same roof. The strains and stresses of this kind of living on the individual, the general structure of a society emerging from it, and the complexities of the caste system, are inexhaustible subjects for us. And the hold of religion and the conception of the gods ingrained in us must necessarily find a place in any accurate portrayal of life. Nor can we overlook the rural life and its problems, eighty-five out of a hundred Indians being village folk.

English has proved that if a language has flexibility any experience can be communicated through it, even if it has to be paraphrased rather than conveyed, and even if the factual detail, as in the case of the Apple Pie, is only partially understood. In order not to lose the excellence of this medium a few writers in India took to writing in English, and produced a literature that was perhaps not first-rate; often the writing seemed imitative, halting, inept or an awkward translation of a vernacular rhetoric, mode, or idiom; but occasionally it was brilliant. We are still experimentalists. I may straightaway explain what we do not attempt to do. We are not attempting to write Anglo-Saxon English. The English language, through sheer resilience and mobility, is now undergoing a process of Indianization in the same manner as it adopted US citizenship over a century ago, with the difference that it is the major language there but here one of the fifteen. I cannot say whether this process of transmutation is to be viewed as an enrichment of the English language or a debasement of it. All that I am able to confirm, after nearly thirty years of writing, is that it has served my purpose admirably, of conveying unambiguously the thoughts and acts of a set of personalities, who flourish in a small town named Malgudi supposed to be located in a corner of south India.

English has been with us for over a century, but it has remained the language of the intelligentsia, less than ten per cent of the population understanding it. In view of this limitation our constitution provides for the changing over of the official language to Hindi in due course. Interestingly, side by side, special institutes are established where English teachers are trained, and the subject occupies a high place in all universities. I feel, however, that it must reach the marketplace and the village green if it is to send down roots. In order to achieve this, the language must be taught in a simpler manner, through a basic vocabulary, simplified spelling, and explained and interpreted through the many spoken languages of India. When such a technique of propagation is perfected, we shall see English, whatever its official status, assimilated in the soil of India and growing again from it.

WHEN INDIA WAS A COLONY

A SUDDEN OUTBREAK of Anglo-India has occurred in the cinema world, involving million-dollar budgets and movement of actors and equipment on a global scale—a minor, modern version of such historic globetrotters as Hannibal, Alexander, Napoleon and heaven knows who else, who moved their hordes and elaborate engines of destruction across continents. Their Indian-oriented counterpart today carries an elaborate load of equipment of a different type—to set up his camp in a strange land, to create illusions of his own choice.

Sir Richard Attenborough's South Africa (of *Gandhi*) was in Poona, David Lean's Chandrapore (of A *Passage to India*, which has recently completed filming) was located in Bangalore, Ootacamund and in Kashmir. First *Gandhi*, now A *Passage to India*, and, in between, *The Far Pavilions, Heat and Dust, Kim* and what-not. It's a trend and a phenomenon.

Anglo-India apparently has a market, while a purely Indian subject has none, being perhaps too drab for a commercial film-maker. India is interesting only in relation to the 'Anglo' part of it, although that relevance lasted less than 200 years in the timeless history of India.

I suspect that a film-maker values, rather childishly, the glamour of the feudal trappings of the British Raj, with Indians in the background as liveried menials or for comic relief. In Attenborough's *Gandhi*, Indians are usually shown in a mass, while the few Europeans—Viceroys, Governors and Generals—are clear-cut individuals, in full regalia wherever it is warranted. Indian personalities, such as Prime Minister Nehru, the Congress party leader Vallabhbhai Patel and Maulana Azad, the Muslim nationalist, lack substance; even Mohammad Ali Jinnah, the founder of Pakistan, is presented slightly, and not as a dynamic man. Other Indian leaders who were associates of Gandhi and who suffered and sacrificed along with him and were responsible for major decisions are left out.

This inadequacy must be a result of bewilderment, to put it mildly. The Indian character was puzzling and the Englishman suppressed his curiosity as bad manners. Incidentally, he was like the American who came later under different circumstances but chose to live like Indians, tasted Indian food, wore Indian dress and tried to understand everything about Indian life.

The Englishman preferred to leave the Indian alone, carrying his home on his back like a snail. He was content to isolate himself as a ruler, keeper of law and order and collector of revenue, leaving Indians alone to their religion and ancient activities. He maintained his distance from the native all through. Indeed, the theme of E.M. Forster's *A Passage to India* was that an unbridgeable racial chasm existed between colonial India and imperial England.

I had a few occasions to meet Forster, whenever I visited London. I enjoyed those visits to Cambridge. We would spend about an hour talking of books, Indian writing and Indian affairs in general. His interest in India was deep and abiding. My second novel, *The Bachelor of Arts,* was launched some years before with his blessing, and owed its survival to his brief comment printed on the jacket. Since then, he had kept in touch with my writing. He would always ask: 'What next?' Once, when I mentioned my next one, a book of mythology, *Gods, Demons and Others,* he paused for a moment and genially asked, 'Who is left out?'

Forster would offer me tea in his room and escort me halfway down to the station. When he visited London, he would send me a note and spend a little time with me before catching his train at King's Cross. When he inscribed a copy of *A Passage to India,* he was apologetic that he could lay hands only on a paperback, at a second-hand bookshop, and gave it with the remark, 'You will find it amusing. But don't read too much into it . . .'

I had heard a rumour in New York that David Selznick or someone had offered $250,000 for a movie option on *A Passage to India,* but that Forster had rejected it. When I asked him about it, he just said, 'I am not interested.' When I questioned him further, he said, rather petulantly, 'No more of it. Let us talk of other things.' He was, however, happy with the stage adaptation of his novel by Santha Rama Rau, who had worked in close consultation with him all through.

How did a little island so far away maintain its authority over another country many times its size? It used to be said by political orators of those days that the British Isles could be drowned out of sight if every Indian spat simultaneously in that direction. It was a David-Goliath ratio, and Britain maintained its authority for nearly two centuries. How was the feat achieved? Through a masterly organization, which utilized Indians themselves to run the bureaucratic and military machinery. Very much like the *Kheddah* operations in Mysore forests, where wild elephants are hemmed in and driven into stockades by trained ones, and then pushed and pummelled until they realize the advantages of remaining loyal and useful, in order to earn their ration of sugarcane and rice. Take this as a symbol of the British rule in India.

The Indian branch of the army was well-trained and disciplined, and could be trusted to carry out imperial orders. So was the civil service. Instead of taking the trouble to understand India and deal directly with the public, Britain transmuted Indians themselves into Brown Sahibs. After a period of training at Oxford and Cambridge, first-class men were recruited for the Indian Civil Service. They turned out to be excellent administrators. They were also educated to carry about them an air of superiority at all times and were expected to keep other Indians at a distance.

I had a close relative in the ICS who could not be seen or spoken to even by members of his family living under the same roof, except by appointment. He had organized his life in a perfect colonial pattern, with a turbaned butler knocking on his door with tea in the morning; black tie and dinner jacket while dining with other ICS men, even if the table were laid in a desert; dropping of visiting cards in 'Not at Home' boxes brought by servants when they formally called on each other. At home, when he joined the family gathering, he occupied a chair like a president, laughed and joked in a measured way; the utmost familiarity he could display was to correct other people's English pronunciation in an effort to promote Oxford style.

The ICS manual was his Bible that warned him against being too familiar with anyone. He was advised how many mangoes he could accept out of a basket that a favour-seeker proffered; how far away he should hold himself when a garland was brought to be slipped over his neck. It was a matter of propriety for an average visitor to leave his vehicle at the gate and walk down the drive; only men of certain status could come in their cars and alight at the portico.

The ICS was made up of well-paid men, above corruption, efficient and proud to maintain the traditions of the service, but it dehumanized the man, especially during the national struggle for independence. These men proved ruthless in dealing with agitators, and may well be said to have out-Heroded Herod. Under such circumstances, they were viewed as a monstrous creation of the British. An elder statesman once defined the ICS as being neither Indian nor civil nor of service. When Nehru became the Prime Minister, he weeded out many of them.

Nomination to high offices, conferment of the King's or Queen's birthday honours in which titles were announced from knighthood to Rai Saheb (the lowest in the list) that could be prefixed to names; such men also enjoyed privileges and precedence in the seating arrangements during public functions and official parties. This system brought into existence a large body of Indians who avidly pursued titles and exhibited loyalty to the government, ever hoping to be promoted to the next grade in the coming year.

There were also instances of rejection of titles as a patriotic gesture. The Bengali poet Rabindranath Tagore returned the knighthood after the 1919 Jallianwalla Bagh massacre (General Dyer ordered troops to fire on a crowd of Indians assembled for a political meeting in a narrow, enclosed space, expertly presented in Attenborough's *Gandhi).*

The British managed to create a solid core of Anglophiles who were so brainwashed that they would harangue and argue that India would be in chaos if the British left, and would congratulate Churchill on his calling Mahatma Gandhi 'half-naked fakir' (although Gandhi himself commented, 'I am glad my friend Churchill recognizes my nakedness, but I feel I am not naked enough').

The map of India was multicoloured: red patches for British India and the yellow ones for the independent states under the rule of maharajahs and nawabs. At the head of a British province was a Governor, a chosen man from Britain, one who was not expected to display any special brilliance, but possessed enough wit to keep his territory in peace, get on with the local population in general, report to the Viceroy in Delhi and carry out his orders. He in turn took his orders from London. The Secretary of State for India was at the apex, with the British Parliament at his back.

The Governor of a province lived like a sultan with undreamt of luxury. He was loaded with the trappings of authority and housed in a mansion set in a vast parkland. During summer, he moved with his entire retinue and the secretariat to a hill station and there lived in a style so well described by Kipling. His Excellency generally divided his time between horse racing and polo, golf and swimming. He presided over elegant public functions, such as flower shows and school prize-distributions. The Governor (and, of course, his family) lived a life of quiet splendour and came in contact with only the upper classes of society and never noticed poverty or squalor. His geographical outlook was limited to government-house vistas, parade routes, and whatever he could glimpse of the landscape from his saloon while travelling in a special train. Most of the Governors were generally kept above want and were believed to be incorruptible, although a couple of names were associated with dark tales of expecting, under the roses in a garland, gold sovereigns or currency notes; of engaging themselves in titillating encounters with society butterflies and so forth, all unverifiable, of course, but whispered about in the bazaar.

A province was divided into districts. At the head of a district was a Collector (until the late 1930s, always a British ICS man) and, under him the Indian subcollector in the subdivisions, who would be responsible for the collection of revenue in the villages.

The native states, more that 500 in number, existed earlier as so many principalities ruled by hereditary princes, all independent of each other at one time. Through intricate historical processes, wars and mutual rivalries that offered ready opportunities for the British to intervene, they were brought, in course of time, under the sovereignty of Delhi, and had to pay subsidies. As long as the subsidy was regularly paid and subversive activities were suppressed, the ruler of a state was left alone to pursue his life of pleasure and court intrigue. In order to keep an eye on the Maharajah, there was a resident representing the crown, living in the cantonment area (also known as 'civil lines', as in *A Passage to India*).

Every capital had a cantonment, which was better town-planned and more comfortable than the downtown districts sprawling around the Maharajah's palace. A cantonment had barracks with soldiers under a commandant to help the government in any possible emergency. The Resident was a puppeteer behind the throne. He and his European community formed a special class living in the cantonment and enjoying exclusive privileges. It would be the Maharajah's duty to guarantee from time to time enough tigers and wildlife for his white masters when they desired to hunt. Especially when the Viceroy visited the state. His Highness must make sure that the honoured guest could pose for photographs with at least one tiger stretched under his feet.

Before this point could be reached, preparations would be made weeks ahead—spotting the quarry, building platforms on trees for the huntsmen to remain in safety while aiming at the tiger, which would follow the scent of a bleating goat tethered near a waterhole. After a ride on an elephant through the jungle, His Excellency would sit up on a *machan* with his party, with their guns at the ready. It was a foregone conclusion that the Viceroy could never miss. However, in the darkness one can never say whose shot kills. But the credit always goes to the honoured guest, although back at home he might not hurt a fly. It would be whispered sometimes that a captive tiger driven crazy by beaters' drums and torches, and famished, and half-dead, already might well have collapsed at the very sound of a rifle shot; thereupon news would be relayed that the VIP had bagged one or more tigers that were terrorizing the countryside.

The banquet that concluded the visit of the Viceroy lent a touch of comic opera—the solemnity, the stiff formality and the steel-frame gradation in the seating plan were inflexible. When pudding was to be served the band in attendance should always strike up 'Roast Beef of Old England'.

I live in Mysore, once a native state, where the annual nine-day celebration called Navaratri was a season of festivity in the palace. At this time, the Maharajah sat in the evenings on his ancient throne in the durbar hall. Invitees would sit cross-legged and barefoot on the throne and resume their seats. On a certain day, a European reception would be held, when the Resident would arrive in state with several European guests. The timing of the Resident's arrival was fixed with precision to a split second, so that he would enter the hall neither before nor after the Maharajah, but at the same time with him, when the guns fired the salute.

On this occasion, the throne would quietly have been moved out of sight as it was too sacred and no one could go before it with shoes on. But Europeans could not be told to remove their shoes and so a silver chair would be substituted for the Maharajah with a footstool, and a parallel silver chair provided at its side for the Resident, also with footstool, whose imperial status would thus be preserved and protected. In that situation, when the European guests bowed before the Maharajah, it was shared by the Resident.

It was of the utmost importance to preserve British superiority under any circumstance. In the railways, they had reserved carriages for 'Europeans Only', into which no Indian would dare to step. Certain shops in the cantonment catered exclusively to Europeans; memsahibs could buy groceries without feeling contaminated by the stares of Indians. Theatre entrances and seats were marked 'Europeans Only'. Exclusiveness was important and inevitable. One noticed it even in hospitals, where European wards and Indian wards were segregated.

In 1924, there was a public outcry against this system. A young student needed urgent medical help and would not be admitted to the General Hospital, Madras, because there was a vacancy only in the European ward and none in the Indian ward. The young man died. Following this, there was a furore in the Madras Legislative Assembly. Satyamurthy, one of the boldest among Indian patriots, whose forthright comments and questions confounded the British rulers and their Indian friends, said:

'Then, sir, the last sentence is: "On the day in question, there were five vacant Indian beds and seven cases were admitted." Now, we are all told that we ought not to be racial in this country. We ought to rise above racial prejudice and that we ought to be cosmopolitan. I try my best to be like that, but my best at times fails when I am reminded that in my own country, in our own Indian hospitals maintained by the Indian taxpayer's money and run, above all, by an Indian minister, there should be beds which should be called "non-Indian" beds. Why, in the name of common sense, why?

'Have you ever heard, Mr President, of any country in the world except ours where beds are being maintained for patients on racial considerations? Do you find in England beds for Indians in those English hospitals specially maintained at the expense of the taxpayer? Do you know what it means, Mr President? You may go in mortal illness to the General Hospital—I trust you will not'—laughter—'but if you had to go, although all the available European beds be vacant, you will not be taken in because you are an Indian, whereas a fifth-rate European without a name can be admitted and given a European bed because he has the European blood. Can flesh and blood stand this? Is it right? I should like to know from the Honorable Minister,' continued Satyamurthy, 'why he maintains in this country at the expense of the taxpayer this racial distinction in hospitals? It seems to me that the time has arrived when we must speak up against this . . .'

There used to be heard a traditional rumour that in the days of the East India Company the thumbs of weavers of Dacca muslin (the finest fabric in the world) were cut off in order to prevent competition with textiles from Manchester and Lancashire. This may sound bizarre but the story persisted for decades. The British were essentially merchants and India was primarily a market. The British temperament seemed to have been market-oriented—even in the 1930s and 1940s. An adviser and secretary to the Maharajah whom I shall name Sir Charles Blimp (with apologies to the cartoonist David Low) promptly sabotaged a proposal for starting an automobile factory in Bangalore when land, machinery, capital and management were ready. He 'strongly' advised the young Maharajah not to approve the proposal and said, 'Indians lack experience and cannot run an automobile factory successfully.'

All the while, he looked benignly on the Maharajah's monthly import of a new Daimler, Austin or Rolls-Royce, with special fittings for his garage, which was already crowded with cars, like the showroom of an automobile dealer. This 'adviser' to the young Maharajah was a beefy, red-faced giant before whom any Indian looked puny and felt overwhelmed when he raised his arm as if to strike and issued commands. The man believed that that would be the only practical way to handle Indians. He drove his staff of 'writers' (clerical staff) to slave for him round the clock, cooped them up in a shed under a hot tin roof at the farthest end of his spacious compound, summoned them through a buzzer every ten minutes to the main building where he was settled under a fan with, perhaps, Lady Blimp 'doing fruits'. They never swerved even by a second from their ritual eating, while his clerks found it difficult to break off for lunch, as he would invariably growl, 'Why are you fellows always hungry?' Poverty and want were normally unnoticed by this gentleman.

Poverty, however, was in the province of the missionary who lived among the lowliest and the lost. Although conversion was his main aim, he established hospitals and schools and in many ways raised the standard of living and outlook of the poorer classes. Before reaching that stage, the missionary went through much travail. He viewed Indians as heathens to be saved by loud preaching.

The street-corner assembly was a routine entertainment for us in our boyhood at Madras. A preacher would arrive with harmonium and drum and, facing heavy odds and violent opposition, begin a tirade against Indian gods. A crowd would gather around and, gradually music and speech would be drowned in catcalls, howls and yelling, and the audience would not rest till the preacher was chased off. It was a sort of martyrdom and he could have saved his skin and got a hearing but for a naïve notion that he should denigrate our gods as a preparation for proposing the glory of Jesus.

Even in the classroom, this was a routine procedure. I studied in a mission school and the daily Scripture class proved a torment. Our Scripture master, though a native, was so devout a convert that he would spend the first ten minutes calling Krishna a lecher and thief full of devilry. How could one ever pray to him while Jesus was waiting there to save us? His voice quavered at the thought of his God. Once, incensed by his remarks, I put the question, 'If Jesus were a real God, why did he not kill the bad men?' which made the teacher so angry that he screamed, 'Stand up on the bench, you idiot.'

The school textbooks were all British-manufactured at one time, compiled by Englishmen, published by British firms and shipped to India on P. and O. steamers. From a child's primer with 'A was an apple' or 'Baa, Baa, Black Sheep' to college physics by Dexter and Garlick, algebra by Ross and logarithm tables compiled by Clark, not a single Indian name was on any book either as author or publisher. Indian history was written by British historians— extremely well documented and researched, but not always impartial. History had to serve its purpose: everything was made subservient to the glory of the Union Jack. Latter-day Indian scholars presented a contrary picture. The Black Hole of Calcutta never existed. Various Muslim rulers who invaded and proselytized with fire and sword were proved to have protected and endowed Hindu temples. When I mentioned this aspect to a distinguished British historian some years ago in London, he brushed aside my observation with: 'I'm sorry, Indians are without a sense of history. Indians are temperamentally non-historical.'

We had professors from English universities to teach literature, which I always feel was a blessing. But the professor's contact was strictly limited to the classroom. When he left the class, he rushed back to his citadel of his professor's quarters and the English club where no Indian was admitted except a bearer to serve drinks. Our British principal never encouraged political activities or strikes, which were a regular feature in our days, whenever Gandhi or Nehru gave the call or were arrested.

The hardiest among the British settlers was the planter who, born and bred in his little village in England, was somehow attracted to India, not to a city and its comforts but to a deserted virgin soil on a remote mountain tract where he struggled and built up, little by little, a plantation and raised coffee, tea and cardamom, which remain our national assets even today. He was firmly settled on his land, loved his work, now and then visiting a neighbour fifty miles away or a country club a hundred miles off. He loved his isolation, he loved the hill folk working on his plantation, learned their language and their habits and became a native in all but name.

AFTER THE RAJ

'THE RAJ' BY itself is meaningless. It could be a prefix or suffix to a proper name. You may say 'Raja' (king or ruler) or 'Rajya' (kingdom) in any Indian language. The Raj in its present form is a vacuous hybrid expression neither Indian nor British, although the OED (which is a sacred cow for us in India, while other dictionaries are useful, they are not necessarily revered as the OED), has admitted it for a definition.

The Raj concept seems to be just childish nonsense, indicating a glamorized, romanticized period piece, somewhat phoney. The Briton did not come to India for his health or to try on 'crown and jewel'. He came on serious business; empire building was no light job. It was tight-rope-walking all the time in a strange land, thousands of miles away from home; making chess moves against inscrutable aliens in a baffling culture. The feudal trappings were incidental to his mission, serving to create a show of authority among the natives. But the fiction-writer never bothered to write about the pioneers' trials, extracting from the subject only the elements of adventure and melodrama. So he wrote of shallow, but sometimes glittering men and women engaged only in love, fights, intrigues and adventures. It is the type of novelist who is in the news today, whose writings provide the stuff for million-dollar TV and film entertainments, against a background supposed to represent India.

Even great writers such as Kipling and E.M. Forster, when they wrote about India, exhibited only a limited understanding, inevitable owing to their racial and other circumstances. The authentic comprehensive Indian theme if attempted at all will have to be pieced together laboriously, bit by bit, like a jigsaw puzzle, and even then one cannot claim to have obtained a total or final picture. India is too vast and varied in characteristics, types, outlook and cultural mores, though under a climate of common heritage. Any generalization about India must necessarily sound like the definition of the elephant in the fable, in which five blind men describe it according to the portion of the creature felt by each with his finger. Although I am an Indian and my stories have an Indian locale, I would not venture to generalize about the whole of India or about my countrymen living beyond my horizon which is south India. I feel more amused than angry when an English writer professes to present the picture of India or a *typical* Indian. Kipling's knowledge was confined to the barracks, mendicants in the bazaar, domestic servants, minor officials, sunburnt bureaucrats and their memsahibs who retreated to hill stations in summer and during those temporary separations from the family (possibly) engaged themselves in minor sexual activities. Only this last aspect is likely to appeal to a film producer. E.M. Forster's *Passage to India* is the work of a writer who has honestly tried to understand this country and the people he met. Though limited in perspective its authenticity cannot be questioned. But this authenticity and the limitations thereof would not do for a multi-million-dollar project. To the film director changes seem inevitable. If one may believe his statements appearing in the press, a mere hint of a rape in the cave in Forster's novel is inadequate for a film treatment, it must be made explicit in some way; and then a heroine who is a prig and an inquisitive bore as in the original is an impossibility for the cinema: she must have feminine charm and appeal, and marry her man in the end. And so, Adela Quested is transformed into a charming victim of Indian contacts, who achieves her romantic aims finally, whatever might have been the author's plans for her.

I have myself suffered in the hands of a film producer a similar issue. In my novel *The Guide*, the hero and the heroine part halfway through the story and never meet again. But in the film version she is brought back with much ado at the last moment to throw herself at the feet of the dying hero. 'We have paid the star three lakhs for her role and that's a lot of money. How can we let her get off midway? She will damn well stick till the end,' explained my director while mangling my story.

At one time the simpleton's view of India persisted in England. Cobras, the rope-trick, and *sadhus* lying on spikes were supposed to be the normal daily conditions of our existence. At Shropshire, which I once visited, an old lady asked, 'From India, sir? Tell me how do you carry on day to day with all those cobras crawling all around?' This was an extreme degree of ignorance but it was typical at one time. Most people in England, especially those living outside London, were unaware that India was no longer a colony. But now, the media's focus on Indian conditions has brought about much improvement in public knowledge. Also, the Festival of India held in London some years ago, extended over several months, has been very enlightening as many of my friends in England have told me.

History shows that India and Britain came close to each other for over a century, engaged (to quote an origin I forget) in an unholy wedlock, followed by a deadlock, and ending in a divorce. At first, the Briton set foot on Indian soil as a trader, established himself among the natives adroitly, consolidated his position through military force and intrigue, remote-controlled from England. Until the time of the Sepoy Revolt in 1857 the Indian attitude to Britain was one of acceptance. With the political awakening in India, the British maintained their authority through a velvet-glove, iron-hand technique. With the growing tempo of the demand for independence, the velvet lining wore out, and a phase of strife and suffering ensued in the country, culminating in Gandhi's categorical statement in 1942 that the only solution to the problem lay in the British quitting India unconditionally.

'Quit India' became a potent *mantra* inscribed on every wall of every city, town and village, and when people chanted the phrase the rulers lost their heads, prohibited by force the sound of it and erased the message from the walls with tar and brush, but it was ineffectual;

the movement continued until a certain day in 1947, when the last contingent of British troops marched through the Gateway of India on their way out.

With all the irritants removed, a period of mutual goodwill began between the two countries. Britain was no longer an overlord but a friendly nation. Certain values of British culture and life were always valued but now the appreciation was redoubled. English language and literature continued to form an integral part of our education. Shakespeare and Shaw and Eliot are read with enjoyment. British publishers look for Indian writers, feeling encouraged by the growing interest in India in their country. My first novel in 1934 could find a British publisher only with much difficulty, and I think the publisher regretted it later, with not even a hundred copies selling. Today, my publisher feels encouraged to keep all my novels in print in a uniform edition. The British Council in major cities has established excellent libraries and from time to time also arranges to bring in lecturers, repertories and concerts for the edification of the Indian public. Oxford, Cambridge and the London School of Economics still attract young scholars with ambition. In sports, cricket which the British introduced less than a century ago is now deep-rooted and flourishing. Today, cricket tournaments are a national event. Even champions of the past such as Hobbs, Sutcliffe and Tate in England are cherished memories in India, along with their Indian counterparts of those days such as Ranjitsinhji, Pataudi, Nayudu and Mankad. Contemporary cricket stars of England, Botham, Gower, Willis with their Indian counterparts, Kapil Dev, Gavaskar and Kirmani attract a crowd of millions when they play.

In the business world too, the Indo-British partnership is successful. A recent business report mentions that among the recent collaboration arrangements between Indian and foreign countries, the United Kingdom has sixty-three collaborations. The relationship between India and Britain continues to flourish.

IN THE CONFESSIONAL

A WRITER FEELS pleased when he meets one of his readers. It is a piece of vanity which is generally forgiven in a writer. People generally think, 'Probably it is the only reward the poor worm receives for his work, let us tolerate him.' A writer feels gratified when a stranger nods knowingly at the mention of his name, but he soon pays the price for his satisfaction. 'Oh, yes,' says the stranger, 'You are So-and-so. I have heard a lot about you.' If the writer is wise and experienced, he must leave the stranger alone at this point and go away, with the flattering thought that his words are really read. But he probes further and gets the answer. 'You write on astronomy, don't you? I have read every word that you have written. I never miss it. Very illuminating, very illuminating,' and you, as one who cannot locate even the Pole Star, realize that you are being mistaken for someone else. You feel like a miserable pretender to a throne, about to be denounced.

There is the reader who displays the utmost enthusiasm on meeting you. He appears so warm and gratified that you think that here, after all, you have met your ideal reader. It has always been your hope that you would come across this ideal person some day, a man who by his very warmth would make you feel that you have been doing some important work, vital for human welfare. But it turns out to be a very short-lived gratification. Disillusionment is actually around the corner. While you are hoping that you are about to have the pleasure of listening to his reaction to your latest weekly effort, he asks suddenly, 'I am proud to meet you, but may I know what you generally write about?' This is an unanswerable question for a writer. You blink for a moment and reply. 'Well, mostly fiction . . .' and he asks with a slightly sour face, 'Fiction, what sort of fiction?' You feel that you are now with your back to the wall. It was bad to have met this man and encouraged him to talk, now there is no escape; you will have to face it fully, and you mutter a feeble explanation of your outlook on fiction. It is a sort of rambling explanation. All the time you are talking, you have a feeling that you are issuing a self-certificate. But mercifully your explanations are cut short by the other's remark, 'I never read fiction. I have done with fiction in my adolescence. However, I am glad I have seen you, having heard so much about you, and you know I love to meet writers.' And so at the next chance of meeting a reader, you carefully avoid any reference to fiction and when you have to explain what you do, you say, 'I write sketches, essays and skits, and light commentaries on contemporary matters,' only to rouse the man into saying, 'Yes, yes, I am sure I have enjoyed reading your short bits, but why don't you attempt something bigger, say a novel? I am sure you can do it. They say there is a lot of money in novels,' and you take the line of least resistance and say, 'Thanks for the suggestion. I will try if I can make good there.'

There is another type of worry from a reader who overrates you. You have perhaps written a few bits which have touched off your reader's sense of irony or humour, or lampooned or attacked something which happened to be also his pet aversion. It has tickled him so much that he views you—that most dangerous of reputations to acquire—as a humorist, and when he meets you he is prepared for a hearty laugh. He watches your face and lips anxiously, and you cannot say, 'Rather a hot day, isn't it?' without sending him into paroxysms of laughter. He discovers a sly wit hidden in the statement. He has made up his mind that your very look, your very breath is humorous. He views you as one who performs clowning feats in print. One person went to the extent of saying to me with a lot of patronage, 'Continuing to amuse humanity? Very good!'

There is the type of reader who demands to be told the moment you are introduced as a writer: 'What books have you written? Give me a list of your works.' And you recite the names of your books, the handful of titles you have produced in your decades of writing, only to provoke the other into saying, 'Only ten books for so many years! Can't you write fifty books a year? I have heard that the late Edgar Wallace used to write two books a week . . . . Anyway please let me have a complete set of your books; of course you must send the bill along! I like to encourage Indian authors. I also want our children to read books by modern Indian authors.' You promise him your cooperation, although you might perhaps do him a service if you told him that you are only an author and not a bookseller, or that the books you have written may not come under the definition of children's books. This man may also display his partiality for facts and figures. He will demand to be told what you were paid for that film story or how much per column you get from such and such paper or what royalty your books fetch. You might probably answer that these facts ought to interest only your income-tax officer, but still you give a reply, out of politeness, as near the truth as possible. He is frankly disappointed that your sales are not on the million level.

The trouble is that the writer, unlike others who have anything to do with the public, works blindfolded. The stage actor has the chance to see how the public reacts to his performance, the musician has unmistakable response shown to him, the painter can stand aside at his own exhibition and listen to the remarks of his public, but the writer alone has no chance of studying his reader's face or hearing his immediate comment. It is well it is so. It is nature's protective arrangement, I suppose. For it is a well-known axiom that either the writer proves superior to his work or it is the other way round. A meeting of a writer and his reader invariably produces disillusionment, which might as well be avoided. I remember one person who went away in chagrin after coming to see me. He had found in my shelves other people's books, and not my own in golden editions as he had expected. My talk was not scintillating and, above all, I was different from the picture he had of me in his mind.

MISGUIDED 'GUIDE'

THE LETTER CAME by air mail from Los Angeles. 'I am a producer and actor from Bombay,' it read, 'I don't know if my name is familiar to you.'

He was too modest. Millions of young men copied his screen image, walking as he did, slinging a folded coat over the shoulder carelessly, buffing up a lock of hair over the right temple, and assuming that the total effect would make the girls sigh with hopeless longing. My young nephews at home were thrilled at the sight of the handwriting of Dev Anand.

The letter went on to say, 'I was in London and came across your novel *The Guide*. I am anxious to make it into a film. I can promise you that I will keep to the spirit and quality of your writing. My plans are to make both a Hindi and an English film of this story.' He explained how he had arranged with an American film producer for collaboration. He also described how he had flown from London to New York in search of me, since someone had told him I lived there, and then across the whole continent before he could discover my address. He was ready to come to Mysore if I should indicate the slightest willingness to consider his proposal.

I cabled him an invitation, already catching the fever of hurry characteristic of the film world. He flew from Los Angeles to Bombay to Bangalore, and motored down a hundred miles without losing a moment.

A small crowd of autograph-hunters had gathered at the gate of my house in Yadava Giri. He expertly eluded the inquisitive crowd, and we were soon closeted in the dining-room, breakfasting on *idli*, *dosai*, and other South Indian delicacies, my nephews attending on the star in a state of elation. The talk was all about *The Guide* and its cinematic merits. Within an hour we had become so friendly that he could ask without embarrassment, 'What price will you demand for your story?' The cheque-book was out and the pen poised over it. I had the impression that if I had suggested that the entire face of the cheque be covered with closely knit figures, he would have obliged me. But I hemmed and hawed, suggested a slight advance, and told him to go ahead. I was sure that if the picture turned out to be a success he would share with me the glory and the profits. 'Oh, certainly,' he affirmed, 'if the picture, by God's grace, turns out to be a success, we will be on top of the world, and the sky will be the limit!'

The following months were filled with a sense of importance: Long Distance Calls, Urgent Telegrams, Express Letters, sudden arrivals and departures by plane and car. I received constant summonses to be present here or there. 'PLEASE COME TO DELHI. SUITE RESERVED AT IMPERIAL HOTEL. URGENTLY NEED YOUR PRESENCE.'

Locking away my novel-in-progress, I fly to Delhi. There is the press conference, with introductions, speeches and overflowing conviviality. The American director explains the unique nature of their present effort: for the first time in the history of Indian moviemaking, they are going to bring out a hundred-per-cent-Indian story, with a hundred-per-cent-Indian cast, and a hundred-per-cent-Indian setting, for an international audience. And mark this: actually in colour-and-wide-screen-first-time-in-the-history-of-this-country.

A distinguished group of Americans, headed by the Nobel Prize winner, Pearl Buck, would produce the film. Again and again I heard the phrase: 'Sky is the limit', and the repeated assurances: 'We will make the picture just as Narayan has written it, with his cooperation at every stage.' Reporters pressed me for a statement. It was impossible to say anything but the pleasantest things in such an atmosphere of overwhelming optimism and good fellowship.

Soon we were assembled in Mysore. They wanted to see the exact spots which had inspired me to write *The Guide*. Could I show them the locations? A photographer, and some others whose business with us I never quite understood, were in the party. We started out in two cars. The American director, Tad Danielewski, explained that he would direct the English version first. He kept discussing with me the finer points of my novel. 'I guess your hero is a man of impulsive plans? Self-made, given to daydreaming?' he would ask, and add, before I could muster an answer, 'Am I not right?' Of course he had to be right. Once or twice when I attempted to mitigate his impressions, he brushed aside my comments and went on with his own explanation as to what I must have had in mind when I created such-and-such a character.

I began to realize that monologue is the privilege of the film-maker, and that it was futile to try butting in with my own observations. But for some obscure reason, they seemed to need my presence, though not my voice. I must be seen and not heard.

We drove about 300 miles that day, during the course of which I showed them the river steps and a little shrine overshadowed by a banyan on the banks of Kaveri, which was the actual spot around which I wrote *The Guide*. As I had thought, nothing more needed to be done than put the actors there and start the camera. They uttered little cries of joy at finding a 'set' so readily available. In the summer, when the river dried up, they could shoot the drought scenes with equal ease. Then I took them to the tiny town of Nanjangud, with its little streets, its shops selling sweets and toys and ribbons, and a pilgrim crowd bathing in the holy waters of the Kabini, which flowed through the town. The crowd was colourful and lively around the temple, and in a few weeks it would increase a hundred fold when people from the surrounding villages arrived to participate in the annual festival—the sort of crowd described in the last pages of my novel. If the film-makers made a note of the date and sent down a cameraman at that time, they could secure the last scene of my novel in an authentic manner and absolutely free of cost.

The producer at once passed an order to his assistant to arrange for an outdoor unit to arrive here at the right time. Then we all posed at the portals of the ancient temple, with arms encircling each other's necks and smiling. This was but the first of innumerable similar scenes in which I found myself posing with the starry folk, crushed in the friendliest embrace.

From Nanjangud we drove up mountains and the forests and photographed our radiant smiles against every possible background. It was a fatiguing business on the whole, but the American director claimed that it was nothing to what he was used to. He generally went 5,000 miles in search of locations, exposing hundreds of rolls of film on the way.

After inspecting jungles, mountains, village streets, hamlets and huts, we reached the base of Gopalaswami Hill in the afternoon, and drove up the five-mile mud track; the cars had to be pushed up the steep hill after encroaching vegetation had been cleared from the path. This was a part of the forest country where at any bend of the road one could anticipate a tiger or a herd of elephants; but, luckily for us, they were out of view today.

At the summit I showed them the original of the 'Peak House' in my novel, a bungalow built fifty years ago, with glassed-in verandas affording a view of wildlife at night, and a 2,000-foot drop to a valley beyond. A hundred yards off, a foot-track wound through the undergrowth, leading on to an ancient temple whose walls were crumbling and whose immense timber doors moved on rusty hinges with a groan. Once again I felt that here everything was ready-made for the film. They could shoot in the bright sunlight, and for the indoor scenes they assured me that it would be a simple matter to haul up a generator and lights.

Sitting under a banyan tree and consuming sandwiches and lemonade, we discussed and settled the practical aspects of the expedition: where to locate the base camp and where the advance units consisting of engineers, mechanics, and truck drivers, in charge of the generator and lights. All through the journey back the talk involved schedules and arrangements for shooting the scenes in this part of the country. I was impressed with the ease they displayed, in accepting such mighty logistical tasks. Film executives, it seemed to me, could solve mankind's problems on a global scale with the casual confidence of demi-gods, if only they could take time off their illusory pursuits and notice the serious aspects of existence.

Then came total silence, for many weeks. Finally I discovered that they were busy searching for their locations in northern India. This was a shock. I had never visualized my story in that part of India, where costumes, human types and details of daily life are different. They had settled upon Jaipur and Udaipur in Rajaputana, a thousand miles away from my location for the story.

Our next meeting was in Bombay, and I wasted no time in speaking of this problem. 'My story takes place in south India, in Malgudi, an imaginary town known to thousands of my readers all over the world,' I explained. 'It is south India in costume, tone and contents. Although the whole country is one, there are diversities, and one has to be faithful in delineating them. You have to stick to my geography and sociology. Although it is a world of fiction there are certain inner veracities.'

One of them replied: 'We feel it a privilege to be doing your story.' This sounded irrelevant as an answer to my statement.

We were sitting under a gaudy umbrella beside a blue swimming pool on Juhu beach, where the American party was housed in princely suites in a modern hotel. It was hard to believe that we were in India. Most of our discussions took place somewhat amphibiously, on the edge of the swimming pool, in which the director spent a great deal of his time.

This particular discussion was interrupted as a bulky European tourist in swimming briefs fell off the diving plank, hit the bottom and had to be hauled out and rendered first aid. After the atmosphere had cleared, I resumed my speech. They listened with a mixture of respect and condescension, evidently willing to make allowances for an author's whims.

'Please remember,' one of them tried to explain, 'that we are shooting, for the first time in India, in wide screen and Eastman Colour, and we must shoot where there is spectacle. Hence Jaipur.'

'In that case,' I had to ask, 'why all that strenuous motoring near my home? Why my story at all, if what you need is a picturesque spectacle?'

I was taken aback when their reply came: 'How do you know that Malgudi is where you think it is?'

Somewhat bewildered, I said, with what I hoped was proper humility, 'I suppose I know because I have imagined it, created it and have been writing novel after novel set in the area for the last thirty years.'

'We are out to expand the notion of Malgudi,' one of them explained. 'Malgudi will be where we place it, in Kashmir, Rajasthan, Bombay, Delhi, even Ceylon.'

I could not share the flexibility of their outlook or the expanse of their vision. It seemed to me that for their purpose a focal point was unnecessary. They appeared to be striving to achieve mere optical effects.

I recalled a talk with Satyajit Ray, the great director, some years earlier, when I had met him in Calcutta. He expressed his admiration for *The Guide* but also his doubts as to whether he could ever capture the tone and atmosphere of its background. He had said, 'Its roots are so deep in the soil of your part of our country that I doubt if I could do justice to your book, being unfamiliar with its milieu. . . .' Such misgivings did not bother the American director. I noticed that though he was visiting India for the first time, he never paused to ask what was what in this bewildering country.

Finally he solved the whole problem by declaring, 'Why should we mention where the story takes place? We will avoid the name 'Malgudi.'' Thereafter the director not only avoided the word Malgudi but fell foul of anyone who uttered that sound.

My brother, an artist who has illustrated my stories for twenty-five years, tried to expound his view. At a dinner in his home in Bombay, he mentioned the forbidden word to the director. Malgudi, he explained, meant a little town, not so picturesque as Jaipur, of a neutral shade, with characters wearing *dhoti* and *jibba* when they were not bare bodied. The Guide himself was a man of charm, creating history and archaeology out of thin air for his clients, and to provide him with solid, concrete monuments to talk about would go against the grain of the tale. The director listened and firmly said, 'There is no Malgudi, and that is all there is to it.'

But my brother persisted. I became concerned that the controversy threatened to spoil our dinner. The director replied, in a sad tone, that they could as well have planned a picture for black and white and narrow screen if all one wanted was what he contemptuously termed a 'Festival Film', while he was planning a million-dollar spectacle to open simultaneously in 2,000 theatres in America. I was getting used to arguments every day over details. My story is about a dancer in a small town, an exponent of the strictly classical tradition of South Indian Bharat Natyam. The film-makers felt this was inadequate. They therefore engaged an expensive, popular dance director with a troupe of a hundred or more dancers, and converted my heroine's performances into an extravaganza in delirious, fruity colours and costumes. Their dancer was constantly travelling hither and thither in an Air-India Boeing, no matter how short the distance to be covered. The moviegoer, too, I began to realize, would be whisked all over India. Although he would see none of the countryside in which the novel was set, he would see the latest US Embassy building in New Delhi, Parliament House, the Ashoka Hotel, the Lake Palace, Elephanta Caves and what-not. Unity of place seemed an unknown concept for a film-maker. (Later Mrs Indira Gandhi, whom I met after she had seen a special showing of the film, asked, 'Why should they have dragged the story all over as if it were a travelogue, instead of containing themselves to the simple background of your book?' She added as an afterthought, and in what seemed to me an understatement: 'Perhaps they have other considerations.')

The cooperation of many persons was needed in the course of the film-making, and anyone whose help was requested had to be given a copy of *The Guide*. Thus there occurred a shortage, and an inevitable black market, in copies of the book. A production executive searched the bookshops in Bombay, and cornered all the available copies at any price. He could usually be seen going about like a scholar with a bundle of books under his arm. I was also intrigued by the intense study and pencil-marking that the director was making on his copy of the book; it was as if he were studying it for a doctoral thesis. Not until I had a chance to read his 'treatment' did I understand what all his pencilling meant: he had been marking off passages and portions that were to be avoided in the film.

When the script came, I read through it with mixed feelings. The director answered my complaints with, 'I have only exteriorized what you have expressed. It is all in your book.'

'In which part of my book?' I would ask without any hope of an answer.

Or he would say, 'I could give you two hundred reasons why this change should be so.' I did not feel up to hearing them all. If I still proved truculent he would explain away, 'This is only a first draft. We could make any change you want in the final screenplay.'

The screenplay was finally presented to me with a great flourish and expression of fraternal sentiments at a hotel in Bangalore. But I learned at this time that they had already started shooting and had even completed a number of scenes. Whenever I expressed my views, the answer would be either, 'Oh, it will be rectified in the editing,' or, 'We will deal with it when we decide about the retakes. But please wait until we have a chance to see the rushes.' By now a bewildering number of hands were behind the scenes, at laboratories, workshops, carpentries, editing rooms and so forth. It was impossible to keep track of what was going on, or get hold of anyone with a final say. Soon I trained myself to give up all attempts to connect the film with the book of which I happened to be the author.

But I was not sufficiently braced for the shock that came the day when the director insisted upon the production of two tigers to fight and destroy each other over a spotted deer. He wished to establish the destructive animality of two men clashing over one woman: my heroine's husband and lover fighting over her. The director intended a tiger fight to portray depths of symbolism. It struck me as obvious. Moreover it was not in the story. But he asserted that it was; evidently I had intended the scene without realizing it.

The Indian producer, who was financing the project, groaned at the thought of the tigers. He begged me privately, 'Please do something about it. We have no time for tigers; and it will cost a hell of a lot to hire them, just for a passing fancy.' I spoke to the director again, but he was insistent. No tiger, no film, and two tigers or none. Scouts were sent out through the length and breadth of India to explore the tiger possibilities. They returned to report that only one tiger was available. It belonged to a circus and the circus owner would under no circumstance consent to have the tiger injured or killed. The director decreed, 'I want the beast to die, otherwise the scene will have no meaning.' They finally found a man in Madras, living in the heart of the city with a full-grown Bengal tiger which he occasionally lent for jungle pictures, after sewing its lips and pulling out its claws.

The director examined a photograph of the tiger, in order to satisfy himself that they were not trying to palm off a pi-dog in tiger clothing, and signed it up. Since a second tiger was not available, he had to settle for its fighting a leopard. It was an easier matter to find a deer for the sacrifice. What they termed a 'second unit' was dispatched to Madras to shoot the sequence. Ten days later the unit returned, looking forlorn.

The tiger had shrunk at the sight of the leopard, and the leopard had shown no inclination to maul the deer, whose cries of fright had been so heart-rending that they had paralysed the technicians. By prodding, kicking and irritating the animals, they had succeeded in producing a spectacle gory enough to make them retch. 'The deer was actually lifted and fed into the jaws of the other two,' said an assistant cameraman. (This shot passes on the screen, in the finished film, in the winking of an eye, as a bloody smudge, to the accompaniment of a lot of wild uproar.)

Presently another crisis developed. The director wanted the hero to kiss the heroine, who of course rejected the suggestion as unbecoming an Indian woman. The director was distraught. The hero, for his part, was willing to obey the director, but he was helpless, since kissing is a cooperative effort. The American director realized that it is against Indian custom to kiss in public; but he insisted that the public in his country would boo if they missed the kiss. I am told that the heroine replied: 'There is enough kissing in your country at all times and places, off and on the screen, and your public, I am sure, will flock to a picture where, for a change, no kissing is shown.' She stood firm. Finally, the required situation was apparently faked by tricky editing.

Next: trouble at the governmental level. A representation was made to the Ministry dealing with films, by an influential group, that *The Guide* glorified adultery, and hence was not fit to be presented as a film, since it might degrade Indian womanhood. The dancer in my story, to hear their arguments, has no justification for preferring Raju the Guide to her legally-wedded husband. The Ministry summoned the movie principals to Delhi and asked them to explain how they proposed to meet the situation. They promised to revise the film script to the Ministry's satisfaction.

In my story the dancer's husband is a preoccupied archaeologist who has no time or inclination for marital life and is not interested in her artistic aspirations. Raju the Guide exploits the situation and weans her away from her husband. That is all there is to it—in my story. But now a justification had to be found for adultery.

So the archaeological husband was converted into a drunkard and womanizer who kicks out his wife when he discovers that another man has watched her dance in her room and has spoken encouragingly to her. I knew nothing about this drastic change of my characters until I saw the 'rushes' some months later. This was the point at which I lamented most over my naïvete: the contract that I had signed in blind faith, in the intoxication of cheques, bonhomie, and back-slapping, empowered them to do whatever they pleased with my story, and I had no recourse.

Near the end of the project I made another discovery: the extent to which movie producers will go to publicize a film. The excessive affability to pressmen, the entertaining of VIPs, the button-holing of ministers and officials in authority, the extravagant advertising campaigns, seemed to me to drain off money, energy and ingenuity that might be reserved for the creation of an honest and sensible product.

On one occasion Lord Mountbatten was passing through India, and someone was seized with the sudden idea that he could help make a success of the picture. A banquet was held at Raj Bhavan in his honour, and the Governor of Bombay, Mrs Vijayalakshmi

Pandit, was kind enough to invite us to it. I was at home in Mysore as Operation Mountbatten was launched, so telegrams and long-distance telephone calls poured in on me to urge me to come to Bombay at once. I flew in just in time to dress and reach Raj Bhavan. It was red-carpeted, crowded and gorgeous. When dinner was over, leaving the guests aside, our hostess managed to isolate his Lordship and the *Guide* makers on a side veranda of this noble building. His Lordship sat on a sofa surrounded by us; close to him sat Pearl Buck, who was one of the producers and who, by virtue of her seniority and standing, was to speak for us. As she opened the theme with a brief explanation of the epoch-making effort that was being made in India in colour and wide-screen, with a hundred-per-cent-Indian cast, story and background, his Lordship displayed no special emotion. Then came the practical demand: in order that this grand, stupendous achievement might bear fruit, would Lord Mountbatten influence Queen Elizabeth to preside at the world premiere of the film in London in due course?

Lord Mountbatten responded promptly, 'I don't think it is possible. Anyway, what is the story?'

There was dead silence for a moment, as each looked at the other wondering who was to begin. I was fully aware that they ruled me out; they feared that I might take 80,000 words to narrate the story, as I had in the book. The obvious alternative was Pearl Buck, who was supposed to have written the screenplay.

Time was running out and his Lordship had others to talk to. Pearl Buck began, 'It is the story of a man called Raju. He was a tourist guide . . .'

'Where does it take place?'

I wanted to shout, 'Malgudi, of course.' But they were explaining, 'We have taken the story through many interesting locations—Jaipur, Udaipur.'

'Let me hear the story.'

'Raju was a guide,' began Pearl Buck again.

'In Jaipur?' asked His Lordship.

'Well, no. Anyway he did not remain a guide because when Rosie came . . .'

'Who is Rosie?'

'A dancer . . . but she changed her name when she became a . . . a . . . dancer . . .'

'But the guide? What happened to him?'

'I am coming to it. Rosie's husband . . .'

'Rosie is the dancer?'

'Yes, of course . . .' Pearl Buck struggled on, but I was in no mood to extricate her.

After several minutes Lord Mountbatten said, 'Most interesting.' His deep bass voice was a delight to the ear, but it also had a ring of finality and discouraged further talk. 'Elizabeth's appointments are complicated these days. Anyway her private secretary Lord— must know more about it than I do. I am rather out of touch now. Anyway, perhaps I could ask Philip.' He summoned an aide and said, 'William, please remind me when we get to London . . .' Our producers went home feeling that a definite step had been taken to establish the film in proper quarters. As for myself, I was not so sure.

Elaborate efforts were made to shoot the last scene of the story, in which the saint fasts on the dry river's edge, in hopes of bringing rain, and a huge crowd turns up to witness the spectacle. For this scene the director selected a site at a village called Okhla, outside Delhi on the bank of the Jamuna river, which was dry and provided enormous stretches of sand. He had, of course, ruled out the spot we had visited near Mysore, explaining that two coconut trees were visible a mile away on the horizon and might spoil the appearance of unrelieved desert which he wanted. Thirty truckloads of property, carpenters, lumber, painters, artisans and art department personnel arrived at Okhla to erect a two-dimensional temple beside a dry river, at a cost of 80,000 rupees. As the director kept demanding, 'I must have 100,000 people for a helicopter shot,' I thought of the cost: five rupees per head for extras, while both the festival crowd at Nanjangud and the little temple on the river would have cost nothing.

The crowd had been mobilized, the sets readied and lights mounted, and all other preparations completed for shooting the scene next morning when, at midnight, news was brought to the chiefs relaxing at the Ashoka Hotel that the Jamuna was rising dangerously as a result of unexpected rains in Simla. All hands were mobilized and they rushed desperately to the location to save the equipment. Wading in knee-deep water, they salvaged a few things. But I believe the two-dimensional temple was carried off in the floods.

Like a colony of ants laboriously building up again, the carpenters and artisans rebuilt the set, this time at a place in western India called Limdi, which was reputed to have an annual rainfall of a few droplets. Within one week the last scene was completed, the hero collapsing in harrowing fashion as a result of his penance. The director and technicians paid off the huge crowd and packed up their cameras and sound equipment, and were just leaving the scene when a storm broke—an unknown phenomenon in that part of the country—uprooting and tearing off everything that stood. Those who had lingered had to make their exit with dispatch.

This seemed to me an appropriate conclusion for my story, which, after all, was concerned with the subject of rain, and in which nature, rather than film-makers, acted in consonance with the subject. I remembered that years ago when I was in New York City on my way to sign the contract, before writing *The Guide*, a sudden downpour caught me on Madison Avenue and I entered the Viking Press offices dripping wet. I still treasure a letter from Keith Jennison, who was then my editor. 'Somehow I will always, from now on,' he wrote, 'associate the rainiest days in New York with you. The afternoon we officially became your publishers was wet enough to have made me feel like a fish ever since.'

A LITERARY ALCHEMY

'WHAT IS SO special about *The Golden Gate?*'

'It is a novel in verse form, three hundred and odd pages, written by a young Indian, and it seems to me no small achievement.'

'Poetry? I don't read poetry. I had enough of it in the classroom long ago. I'm not prepared to struggle anymore to squeeze any sense out of a stanza, with notes and annotation and explanation. I have had enough of it. Today, I'm impervious to poetry. Even "Baa Baa Black Sheep" would need an annotator for me today.'

'Nonsense, I won't believe you. It's a pose many persons adopt to show how mature they are. Of course, memories of one's experience in a classroom could produced a trauma, in which state all poetry and prose might sound dreadful. However, I do not doubt that you secretly dip into Palgrave's *Golden Treasury* from time to time.'

'How do you know?'

'I noticed a copy on your table this morning, and it looks well thumbed.'

'You are right. I enjoy going over lines such as, "The curfew tolls the knell of parting day" or "Awake! For Morning in the Bowl of Night/Has flung the Stone that puts the Stars to flight:/And lo! the Hunter of the East has caught/The Sultan's Turret in a Noose of Light."'

'I like particularly Shakespeare's sonnet, "When to the sessions of sweet silent thought/I summon up remembrance of things past,/I sigh the lack of many a thing I sought . . ." It is good to start the day with a few lines of the *Golden Treasury* in addition to any religious hymn or prayer one may be accustomed to.'

'You were talking about *The Golden Gate*.'

'Yes. Coming back to it—an extraordinary work. I've never come across any other modern writer who has ventured almost recklessly to narrate a story in verse. The book was recommended to me at a dinner party by a lady in such ecstatic terms that it produced a contrary effect as it always happens when someone recommends anything too obviously. I resist it. Now *The Golden Gate* seemed to be the in thing, like the American fashion to display the Book of the Month choice on the hall table. Whether it is read or not is another matter.'

'You started with *The Golden Gate* but are straying from the subject.'

'Yes. When the lady recommended it at the dinner, my host dashed out, went down to the book stall and brought me a copy. Next day, I opened the first page, glanced through a few lines; the lady's overzealous recommendation still rankling in my mind, I put away the book. Weeks later, the author, Vikram Seth, appeared in a TV interview and I realized, here was a genuine writer with the right values, gift and outlook, not writing in order to blow off steam or to reform society, but a genuine artist who takes pleasure in writing. Here I found rhyme, reason and humour, and above all sensed a rhythm which "vibrates in the memory" even after the book is shut and put away. Vikram Seth shows absolute mastery of the English language, and has created a unique literary alchemy. Yes, this is a book fit to be kept beside Palgrave's *Golden Treasury for* frequent literary refreshment.'

*

Passing from literature to language, 'Indian English' is often mentioned with some amount of contempt and patronage, but is a legitimate development and needs no apology. We have fostered the language for over a century and we are entitled to bring it in line with our own habits of thought and idiom. Americans have adapted the English language to suit their native mood and speech without feeling apologetic, and have achieved directness and unambiguity in expression.

I noticed in the *Hindu* 'Know Your English' column, Professor Subrahmanian referring to the expression 'needful' as being permissible. I was relieved to note it since I have always felt 'Do the Needful' as being a practical, compact, and comprehensive tabloid expression. In our college days, Prof. J.C. Rollo, who was a purist, would spend the first quarter of an hour to denounce Indianisms; 'needful' was one such. He said, 'Avoid like the plague the expression "needful". Never say, "do the needful" under any circumstance.' He was also opposed to the expression 'and oblige'. 'You may say, "I will be obliged if you etc." but never, "and oblige" at the end of a letter. It's hideous.'

I have always rebelled against Prof. Rollo's decrees, feeling that 'Please do the needful' and 'and oblige' are a brilliant combination which conveys all the meaning, command and request in a couple of phrases. 'Do the needful and oblige' is a masterpiece of economy and contribution to the English language.

REFLECTIONS ON FRANKFURT

TO ME THE word 'fair' generally conjures up a vision of sprawling sheds in a field, blinding illuminations, deafening announcements from loudspeakers, dust, bustle and congestion. I had imagined books, instead of cosmetics and gewgaws, displayed in a similar background in Frankfurt also.

'Where is the Fair?' I had asked, though standing in front of the permanent exhibition buildings—mansions in several blocks to accommodate about 8,000 booksellers and publishers representing over 120 countries, and with enough space for a total of 1,00,000 visitors to move around freely.

Ice-cream, coffee and snacks available at every corner, to mitigate the fatigue of rambling and browsing in this vast universe. One's feet and legs protest and grow heavy in spite of the facilities provided for movement with a free continuous shuttle service between the buildings, and escalators and mobile belts within the halls themselves.

Preceding the formal opening of the book fair, meetings of Indian authors and publishers were held at the City Hall auditorium where one heard recitations, readings and discussions. On the whole, academic in tone, except when authors complained against their publishers on the subject of royalty and payments, and the publishers in their turn spoke of the difficulties they experienced from suspicious writers. Mrs Kamala Das said that her best-selling book in English never brought her adequate returns, although her publisher a few moments earlier had in his speech claimed her as their best-selling author. Ms Qurratulain Hyder, eminent Urdu writer, said that her books have been selling in India and all neighbouring countries in thousands for a quarter of a century now, but her publishers never paid her any royalty; they brought out new editions of her works under different imprints and pretended they were pirated editions.

Another speaker held the audience spellbound with a blistering attack on the Sahitya Akademi with which he had been associated officially for years. There was much justice and logic in what he said, but the general feeling was that this was not the occasion nor place to expose our weak points and failures.

Equally outrageous was the speech by a lady, one of the guests from India, at the podium where she was expected to speak on tradition and change or some such theme. While the speakers who preceded her confined themselves to the subject, our lady commenced her speech with, 'Friends and Germans'. One almost expected her to say, 'I've come to bury Caesar, not to praise him.' She almost fulfilled this expectation by launching on a tirade against the German character. According to her, all Germans were unfriendly, grim and unsmiling, whereas the Indian tradition was to smile and greet and show hospitality to all strangers. The speaker suggested that the German government would do well to appoint official smilers on a salary of DM 1,000, whose only business would be to stand in street corners and keep smiling. Finally, she wailed: 'All I am asking for is love from Germans.' We felt embarrassed as this was an extravagant demand and her attack totally unwarranted, since we had experienced nothing but royal hospitality and kindness from our hosts. We were put up in excellent hotels, provided with transport and with every comfort one could want.

*

I heard rumours in Frankfurt and then in Paris and London that I was to be awarded the Nobel Prize this year (1986). Some Paris newspapers carried the 'shortlisted' names of three writers in the

Third World, as the committee had decided to award the Prize to the Third World this year to overcome the charge of being biased in favour of American and European writers. I was greeted and congratulated here and there. I could not be sure this honour would be welcome at this stage of my life. I had mixed feelings about it. I am already a victim of excessive public attention. Frankly, I feel uneasy (and angry) when cameras are pointed at me, and try to avoid interviews, greetings, and attempted 'felicitations', and above all unnecessary correspondence. I love to be left alone and not noticed whatever reception my writing might have. And the prospect of becoming a 'laureate' was nightmarish. Thank God, it passed.

If my name actually did come up, and then was dropped, I speculate on the arguments one might have overheard from the committee room before the decision on 16 October.

'For half a century Narayan has been building up a world of his own and peopled it with a variety of characters, who have ceased to be fictional, but are recognized and loved in any part of the world by Narayan's readers . . . it is an achievement which should be treated as a contribution to world literature,' argued one.

'To a certain extent, yes,' said the arbiter. 'This author's work is diverting, amusing and readable, but possesses none of the elements that go to make great literature.'

'What are those elements of great literature?'

'All great literature must echo the soul of man. The struggles, agonies and anguish in the soul of the individual must be reflected in the work, against the background of historical and social convulsions of the countries in which the individual finds himself tossed about as a helpless victim. All the grimness of existence must find a place in a writer's work. Above all, a certain degree of obscurity and difficulty of idiom in the text enhances the stature of a literary work.

'Applying these tests, Narayan's work fails. His writing is too simple, and too readable, requiring no effort on the part of the reader. Mere readability is not enough. A reader must be put to work and must labour hard to get at the meaning of a sentence; only then can he feel triumphant at having mastered a page.

'Narayan's further defect lies in his light hearted tone under all circumstances. This is a grave defect. Humour is all very well up to a point, but it is not everything in literature. Humour has a tendency to stimulate frivolity. Our founder and benefactor, Alfred Nobel, you must remember, invented dynamite, which is no joke, and it would be inappropriate to award the prize in his name to a writer who is uncommitted to the serious and sinister problems of existence.

'Narayan has produced quite a body of work to fill up bookshelves and shows promise. He has created a new map called Malgudi in which his characters live and die. Story after story is set in the same place, which is not progressive, a rather stagnant background. Narayan's stories fail to reflect the dynamism of India's civilization or aspirations.

'We hope some day Narayan will develop into a full-fledged writer deserving our serious consideration.'

LOVE AND LOVERS

WHEN I FEEL the need for an academic discussion, I walk across to the professor's study and wait for him to open a subject. Normally a monologist, today he was in a cross-examining mood. After a few perfunctory observations on the weather and corruption in public life, he suddenly shot out an angry question, 'Is literature dying in our country?'

'Not seen its obituary yet,' I replied, in keeping with this mood of enquiry.

'Where is Tolstoy or Dostoyevsky?' he asked with passion.

'Rather hard to say, but definitely not in this world, not been around for a long time now.'

'You don't have to tell me that, I am asking where is our Tolstoy or Dostoyevsky? Why has our country not produced a Tolstoy or Dostoyevsky?'

'For the same reason it hasn't produced a Grand Canyon or Aurora Borealis. Certain things in this world, including men of genius, are gifts from a mysterious source, and cannot be made to order, or duplicated internationally like cosmetics or drugs. As for me, I am content to read Tolstoy or anyone in translation, without sighing that we do not have a replica in our country.'

'Which shows you have no national pride or aspiration. No wonder you are not taken seriously. Have you ever tried to place your finger on the pulse of our nation or made any attempt to echo our national aspirations?'

'No, because I am interested only in the individual, and I am extremely suspicious of the phrase 'national aspiration'. It is pretentious and phoney. Each person has a private universe and lives many lives. You will be nearer the mark if you speak of the problems, hopes, and aspirations of a person: say a doctor's hope to see more sick people coming in; the sick man hoping that his doctor is a minor god capable of holding him back from the grave; the politician's jugglery to win votes; the voter's fleeting euphoria of being a king-maker; the boy's hope that his school roof would have collapsed at week-end; the policeman's dream that the thief would walk in with the stolen property and save him all the trouble; the cobbler at the street-corner watching passing feet for worn-out soles; the householder's concern to keep his budget and family in proper shape; the snake charmer with his assets curled up in the bamboo basket; the peripatetic knife-grinder's cry down the street on a hot afternoon, an infinite variety of lives overlapping and complementing one another. I am moved by such patterns of life, and not by your 'national aspiration'. What is it really? Do you visualize six hundred million to look skyward on a given day and shout their aspiration in a single voice?'

'Now let us dismiss this aspect, as you implicitly admit your failure as a national interpreter. You probably assume and want me to accept you as an expert on the individual. May we examine your writing from his point of view? Are you going to tell me that you portray the individual in his fulness? There are areas you have neglected. For example, do you deal with man-woman relationship with any seriousess? Aren't you prudish when it comes to sex?'

'Not exactly prudish, only I take the hint. When a couple, even if they happen to be characters in my own novel, want privacy, I leave the room; surely you wouldn't expect one, at such moments, to sit on the edge of their bed and take notes?'

'Why not? Just what would be expected of a novelist concerned with realism. I have closely studied your handling of this particular aspect, and found you wanting. Take your earliest *Dark Room* where the head of an office seduces his pretty trainee. Your latest *Painter of Signs* where Daisy and Raman are thrown physically together for days on end, and then of course your *Guide,* that masterpiece of glorified adultery, in all these and others, while one expects a great deal from your pen as a realist, you dismiss the time hastily; the utmost you afford the reader is a quick eavesdropper's or keyhole-viewer's report, slurring over the dynamism of love.'

'Is there any need for elaboration? I find that the very mention of a darkened room with whispers coming through the bolted door, stirs your imagination to such an extent that you ask for more. I am confident that at a certain point I can safely leave it all to the reader's imagination without fettering it with wordy descriptions. Particularly after D.H. Lawrence, no writer can have anything original or fresh to say about lovers. However, to please you, I am prepared to add a footnote at appropriate places in my novels: "For further details look up *Lady Chatterly's Lover.*" Even the authors of American bestsellers, which provide its readers bed scenes at regular intervals, say once every five thousand words, exhibit nervousness while seeking new phrases for an old experience, and often let their narrative degenerate into a sort of popular treatise on anatomy.'

'How can any honest writer avoid sex where it serves an artistic purpose?'

'Could you please define the phrase "artistic purpose"? Once I served on a censorship enquiry committee. Every film-producer who appeared before us pleaded for a liberal interpretation of the code where sex and nudity served an artistic purpose; it turned out on scrutiny that they only wanted freedom to copy the new-wave Swedish or French films, in which the costume-departments have obviously been abolished, and the camera does not move beyond a double-bed all through the story.'

'You are putting it crudely . . . but you have no right to skip any fundamental human experience . . .'

'Experience is vast and one is forced to be selective. If every bodily function and physical and mental activity is to be recorded without any omission, not all the world's paper supply will suffice even for a single novel. Anyway I now have an idea of what you are looking for. Why don't you go and contemplate the sculptural masterpieces at Khajuraho to start with? There you will find an

exuberance, beside which Swedish films will look like the work of
starched Puritans.'

'I have never visited Khajuraho,' he said with a sigh.

'Nor I, like a million others in our country, I have only seen them
in colour slides projected at the homes of some friends in America.
Why don't you visit our famous temples?'

'Oh, I don't believe in idol worship . . .'

'Makes no difference. You may avoid the *sanctum sanctorum*,
where the sculptor has probably shaped God's image with restraints
and reverence—but after finishing the main image he appears to
have gone wild when carving the pillars and cornices. Words cannot
match the sculptor's art in directness, although a finicky person is
likely to find it embarrassing.' The professor became pensive for a
moment as he remarked, 'Oh how little we know of our own
treasures! We have to discover them only through foreigners!'

'Ancient sculptors seemed to have anticipated the philosophy of
tourism and did their bit to attract visitors from beyond the "seven
seas".'

'Yes, yes, quite a plausible hypothesis. Travel is important, sir.
Bharat Darshan should find a place in every education programme. I
shall promote the idea at all conferences hereafter.'

THE NOBEL PRIZE AND ALL THAT

THESE DAYS EVERYONE feels the right to comment on any subject not necessarily concerning them. The flood of printed material available to an individual for browsing at the news-stand, the circulating library around the corner, the free reading room, or on an obliging neighbour's book-shelf, not to speak of the radio and TV, fills the eyes and ears, and (one hopes) also the mind to overflowing with information, facts and fancies, so that everyone feels convinced that he knows everything and comments freely on every subject.

Five years ago no one would bother about the Nobel Prize, as to who got it or missed it. One would glance at the announcement without any reaction and pass on to the next item in the newspaper.

Now the month of October has become a season of general speculation about the Nobel winners, especially for Peace and Literature. The awards for Science and Medicine sound too technical and beyond the understanding of the average citizen, who accepts those announcements without a murmur, feeling: 'Lucky fellows, let them flourish, God knows what they have achieved. However not our business . . .'

The awards for Peace and Literature, on the other hand, provoke universal comment on the following lines: 'Oh! this is sheer politics and nothing less. So and so is a war-monger, racketeer in arms, smuggler, CIA agent—and to say he has striven for world peace, preposterous!' If the recipient's name is unfamiliar, the comment would be: 'Who is this character? Which corner of the globe does he inhabit? No one has heard of this man or his country! And to say that he was dedicated to the cause of world peace, too ridiculous for words!'

The prize for Literature when announced causes the utmost flutter among the speculators. The proliferation of lotteries, with the promise of a Bumper Prize of crores on the following morning, has created a chronic gambler's temperament in everyone. The speculator, even if he is beyond the pale of the ever-hopeful literary fraternity, would like to back a favourite every year just to enjoy a vicarious thrill if his candidate wins, and then reacts bitterly when the announcement actually comes. 'Never heard of this poet, where was he hidden all these centuries? Who is he? What on earth is his language? The Nobel Committee has a genius for ferreting out obscure languages and writers.'

Another might say, 'If you were a Russian citizen at one time and expelled or likely to be expelled from your native land and then wrote poems and novels, you have a ninety per cent chance of becoming a Nobel Laureate.'

'Statistics prove that the Third World writers, with occasional exceptions, are normally ignored.' William Golding, the British Nobel winner, is reported to have stated that it was time that Asian writers were given their share of recognition by the Nobel Committee, as if one were talking of an equitable distribution of cabbage soup in a relief camp.

Geographical, topographical, hemispherical, or ethnic considerations are irrelevant in literature. One cannot, for instance, compel a selection committee to turn its attention to Antarctica since the claims of that part of the world have been consistently overlooked. On the other hand it must also be said that if the soil (or rather the snow) of Antarctica produces a literary masterpiece it is bound to emerge like a shining star in the firmament even if the Nobel Committee remains ignorant of its existence. A classic does not have to wait for the Nobel stamp of approval. World masterpieces, plays of Shakespeare, Dante's *Divine Comedy*, and the *Ramayana*, were known before Alfred Nobel lighted the first fuse.

However, the Nobel-Award-watchers seem to be self-appointed

busybodies. Alfred Nobel the dynamitician might not have possessed deep or wide conceptions of science or literature or other subjects, but created an endowment because he liked to do so.

Alfred Nobel might not have been aware of the subtler aspects of language or literature, but seems to have just specified, rather naïvely, that a work should promote 'idealism'. If his condition is strictly followed, the only literatue qualifying for the Nobel Prize would have been *Self Help* by Samuel Smiles, or *How to Win Friends and Influence People;* or *Baby Care* by Dr Spock. But judges have stretched the notion of 'idealism' so that Hemingway and Neruda, Patrick White, Canetti, and others could be chosen for the award.

That the award is practically confined to the West is a general complaint but seems inevitable. European languages are the only ones known to the judges. Alfred Nobel could well have thought that all the non-European continents were areas of darkness, populated by human beings who had not yet evolved an alphabet. Even if he had mentioned the word 'global' anywhere, he could have only meant the Western world. At some point, the Nobel Committee might legitimately turn round and say: 'It is none of your business to criticize us. We are the executors of a certain individual's will and testament. Nobody can question our authority or judgement.'

'Accepted, but here are a few suggestions to enhance your efficiency. Beyond sixty if an author is already established, your recognition will not be of any real value; at that stage he cannot become more famous or richer by your recognition; as GBS has said, "Your money is a life-belt thrown to a swimmer who has already reached the shore in safety." So you must set an age-limit for the recipient in literature. Secondly, the recipient should be of an age when he can travel comfortably to Stockholm, to receive the honour without a physician in attendance.'

Kawabata, though he was comparatively junior to most awardees, said: 'I had to travel to Stockholm all the way, and felt exhausted. It took a long time to recoup my strength.'

'What did you do with the money?'

'Nothing much. Only thing I could think of buying was a wooden chair in Denmark or Sweden, I forget; it is for guests like you who cannot sit down on the floor comfortably. There you see it on the veranda.'

A few weeks later he ended his life leaving a note that he had nothing more to live for and saw no reason to continue to exist, although he had disapproved of the idea of suicide when we discussed the subject earlier.

I heard that John Steinbeck had to flee to an unknown destination to escape the mail mounting up in stacks in his parlour, when he became a Nobel Laureate. Shaw mentions that the volume of correspondence following the Nobel Award (though he declined it) was unmanageable, leaving him no time to write his plays; he was forced to cry out: 'I can forgive Alfred Nobel for having invented dynamite. But only a fiend in human form could have invented the Nobel Prize.'

THE WRITERLY LIFE

'ARE YOU STILL writing?' I am sometimes questioned. It may be no more than an attempt on the part of a visitor to make polite conversation, but, alas, I do not like it. The question seems to be in the category of 'Have you stopped beating your wife?' which cannot be answered with a simple 'yes' or 'no'. The questioner has come prepared for a long afternoon's chit-chat and his question may be only an opening gambit. Assuming it might be so, I generally respond to his query with vague sounds at the throat or mumble about the weather, and then if necessary proceed to familiar topics such as corruption, bribery and nepotism, and their subtleties and variations noticeable in public life, the inside story of some corporate take-over scandal, and so on, practically a resumé of the newspaper headlines of the morning. Most times I succeed in warding off the questioner. All the same, the question itself causes uneasiness, particularly the *still* in the query. Probably, the questioner sees me differently from the image I am accustomed to in the mirror during the morning shave, when I do not pause to note the pouches and webs under the eye, the sagging jowl, and other marks of years. Or perhaps this man is in possession of some scientific information to prove that prolonged gripping of pen between the thumb and forefinger results in deadly symptoms, proved by experiments with strait-jacketed monkeys trained to drive the quill non-stop. To please the visitor if he persists with his question I may say, 'Oh no, how can I? One must retire at the right time. Our *Shastras* have decreed *Vanaprastha* at some point in one's life. Even governments have fixed fifty-five or fifty-eight years (depending upon the mood of the chief minister of the hour) for the retirement of government officials. One must make way for the younger generation, you know.' This sentiment, I hope, sounds noble enough for the man to leave me alone. But he may suddenly turn round and declare, 'Impossible, sir, impossible. How can there be retirement for a writer! You must go on giving pleasure to the public,' as if I were a performing artiste. It is at this point that I decide to get the ultimate weapon out to quell the questioner. 'Did you like the ending of my *Man-Eater of Malgudi,* where the evil man hits his skull with his own fist and collapses?' He looks perplexed and says, 'Tell me, what's the story about?'

'It has taken me nearly eighty thousand words to tell that story. If you haven't read it, don't worry about it.'

'That particular book I have not been able to get. Where is it sold, what is its price?'

I go on to the next question. 'Can you tell me if Raju in *The Guide* dies at the end of the story, and whether it rained, after all?'

'Is that also a novel? I only saw the film, but not fully. I had to go away somewhere.'

'Perhaps,' I added, 'the electricity also failed. Quite a possibility, you know, with the services being what they are.' I could put in a fresh question every two minutes like the *Yaksha* in the *Mahabharata.* But I desist, saying to myself that no man is under any compulsion to read my books even if he likes to talk about them. And then, I am in complete agreement with him when he says, 'In these days what with the office work and the hunt for kerosene and gas all the time, so little time is left.' 'Truer words were never uttered,' I say. Feeling encouraged, he ventures to explain, 'My little daughter has one of your stories about a dog in her school book, she is a bright girl and speaks to me about you, you know.'

I really do not mind daughter-guided innocent enthusiasts of this type, but the man who really puts me off is the academician who cannot read a book for the pleasure (if any) or the pain (in which case he is free to throw it out of the window). But this man will not read a book without an air of biting into it. I prefer a reader who picks up a book casually. I write a story or a sketch primarily because it is my habit and profession and I enjoy doing it. I'm not out to enlighten the world or improve it. But the academic man views a book only as raw material for a thesis or seminar paper, hunts for hidden meanings, social implications, 'commitments' and 'concerns', or the 'Nation's ethos'. When he finds a novel yielding none of these results he will busy himself over the work in other ways. A certain English professor has managed to draw an intricate map of Malgudi with its landmarks laboriously culled out of the pages of all my novels. To see an imaginary place so solidly presented with its streets and rivers and temples, did not appeal to me; it seemed to me rather a petrification or fossilization of light wish-like things floating across one's vision while one is writing.

Another scholar sought the following clarification: 'In one of your novels you mention that the distance between Trichy and Malgudi is 150 miles, but you have placed Malgudi midway between Trichy and Madras while Trichy is only a night's journey from Madras. Also in a certain novel you have put the distance from Malgudi railway station to Albert Mission as three miles while in another . . .' He was offended when I replied, 'If you are obliged to calculate such distances you should employ not an ordinary measuring tape but a special one made of India rubber, since distances in fiction are likely to be according to Einstein's theory.'

The man who really charmed me was a slightly drunken stranger who was introduced to me as one of my admirers at a friend's house. The man looked me up and down sceptically and said, 'You are the novelist? No, you can't be.'

'Why not?' I asked.

'All the time I had pictured in my mind the author of my favourite novels such as *The Guide* etc. so differently. Now you look like this. You must be an impostor.'

'Absolutely right,' I cried, 'you are the first sane person I have come across. So difficult to convince others that I'm not myself.'